D0948657

Additional praise for Project Risk Management: Essential Methods for Project Teams and Decision Makers

This book provides an overview of the risk landscape and zeroes in on the top most practical and efficient risk methodologies. This no-nonsense angle stems from Yuri's hands-on experience with a number of mega- projects. A must-read for all project practitioners who wish to separate the wheat from the chaff!

Manny Samson, President, MRK2 Technical
Consulting Limited

Over the years that I received Yuri's risk management support, I have found his approach to identifying, addressing, and assessing the project risks very efficient, refreshing, and thought provoking, even in areas of work and projects that were new to him!

Martin Bloem, PQS, Principal, Project
Cost Services Inc.

Dr. Raydugin's practical approach to risk management provides the reader with a refreshing and rich experience to an old subject. His thorough examples and attention to details allows the reader to unlock the black box mysteries of risk management to further enhance the project management toolbox. This is a must-read for project management practitioners of all levels in all industries.

Mikhail Hanna, PhD, PMP, Manager of Project Services,
SNC-Lavalin Inc., and Project Management Lecturer

Project Risk Management

Founded in 1807, John Wiley & Sons is the oldest independent publishing company in the United States. With offices in North America, Europe, Asia, and Australia, Wiley is globally committed to developing and marketing print and electronic products and services for our customers' professional and personal knowledge and understanding.

The Wiley Corporate F&A series provides information, tools, and insights to corporate professionals responsible for issues affecting the profitability of their company, from accounting and finance to internal controls and performance management.

Project Risk Management

Essential Methods for Project Teams and Decision Makers

YURI RAYDUGIN

WILEY

Library of Congress Cataloging-in-Publication Data:

ISBN 978-1-118-48243-8 (Hardcover)
ISBN 978-1-118-74624-0 (ebk)
ISBN 978-1-118-74613-4 (ebk)

Printed in the United States of America

10 9 8 7 6 5 4 3 2 1

To my uncle Yuri, Lt., 97th Special Brigade, 64th Army, killed in action October 27, 1942, in Stalingrad, age 19.

To my parents, Nina and Grigory, my wife, Irina, and my sons, Eugene and Roman.

To my former, current, and future co-workers.

Contents

PART IV: RISK MANAGEMENT CASE STUDY: PROJECT CURIOSITY

Foreword

ASKED THE AUTHOR why he would want me to write a foreword to a book on risk management when this is not an area of my expertise. He replied that I was exactly the type of reader the book was aimed at—"decision makers and project team members." He wanted the book to be a resource for both decision makers and project team members like myself. The book is written at a high level without encumbering it with much mathematics, but still has enough detail that the importance of a thorough assessment of the uncertainties in a project for the successful management of the project would be clear! This intrigued my curiosity, so I agreed to read the book. To my surprise, I found it an enjoyable read with tips on how to address issues that I might have ignored (e.g., *broiler black swans*) or not even realized existed (e.g., *unknown unknowns*). There is even some Russian humor, such as in the sidebar on "flying to the sun." Such gems like avoiding risk in flying to the sun by only flying at night made me laugh, but I can see how similarly ridiculous risk avoidance strategies could pass muster if the right people aren't at the table.

Although not specifically called *expert* opinion, the problem of *anchoring* or *subconscious bias* on the part of experts as well as *hidden agendas* or *conscious bias* is pointed out as a failure of the process to properly quantify risks (uncertainties). The hierarchy or *vertical integration* of risk management is particularly sensitive to this. If the error occurs at the corporate level and is passed down to the business unit charged with delivering the project, an impossible situation arises. However, this is not the focus of this book; rather it is concerned with uncertainty issues at the business-unit and project levels, but still there has to be communication across corporate levels.

Although I earlier mentioned two terms that might be considered jargon, the book attempts to minimize their use and even suggests alternative terminology. I had a special reason for mentioning these two because they are particularly applicable to the oil and gas industry. The best recent example of *unknown unknowns* is the explosion in the supply of natural gas. The United States is going from a country that was building terminals to import LNG (liquefied natural gas) to now building export terminals for surplus gas. This has developed over the past 10 years due to technology breakthroughs with regard to horizontal drilling and multistage fracturing, which allows natural gas to be developed commercially from tight petroleum source rocks. This has far-reaching implications as natural gas is a cleaner-burning fuel than coal and therefore internally will be the fuel of choice for utilities in the future, replacing coal. The integration of unknown unknowns seems to be an impossible task at first glance. Some light at the end of the tunnel appears in this book through correlation of past experience as to their severity by industry.

A *black swan* is an event that is a game changer when it occurs in a project's external environment but that has a very low probability of happening. A *broiler black swan* is politically or commercially motivated and may hide a hidden agenda. An example of this is the development of the oil sands of Alberta, which has been labeled the filthiest oil on the planet and has been subject to condemnation globally by environmentally motivated groups. The author does not offer solutions to these issues; rather he is concerned with their identification and impact on the project. Once they are identified, methods to reduce their impact would be part of the risk management plan.

Being a scientist and reading a practical book on risk management authored by an engineer who has also dabbled in science and business is rather a novel exercise. Certainty is paramount in the engineer's discipline while uncertainty is the scientist's mantra. My discipline, geology, where decisions are made based on relatively few data, is probably one of the most important disciplines in which to apply a quantitative approach to risk management. Being from the old school, where risk was addressed in a strictly deterministic manner, it was nice to see that the author supports the premise that the uncertainties are first identified, assessed, and addressed in a deterministic manner in the initial project phases, followed by integrated probabilistic cost and schedule risk analysis (based on expert opinion and Monte Carlo statistical methodology) to define project reserves and sensitivities (including reputation, environment, and safety). Deterministic analysis is concerned with approval and implementation of addressing actions. Probabilistic analysis is concerned with optimization of baselines and allocation of adequate reserves to ensure a high probability of project success. Issues occur when moving from deterministic to probabilistic analysis. One should be aware from the start of the need to convert deterministic data to probabilistic inputs. Double counting is an issue. There is a need to get correlations properly introduced in the probability model when the uncertainties aren't truly independent. This book addresses these issues.

Not being a statistician, I appreciate the author's explanation of the difference between deterministic modeling and the probabilistic approach using the Monte Carlo method: "The Monte Carlo method . . . mimics . . . thousands of fully relevant albeit hypothetical projects." An analogy to this would be government. The ideal ruler of a country is a monarch who makes all the decisions (akin to the deterministic model) while rule by the people (akin to the probabilistic model) is focused on compromise. The best system depends on the situation and the individual monarch. Neither is perfect, and checks and balances are needed, which have evolved into a system where there are elected representatives of the people (with biases) with the lead representative being a "monarch with diminished powers" due to the checks and balances in place. This is exactly what the author proposes, the "integration of deterministic and probabilistic assessment."

It is interesting that the author is a nuclear engineer, and that Monte Carlo techniques were developed to help build the atomic bomb and now have come full circle where they are the most widely applied method in risk management. One of the strengths (and there are many) of this book is that the author is able to explain many of the procedures developed for risk assessment by analogy to physics principles while keeping the mathematics to a minimum. This is consciously done based on experience, as the author says: "My practical experience of introducing mathematical definitions related to utility functions . . . was a real disaster."

I fully agree with the author when he quotes Leonardo da Vinci: "Simplicity is the ultimate sophistication." Following this theme, Plato advised that the highest stage of learning is when experience allows one to understand the forest, and not just the trees (not Plato's phraseology—he used the analogy of a ladder); perhaps a slight connection can be made with Nike, which popularized the expression "Just Do It!" This would suggest that the risk assessment is only as good as the quality of the expert opinion given. Risks are identified and their importance assessed so that the focus is on only the most important risks. The less important risks are adequately addressed so that they are within the companies' risk tolerance. The more important risks are also addressed and tracked to be able to respond quickly if they approach being *critical* (nuclear terminology again). The author states, "Unfortunately, it is not unusual that project risks are identified and addressing actions are proposed just for show. This show is called a decision gate." I think this is only a warning. Decision gates play an important role in both risk management and work plans. While deterministic scoring methods have their place, probabilistic assessment methods can be a utopia for practitioners who do not fully understand uncertainty assessment. To avoid falling into these traps, it is important to have someone well versed in risk management (a risk manager) to lead the team.

The book is nicely laid out in four parts. The first part looks at the risk management process at a high level, followed by more detailed descriptions of deterministic methods, followed by the probabilistic Monte Carlo method. Finally, a detailed example is presented on carbon capture and storage, illustrating the methodology of risk management step by step to the final outcome. The book accomplishes its purpose of being a practical recipe book for the non-expert who is a decision maker or a project team member and who wishes to understand how to conduct a robust risk management process while avoiding the many pitfalls.

Dr. Bill Gunter, P. Geol.,
Honorary Nobel Laureate,
Alberta Innovates—Technology Futures

Preface

THAT WAS THE DAY—when a grandiose multibillion-dollar mega-project that I had recently joined was pronounced dead. It had drilling pads, processing facilities, an upgrader, pipelines, roads, camps, and an airfield in its scope. It turned out that several critical risks were not properly addressed, which made uncertainty of the project outcome unacceptably high. As a result of a decision gate review, a few-million-dollar de-risking project was announced instead to prove core *in situ* technologies standing behind the project and address some other critical risks stemming from the key project assumptions.

"The King is dead, long live risk management!"

This was a pivotal point in my ongoing interest in project risk management, one that defined my career path for many years ahead.

There were two valuable lessons learned related to that project. First, despite the fact that the majority of the project team members were high-level specialists in project management, engineering, procurement, construction, project services, stakeholder relations, safety, environment, and so on, they were not comfortable enough in selection and application of project risk management methods. Second, even though decision makers at the divisional and corporate levels had tons of project development experience, they did not pay due attention to some particular categories of uncertainties. In both cases, the situation was exacerbated by manifestations of bias based on a degree of over-confidence and desire to push the project through decision gates to sanctioning. Another bias factor that blindfolded decision makers was the impressively growing price of oil at that time.

These two lessons led to a quest for a few simple but really effective, adequate, and practical methods of project risk management. Those methods should be understandable enough by both project teams and decision makers. To simplify, *input–black box–output* engagement relations between project teams, risk management, and decision makers were contemplated.

In this simplified picture of the risk management world, project team members should provide high-quality unbiased information (input) related to their disciplines to feed just a few risk methods. To do this they should know the logic behind required input information as well as its specs. It would not hurt if project team members were aware of outputs expected after processing the information they provided.

Similarly, decision makers should not merely be familiar with information required as inputs to the risk management black box. They should be utterly comfortable with interpretation of results (output) coming from the black box as outputs and be able to use them in informed, risk-based and, again, unbiased decision making.

To assure quality inputs and outputs project team members and decision makers (project practitioners) should know the methods of project risk management well enough. In a way, the black box should be seen by them as a practical risk management *toolbox* (not a mysterious black box) that contains a small number of slick and handy instruments. The practitioners would not be able to use all of those tools on their own, but they certainly should be familiar with their purpose, value, and applicability.

Obviously, this approach requires a project risk manager who maintains the toolbox and applies the tools in the right ways. This book defines his or her role as a custodian of the toolbox and should help to ensure that the correct inputs and outputs are provided and used.

This book is based on my project risk management involvement in almost two dozen mega-projects in the owners' and the engineering, procurement and construction (EPC) organization environment, but I won't name them since I'm bound by multiple confidentiality agreements (unless my participation was recognized in project reports available in the public domain). The majority of those projects belong to oil and gas, petrochemicals, and the energy industry. Pipeline, conventional oil, heavy oil and oil sands production, conventional and unconventional gas extraction, refinery, upgrader, chemical plant, CO_2 sequestration, power generation, transmission line, gasification, and liquefied natural gas (LNG) projects are among them. Only the people I worked with on those projects could have guessed that some of them (both projects and people) would implicitly shine through this book. My former and current co-workers may also recognize and recall our multiple discussions as well as training sessions I provided.

The methods and insights described in this book are applicable to more than just mega-projects. The same methods and insights could be relevant to a few-hundred-thousand-dollar tie-in project, a major project to construct a several-hundred-kilometer pipeline in Alberta, and a pipeline mega-project connecting Alberta with refineries in the southern United States or eastern Canada or LNG export terminals in British Columbia. (According to common industry practice, a project is conditionally defined as *mega* if it has a budget of at least $1 billion. Capital projects of more than $10 million to $100 million or so could be considered *major* depending on their complexity and organization.)

Are the methods and insights of this book applicable to other industries? Yes and no. They are certainly applicable to any infrastructure, civil engineering, mining, metallurgy, chemicals, wind or nuclear power generation projects, and so on, regardless of their sizes. However, this book probably gets too much of capital projects' flavor to be directly applicable to IT, pharmaceutical, consumer goods, defense, air/space initiatives, and so on, especially if R&D activities are part of those projects. I am not familiar enough with those industries and the project development practices adopted there. Prudently speaking, some efforts would be required to convert the insights of this book and make them fully adaptable to them. At the same time, a general discussion on applicability of the project risk management methods of this book to R&D projects is provided. (This does not mean that I discourage representatives of those industries to buy this book. On the contrary, I strongly believe that the main ideas and principles of risk management are universal.)

This book is not an academic study. It is rather an attempt to share my practical experience and learned lessons. This should possibly exempt me from a requirement of the extensive literature review that is common in academic books. There are three reasons for this.

First, project practitioners usually do not have regular access to academic journals. Or they simply do not have enough time for regular literature reviews. Second, it will not be an exaggeration to say that most project practitioners, including risk managers, do not read a lot of academic books. Even if they do, they do not often apply the risk management methods found in academic books to practice. Quite often risk management methodologies are forced by vendors of corresponding risk management software packages. Along with their IT tools they impose their understanding of risk management, which is not always adequate. Third, to engage project practitioners and not scare them away, I use references to a very few, really good academic books as well as to some relevant academic articles that I did read (or wrote), but only where absolutely necessary.

Some authors of academic articles might discover that this book reflects on ideas that are similar to theirs. This shows my practical contribution to support and confirmation of those ideas, which is done even without my knowledge of their origin. Where there are contradictions with some brilliant ideas, please write such misalignments off as my being biased, under-informed, or too practical.

This book is not a quest for full completeness of all known project risk management methods. On the contrary, this is a quest for *selective incompleteness.* Only the few practically important risk methods that make a real difference in the real project environment are part of this book. The rest of them are either briefly discussed just to outline the "edge of practical importance" or not cited at all.

On the other hand, there is a certain *completeness* of risk methods as they represent a sufficiently minimal set that covers all main aspects of modern risk management of capital projects and all types of uncertainties, called *objects* in this book. No more and no less than that! The attempt by authors to include all known risk methods and produce a sort of risk management *War and Peace* is one of the key reasons that practitioners are reluctant to read academic books: it is not always clear what is really important for practice when reading those types of books. A limited number of methods are required when managing the risks of real capital projects. The rest of them are not very relevant to practice. This explains the words "Essential Methods" in the book's subtitle. Several preliminary subtitles discussed with my publisher actually contained words such as "Pareto Principle," "20/80 Rule," "Lean Approach," and so on. Even though these were not used, in essence I preach (but do not pontificate upon) these concepts here.

The style of the book is close to a field manual or travel notes on a journey in the field of risk management. I tried not to use a "high horse" for that journey, which is not always true of the risk management book genre. Needless to say, pontificating on a risk topic is an absolute taboo.

Although the title of this book is *Project Risk Management*, I understand this as "project uncertainty management." This contradiction is explained by the fact that the purpose of risk management is to reduce overall uncertainty of project outcome. *Risks*, in the narrow understanding of the term, are just one of several uncertainty factors contributing to overall outcome uncertainty. The term *risks* in a wider understanding could mean almost everything and nothing. As the term *uncertainty* is less often used in project management and currently less searchable online, it was decided to keep the word *Risk* in the book title. Part I of the book begins with a discussion on all main categories of uncertainties (or *objects* of uncertainty management) that together give rise to overall project outcome uncertainty.

Selection of adequate methods for managing a particular category of uncertainty depends on the nature of the challenge. Physicists like to speculate about a method's or model's *distance to reality*. Many fundamental discoveries and their explanations in physics were done using simple but sufficient analytical techniques way before the age of computers. Even powerful computers that facilitate modeling sometimes make errors and mistakes. A selected risk method should be simple enough to be understandable by practitioners but adequate enough to produce meaningful results. We do try to find that golden mean in this book. The level of practicality and simplicity depends on particular risk management topics. If the reader finds some topics too simple and some too complicated, it is due to my searching for a robust trade-off between simplicity and adequacy.

For example, we will discuss features of robust deterministic methods for initial identification, assessment, and addressing project risks in Part II of the book. These are also good for selection of engineering design and procurement options, managing procurement risks, and evaluating cost escalation, being straightforward but pretty informative for those tasks. At the same time they are utterly useless for identifying project sensitivities, developing and allocating project reserves, and evaluating overall cost and schedule uncertainty associated with a project. They have too big a distance to reality for those challenges. In Part III, probabilistic (Monte Carlo) methods are discussed, including information on required inputs and using results in decision making. I tried to refrain from making their distance to reality too short in order to avoid excessive complexity.

However, it is pointless to promote more sophisticated probabilistic Monte Carlo techniques as a replacement for deterministic scoring methods in all situations. In the same way, quantum mechanics is not required for good-old mechanical engineering!

Probabilistic Monte Carlo techniques stemmed from statistical quantum mechanics and came of age in the 1940s in the study of the behavior of the neutron population, which had a certain relevance to the Manhattan project and its Russian counterpart. Branching out from deterministic to probabilistic risk methods in risk management resembles the transition from classic Newtonian physics to the quantum physics of Schrödinger et al.

Deterministic risk methods usually view uncertainties individually in their isolation from the other uncertainties. Probabilistic methods treat them as a population when uncertainties losing their individuality could be correlated with each other and mapped to baselines to collectively represent overall project risk exposure quantitatively. (This slightly resembles statistical behavior of the neutron population in a nuclear reactor, for example.) My challenge here is to describe some pretty sophisticated probabilistic methods used in project risk management, including their inputs and outputs, in very simple terms.

Hence, my overall goal is for a project practitioner to consider my book valuable despite the fact (or rather because) it is not a comprehensive academic volume. I would not even resent if an experienced risk manager, seasoned consultant, or sophisticated academician called it rather simple. Let's keep in mind what Leonardo da Vinci said: "Simplicity is the ultimate sophistication."

To explain the last statement I need to reflect on my background a bit. My teenaged skydiving experience aside, my first formal learning of risk management took place as part of the engineering and scientific curriculum at an engineering nuclear physics department. That was a fascinating experience! The level of complexity and sophistication was enormous, to say the least. But what we were taught was constructive simplicity based on the following "two commandments":

1. Do not come up with a solution that is more sophisticated than is required!
2. Do not come up with a solution that is overly simple and inadequate!

I know that this was an attempt to address certain types of technical risks as well as psychological and organizational bias. It was also an attempt to teach young kids to use what is now called "out-of-the-box" thinking.

Whenever the topic of out-of-box thinking comes up in conversations with my friends and co-workers I usually reply that employment as a scientist implied full *absence of in-box thinking*, which was just part of the job description. There was no box or out-of-box thinking at all; there was just independent thinking. My readers should find traces of this in the book.

A while ago I asked myself if I should get rid of those lessons learned living and working in North America. Probably not! Comparing education in Europe and in North America I cannot help but share my observation: the purpose of education in Europe is knowledge, whereas the purpose of education in North America is immediate action. (My son's university curriculum provides additional confirmation of this.) Neither system of education is better than the other. In some cases the North American system is much better, but not always. I feel that a broader knowledge base helps one find optimal solutions that are as simple as possible and as adequate as required. At least it should prevent psychological impulses to buy more sophisticated and expensive hardware and software tools or hire more expensive consultants in fancier ties when a challenge with any degree of novelty is looming.

Upon getting my Ph.D. in physics and mathematics in the late 1980s, I felt that I had a big void in my education related to various aspects of business and management. So, my next degree was from Henley Management College.

Henley-on-Thames is a lovely and jolly old English town with unbelievably high property prices, which eventually encouraged me to choose Canada as my next destination. One key discovery on my journey to the Henley MBA was the substantial cross-pollination between mathematics and business. Mathematical methods were broadly used in business for decision making, although often in a relatively naive form. But that naïveté seemed to be justified by a quest for practicality and simplicity of applications. This made me a proponent of informed risk-based decision making whenever a decision should be made. Building simple but fully adequate decision-making models still makes my day.

Simplicity of applications is what I kept in mind when writing this book. However, the quest for adequacy of the discussed methods defined the exact level of acceptable simplicity. It's like a simple supply-and-demand curve in economics that defines how much is required and at what price. "Everything should be made as simple as possible, but not simpler," as Albert Einstein used to say.

Besides anonymous examples from mega-projects I took part in, I refer to my pre-Canadian experience for additional allusions, explanations, stories, and anecdotes. For instance, I use several analogies from physics that seem to be related to risk management. Please do not regard those insights as terribly deep philosophically. However, some of them may shed additional light on the topics of this book for readers with a technical background.

Several risk-related topics are not included in this book for the sake of staying focused. For instance, features and detail comparison of risk management in owner and EPC environments, risk management in business development, integration of project risk management with corporate risk management, probabilistic project economics, process hazard analysis (PHA)/ hazard and operability (HAZOP) studies, advanced schedule risk analyses of resource loaded schedules, and so on, are not discussed in this book but could become subjects for my next book, which depends on readers' and editors' support.

As is often done in physics, this book is based on a few *first principles*.

First, the three-dimensional (3D) nature of risk management is introduced. The importance of a fourth dimension (time) is also pointed out. These include vertical (work package–project–business unit–corporation), horizontal (all project disciplines), and in-depth (partners, vendors, contractors, investors) dimensions.

Second, it is shown that to be adequate in risk management we need to talk about *uncertainty* management, not risk management. *Degrees of freedom* of uncertainties are introduced, including time. Based on those a comprehensive list of uncertainty "objects" is formulated to ensure that we do not miss or overlook anything major.

Third, main external and internal "uncertainty changers" are introduced that should influence and transform project uncertainty exposure in the course of project development and execution. Uncertainty addressing actions are positioned as one of the key internal uncertainty changers and risk management controls.

Fourth, each of the identified uncertainty object types need adequate but constructively simple methods to get managed. A minimal but comprehensive set of the most efficient and adequate methods (both deterministic and probabilistic) is selected. Those are discussed one by one in Parts II and III of the book.

Some topics are repeated several times in the book with increasing levels of detail and complexity. So, readers interested in getting to the bottom of things through the layers of information should read the whole book. Corresponding chapters could be used for reference purposes independently.

Part I may be seen as a "helicopter view" of risk management. Parts II and III are devoted to specific deterministic and probabilistic methods. Finally, Part IV provides a simplified "straw man" case study of a hypothetical project, Curiosity, where key concepts and methods introduced in Parts I, II, and III are demonstrated again, practically showing their power and value. A simplified sample project base estimate, project schedule, risk register, and integrated cost and schedule risk model are introduced to link the deterministic and probabilistic methods overviewed in this book.

It was possible to devote the case study of Part IV to various types of capital projects, from off-shore oil production, to power generation, to LNG, and so on. I decided to develop a simplified case study of a carbon capture and storage (CCS) project for several reasons. This type of project promotes a "green" approach, has a higher level of complexity, deals with new technologies, includes integration of three subprojects (CO_2 capture, pipeline, and geological sequestration), and is characterized by close involvement of external stakeholders, including branches of government. It also has severe commercial risks related to immaturity of the CO_2 market and the lack of infrastructure to deliver CO_2 for enhanced oil recovery (CO_2-EOR). At the same time, putting aside some obvious features of CCS projects, the uncertainty exposure of a CCS project is comparable to that of any capital project. Similar methods would be used to manage the uncertainties of any type of capital project as those methods are universal.

However, the key reason for selecting a CCS project for the case study was that Dr. Gunter, my former co-worker and a top world expert in CCS, kindly agreed to write a foreword to my book. As I had done risk management for more than one CCS project, his interest facilitated my choice immensely. I highly appreciate the valuable comments and insights that Dr. Gunter has contributed to the shaping of this book.

This book can be used not only by project practitioners but also by instructors who teach courses related to project risk management including PMP certification. To facilitate teaching, additional instructor's ancillaries can be found on www.wiley.com in the form of PowerPoint presentations. These presentations are developed on a chapter-by-chapter basis for all four parts of the book.

The information provided in this book is fully sufficient for the development and implementation of a lean, effective, and comprehensive risk management system for a capital project.

Acknowledgments

THANK MY FAMILY for support in writing this book, which turned out to be a second full-time job for several months. It deprived us of Christmas holidays, many weekends, and most evenings together.

I highly appreciate the valuable contributions that Dr. Bill Gunter has made. It would be a very different book without his support.

Although I cannot mention them all, there are dozens of former and current co-workers whom I would like to thank. They all contributed directly or indirectly to this book and made it possible, sometimes without knowing it. I am grateful to Manny Samson and Martin Bloem, two of the top cost-estimating specialists in the industry, who shaped my practical understanding of risk management. They set limits on my attempts to be too sophisticated and theoretical.

I often recall working together with prominent scientists Professor Valentine Naish and Corresponding Member of Russian Academy of Sciences Professor Eugene Turov. I will always remember them and their professional and moral authority.

Special thanks go to Doug Hubbard for his practical support in publishing this book. The influence of his excellent books on my writing style cannot be overestimated.

PART ONE

Fundamental Uncertainty of a Project Outcome

I N WORDS ATTRIBUTED TO Abraham Lincoln, Peter Drucker, Steve Jobs, and several other prominent individuals, the best way to predict the future is to create it. Project development could be understood as an activity to predict future project outcome through creating it. The role of risk management is to ensure a certain level of confidence in what is supposed to get created as a result.

CHAPTER ONE

Nature of Project Uncertainties

Questions Addressed in Chapter 1

- What could be expected as a project outcome?
- What factors are behind deviations from the expected project outcome?
- Do we really know what we try to manage?
- What degrees of freedom do uncertainties have?
- What are major uncertainty objects and their changers?
- When is a decision really a decision and when it is an opportunity?
- Is it really risk management? Or is it actually uncertainty management? ■

MULTIPLE FACTORS INFLUENCE OVERALL project outcome. Their nature and influence depend on how a project is developed and executed, what are project objectives and expectations of stakeholders, and so on. It is not possible to manage factors influencing project outcome without properly understanding their definition. Only when all relevant uncertainty elements are pinned down and all factors leading to uncertainty changes

3

are clearly understood can a minimal set of adequate methods be selected to manage all of them effectively.

Those multiple uncertainty elements are called uncertainty *objects* in this book. Systematic definitions are proposed for all of them from *first principles* based on the intrinsic nature of project uncertainties along with main factors that change the objects (*uncertainty changers*). The purpose of these definitions is not to come up with linguistically flawless descriptions of the objects, but to reflect on their intrinsic nature. The *degrees of freedom* are used to classify various realizations of uncertainties. This formalized systematic consideration, which resembles symmetry analysis of physical systems, is converted to specific and recognizable types of uncertainties and changers that pertain to any capital project.

PHASES OF PROJECT DEVELOPMENT AND PROJECT OBJECTIVES

Phases of project development used in industries vary as do their definitions. They are also different in the same industry, for instance, in the case of project owners and contractors. We will use a simplified set of project phases that is common in the oil and gas industry in the owner environment (see Table 1.1).

The first three phases are often combined to front-end loading (FEL). They precede final investment decision (FID), which is supposed to be made by the end of Define, which is a crucial point for any project (no FID, no project's

TABLE 1.1 Project Development Phases

Project Phase	Description
Identify	Commercial and technical concept is pinned down; its feasibility is considered proven by the end of Identify.
Select	Several conceptual options are outlined; one is selected for further development by the end of Select.
Define	Selected option is developed, including all baselines; it is sanctioned by the end of Define [final investment decision (FID)].
Execute	Approved project is being implemented and completed by the end of Execute.
Operate	After commissioning and startup, project is in operations during its lifetime and decommissioned by the end of Operate.

future). All project objectives and baselines are supposed to be well developed prior to FID to be reviewed and (hopefully) sanctioned.

The main focus of this book is on phases preceding FID (i.e., on FEL). For this reason two main project lifecycle periods could be introduced conditionally and told apart: "Now" (FEL) and "Future." Operate certainly belongs to Future, which could include dozens of years of project lifetime before decommissioning. Execute seems to hide in a gray area since it's the beginning of Future. It starts at FID and doesn't end until the project is complete. One could imagine the high spirits of a project team, decision makers, and project stakeholders when a project FID is made and announced. The boost in energy, enthusiasm, and excitement following the positive FID is certainly an attribute of a "Now-to-Future quantum leap."

After positive FID a project is likely to have future. So, decision makers, team members, and stakeholders are interested in knowing what sort of actual future characteristics it might get upon completion. If we regard project objectives and baselines as a sketchbook put together for FID, how close would the original (i.e., project completed in Future) resemble sketches done Now?

The answer to this question becomes clear in the course of project execution. By the end of Execute there will be a pretty clear picture. The original could appear even more beautiful and attractive than the sketches of the past. This is a sign of the project's success. But the original could also get ugly, with sketches being quite irrelevant to reality.

To continue the artistic analogy, the sketches may be done using various styles and techniques. The variety of styles could resemble anything from cubism, expressionism, and pop art, to impressionism, to realism. (Guess what these styles could mean in project management!) A "project development style" adopted by a project in FEL depends on many factors: from maturity of the company project development and governance processes and biases of team members and decision makers, to previous project development experience, to stakeholders' expectations and activism. But what is even more important is the "project execution style." Its abrupt change right after FID could make pre-FID sketches completely irrelevant (see Figure 1.1).

QUEST FOR PREDICTABILITY OF PROJECT OUTCOME

Figure 1.1 represents a concept of a value associated with project definition and execution. The term *definition* means here all activities related to FEL, and not only to the Define phase, whereas the term *value* could be perceived as an

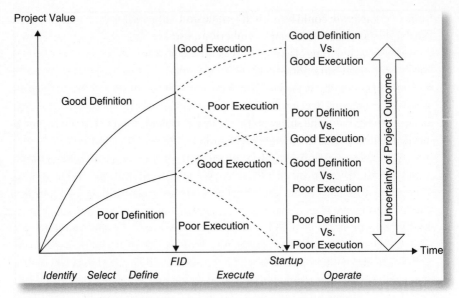

FIGURE 1.1   Project Definition, Execution, Value, and Outcome

amalgamation of project objectives, baselines, and stakeholders' expectations compared with the completed project. (In a simplified interpretation it could relate to either project cost or duration.) According to Figure 1.1, a project value may be characterized by a broad spectrum of outcomes, from unconditional success to complete failure. According to benchmarking data and the definition of project failure by the IPA Institute, a staggering 56% of major projects fail due to

- Budget overspending for more than 25%, and/or
- Schedule slipping for more than 25%, and/or
- Severe and continuing operational problems holding for at least one year.[1]

Imagine what the failure numbers would be if we used 15 or 20% thresholds instead.

Project definition and execution is a battle against multiple factors of uncertainty of the project outcome. Multiple uncertainties and deviations from project objectives should be understood as inputs to project definition and execution that drive overall uncertainty of outcome. Depending on features of project development and execution, this could be either an uphill or downhill battle. Accumulated deviations from multiple project objectives and baselines upon project completion could be both favorable and unfavorable to various degrees. Decision makers, project team members, and stakeholders have a vested interest in the final outcome of a project. Was this delivered within scope and quality, according to the sanctioned budget and by the approved completion date, or was the discrepancy between baselines and reality appalling? Were changes done during project development and execution? Were they properly taken into account? What was the safety record or environmental impact in the course of project delivery? Has the owner's reputation suffered?

All these questions emphasize multiple dimensions of project goals and uncertainty of project outcome. All project disciplines—engineering, procurement, construction, quality, project services, safety, environment, stakeholder management, and so on—take part in shaping corresponding baselines and managing multiple uncertainties at the work package and project levels. Project risk management has unique positioning, though. It not only evaluates the credibility of all project baselines but must identify and manage deviations from them in all their thinkable realizations due to multiple uncertainties.

SOURCES AND TYPES OF DEVIATIONS FROM PROJECT OBJECTIVES

Multiple uncertainty factors give rise to the overall project outcome and, hence, to deviations from the initially stated project objectives and baselines. A combination of all particular deviations from objectives in the course of project development and execution contributes to the overall uncertainty of the project outcome.

Any project objectives or baselines, such as project base estimates, schedules, or engineering design specifications, are models that try to mimic future project reality. As mentioned in the Preface, each such model may be characterized by its *distance to reality*.[2] It would not be an exaggeration to say that those baselines have quite a large distance to reality by default. All of those baselines are developed in a perfectly utopian uncertainty-free world. For instance, all costs, durations, or performance parameters are *one-point numbers*, implying that they are fully certain! Such a wonderful level of certainty could be achievable only if all stakeholders of a project welcome it North-Korean style; all subcontractors and suppliers cannot wait to ensure the highest possible quality and just-in-time delivery, demonstrating Gangnam-style excitement; technology license providers and financial institutions greet the project by performing Morris dancing enthusiastically; and regulatory bodies are engaged in encouraging Russian-Cossack-style dancing. It is a nice, utopian picture of a project environment (although those dances more often resemble daily Indo-Pakistani border military dancing of carefully choreographed contempt).

All those multiple uncertainties give rise to multiple deviations from the utopian risk-free baselines shaping the project reality. Let's introduce a set of standard project objectives in this section as well as reviewing the reasons for deviations from them that are observed in any capital project. Traditionally, three project objectives have been considered (triple constraint, iron triangle, etc.):

1. Scope/Quality/ Performance
2. Capital expenditure budget (CapEx)
3. Schedule

These three objectives imply constraints on each other to exclude apparent dichotomies, as fast delivery of a good project cheaply is not quite possible.

First, there should be a reason for undertaking a project. This should bring up a certain level of utility in Operate. Usefulness of a capital project could relate to characteristics of a structure to be constructed (a building of a certain size and purpose, a bridge of expected load rating, etc.) or to performance of a production facility of a certain production output (barrels of oil or cubic feet of natural gas produced and/or processed per day, tons of fertilizer produced per month, tons of carbon dioxide captured and sequestered in aquifer per year, etc.). Both structures and production facilities should be durable enough in the course of their operations, which brings up topics of reliability, availability, and maintainability.[3] A budget for operating and maintaining a facility (*operating expenditure budget—OpEx*) should be reasonable economically to support the required level of reliability and availability and, hence, planned operating income. The Scope/Performance/Quality objective is the first of the classic triple constraints. There are many uncertainty factors that could lead to deviations from this objective.

Second, a structure or facility of concern should be delivered according to an approved capital expenditure budget (CapEx). A base estimate of a project takes into account all required expenses to deliver it. Needless to say, accuracy of the base estimate depends on phase of project development. The level of engineering development is a major driver of accuracy for every cost account. For instance, when developing a concept design of a production facility, the amount of pipes of small (few inches) diameter is not quite clear. To estimate inevitable additional expenditures that will be justified later, corresponding design allowances are used to address uncertainties related to material takeoff. If a project is unique and adopts a new technology, the required design allowances could be quite high. In the case of repetitive projects it could be just a few percentage points of corresponding base estimate cost accounts.

Each work package could have an estimate of specific accuracy level in a given phase. Besides level of engineering development, accuracy of a package estimate strongly depends on progress of procurement activities, with highest accuracy expected when the prices are locked in. Nobody doubts that there will be the price of, say, construction materials in the base estimate of a given project. (Formally speaking, the probability of the presence of this cost in the base estimate is exactly 100%.) It is usually questionable which particular price it would be. Moreover, if several estimators are asked to prepare an estimate of a project or its work packages independently, no doubt there will be a visible spread of their numbers. Differences in the estimate numbers could be explained by variations of historic data and methods used for estimating as well as the personal experience and qualifications of the estimators. Some of them are more aggressive (optimistic) by nature and some are more prudent (pessimistic). The latter example is one of the realizations of psychological bias in project management that will be discussed in this book, which is also realization of a general uncertainty.

A base estimate is normally developed in the currency of a base period. One dollar (or ruble, yuan, dinar, yen, euro, and so on) today won't have the same purchasing power several months or years from now when estimated items will be actually purchased. The issue here is not just general inflation, which is normally equal to a few percentage points per year in North America. General inflation, which is usually measured as consumer price index (CPI), has almost nothing to do with future prices of line pipes or structural steel, or the cost of labor in Texas or Alberta. For example, prices of several types of line pipes grew 20–40% in 2008 before dropping drastically by year-end. Supply–demand imbalances in particular industry segments could exceed CPI manifold.

Cost escalation is a special type of general uncertainty that could be predicted relatively adequately using the correct sets of macroeconomic indexes. Obviously, prices do not rise indefinitely. Drops in prices of materials, equipment, and services used by capital projects could be significant. Cost de-escalation could be predicted and used for selecting the right purchasing time. These last two statements could generate some skeptical remarks. To "predict" here means to forecast the general upward or downward trend of prices in a particular segment, not an absolute level of prices. For instance, existing escalation models for line pipes based on right macroeconomic indexes forecast annual growth of around 10–15% in the first three quarters of 2008. It was much less than actual growth, but informative enough for sober decision making.

If some materials or services are purchased abroad, currency exchange rate volatility causes additional uncertainty in the CapEx. It could be managed similarly to cost escalation/de-escalation. The capital expenditure budget (CapEx) objective is the second of the three traditional constraints.

As a project is supposed to get delivered not only on Scope and on Cost but on time, too, the third classic constraint is Schedule, meaning project duration. A schedule developed as a project baseline has a completion date, not a range of dates. Similarly, all normal activities of the schedule will have unambiguous one-point durations. Is it too bold to state certainty like this? Of course, actual durations of most (if not all) of the normal activities will differ from the model. The Schedule is just a model that has its own distance to reality, too. The real project completion date will differ from the planned one. I recall several occasions when mega-projects developed behind the Iron Curtain were completed right as declared, which had deep political and reputational meaning back then. All of those projects were complete disasters in terms of CapEx, and especially Scope/Quality/Performance, though. My recent experience points to the fact that this can happen on both sides of former Iron Curtain.

Again, the level of project development (especially engineering and procurement development) as well as methods and data used for planning are major drivers of duration general uncertainties. We know there will be *a* duration for a particular normal activity. We just don't know exactly *what* the duration would be. Similar to estimating, if several schedulers take on schedule development independently, durations of normal activities and overall project durations would not be the same, bringing up corresponding spreads. Again, different historic information and methods could be applied by different schedulers who themselves could have different levels of experience, expertise, and aggressiveness. Moreover, schedule logics proposed by different schedulers could differ.

It is obvious that if an engineering or construction team is deployed to deliver a particular project, there will be incurred costs in case of schedule delays. Construction crews, engineering teams, rented equipment or buildings, and so on should be paid for no matter whether those work or stay idle. This brings up an additional general uncertainty factor that should be taken into account to assess schedule-driven costs, or rather, schedule-delay-driven cost impacts. We will use "burn rates" that may be treated as general uncertainties to integrate probabilistic cost and schedule analyses.

The deviations from the three classical project objectives described earlier are actually part of "business as usual," being attached to Scope, Cost, or Schedule baselines. No unexpected factors or events that are not part of baselines are contemplated. However, in place of precise baseline one-point values we actually assume ranges of those values. In an attempt to reflect on this ambiguity, project engineers, estimators and schedulers introduce the most reasonable or likely representatives of those scope, cost, and schedule ranges as one-point values surrounded by an entourage of the other values from the ranges. Obviously, the spread associated with the existence of the entourage relates to an ambiguity of possible impacts on objectives, and not probabilities of the impacts. There is no uncertainty associated with the impact's existence that is absolutely certain. Let's call those one-dimensional uncertainties of just impact ambiguity *general uncertainties*.

However, myriad unplanned events might occur in a real project. If they occur, those could be seen as "business unusual" as they are not part of baselines at all. Probabilistic methods allow one to take those uncertain events into account but outside of baselines and through attaching to them probabilities of occurrence. Project delays related to the permitting process or additional requirements related to protection of the environment that are imposed as conditions of project approval by the government are examples of uncertain events that impact Scope, Cost, and Schedule objectives. However, their exact impacts and probabilities stay uncertain. Being associated with business unusual, they have not one, but two dimensions of uncertainty, both uncertainty of impact and uncertainty of occurrence. Let's call the business-unusual events *uncertain events*.

However, uncertainty of impact means *general uncertainty*. Hence, general uncertainty merged with uncertainty of likelihood gives rise to an uncertain event.

Mathematically, general uncertainties may look like a subclass of uncertain events when probability gets to 100%. Technically, this is correct. However, our previous discussion on "business as usual" versus "business unusual" dictates to tell them apart. Philosophically speaking, when an uncertain event is losing one dimension of uncertainty becoming absolutely certain in terms of happening (100% chance of happening), it redefines the whole nature of the uncertainty as the "game of chance" is over. It's like gambling in Las Vegas and knowing for sure that you will beat the wheel every time it spins. Unclear would be only the size of each win. How can a casino profitably operate like that?

What technically happens when an uncertain event actually occurs? In place of probability of a possible deviation from project objectives equal to, say,

5%, the deviation suddenly becomes a reality. It becomes a fact or *given* with probability of 100% as no game of chance is involved anymore. This directly leads to impact on project objectives. As an uncertain event loses one uncertainty degree of freedom it becomes a general uncertainty if its impact is not yet fully understood. When the impact of that former uncertain event that turned to a general uncertainty eventually becomes known, it becomes an issue and redefines project baselines. An issue loses both characteristics of uncertainty. It is certain in terms of both likelihood (100%) and impact (no range/one-point value).

If an uncertain event has occurred, it is too late to proactively prevent this. The only way to address this is to try to screen out impacts on project objectives through some recovery addressing actions. This should be considered part of reactive crisis management. Ideally those reactive actions should be planned beforehand for cases in which risk prevention does not work. Crisis management is usually more costly than preventive actions. An ounce of prevention is worth a pound of cure!

Imagine a situation where an uncertain event characterized by a probability of occurrence has a clear impact without any impact range. It would belong to the category of *discrete uncertain events* in terms of impact when impact on or deviation from objectives is fully predictable. For instance, in the case of circus equilibrists who are working without a safety net, the probability of failure is quite low although the possible safety impact is rather certain.

Some uncertain events could have very low probabilities and extremely high impacts. So, they cannot be viewed as moderate deviations from project objectives. Their possible impacts might be comparable in magnitude with baselines. Being in the same or higher "weight categories" with baselines, natural disasters, some *force majeure* conditions, changing regulations, opposition to projects, general economic crises, and so on could lead to devastating scope changes, critical cost increases, and knockout schedule delays. In a sense, those events destroy initial baselines or fully redefine them. For instance, if a pipeline project that had an initial duration of two years was delayed due to opposition and strict environmental requirements for three years, all its initial baselines should be redone. Moreover, the project owner might just cancel the project and pursue some other business opportunities. Eventually, if approved and moved forward, it will be a different project with different scope, cost, and schedule.

Uncertain events like this are called "show-stoppers" (a knockout blow on objectives), "game changers" (a knockdown blow on objectives), or "black swans" among risk practitioners.[4] Despite the fact that those are part of enterprise or corporate risk management (ERM), they should be identified, monitored, and reported by the project teams. A project team cannot effectively manage events like this unless a sort of insurance coverage is contemplated in some cases. The owner's organization should assume ownership of the show-stoppers and game changers in most cases. For this reason, such supercritical project uncertain events are also called "corporate risks."

Using some analogies from physics, we may compare baselines with base states of a physical system. For instance, a crystal lattice of a solid matter at zero degree Fahrenheit represents its base state. If temperature slightly increases, linear vibrations of atoms around their equilibrium positions take place. Those independent small deviations from a base state are called *phonons*. Degrees of deviations are relatively small and don't disrupt the base state. We may conditionally compare those linear vibrations with general uncertainties. However, if temperature further rises, some new nonlinear effects occur when phonons are examined as a population or superposition of quasi-particles. Their collective behavior gets clear statistical features. In some situations this behavior modifies characteristics of the solid matter. We may compare this with correlated uncertain events. If temperature further increases, the energy of the population of phonons, which obtain clearly nonlinear behavior, could be enough to change the base state. *Phase transition* occurs, leading to a change in crystal lattice type. Isn't this a game changer? If temperature further increases and reaches the solid's melting point, there is no solid matter anymore. This sounds like a show-stopper in the case of corporate risks. Moreover, some impurities or defects of a crystal lattice that are not expected in ideal solid matter could be compared with some unknown uncertainties.

We don't want to exaggerate the depth and significance of this analogy between solid state physics and project risk management. However, it could be informative for readers with a technical background.

Besides the traditional triple constraint objectives, organizations use additional project constraints these days. For example, a project might be delivered on Scope, on Cost, and on Schedule, but it resulted in multiple fatalities, had a devastating environmental impact, and ruined the organizational reputation. Concerning fatalities, polluted environment, or devastated reputation, shouldn't an organization be ready to ask "How much should we pay to compensate for occurred environmental, safety, and reputation risks?"[5] Or should it rather manage corresponding "soft" objectives and deviations from them consistently? The following "soft" objectives are widely used or should be used these days to make risk management more comprehensive:

- Safety
- Environment
- Reputation

The Safety objective will be understood as *health and safety (H&S)* in this book in most cases.

These soft objectives are normally treated as additional "goal-zero" types of constraints: no fatalities and injuries, no negative impacts on Environment and Reputation. A longer list of additional constrains could be adopted by a project to also reflect on stakeholders' management, legal objectives, profit margin goals, access to oil reserves or new contracts, and so on. Those objectives are more often used at the corporate level.

Deviations from these goal-zero-type objectives might be also realized as both general uncertainties and uncertain events. It is the same in the case of Scope, Cost, and Schedule objectives—those could become "corporate risks."

There is an obvious inconsistency in the terminology of modern risk management. First, the word *risk* means something unfavorable. However, when *risk* is used in risk management it covers both upside (favorable) and downside (unfavorable) deviations from objectives. Second, when the term *risk* is used this implies some probability of occurrence, even according to the ISO 31000 standard.[6] However, general uncertainties have certainty of occurrence. To fully resolve these two inconsistencies we have to presume the following four categories:

1. Downside uncertain events
2. Upside uncertain events
3. Downside general uncertainties
4. Upside general uncertainties

All deviations from project objectives discussed so far are understood as *known*. They are normally identified and put on a project's radar screen. We know that they should be part of risk management activities due to one or both dimensions of uncertainties. In other words, their relevance to a project is believed to be fully certain.

The bad news is that some deviations could be overlooked and would not appear on the risk management radar screen at all (at least until they occur). Following the fundamental observations of modern philosopher Donald Rumsfeld, we cannot help introducing the unknown–unknown part of his picture of the world (see "Unknown Unknowns"). Those stealth types of objects may be called *unknown unknowns*. We will call them *unknown uncertainties*.

UNKNOWN UNKNOWNS

"There are known knowns. These are things we know that we know. There are known unknowns. That is to say, there are things that we know we don't know. But there are also unknown unknowns. There are things we don't know we don't know."

Donald Rumsfeld

Discussing various types of uncertainties earlier we implicitly assumed that unbiased workers, who have plenty of time and resources, identify, assess, and address risks using ideal risk methods that they fully understand. Unfortunately, project teams usually work under a severe time crunch; they are normally understaffed; workers have different perceptions of possible risks depending on their previous experience and background; and they have various levels of training and understanding of risk methods. Moreover, some of them could be interested in identification (or non-identification) of particular risks and particular assessments and addressing. Even more significant, a company might not have adequate risk methods in its toolbox at all.

The various systematic inconsistencies outlined earlier are referred to in risk management as *bias*. Bias could stem from features of both organizational aspects of risk management and its psychological aspects. The main types of bias will be discussed in Part II. All of them could have an impact on identification and assessment of general uncertainties and uncertain events through introducing systematic identification and assessment errors.[7] Some of them may even lead to overlooking uncertainties during identification, making them the infamous unknown unknowns. But room for unknown uncertainties could serve as a measure of quality of a project risk management system.

KEY OBJECTS OF RISK (OR UNCERTAINTY) MANAGEMENT: DO WE REALLY *KNOW* WHAT WE TRY TO MANAGE?

The previous section brought up quite a few possible deviations from project objectives that define overall uncertainty of project outcome. Surprisingly, discussion on definitions of terms such as *risk, opportunity, threat, chance, possibility, uncertainty, ambiguity, issues, consequences, likelihood*, and so on can be found in many modern publications on risk management and professional forums. Implicit links among these terms as well as nuances of their meanings in various languages are still being discovered and fathomed. It seems that all those discussions have a linguistic nature that does not necessarily have a lot to do with the fundamental nature of uncertainty.

Those are all signs of lack of solid structure and logic in risk management as a discipline. Do you think that representatives of more mature disciplines such as mechanical engineering discuss fundamental differences between compressor and pump stations?

It seems to me that having English as a second language is a benefit that justifies ignoring all those nuances. It also seems that project team members and decision makers, even if they are native English-language speakers, are not very interested in those nuances, either. At the same time a need to apply first principles related to the fundamental nature of uncertainty to clarify all those definitions has been on my mind for a while.

The recent ISO 31000 standard was an attempt to draw the line at these endless and often futile discussions. As a general guideline supposedly applicable to any industry, the ISO 31000 standard doesn't provide and is not expected to provide a toolbox to adequately assess and manage all types of uncertainties that usually give rise to overall uncertainty of project outcome. Some concepts, definitions, and tools that are required for this are either missing or confusing. For instance, the standard defines risk as a potential event as well as the effect of uncertainty on objectives that is characterized by consequences and likelihood of occurrence. This is a core definition that I fully support but in the case of uncertain events only. What if there is no event but there is uncertain impact on project objectives? In other words, what if a given (not potential) uncertainty exists only due to deficiency of knowledge about impact on objectives, with likelihood of the impact being 100% certain? What if probability of event is uncertain but possible impacts is fully and clearly defined? What would be the classification and role of uncertain events that did occur (issues)? How about various types of biases and unknown uncertainties? Do we need an ISO 310000-A standard to manage additional uncertainties like this?

This section is devoted to the introduction of a comprehensive set of practical definitions that can be used in modern project risk management regardless of whatever names or tags we attach to those. A key incentive to do this is to come up with a clear-cut set of basic notions that can be utilized in practice (not in theory) of risk management of capital projects. Hence, they could be used by project teams and decision makers as international risk management lingo. We don't intend to develop definitions that fit all risk methods, all industries, or all types of (past, current, and future) projects, or that comply with "Risk Management Kremlin's" requirement. There is no intent to dogmatize risk management of capital projects, either.

Let's call these definitions *uncertainty objects*. All of them have been already introduced indirectly in the previous section in a narrative way. They will be meaningful regardless of the linguistic labels we attach to them. We will keep them in our toolbox, not because of labels and nuances related to them, but because of the utility and consistency they provide when waging war against uncertainty of project outcomes. Table 1.2 recaps the discussion of the previous section in a structured way. (The reader could change the labels of the objects to his or her taste or according to his or her native language as soon as their fundamental nature and role are well understood.) The contributions to project cost and schedule reserves mentioned in Table 1.2 are discussed in Chapters 12 and 14.

All new objects are adequately described by combinations of words that contain the word *uncertainty*, and not the word *risk*. The term *risk* plays a rudimentary role in Table 1.2. In a way, the term *risk* becomes irrelevant. (What an achievement given the title of this book!)

We may use a physics analogy describing relations among molecules and atoms to better understand what happened. In place of the traditional object risk ("a molecule") we have new objects ("atoms"). Those new objects are defined by possibilities of upside or downside deviations in the case of general uncertainties or uncertain events, which could be known (identified by a project team) or stay unknown until they occur. To further follow the physics analogy, we may define *three degrees of freedom* associated with an uncertainty:

1. Uncertainty of impact (general uncertainty) versus uncertainty of impact *and* likelihood (uncertain event)
2. Downside (unfavorable) deviation versus upside (favorable) deviation
3. Known (identified) uncertainty versus unknown (unidentified) uncertainty

These three degrees of freedom generate eight main uncertainty types as Figure 1.2 implies:

1. General Uncertainty (GU)—Downside (↓)—Known (K) {GU↓K}
2. General Uncertainty (GU)—Upside (↑)—Known (K) {GU↑K}

TABLE 1.2 Key Uncertainty Objects

Uncertainty Type	Uncertainty Object	Deviation From	Upside or Downside?	Comments
N/A	Project Baselines	N/A	N/A	Hypothetical set of one-point values that are proclaimed fully certain to represent uncertainty-free project objectives.
Given [probability: certain; impact: certain]	Issue	Any objective	⇅	Issues redefine baselines. Issues appear when a general uncertainty becomes certain in terms of impact or uncertain event occurs and becomes certain in terms of both probability and impact. An issue can be associated with either upside or downside deviation depending on the nature of a realized uncertainty.
	Design Uncertainty	CapEx, Scope	→	**Design allowance** is used to address design uncertainty. Normally it is not part of risk management although should be kept in mind when assessing the other objects.
Known (or Unknown) General Uncertainty [probability: certain; impact: uncertain]	General Cost Uncertainty	CapEx		Applicable to each estimate's cost account. Contribute to **project cost contingency.**
	General Duration Uncertainty	Schedule		Applicable to each normal activity. Contribute to **project schedule reserve.**
	Cost Escalation	CapEx	⇅	Taken into account through **escalation reserve**; in case of de-escalation could be used for selection of purchasing time.
	Currency Exchange Rate Uncertainty	CapEx		Taken into account through **exchange rate reserve**. Could be avoided/transferred through hedging.

	Schedule Driven Costs	CapEx		Distribution of completion dates and associated range of schedule delays converted to extra costs; taken into account through application of burn rates in integrated probabilistic cost and schedule risk models as a cost general uncertainty and give rise to **project cost reserve**. Burn rates could be considered *auxiliary* general uncertainties.
	Organizational Bias	Any objective		Systematic errors in identification and assessment of all project uncertainties. Due to human nature and business realities, bias pertains to all project teams to a certain degree as a general uncertainty. In some cases may lead to upside deviations from project objectives. Various anti-bias and calibration methods should be in place to suppress these systematic errors.
	Subconscious Bias	Any objective		
	Conscious Bias	Any objective		
Discrete Uncertain Event [probability: uncertain; impact: certain]	Discrete Uncertain Event	Any objective	⇅	(Known or unknown) uncertain events with clearly predictable one-point impacts on objectives could be singled out as discrete uncertain events. Known discrete uncertain events of cost impacts contribute to **project cost risk reserve** along with uncertain events.
	Downside Uncertain Event	Any objective	→	Those two categories are traditional subjects of risk management that are called *risks* or separately *threats* and *opportunities* in risk jargon. Known uncertain events of cost impacts give rise to **project cost risk reserve.**
	Upside Uncertain Events	Any objective	←	

(Continued)

TABLE 1.2 (Continued)

Uncertainty Type	Uncertainty Object	Deviation From	Upside or Downside?	Comments
Known Uncertain Event [probability: uncertain; impact: uncertain]	Unacceptable Performance and LDs	CapEx, Scope, Quality/Performance, Reputation	→	These could be standalone downside uncertain events depending on corporate financial reporting. If *Quality/Performance* objective is not met upon project completion, **performance allowance** would be used to address poor performance (performance warranty). In case some clauses stipulated by a project contract (consequential damages, schedule delays, turnover of key personnel, etc.) are not obeyed, **liquidated damages** may be incurred.
	Known Show-Stopper/Game Changer	Any objective	→	Probability of occurrence is usually very low and impacts are devastating that destroy (show-stopper: knockout impact) or drastically redefine (game changer: knockdown impact) baselines. Considered part of corporate risk management and not included in project reserves.
Unknown Uncertain Event [existence: uncertain]	Unknown Downside Uncertain Event	Any objective	→	Stays unidentified until occurs; new technology and geography as well as various types of bias are major sources. Also project changes (baseline's redefinition) in case changes are not adequately managed could be a source. May be covered by a special cost or schedule **unknown–unknown reserve (allowance)**.
	Unknown Upside Uncertain Event	Any objective	←	Stays unidentified until occurs; new technology and geography as well as various types of bias are major sources.
	Unknown Show-Stopper/Game Changer	Any objective	→	Being type of unknown, stays unidentified until occurs; new technology and geography as well as various types of bias are major sources. Also project changes (baseline's redefinition) in case changes are not adequately managed could be a source. Probability of occurrence is usually very low and impacts are devastating that destroy (show-stopper: knockout impact) or drastically redefine (game changer: knockdown impact) baselines. Considered part of corporate risk management.

3. General Uncertainty (GU)—Downside (↓)—Unknown (U) {GU↓U}
4. General Uncertainty (GU)—Upside (↑)—Unknown (U) {GU↑U}
5. Uncertain Event (UE)—Downside (↓)—Known {UE↓K}
6. Uncertain Event (UE)—Upside (↑)—Known {UE↑K}
7. Uncertain Event (UE)—Downside (↓)—Unknown {UE↓U}
8. Uncertain Event (UE)—Upside (↑)—Unknown {UE↑U}

Moving from molecules to atoms represented a natural path of science when accumulated knowledge allowed one to better fathom objects of Nature and describe them more adequately and in more detail. The same thing happens when we better understand what we used to call "risk."

One may wonder about the placement of some additional or missing objects such as issues and discrete uncertain events in Figure 1.2. Those were discussed in the previous section and mentioned in Table 1.2. We might make another step "from atoms to electrons, protons, and neutrons" on the way to higher complexity and better understanding. This should double the size of the cube in Figure 1.2. As a result, in place of two categories describing probabilities and impacts we should get four (see Figure 1.3):

1. Issue (probability: certain; impact: certain)
2. General uncertainty (probability: certain; impact: uncertain)
3. Discrete uncertain event (probability: uncertain; impact: certain)
4. Uncertain event (probability: uncertain; impact: uncertain)

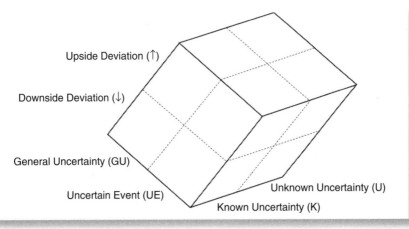

FIGURE 1.2 Three Uncertainty Degrees of Freedom

The addition of extra objects generates a bit too much complexity, which could be overshooting the purpose of this book. Let's keep increasing the level of complexity to academic studies and books. To keep things simple, let's treat an issue as limiting realization of a general uncertainty when impact uncertainty vanishes. Similarly, a discrete uncertain event should be understood as limiting realization of an uncertain event when the possible impact is fully certain. This convention should allow one to avoid adding extra objects to Figure 1.2, which is informative enough. At the same time, all major objects of risk management are comprehensively defined from first principles by Figures 1.2 and 1.3. Moreover, the arrows in Figure 1.3 represent possible transformations among discussed objects in the course of project development and execution.

To be consistent let's summarize this discussion through formal introduction of *four degrees of freedom* of uncertainties as follows:

1. Probability: certain (100%) versus uncertain (< 100%)
2. Impact: certain (one-point) versus uncertain ("range")
3. Favorability: upside (favorable) versus downside (unfavorable)
4. Identification: known (identified) versus unknown (unidentified)

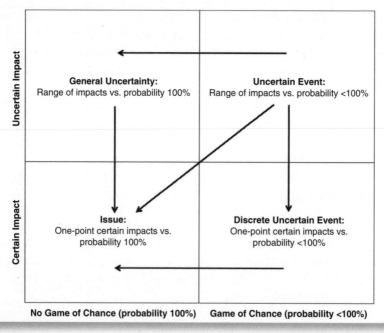

FIGURE 1.3 Uncertainty versus Certainty of Impacts and Likelihoods

These four academic uncertainty degrees of freedom (introduced for consistency) will not be used in this book. We will ignore them and will use practical uncertainty objects generated by those degrees described by Table 1.2 and Figures 1.2 and 1.3.

I'm sorry for using an approach that looks more and more like quantum physics. For readers who don't appreciate analogies from science we may turn to a linguistic analogy such as associating the English language with England. Due to the enormous popularity and success of the English language all over the world in the past few decades and the existence of a number of dialects, accents, and versions, the English language is not associated just with England anymore, as it was in the times of Shakespeare.[8] To me, it's about the United States or Canada these days, despite the fact that I did go to business school in England. For some people it could be about Australia or India, South Africa or Zimbabwe. Even the highly successful 2012 Summer Olympic Games that were hosted in London, England, won't change this much. So, geographically we may distinguish English English, American English, Canadian English, Australian English, East Indian English, and so on, not to mention the multiple versions of English used in the rest of the United Kingdom as well as Spanglish, Chinglish, or Russglish, which I speak fluently.

Should we not treat and interpret words such as *risk management* and *risk* in a similar way? The word *risk* sounds like a linguistic analogy to *English*, and *risk management* to *English English*. I feel that more appropriate and comprehensive would be the words *uncertainty* and *uncertainty management*, which reflect much better the spectrum of objects required to handle overall uncertainty of project outcomes. In light of the more precise and clear definitions of uncertainty objects introduced by Table 1.2 and Figures 1.2 and 1.3, the word *risk* sounds more like a vague piece of jargon that could mean everything and nothing.

Should risk analysts, coordinators, managers, and subject matter experts (SMEs) agitated by these speculations rush in with proposals to management to change their job titles accordingly? Probably not (yet). We should not break with traditions so easily even when they no longer reflect reality. We should cherish them even without any visible reason. I will keep my current good old title of Director, Risk Management, intact. Moreover, I would not support such proposals from my co-workers even if I do understand them. Once again, it's not about labels or titles. So let's keep it calling "risk management," meaning "uncertainty management."

Although I tend to use traditional words and phrases such as *risk, risk register, risk management*, and *risk management plan*, all those r-words should be understood as u-words in all cases. Another main reason to continue using the word *risk* every now and then in place of *uncertainty* is that it is conveniently short, containing only four letters and one syllable.

 ## UNCERTAINTY EXPOSURE CHANGERS

Table 1.2 presents key uncertainty objects that are understood as static and that outline a snapshot of overall project uncertainty exposure in a given moment. What is missing in this picture is time and uncertainty dynamics. So, if you thought that the four uncertainty degrees of freedom are enough, you would be wrong. The fifth degree of freedom is time. As time actually introduces changes or dynamics of project uncertainties objects, in place of that additional degree (time) we will use its representative objects, as follows.

Overall project uncertainty exposure is volatile and depends on a lot of ongoing changes and activities in a project's internal and external environment. Let's call them *uncertainty exposure changers* or just *changers*. They may be external and internal to a project, but they also may be controllable and uncontrollable by a project team.

External uncertainty exposure changers include any dynamics or transformations of givens and facts that are causes of uncertainties relevant to a project. For instance, changes in tax or environmental regulations could be introduced as external uncertainty changers.

Internal uncertainty exposure changers include any decisions and choices relevant to a project done by a project team. Amendments of project-related assumptions are also qualified for this category. These changers influence dynamics and transformation of causes of uncertainties relevant to a project. Decisions, choices, and amended assumptions should not be considered risk management controls since they are usually aimed at shaping project objectives and baselines.

Uncertainty addressing actions make up a special group of internal uncertainty changers. As discussed in Chapter 5, there are two major types of addressing actions: preventive and recovery. Uncertainty addressing actions should be considered major risk management controls to amend project uncertainty exposure in a focused way.

Another angle from which to view changers is the degree of influence a project team has over them. In other words, can a project team guarantee that a changer leads to expected and predictable results planned by the project team for certain? If the answer is somewhat uncertain, this could be considered uncontrollable. For example, implementation of a decision may depend on an approval or a commitment by third parties or stakeholders. Even if an approval is expected from top management of the same organization, this introduces an uncertainty aspect to a project, anyway. For example, a project team might ask management about early procurement of long lead items prior to a final investment decision. Even if a project team builds a strong case to support this, the final decision is uncertain and depends on management. As a result, the decision should be regarded as an upside uncertain event (or *opportunity* in risk jargon) with some probability of happening.

Similarly, any uncertainty addressing action could fully or partially fail. Potential of failure is reciprocal to the control a project team has over implementation of the action.

Volatility of external uncertainty changers is comparable to volatility of the stock markets as this includes volatility of the general economic situation and activities of multiple project stakeholders. It is unlikely that a project team would have much control over external uncertainty changers. The only method to influence them somehow relates to implementation of uncertainty addressing actions (internal changers). Obviously, such addressing actions do not often lead to full control of external changers. For instance, a project team may try to build relations with external stakeholders (e.g., local communities) in order to reduce or avoid a risk of opposition to the project. In some very rare cases this might lead to full control of the external stakeholders' intentions that allows them to fully avoid the risk of opposition.

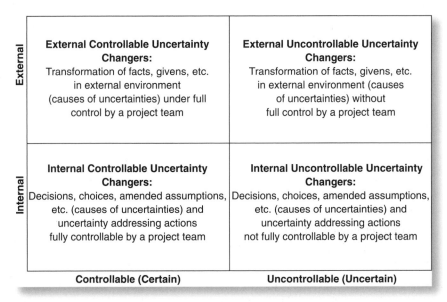

FIGURE 1.4 Main Types of Project Uncertainty Changers

The bottom line is that uncertainty changers could be external and internal and wage a tug of war with each other. They could be either controllable/certain or uncontrollable/uncertain (see Figure 1.4). This approach is supported by a main uncertainty identification tool (bowtie diagram) discussed in Chapter 4. The bowtie diagram includes causes of uncertainties, addressing actions, and risk breakdown structure (RBS) describing the external and internal project environment. In addition, this discussion leads to the important topic of proper assessment of uncertainties after addressing (Chapter 5) due to the possibility of an action's failure.

 ## CONCLUSION

This chapter links overall uncertainty of a project outcome with all major contributing uncertainty factors (objects) that give rise to this. The degrees of freedom of uncertainties were introduced to explore and generate a rich spectrum of uncertainty objects.

Dynamics of uncertainty objects was introduced through internal and external changers. These could be either controllable (certain) or uncontrollable (uncertain).

As soon as all major objects of project uncertainty are revealed and the main types of uncertainty changers are singled out, focused selection of adequate methods to handle uncertainty objects should commence. There is no silver bullet that allows control of all uncertainties in a consistently efficient way. A tailor-made approach is required to match challenges with methods. The number of adequate and crucial methods to handle all types of uncertainties is quite small. The rest of the book is devoted to a detailed overview of the limited number of the most efficient and adequate methods that zero in on particular types of uncertainties and their changers.

 ## NOTES

1. IPA Institute, "Successful Mega Projects" Seminar (Calgary, Alberta, Canada 2009), p.18.
2. A. Dubi, *Monte Carlo Applications in System Engineering* (Hoboken, NJ: John Wiley & Sons, 2000).
3. C. Ebeling, *An Introduction to Reliability and Maintainability Engineering* (Long Grove, IL: Waveland Press, 1997).

4. C. Chapman and S. Ward, *Project Risk Management: Processes, Techniques and Insights* (Chichester, England: John Wiley & Sons, 2003).

5. One European organization recently "found an answer" to this question as a result of an infamous incident in the Gulf of Mexico. The price tag is several billion dollars in legal damages and counting; environment and company reputation are severely damaged; several people are dead. No doubt, it is more reasonable to manage risks of safety, environment and reputation impacts before they happen (preventive approach) than pay a huge price (and not only in monetary terms) after they occur (crisis management).

6. ISO 31000 International Standard: *Risk Management: Principles and Guidelines* (Switzerland: International Organization for Standardization, 2009).

7. D. Hubbard, *The Failure of Risk Management: Why It's Broken and How to Fix It* (Hoboken, NJ: John Wiley & Sons, 2009).

8. R. McCrum, W. Cran, and R. MacNeil, *The Story of English* (London: Faber & Faber, 2011).

CHAPTER TWO

Main Components of a Risk Management System

Questions Addressed in Chapter 2

- What happens when projects do not have risk management plans?
- What happens when projects do not have *good* risk management plans?
- What are the three (actually four) dimensions of risk management?
- What are the roles of broiler black swans and red herrings in risk management?
- What are the roles of the game changers and show-stoppers in project risk management?
- What roles did Fyodor Dostoyevsky and Dr. Feynman play in risk management?
- When the cart gets put before "two horses" in risk management, how do we put it back?
- How does automation allow you to make mistakes easier and more comfortably? ■

A PROJECT RISK MANAGEMENT SYSTEM is like a symphony orchestra that includes many instruments and performers. It requires the proper structure and fine tuning and its parts should be well synchronized to ensure proper overall performance and to exclude cacophony. This chapter provides a high-level overview of the components of an adequate project risk management system. Subsequent chapters describe all the required details. A project risk management plan is like a "full score" that is used by a project team to play in unison like an orchestra. This document ensures that the project risk management system adopted by an organization is a differentiator (supposedly a positive one) and a strong competitive advantage for the organization.

Three components of a project risk management system—organizational framework, risk management process, and risk management tools—are introduced in this chapter. In a good project risk management plan, those components should be defined in detail. The three dimensions of an organizational framework are introduced to highlight a *line-of-sight* concept of project risk management.

Various obstacles that may impede efficiency of a project risk management system are discussed. In that regard the secondary role of tools in risk management is accentuated.

RISK MANAGEMENT PLAN

To adequately identify and manage various project uncertainties a project team should develop a very structured, clear, and engaging system that includes steps of identification, assessment, and addressing (i.e., risk management process). Responsibilities of project team members in the risk management process should be clearly defined. An organizational risk framework should take into account the type of business an organization is in. The organizational framework should include not only responsibilities of the team members but their engagement in the risk management process where project uncertainties could be identified, assessed, and addressed. In addition, risk reporting and escalation should be clearly established to exclude situations where some uncertainties are overlooked and not taken care of. This gets us back to the role of organizational bias, briefly discussed in Chapter 1. Conscious and subconscious types of bias could be notoriously influential in the risk management process, too. These three types of bias (especially organizational bias) could be seen as a "risk to risk management." Proper risk management "health self-checks" should be included in the project risk management plans as part of the organizational risk framework.

Both the risk management process and the organizational framework should be supported by effective risk management tools. Their optimal functionalities and structure depend on the type of managed uncertainties. A well-known risk management tool is a *risk register*. Some project teams develop a single project risk register that covers all possible types of uncertainties in all project disciplines. Such a grandiose document could easily contain hundreds and hundreds of items that cannot be effectively managed and used. It is preferable to have several specialized and communicating registers and logs and to set a hierarchy of them in a project uncertainty repository.

Probabilistic risk assessments require specialized software packages based on applications of the Monte Carlo technique. The particular tools used for probabilistic assessments as well as types of analyses (probabilistic schedule, cost, integrated cost and schedule analyses, etc.) should be reflected in the project management plans, too.

A project risk management plan is a short working document that puts together and synchronizes the three main components of a risk management system:

1. Organizational framework
2. Risk management process
3. Risk management tools

It is difficult to develop a risk management plan that covers the three components for all phases of project development and execution. It should be revised and updated right after the end of each phase. Unfortunately, it is often done right before the end of a phase instead, just to pass a coming decision gate. This is the sign of a formal and inefficient risk management system. For instance, simple scoring techniques are used for assessments in the early phases, such as Identify and Select. At the same time, by the end of Select and in Define, probabilistic methods are regularly used for assessments and project reserve reevaluations. Regular probabilistic assessments are required in Execute to redefine required contingencies and to draw them down. The corresponding shift from scoring to probabilistic methods should be reflected in the project risk management plan. In the course of project development and evolving of the project, the uncertainty exposure and project risk management system should also evolve.

A project risk management plan should be written in close cooperation with representatives of the other project disciplines. In some cases specialists from other organizations (joint venture partners; engineering, procurement and construction [EPC] contractors; etc.) should be engaged, too. The reason for this is very simple. The other project disciplines are responsible for shaping the project objectives and baselines, whereas the purpose of the risk management is consistent identification, assessment, and addressing of the deviations from the objectives and baselines. These tasks cannot be fulfilled without engagement of those disciplines.

It would not be an exaggeration to state that if a project does not have a formalized risk management plan, there is no risk management. Of course, some activities resembling and mimicking project risk management are possible. However, their reliability cannot be high due to lack of system, structure, and consistency and would likely bring up negative value by failing to meet expectations. The key message here is very simple. The real value of a risk management system is measured not by types of uncertainties or instances when those uncertainties are managed properly. Its real value is reciprocal to the size of the room left for missed and unmanaged uncertainties. We will get back to this theme when we discuss unknown uncertainties.

One may feel that in some cases the absence of a risk management system could be a lesser evil than having a misleading risk management system in place. Hopefully, such a project has a good crisis management plan, at least.

The rest of this chapter is devoted to a high-level description of the three main components of a risk management system. Inevitably, I need to repeat some general banalities about a risk management system along with some fresh ideas. However, subsequent chapters discuss these components in detail using practical insights.

 ## ORGANIZATIONAL FRAMEWORK

The organizational framework is the most important element of a risk management system related to organizational governance. It should reflect which business an organization is in, which, in our case, is project development and execution. It defines what project objectives and what types of deviations from them should be the focus of risk management and how those deviations should be managed and reported. We also use the term *organizational context* as a synonym for *organizational framework*. Either term should be viewed as a component of the broader organizational governance.

The four key elements of an organizational framework of capital megaprojects are:

1. Description of the challenges a project has (objectives and deviations from them) and the approach for how risk management is to meet those challenges

2. Responsibilities of project team members
3. Types and frequencies of risk review activities
4. Risk reporting and escalating

The main concept used to define these elements is called *line-of-sight* to ensure that uncertainties of various origins and levels of severity are not overlooked. Three dimensions (3D) of risk management should be introduced to structure the line-of-sight:

1. *Vertical (hierarchy):* integration of the risk management system at work package–project–business unit–corporate levels
2. *Horizontal (disciplines):* integration of various project disciplines from engineering, procurement and construction to safety, project services, etc.
3. *In-Depth (coordination):* integration of risk management activities among project owners, partners, EPC contractors, and major stakeholders

Figure 2.1 represents the vertical, horizontal, and in-depth dimensions of an organizational framework and risk management integration. As discussed in Chapter 4, these three dimensions should be kept in mind when defining an adequate *risk breakdown structure (RBS)* to be adopted by a project.

FIGURE 2.1 Three Dimensions of Risk Management

As in physics, there is a fourth dimension missing in risk management: time. As it is quite difficult to develop figures in 4D, time is not shown explicitly by Figure 2.1. However, it should be always kept in mind as overall project uncertainty exposure and objects contributing to this are constantly evolving. (External and internal uncertainty changers, including uncertainty addressing actions, were introduced in Chapter 1. They are discussed again in Chapter 4.)

The 3D picture of risk management introduced in Figure 2.1 exceeds the scope of this book immensely. We will be focused on the two lower floors of the pyramid (work package and project levels) as related to EPC and project services mostly. On a few occasions we will refer to the business unit and corporate levels. The list of disciplines (*horizontal*) may be expanded to include business development, operations, legal, HR, finances, and so on. Realizations of risk management in those will be mostly left out, too. The *in-depth* dimension will be mostly ignored as well.

If risk management is a standalone project discipline, this is a guaranteed way to its isolation and failure. Its role is to handle deviations from objectives and baselines in all disciplines at the work package, project, and business unit levels. Hence, it should be *integrated* into all cells of the pyramid of Figure 2.1. That is why it is not shown in Figure 2.1.

Besides being a standalone discipline, the isolation of risk management could take various forms. For instance, strangely enough, grandiose risk workshops that are held once a year or so are direct indicators of this. Those actually try to cover all three dimensions simultaneously, which is not possible, of course. I am appalled by recommendations to have major risk workshops like this where two or three dozen representatives of various project disciplines spend days identifying, assessing, and addressing risks that are so different in their nature. Each particular participant is engaged in discussing uncertainties he or she is really interested in and qualified to discuss for no more than 5–10% of the time.

Quite often those workshops are the only risk management activities the participants are ever involved in, which is enough to convince them of the low value of risk management and its ultimate boredom. Low-value-added or negative-value-added risk management activities like this could be called "risk management ritual dances." The logic behind this is: "If we spend two days on a risk management workshop, this should mean we have risk management!" Take a look at "Cargo Cult Science" as a direct allusion. We will discuss the most effective types of risk workshops and other activities to identify, assess, and address risks in Part II.

CARGO CULT SCIENCE

As Richard Feynman, Nobel laureate in physics, wrote in his famous book, *Surely You're Joking, Mr. Feynman!*, "We really ought to look into theories that don't work, and science that isn't science." He presented a story of "cargo cult science" as an allusion to the adequacy of some theories and methods:

> In the South Seas there is a cargo cult of people. During the war they saw airplanes land with lots of good materials, and they want the same thing to happen now. So they've arranged to make things like runways, to put fires along the sides of runways, to make a wooden hut for a man to sit in, with two wooden pieces on his head like headphones and bars of bamboo sticking out like antennas— he's the controller—and they wait for the airplanes to land. They're doing everything right. The form is perfect. It looks exactly the way it looked before. But it doesn't work. No airplanes land. . . . They follow all the apparent precepts and forms . . . but they're missing something essential, because the planes don't land.

> R. Feynman, *Surely You're Joking, Mr. Feynman!*, reprinted by permission of W.W. Norton & Company.[1]

This should be kept in mind when thinking about the credibility and efficiency of various risk management activities and methods.

The three dimensions of risk management and the line-of-sight idea should be kept in mind when establishing a risk responsibility matrix for project team members. Project teams could use one of many known forms of responsibility matrices, such as:

- RACI: Responsible, Accountable, Consult, Informed
- RASCI: Responsible, Accountable, Support, Consult, Inform
- RACIA: Responsible, Accountable, Consult, Informe, Approve
- LACTI: Lead, Approve, Consult, Tasked, Informed

Each of them has its own merits and could be selected by a project team. I am a proponent of a simple RR-matrix where *RR* stands for Roles and Responsibilities. One of the reasons for this is that I do not see much difference in the meanings of the words *responsible* and *accountable*. I tend to confuse their meanings in the context of right applications of those matrixes every time. Table 2.1 represents a typical RR-matrix of a capital mega-project.

TABLE 2.1   Roles and Responsibilities in Risk Management

Roles	Responsibilities
Executive/ Decision Maker	1. Approves project objectives and project risk management plan 2. Regularly reviews the overall project uncertainty exposure. 3. Endorses critical uncertainty severity assessments as recorded in the risk register. 4. Monitors progress of the uncertainty addressing action plans for critical uncertainties.
Project Manager	1. Defines the project objectives and leads development of the project risk management plan. 2. Owns the project risk management system, plan, and risk register. 3. Initiates the creation of a fit-for-purpose risk management process, aligned with project objectives and organizational context. 4. Approves the project's RAM. 5. Regularly reviews the project risk database, focusing on completeness of required information and situations when information should be taken to a higher level of management. 6. Ensures higher-level uncertainties (e.g., business unit or corporate) are communicated to the appropriate level of management. 7. Reviews critical uncertainties and endorses material uncertainty assessments. 8. Resources response plans for critical and material uncertainties. 9. Nominates owners for critical uncertainties. 10. Monitors progress of the uncertainty addressing actions and provides guidance in case there are deviations from the plans. 11. Ensures, through supervision, effective implementation of uncertainty addressing actions. 12. Regularly reviews the effectiveness of the risk management plan as a whole through internal management review or by requesting peer reviews.

Team Lead/ Uncertainty Category Owner (any discipline)	1. Regularly reviews the project risk database, focusing on completeness of required information and situations when information should be taken to a higher level of management.
	2. Reviews assessments of critical and material uncertainties and endorses material severity assessments as recorded in the risk register.
	3. Nominates uncertainty owners.
	4. Resources addressing plans for material severity uncertainties.
	5. Monitors progress of the uncertainty addressing and provides guidance where there are deviations from the plan.
	6. Ensures effective implementation of uncertainty addressing.
Risk Manager	1. Develops project risk management plan, creates and maintains the risk register and ensures overall quality.
	2. Owns and maintains project risk management process.
	3. Proposes the project specific RAM and ensures agreement by project manager and executive.
	4. Ensures that all uncertainties have assigned owners.
	5. Trains, coaches, and supports the uncertainty and action owners.
	6. Generates reports from the risk register to inform the project team and decision makers about progress made in implementation of actions.
	7. Coordinates and facilitates uncertainty reviews and workshops and ensures consistent implementation of selected risk management methods.
	8. Ensures all team members and decision makers are familiar with the project risk management process and tools.
	9. Ensures all team members and decision makers are aware of various types of organizational and psychological bias and manages group dynamics to exclude impact of bias on quality of project risk management.

(Continued)

TABLE 2.1 (Continued)

Roles	Responsibilities
Uncertainty Owner (any discipline)	1. Ensures that his or her uncertainty has a clear, meaningful title and description.
	2. Provides a clear audit trail for updates.
	3. Ensures that his or her uncertainty is properly assessed (before and after addressing) and that the assessment is endorsed at the appropriate level.
	4. Ensures that uncertainty addressing actions are defined and coordinates their implementations with action owners.
	5. Monitors and appraises effectiveness of uncertainty addressing with a view to improvement.
Action Owner (any discipline)	1. Progresses actions per the response plan timing.
	2. Updates the risk register for action status.
	3. Informs the uncertainty owner about any concerns related to the addressing.
	4. Notifies the uncertainty owner of any changes required in resourcing or timing to implement the action.
Team Member (any discipline)	1. Gets familiar with the uncertainties and addressing actions that may impact his or her work.
	2. Continuously identifies uncertainties that may jeopardize the achievement of project objectives.
	3. Provides feedback to uncertainty owners if addressing is found to be ineffective and suggests how to improve.

Types and frequencies of review meetings should be defined in the risk management plan. This has a direct link with the fourth dimension of risk management introduced earlier, which is time. This also leads to the well-known but often poorly followed maxim that risk management should be an ongoing and evergreen activity. A simple rule is that more severe risks should be reviewed more often and at a higher level of the organization. In addition, if a risk is identified at a discipline level that could lead to very high deviations from objectives, it should be escalated to the right level in the organization. For instance, some package risks could be included in project, business unit, and even corporate registers. Chapter 7 contains a more detailed discussion on this topic.

Practical realization of the organizational framework in project risk management is done through risk management process and risk management tools.

RISK MANAGEMENT PROCESS

The risk management process is the second most important element of a risk management system. Traditionally, a risk management process is used for uncertain events (risks). The other objects introduced in Table 1.2, such as various types of general uncertainties, are not subject to this. However, there is no reason why the same process could not be applicable to both uncertain events and general uncertainties of various sorts. First, the purpose of the process is to systematically discover possible deviations from project objectives. Second, assessment of deviation's probabilities and magnitudes should be undertaken. The ultimate goal of the process is to suppress downside deviations to an acceptable level and enhance upside ones. Certainly, this should be done economically; otherwise, it could be more reasonable to accept some deviations "as-is." In other words, the risk management process is an algorithm to identify, assess, and address all possible deviations from project objectives and baselines (see Figure 2.2). The steps of the process are briefly described in this section. Detailed discussion of the steps is undertaken in Part II. In order to support the identification and assessment steps, some preparations are required.

First, the set of project objectives should be highlighted and each objective should be described as a short statement. Second, the deviation's "scanning tools" should be in place, which allow you to systematically scan a project's internal and external environment. Third, a "measuring tape" to assess deviation's probabilities and magnitudes should be brought up.

We introduce a common approach to select a set of project objectives used in risk management in this chapter. The set of objectives is the benchmarking

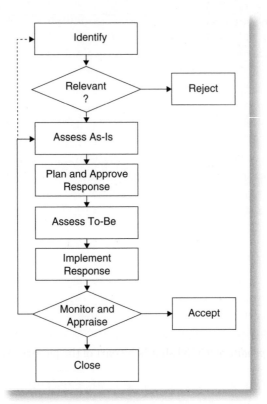

FIGURE 2.2 Risk Management Process

foundation of a project risk management system. This reflects what is important to the organization undertaking the project, to its partners, and to its stakeholders. This sets up the criteria for success or failure of a project. It defines how the measuring tape adopted by the project is structured. The measuring tape (risk assessment matrix [RAM]) is discussed in Chapter 5. The RAM incorporates selected project objectives and has five categories of deviations from them as well as five categories describing probabilities of occurrence. Those categories are used to assess the level of risk severities.

Detailed discussion on the measuring tape (RAM) and scanning tools (bowtie diagram and RBS) is provided in Chapter 4. It is important to keep in mind that the RAM and RBS are the main "vehicles" to adequately represent organizational framework in risk management process and risk management tools.

Project Objectives

As discussed in Chapter 1, a traditional set of "hard" objectives includes a "project triangle" of three constraints:

1. Scope
2. Capital expenditure (CapEx)
3. Schedule (completion date)

These hard objectives are usually well quantifiable. Besides those, some "soft" objectives that are widely used these days include:

1. Safety
2. Environment
3. Reputation

These soft objectives are normally treated as additional goal-zero types of constraints: no fatalities or injuries, no negative impacts on environment and reputation. In addition to the typical objectives put forward, one hard objective is often overlooked pertaining to operations, not project delivery. Project lifetime *operational expenditure (OpEx)* should be part of the picture. Normally, OpEx is included in the project economic models and closely relates to performance of the delivered project. In some cases direct apples-to-apples comparison of CapEx and OpEx is required when considering holistically cost risk exposures during project delivery and in operations. The standard present value (PV) approach may be used to convert annual lifetime OpEx budgets to a base period's money and directly compare the resulting PV of OpEx with CapEx. A discounting factor equal to average cost of capital (to say, 5–7% in North America) should be used to get the PV of OpEx. As a result, the Cost objective could be treated as a sum of CapEx and PV of OpEx where required (see Chapters 9 and 10).

According to this discussion, the following six project objectives will be systematically considered in this book:

1. *Scope*: quality and performance including reliability, availability, maintainability[2]
2. *Cost*: CapEx (plus PV of OpEx, where required)
3. *Schedule*: project duration/ completion date
4. *Safety*[3]
5. *Environment*
6. *Reputation*

These project execution objectives are typical for organizations that own capital projects (project owner organizations) . Depending on the project location, an additional soft project objective could be established related to *Security*. This covers personal security of workers, business continuity, and possible company property losses. We will not further consider this objective in the book.

Some additional project objectives could be selected (*Legal*, *Employee Retention*, *Gross Margin*, etc.) in case of the EPC organizations. A different set of objectives is to better reflect on the organizational context and nature of EPC business. Certainly, different sets of objectives should be selected for business unit and corporate levels in any type of organization. The objectives should reflect the particular organizational context and the area of the pyramid depicted in Figure 2.1.

The Scope objective depends on the nature of a project. In the case of a carbon capture and storage project, it could be about sustained System Capacity of CO_2 capture and injection to aquifer (tons per year). In the case of an oil exploration and production project, it could be about daily oil production rate (barrels per day). For a chemical plant, this would be about monthly production rate of a specified chemical substance (tons per month).

The following example shows how these six objectives may be specified in a risk management plan as short statements:

1. *Scope:* to deliver a facility that has production rate, reliability, availability, etc. according to the approved specification
2. *Cost:* to deliver a facility according to an approved budget
3. *Schedule:* to deliver a production facility by an approved date
4. *Safety:* to comply with all applicable company and industry safety requirements and standards, including zero-goal in terms of safety incidents
5. *Environment:* to comply with all applicable environmental regulations and company standards, including zero-goal in terms of negative impact on environment in construction and operations
6. *Reputation:* to ensure that no negative impact on company reputation or relations with the project's stakeholders occurs during project delivery and in operations

Some additional clarifications and modifications could be required in particular cases. For instance, the words *to deliver* may contractually mean mechanical completion, startup, first oil, sustained operations, and so on. Approved specification, budget, and schedule imply existence of corresponding fully developed baselines. Particular regulations and standards may be cited.

Good reputation and relations with stakeholders might assume the possibility of winning new contracts or future access to oil and gas reserves around the world. One might guess that it is more attractive for companies to be good corporate citizens with access to oil and gas reserves and lucrative contracts than just to be good citizens. At the same time the set of objectives should be rather concise and clear to be used as a quick mnemonic reference when undertaking various risk management activities. Project objectives formulated this way could be considered key objects of risk management, too, as they play the role of benchmarks for deviations from them. In comparison to the uncertainty objects of Table 1.2 those should be formulated in a most certain (specific, measurable, and so on) way.

Steps of the Risk Management Process

The steps of the risk management process could be conditionally grouped in two categories: (1) management of uncertainties and (2) their assessment. The second group provides information for decision making, including assessments of required project reserves. Methods of uncertainty assessments depend on the nature and phase of a project. We discuss two main methods of assessment—deterministic (scoring) and probabilistic (Monte Carlo)—and their modifications in Chapter 3. The steps of the risk management process are briefly reviewed in this section. We will get back to their detailed discussion in Part II. The single most important step of the process is Step 7: Implement Response, which is where the rubber meets the road. The rest of the steps are relevant only for a single reason: to effectively support it.

Step 1: Identify

Uncertainties of various types (the objects of Table 1.2) relevant to a project should be identified first to be managed. A structured approach that ensures that all relevant uncertainties are captured is required. Uncertainties may stem from various parts of the project's environment, both internal and external defining their sources.

EPC and the other major project disciplines and activities are common sources of uncertainties. Some stakeholders might be keenly interested in the success (or failure) of a project. Excessive attention like this could become an additional source of uncertainty to the project outcome. Uncertainties may be induced by shortcomings of processes used by the project, such as interface or change management, features of the decision-making process, and so on.

Interface management and project changes are common sources of uncertainties. These two sources, especially project changes, are systematically overlooked by project teams. For this reason these two often become not just sources of uncertain events but unknown uncertain events. As discussed in Chapter 4, this is a classical situation of organizational bias where many aspects of project changes are systematically overlooked.[4]

Some rare but devastating events, referred to as "black swans,"[5] could lead to complete project disaster or its cancellation. Usually they occur in a project's external environment and have a very low probability of occurrence but crushing impacts on project objectives. (The origin of this term is associated with the saying, "It is about as likely as finding a black swan," which reflects on the very low probability of occurrence.) If they occurred, there is no project as previously contemplated anymore as one or more baselines will be substantially impacted or destroyed. There will be either a different project after the baseline's rework or none at all.

There is no need to be paranoid about black swans, at least in the case of project teams. Viewing black swans from an organizational framework angle, they should be treated in a context of demarcation of responsibilities between project and corporate risk management. Known black swans should be reviewed during the final investment decision (FID) to take into account an organization's risk appetite. The issue here is that an organization's risk appetite strongly depends on the phase of current economic cycle and is subject to organizational bias. In the case of good general economic news, organizational bias in the form of overconfidence could be remarkably amplified, providing decision makers with rose-colored glasses.

Most dangerous objects are unknown or unidentified uncertainties. As discussed in Chapter 4, they have several reasons to stay undercover. Project novelty and various types of bias are the major ones. It is possible to reduce room for them to a certain degree, but never to zero. Of course, black swans could be the most devastating of them. But once again, there is no need for Dostoyevsky-type psychological analysis of fears and concerns related to them,[6] although managing corresponding types of bias based on a good knowledge of Dostoyevsky's works is certainly part of the solution.

Logic reciprocal to this should dictate forbidding all major modes of industrial production and traveling, closing financial markets, canceling most planned capital projects, and so on. As one of the project directors I worked with argued, "If we got paranoid about those so-called 'black swans,' we would have achieved nothing!" If you fear, don't do; if you do, don't fear. Project teams should work on development and execution of projects, and corporate people can afford to be paranoid. Let this be part of their job description.

Unfortunately, some of the black swans could be introduced or generated by various professional activists and lobbyists. Some of them just seek our attention and camera time trying to sound semi-intellectual; some are fronts of serious commercial and political interest groups with hidden agendas. No doubt, some concerns are legitimate and should be addressed. However, recent history provides examples of politically and commercially motivated delays or cancellations of projects in North America, which makes it less competitive. For instance, lack of pipeline capacity to export heavy oil from Alberta in either direction could be a source of additional risk exposure to the whole heavy oil sector in Alberta. I wonder who might profit from this?

I will not further explore this highly political topic, which is outlined well enough for the purpose of risk identification. In any case, we may be talking here about politically and commercially fed "broiler black swans" as opposed to "wild black swans"! The latter are more or less random from the viewpoint of management of a particular project, whereas the former are predetermined by focused activities of certain stakeholders and might come out of the woodwork at any time. Due diligence is required to understand causes or origins of black swans in general, and motivations of external stakeholders in particular when identifying the broiler black swans. The key difference between wild black swans and broiler black swans is that the latter would not necessarily have very low probability of occurrence, being a focused activity of particular project stakeholders. We will discuss probability assessments of broiler black swans in Chapter 5.

I cannot help mentioning the recent severe reputational damage done to a European oil and gas company due to its dubious Arctic drilling experience. A major nongovernmental organization declared that company to be "the worst company of the year in the world." In a nutshell, this type of World Championship and attributed reputational damage will certainly make it much more difficult for that company to get future access to oil and gas reserves globally, develop and execute its projects, and attract qualified specialists. Like the typical broiler black swan, it came out of thin air as it could not be identified or managed beforehand. And in the era of Internet and mass communications it inflicted unproportionally high reputational damage ("black eye") to that company ("black sheep").

Broiler black swans should be considered part of corporate risk management according to the *vertical* dimension of risk management. To address possible political corporate risks like this, the building of broader coalitions is required to ensure sufficient company support at large and support of its major and mega-projects in particular. For this reason, project team members should not waste their time trying to identify all those corporate black swans, or rather *red herrings*. Instead, they should zero in on developing and executing baselines through managing far more relevant project uncertainties.

Show-stoppers or game changers reflect project realities much better. So, we won't use the jargon-type terms such as *black swan*, *sheep*, or *eye* any further. One exception will be "broiler black swan" (Chapter 5) that seems like a very powerful concept to discuss activities of some types of project external stakeholders. Chapter 7 contains additional discussion on show-stoppers, which we consider when a project does not exist anymore (knockout impact on objectives), and game changers (knockdown impact on objectives), or when its baselines should be significantly reworked.

Besides the various sources of uncertainties discussed earlier, there are causes of uncertainties. Project teams should permanently scan the internal and external environment for facts, givens, trends, and so on and try to check them for relevance to the project and capacity to cause deviations from objectives. Assumptions and decisions made during project development are other major incubators of causes.

A powerful risk identification framework called the "bowtie diagram" is introduced in Chapter 4. It integrates sources, causes, events, and impacts on project objectives as well as addressing actions in one compact thinking tool.

The three dimensions of risk management (Figure 2.1) should be kept in mind when identifying uncertainties, although the business unit and corporation levels are excluded from discussion in this book. This means that the scope of uncertainty identification should be absolutely clearly defined every time this activity is planned. The following and similar questions should be clearly answered prior to the identification efforts:

- Is uncertainty identification devoted to one of the work packages?
- Should package uncertainties transferred to a vendor or kept by a project owner be identified?
- Are uncertainties considered only as related to risk exposure of an EPC contractor?
- Are project execution uncertainties belonging to a project owner within the focus of the identification efforts?

Any team member may come up with an uncertainty related to the project. This may not necessarily pertain to the area the individual works in. This may be identified during risk workshops, regular team meetings, interviews, work package procurement activities, engineering and constructability reviews, and so on or may be submitted without being identified during formal meetings. In any case the project risk manager should:

- Check whether the identified uncertainty (or similar) is not already previously identified.
- Discuss it with representatives of relevant project disciplines.
- Describe it using adopted rules (three-part naming based on bowtie diagram structure introduced in Chapter 4).
- Propose an owner.
- Make a conclusion as to whether the identified uncertainty is relevant to the project.

Uncertain events are the primary uncertainty type handled by risk management traditionally. In the case of general uncertainties, they are usually kept outside of risk registers. Namely, they are supposed to be kept in logs of various project disciplines (EPC, estimating, scheduling, safety, environmental, etc.). Addressing them is part of the routine activities of project disciplines focused on development of project baselines.

Even if general uncertainties are not retained as part of the project risk register being kept in a discipline's logs, information on general uncertainties is used when evaluating project reserves by probabilistic methods. The key principle in handling various uncertainties simultaneously is excluding their double counting, or "double-dipping" as practitioners call it.

It is important to dispatch every particular identified uncertainty to the right log/register, depending on its nature and origin. We discuss various project logs/registers and their integration and communication with the project repository in Chapter 8.

Identification should be an ongoing, evergreen process. After initial risk identification, which is usually done in Identify, identification of risks should be done during various project review meetings. Overall review of risks and identification of additional risks should be done before every decision gate and upon initiation of the next phase. Both routine project discipline activities, including work package management, and regular risk reviews should be used for risk identification. Special value improvement exercises (value engineering, constructability reviews, etc.) are common venues for identification, especially for upside uncertainty ("opportunity") identification. The project uncertainty repository is supposed to have a structure that accommodates various risks coming from the three dimensions of risk management (Figure 2.1).

In some cases more than one uncertainty object may be involved to adequately describe a particular project uncertainty. For instance, some general uncertainties bring up unusually high uncertainty levels. This is usually true when more than one baseline scenario could be realized (branching). Those should be included in the risk register for reporting and visibility purposes. For instance, absence of geotechnical data in a new location yields broad uncertainty associated with the cost of a facility's foundation. A proper geotech study program could resolve this uncertainty. However, if it is not planned, a broad range of soils could be discovered upon beginning construction, from sand and clay (with or without boulders) to gravel, to rock, not to mention encountering extremes like swamp or permafrost in some locations. Realization of these extreme scenarios could be treated as an uncertain event.

Similarly, a certain level of labor productivity is usually factored into a base estimate and accompanied by a range as a general uncertainty. If productivity exceeds the established range for any reason, such an occasion could be treated as an uncertain event with some probability.

Step 2: Relevant?

This screening step is aimed at assessment of relevance of an identified uncertainty to the project. For instance, a tsunami in Guinea Bissau and its consequences should not be relevant to a project unless it is located there or some goods and services are bought from that part of the world. At the same time, a similar event in Japan or South Korea, which are common sources of high-quality equipment and materials for capital mega-projects, could be viewed in the light of recent tragic events as an insurable *force majeure*.

Decision about the relevance should be made by the project manager and project risk manager. A decision on where in the project uncertainty repository a particular identified uncertainty should be kept should also be made. The identified uncertainty should get the status "Proposed" in a project uncertainty repository.

Step 3: Reject

Supposedly, this step is not applicable to each identified uncertainty. If a conclusion is made that the identified uncertainty is not exactly relevant to the project, it should be either correspondingly amended or rejected. If rejected, it should still be kept in a project repository with the status "Proposed, Closed."

Step 4: Assess Before Addressing

If a new uncertainty is not rejected, it should be assessed. Usually initial assessment is done using a scoring method based on a project RAM, described in detail in Chapter 3. This assessment is done for the as-is case first. This takes into account addressing measures in place (but not future addressing actions).

In the case of general uncertainties RAM-based assessment could be done using probability equal to 100%. In practice, RAM is not often used for assessment of cost and schedule general uncertainties. Cost estimators may evaluate possible upside and downside deviations from corresponding cost accounts, knowing current level of engineering development, available quotes, and so on, as well as historic information and methods used to develop the estimate. Similarly, schedulers could evaluate the deviations from durations of normal activities. Assessment of cost and schedule general uncertainties is usually required when preparing for probabilistic cost and schedule risk analysis.

According to Figure 2.2, the risk management process could repeat itself several times. Implementation of each addressing action changes assessment as-is because measures in place will include the recently implemented addressing actions. When all planned actions are implemented, the assessment as-is is equal to the assessment to-be defining residual risk exposure.

Ranking of uncertainties could be done at this stage as results of as-is assessments are available. As discussed in Chapter 5, an uncertain event may be qualified as Critical, Material, or Small, depending on its probability and impacts. A corresponding color (red, yellow, or green) will be assigned for visibility and reporting purposes. As it is not unusual that there can be impacts on more than one project objective, top impact score should be taken into account in ranking. One of the key implications of this rule discussed in Chapter 5 is that all project objectives are equally important to a project. Moreover, deviations from them of equal degree are supposed to commensurate to each other. This makes definitions of some projects as "schedule driven" or "cost driven" very dubious. They should rather be "project-objectives-set driven," as there should not be second-class project objectives.

Assessment of uncertainties using deterministic methods is done one-by-one for each particular uncertainty individually. Overall uncertainty exposure is understood simply as a conglomerate of uncertainties of particular categories and levels. This is used for allocation of resources to support particular addressing actions. The situation is different when probabilistic methods are applied for assessment of cost and schedule uncertainty exposure. A whole population of uncertainties is assessed to derive project contingencies jointly. United impacts of all uncertainties are incorporated (mathematically "convoluted") to overall project cost or duration distribution curves reflecting on the overall uncertainty of project outcomes cost- and schedule-wise. Probabilistic Monte Carlo methods are discussed in detail in Part III.

Step 5: Plan and Approve Response

Downside uncertainty response actions are used to reduce impact on project objectives. The goal of the upside uncertainty response actions is to increase their positive impact. Five key strategies of addressing are discussed in Chapter 5 in detail. Those are focused on managing two parameters of uncertainty: probability of occurrence and impact on objectives. A combination of various strategies could be used to address a particular uncertainty.

A project team member who is responsible for a particular uncertainty (owner) should come up with a response plan. It may contain several addressing actions. Each of those actions should have its owner. As a rule the uncertainty owner should be more senior than action owners as his or her role will be a coordination of action owners' efforts to reduce risk severity to an acceptable level. This also means that the corresponding resources required to address uncertainties should be allocated and approved by project leadership, including assignments of the action owners. As discussed in detail in Chapter 7, uncertainties that could have higher impacts on project objectives should be assigned to more senior people in the organization.

Step 6: Assess After Addressing

Uncertainty exposure assessment after addressing depends on what addressing actions are included in such an assessment. Depending on a project schedule and addressing action's nature, implementation of them should be done at a particular point in the future. All planned actions should be gotten over with by the end of the project. In any case it would be too late to implement some as residual uncertainty exposure associated with project delivery will evaporate. Only uncertainties in Operate will hold up. The definition of assessment after addressing and timelines of assessment to-be require further clarification. In other words, this brings up the time dimension of uncertainties again.

Assessment after addressing or to-be should be understood as completion of relevant addressing actions by a particular point in time. This assumes that corresponding actions have implementation windows before that particular point in time. For instance, it would be too early to expect that all addressing actions of an uncertainty that could occur in construction should be implemented before the final investment decision (FID). This particular point in time corresponds to a snapshot of future uncertainty exposure when a particular decision should be made. It could be any major decision gate between phases of project delivery, including FID, or any intermediate milestone to be achieved by a project. Obviously, this approach presumes introduction of several assessments to-be. For instance, it could be "to-be-1" for a decision gate by the end of Select, "to-be-2" or "to-be-FID" corresponding to FID, "to-be-3" based on expected exposure when a major construction milestone is reached, and so on. This approach is used for project cost risk reserve drawdown as discussed in Chapter 14. The drawdown forecasts could be done on a monthly or quarterly basis, depending on expected implementation of addressing actions. Each of those forecasts could be treated as "to-be-i," "to-be-j," "to-be-k," and so on, assessments.

The same principles of assessments are used for to-be assessments as for as-is assessments. However, the to-be assessment should take into account chances that proposed addressing actions might not be successful. It also should keep an eye on the possibility that proposed actions could become the cause of new uncertainties themselves. This introduces the notion of *manageability* that is sometimes used by practitioners. Sometimes uncertainties could be declared as having a high or low level of manageability without proper consideration of proposed actions. The issue with this approach is that risk's impact on one objective could be nicely managed, whereas impacts on the other objectives could be more difficult to handle. So, automation of a thinking process like this is not something I am a proponent of and could be qualified as a sort of organizational bias. Besides, this step is subject to various types of psychological bias as we are talking about changes in *future* uncertainty levels as a result of *future* addressing actions.

A remarkable spinoff from the previous discussion is that it is of paramount importance to define start and finish dates of all addressing actions in project risk registers and constantly monitor progress of their implementation.

Step 7: Implement Response

This could be seen as the most boring but the most important part of the risk management process—where the rubber meets the road. The key point here is that all proposed and approved addressing actions get owners and are included into work plans of corresponding project disciplines, from engineering and procurement, to safety, to stakeholder management.

Step 8: Monitor and Appraise

The progress of the implementation of the addressing actions should be regularly reviewed. If required, amendments of the working plans may be done and new actions proposed. As a result of this step uncertainties might be upgraded, downgraded, closed, or taken.

Step 9: Close

Full mitigation or transfer is usually impossible and residual exposure associated with a particular uncertainty is often still far from zero. However, an uncertainty may be closed due to development of a new reference case as the uncertainty gets avoided. However, a consecutive change of scope done later might reincarnate this. So, if a new reference case is developed, the list of previously closed uncertainties should be reviewed. Some of them could be reopened. In other cases an uncertainty may become irrelevant and closed. For instance, if all environmental permits are timely received, which sometimes happens, risks stemming from permitting should be closed.

Step 10: Accept

If all proposed addressing actions are implemented but residual uncertainty cannot be closed, the uncertainty should be accepted. We discuss five addressing strategies in detail in Chapter 5. One of those is Accept. It might seem that Step 10 and the Accept strategy fully coincide. This is not exactly the case. The standalone Accept strategy means nothing is planned to address a particular uncertainty. The as-is and to-be assessments are equal by default since the beginning. The standalone Accept strategy is a *do-nothing* one. Implement Response (Step 7) is inapplicable as nothing is planned for implementation. However, if some other addressing strategies are planned, the Accept strategy will fully coincide with Step 10, but only when all planned addressing actions supporting the other strategies are implemented.

 RISK MANAGEMENT TOOLS

Sometimes project teams and especially corporate risk people exaggerate the importance of risk management tools used to maintain risk register databases, making them a primary focus of risk management systems. I don't mean that the tools are not important at all. What I mean is that tools should be employed as servants of the two bigger priorities: organizational frame-work and risk management process. The risk tools are supposed to support these two adequately. No need to put the cart before these two horses. The ISO 31000 standard[7] does not even mention the tools for this reason. It is just a tactical decision which tool(s) to use as long as they support strate-gic components of the risk management system, such as the process and the framework. Producers of risk database software packages seem to have exactly the opposite opinion about this.

One indicator that the cart has been put before the horse is that risk register templates don't reflect the points just discussed; project team members try to avoid using that tool, and a project team is engaged in low-value activities to optimize the tool and integrate it with probabilistic tools and some other busi-ness systems. Eventually this becomes an obstacle to increasing risk manage-ment efficiency. From a competitive advantage it could become deadweight.

Developers of software packages and applications must face a similar dilemma regularly. A software platform could be tightly controlled and difficult for users to get tailor-made (*closed architecture*). This usually has a limited num-ber of users and low popularity. Another platform could be broadly open for amendments (*open architecture*) and is usually very popular among users. The issue is that neither are terribly efficient. The right trade-off between openness and closedness usually yields the best efficiency. The question is where to start in the case of project risk management. I am convinced that initial building of a healthy risk management culture cannot be initiated through imposing mandatory tools, even if those tools are really good. The best method to initially build it is to put a minimal number of restrictions or requirements on risk tools. When team members see the value of risk management in the organizational context of their activities they absorb risk management culture better than if a risk tool were given to them.

What tools should they initially use? The right answer is: the ones that they are comfortable with. I don't think this should be Photoshop, but MS Excel with the right risk register template and a minimal level of standard features (drop-down menus, conditional color data formatting, etc.) certainly could be. This should fully support the organizational framework and risk management pro-cess adopted by the project. As a next step, a commercially available software package should be selected and tailor-made to fully support the organizational framework and the process. If it is merely imposed on the project team and is not adequate, a number of inefficient Band-Aid solutions will follow to make the tool adequate. This will disrupt risk management activities regularly and turn away team members from risk management.

IMPOSING RULES VERSUS ADOPTING RULES

This story is believed to have happened in one of the so-called "hidden cities" of the Soviet Union in the late 1940s or early 1950s and has become part of the folklore among Russian scientists and engineers related to decision making.

Clandestine high-security research centers in the middle of nowhere usually devoted to nuclear and missile armament R&D and production have been called "hidden cities." They have advanced R&D and production facilities, high-comfort residential areas, nice shopping centers, and so on, all encircled by a high fence with an armed guard.

Several new R&D buildings were erected in one of these cities. Nice, new grass lawns were developed around the buildings; some pavements were constructed crossing those lawns. Everything looked okay, except for the fact that the pavements were not being used, giving rise to severe damage to the new lawns.

The local administrative supervisor, a tough man with previous military and security background, considered this a personal challenge and ordered the capture and penalizing of any violators of the walkway rules. Corresponding warning posters were put around the lawn; military police were ambushing violators regularly, but this did not help much. As both staff and administration were becoming increasingly frustrated, a new general manager responsible for R&D, who did not have much of a military background, decided to intervene. The following action plan was developed and implemented:

1. All pavements were replaced by grass.
2. Individuals were allowed to walk anywhere on their way from one building to another.

As a result of implementation of this plan:

1. A new walking pattern was identified within a month of "free lawn" use.
2. It was discovered that previously imposed pavements were not actively used, and were virtually useless.
3. Some teams that worked closely together but were located in different buildings were moved together.
4. New pavements were constructed based on the newly discovered walking pattern.
5. All law-and-order enforcement activities were stopped, having become irrelevant.

"Imposing Rules versus Adopting Rules" illustrates the discussion on closedness versus openness and how similar issues could be resolved smartly.

We will continue our discussion of the project uncertainty repository in the next section. The final section of the chapter provides an overview of the tools for probabilistic analyses.

Three Dimensions of the Risk Management and Uncertainty Repository Concept

A key tool traditionally used in risk management is a risk register. Often it is a monstrous document that contains hundreds of items. Many of them have nothing to do with risk management and no one knows how to use and manage this deadweight.

With the proposed paradigm shift from risk to uncertainty management, an *uncertainty repository* should be substituted. This should have several different logs to keep tabs on all uncertainty objects of Table 1.2 represented in the three dimensions of the organizational framework (Figure 2.1). Each work package should have a separate risk inventory that should be used to support the procurement process (Chapter 10); several engineering logs could be created to make decisions on selection of engineering design options (Chapter 9), and so on. We discuss the structure of a well-organized project uncertainty repository in Chapter 8.

Excessive automation of the uncertainty repository could create an illusion of good risk management. Often excessive automation yields negative value when seen as a substitute for analytical skills and deep risk analysis. This resembles the alarming trend that kids are losing their elementary arithmetic skills due to excessive use of calculators, computers, or whatever they use these days. Using mental power in both cases (arithmetic and risk management) in place of devices suggests that one is better engaged in and better understands what he or she is doing. As Warren Buffett once said, "Risk comes from not knowing what you're doing."

Excessive use of automation and "outsourcing risk management brainpower" are possible causes of organizational risks. Simple workable solutions that engage a project team in the thinking process and deep risk analysis are far preferable to inefficient automation for the sake of automation. Keep in mind that space exploration programs developed by Russia and the United States, not to mention their less innocent counterparts related to nuclear physics, were successful way before automation came of age. Those successes were based on analytical thinking.

"First Automated Vending Machines" sheds further light on this discussion. I am not a frenetic proponent of old methods. I am merely an opponent of red herrings in risk management in the form of excessive automation and an open-minded proponent of most adequate and user-friendly tools available at a particular point in time. If a new, more adequate generation of risk software tools is developed that would be a better match for the requirements of advanced project risk management systems, then all those bells and whistles will come of age. The word *adequate* points to full support of the organizational framework and risk management process to make it as simple and user-friendly as practically possible.

FIRST AUTOMATED VENDING MACHINES

My wife, Irina, and son, Roman, attended my graduation at Henley Management College in May 2001, where I received my Henley MBA diploma. To celebrate we decided to go to Paris after staying in Henley-on-Thames and London (also on Thames). Besides visiting the Louvre and the Eiffel Tower, and shopping at Les Champs-Elysées, we went to the *Musée d'Art Moderne*. A temporary exhibit devoted to consumerism and mass marketing in the 20th century was an unexpected addition to the museum's permanent exhibition. It was well aligned with my interests as a new business degree graduate. One exhibit was quite a big booth with a small outlet, two or three buttons, and a coin slot, nothing else. It was the first automated vending machine developed in the United States. Those machines successfully sold hamburgers and soda. Everything looked automated, but there were people inside.

For several reasons, those first manned "automatic" vending machines were the best possible solution then, until the time when the level and economical affordability of real automation became acceptable for mass market applications. In a way, the current level of project risk management resembles the level of the first vending machine's automation. This means we don't need overly sophisticated risk database solutions yet. Here are three arguments to support this viewpoint.

First, the general approach toward risk management of capital projects has yet to be fully crystallized. An international standard, ISO 31000, was developed in 2009. It is quite consistent and logical but a very high-level document that does not seem to provide a lot of practical value. Available risk management certification programs are far from being very impressive, either. I don't mean that general theory is wrong there; it is just too general. Those programs are not even consistent among themselves and often just repeat proper general banalities over and over again.

Second, project risk management is a relatively new discipline.[8] There is no stable cadre of risk managers in the industry yet. The vast majority of mature project risk managers came from other disciplines, mostly engineering and estimating or scheduling a few years ago, and may retire soon. A new generation start their careers in project risk management but often leave the profession, mostly for engineering and project services or project management. This is a typical generalist's occupation that requires a broad, almost encyclopedic education and knowledge of various disciplines, from engineering and commerce to finance, to mathematics. This impedes crystallization of project risk management as a consistent discipline.

Third, the current level of computer technologies is far more advanced than the current level of maturity of project risk management as a discipline. Development of software tools of any kind is technically very easy. Plus, software providers have hefty sales and marketing budgets to convince anyone that their tools are the best in the entire universe. What is difficult is consolidation of the project risk management approach (both organizational framework and process), which will dictate detailed specs for risk management tools. For the time being, providers of risk management tools dictate and impose their understanding of the organizational context and the risk management process on project teams. For this reason I would not recommend implementing risk management tools that are too sophisticated unless they are fully understood, simple, and tailor-made to meet all risk management system requirements.

Hence, the general immaturity of project risk management as a discipline along with the advanced level and power of the near-risk-management IT industry leads to a situation where the cart (IT tools) ends up going before the two horses (the organizational framework and the process).

Some will find my thinking on excessively sophisticated but not well-understood solutions slightly biased. It is biased due to my background in Russian science and engineering. We never looked for the most sophisticated solutions, which were normally sales, marketing, or politics driven. We always looked for the most elegant, simple, and workable solutions possible, which usually were also the most reliable and efficient. Such solutions are called "smart" these days (see "Space Pen versus Space Pencil").

SPACE PEN VERSUS SPACE PENCIL

One may recall that old story (which seems to be true) about NASA spending millions developing a "space pen," whereas the Russians just used pencils. Let's stay with pencils in risk management when thinking about risk software packages, at least for a while!

My bias does not reject a proper level of sophistication when it is really required. For instance, I fully support the use of sophisticated probabilistic tools (discussed in the next section) as those don't have adequate alternatives. But project risk registers do not at all need such an appalling and irrelevant level of sophistication.

All logs, inventories, and registers introduced earlier should feed a project risk (uncertainty) master register, which cannot be done through automation. Not all identified items should be promoted to the master register. The main qualifying tool for this is the RAM discussed in Chapter 5. Three categories are introduced, depending on level of uncertainties: critical/high (red), material/medium (yellow), and small/low (green). These should serve as the threshold criteria for "promotion." Mostly critical (red) and material (yellow) risks before addressing should be promoted to the master register. Most of the small (green) risks should be managed by corresponding disciplines to avoid cluttering the master register. There is an exception related to game changers and show-stoppers: formally, they could be qualified as small risks due to very low probability with very high impacts. Needless to say, when they do happen they cannot be considered small, as they destroy project baselines. They should be included in project master registers as well as in business and corporate unit registers.

We discuss the features of good risk database software packages in Chapter 8. A spec for a simple but workable MS Excel-based DIY template for risk registers will be introduced, too.

Besides RAM, two other tools also integrated with the repository are RBS and the bowtie diagram, which are used for risk identification and are discussed in Chapter 4.

Tools for Probabilistic Analyses

As discussed in Chapter 3, Steps 3 (assessment as-is) and 5 (assessment to-be) of the risk management process (Figure 2.2) presume application of probabilistic methods for development of adequate cost and schedule reserves. There are several commercial software packages that are used for probabilistic cost and schedule risk analyses. Three of them seem to dominate the market, although I might be biased because I use only these software packages. On the other hand, I am aware of tools used by several major companies for their capital projects. All of them use the following three tools:

1. Oracle Crystal Ball
2. @Risk
3. Oracle Primavera Risk Analysis (PertMaster)

We discuss features of the tools for probabilistic risk analysis in Chapter 8 and their practical applications in Part III of the book.

Tools for Cost Escalation and Currency Exchange Rate Modeling

Chapter 11 introduces principles of cost escalation and currency exchange rate modeling. Three major inputs to this are:

1. High-level work package–based cost estimate
2. Project's cash flow, which defines when purchases related to work packages are planned
3. A set of adequate macroeconomic indexes related to the project cash flow

The first two documents are usually MS Excel–based. There are several sources of macroeconomic indexes that could be used. According to my experience, the most valuable source of macroeconomic indexes for projects in North America is Global Insight. Almost 400 indexes related to various industries and geographies are available for the United States. Close to 100 indexes are available for Canada. As for the other countries, the number of indexes is not always adequate for proper modeling.

 CONCLUSION

This chapter provided a broad overview of uncertainty management. Features of good and bad risk management systems were outlined. Three key components and their hierarchy were introduced, accentuating the secondary role of risk management software tools. Three dimensions of risk management that shape the organizational framework of project risk management were described. Features of a good risk management process were outlined to support the organizational framework.

The topic of adequacy of various methods and tools for management of various project uncertainties is further discussed in the next chapter.

NOTES

1. R. Feynman, *Surely You're Joking, Mr. Feynman! (Adventure of a Curious Character)* (New York: W.W. Norton, 1997).
2. The Scope objective could be understood as Scope/Quality/Performance/System Capacity, and so on, depending on the organizational context of a particular project.
3. The Safety objective is understood as the Health and Safety (H&S) objective in most cases.
4. K. Cooper and G. Lee, "Managing the Dynamics of Projects and Changes at Fluor" (Fluor Corporation, 2009, www.kcooperassociates.com/files/SD_Paper_for_Reprint_V3.pdf)
5. N. Taleb, *The Black Swan* (New York: Random House, 2010).
6. F. Dostoyevsky, *The Idiot* (Cambridge,UK: Oxford University Press, 2008).
7. ISO 31000 International Standard: *Risk Management: Principles and Guidelines* (Switzerland: International Organization for Standardization, 2009).
8. J. Schuyler, *Risk and Decision Analysis in Projects* (Newtown Square, PA: Project Management Institute, 2001).

CHAPTER THREE

Adequacy of Methods to Assess Project Uncertainties

Questions Addressed in Chapter 3

- What distances to reality do various risk methods have?
- What is a minimal set of adequate methods that covers all types of project uncertainty objects?
- How may we recognize ersatz or pseudo risk management methods?
- Why is icon painting somehow relevant to risk management? ■

PART II OF THE BOOK is devoted to applications of deterministic methods in risk management. Part III describes the power of the probabilistic technique. Both deterministic and probabilistic methods could be either qualitative or quantitative. This difference might be blurred in some cases. We review these four situations in this chapter in anticipation of more detailed discussion in Parts II and III. To anticipate conclusions coming from this overview, I would state that only deterministic qualitative and probabilistic quantitative methods look fully authentic. Most of the other methods (probabilistic qualitative and deterministic quantitative ones) look like epigone-type ones.

Those could be considered attempts at the merger of authentic risk methods with methods of estimating and scheduling.

It is important to select adequate methods to assess various uncertainties that give rise to overall project outcome uncertainty (Figure 1.1). Adequacy of methods may be introduced through contemplating their *distances to reality*.[1] On one hand, a method should be informative and credible enough to assess corresponding project uncertainties and their contributions to overall uncertainty of a project's outcome. On the other hand, it should not be an ivory-tower exercise. This is a constructive simplicity principle. Moreover, any deterministic or probabilistic technique may be realized through models and tools that have different levels of complexity and detail. If a model or tool is too simple, it won't reflect project reality and uncertainty exposure in a meaningful way. One may see a forest in a distance but not particular trees.

A lot of effort could be spent to develop a very detailed model of project uncertainty exposure that contains detailed descriptions of hundreds of uncertain events, all possible correlations among them, and so on. This would correspond to detailed description of each tree when one cannot see the forest for the trees. I don't know any project manager who would permit spending many resources to develop and run models like this. On the other hand, I know some risk consultants who have come up with speculative stories related to risk exposures based mostly on their gut feelings and not substantiated by any meaningful assessments based on mathematical logic. Those after-lunch discussions might be cozy and amicable but not very valuable for managing risks. In other cases project team members and decision makers have been staggered on reviewing tricky, Gordian-knot-type probabilistic models.

"So what?" is a simple question often used by scientists as an acid test to evaluate relevance and adequacy of various models and techniques. If the answer to this loaded question is somewhat positive, a model, method, or tool might have value. Otherwise, read the "Cargo Cult Science" feature in Chapter 2 again.

Four major classes of methods used for project uncertainty assessment are described in this chapter (see Figure 3.1) along with their applicability and value.

REVIEW OF DETERMINISTIC QUALITATIVE (SCORING) METHODS

Usually, deterministic scoring method is intuitively understood by any project team member. To measure both types of uncertainties, it is based on measuring

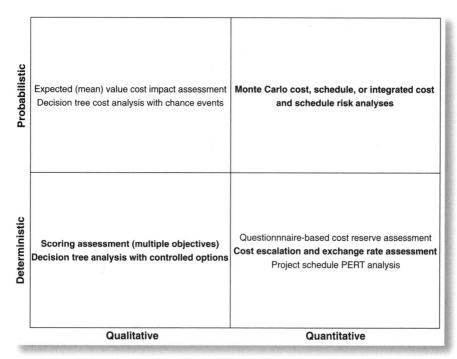

	Qualitative	Quantitative
Probabilistic	Expected (mean) value cost impact assessment Decision tree cost analysis with chance events	**Monte Carlo cost, schedule, or integrated cost and schedule risk analyses**
Deterministic	**Scoring assessment (multiple objectives) Decision tree analysis with controlled options**	Questionnnaire-based cost reserve assessment **Cost escalation and exchange rate assessment** Project schedule PERT analysis

FIGURE 3.1 Deterministic and Probabilistic versus Qualitative and Quantitative Methods of Uncertainty Assessment

deviations from project objectives and their likelihoods. This requires development of an appropriate "measuring tape." As deviations might occur from several project objectives, this measuring tool should be universal enough to be applicable to any project objective, not to mention measuring probabilities.

Scoring Assessment Method (Impacts on Multiple Project Objectives)

Two groups of objectives were introduced in Chapter 2. The first group represents the classic project management triangle: Scope, Cost, and Schedule. These three objectives are easily quantifiable. Deviations from them should be easily quantified, too.

The other three objectives introduced in Chapter 2 (Safety, Environment, and Reputation) are considered "soft" or *goal-zero*-type objectives and not directly quantifiable. Instead, some short scenarios or stories related to deviations are used.

Figure 3.2 represents a sample *risk assessment matrix (RAM)* of a capital project used by a project owner organization. It contains seven project objectives. In most cases we will consider CapEx and PV of OpEx as one Cost objective in this book unless otherwise specified. The generic Scope/Quality/Performance objective is represented by a more specific *System Capacity* objective in the sample RAM.[2]

An EPC contractor might adopt a different RAM for the same project due to a different organizational context. We will discuss an approach to develop a project RAM in Chapter 5.

Among obvious advantages of the scoring method, there is its simplicity and support of the risk management process. The scoring method allows quick assessment of risks before addressing, bringing forward addressing actions and assessment of residual risks. This is a simple and powerful assessment tool that supports risk addressing. It may be easily modified for decision making in engineering (see Chapter 9) and procurement (see Chapter 10). I am considered a proponent of more advanced probabilistic methods due to my background. However, I believe that the deterministic scoring method, despite its shortcomings, is too effective to ignore and drop in favor of Monte Carlo methodology in all situations. Both methods should be in the risk management toolbox and feed each other.

Attempts to promote Monte Carlo methodology in all possible risk management situations would be similar to attempts to impose quantum mechanics as the only methodology in place of quite adequate methods based on classical Newtonian physics in mechanical or structural engineering. The quantum method is just not relevant to mechanical or structural engineering, being a weird and impractical overshooting!

Whatever our preferences, biases, or even hidden agendas, we need to remember that probabilistic methods are applicable only for assessment of uncertainties related to the three quantifiable objectives and are virtually useless for assessments of soft objectives. In the vast majority of cases they are used in project risk management only for assessment of cost and schedule uncertainties and development of corresponding project reserves. A well-developed scoring method is based on keeping in mind multiple project objectives, both hard and soft. (By this reason scoring methods are more powerful and comprehensive than probabilistic Monte Carlo methods.) The key idea of scoring methods is that project objectives selected for risk management are equals. Declaring that some objectives are more important or "more equal than others" (citing George Orwell) and drive a project is a sign

	CCS Project Curiosity: Impact on Project Objectives							Probability				
	CapEx, $M	OpEx, %	Schedule Mos	System Capacity, M tons/year	Safety	Environment	Reputation	<1% Very Low (1)	1%–20% Low (2)	20%–50% Medium (3)	50%–90% High (4)	>90% Very High (5)
Very High (5)	>50	>5	>6	>0.15	Single or multiple fatalities	Massive Effect	International media coverage. Irreparable stakeholder impact	5	10	15	20	25
High (4)	20–50	3–5	3–6	0.1–0.15	Serious personal injury resulting in permanent disability	Major Effect	National media coverage. Substantial stakeholder impact	4	8	12	16	20
Medium (3)	5–20	1–3	1–3	0.05–0.1	Injury in personnel not resulting in permanent disability	Localized Effect	Regional media coverage. Moderate stakeholder impact	3	6	9	12	15
Low (2)	0.5–5	0.5–1	0.5–1	0.01–0.05	Medical treatment of personnel. Lost time incident	Minor Effect	Local media attention. Minor stakeholder impact	2	4	6	8	10
Very Low (1)	<0.5	<0.5	<0.5	<0.01	Minor impact on personnel First aid only. No lost time	Slight Effect	Slight media attention. Little stakeholder impact	1	2	3	4	5

FIGURE 3.2 Sample Risk Assessment Matrix

of organizational bias at the best or misunderstanding of project risk management at the worst.

The Cost objective cannot be more important than Reputation or Safety, just as Schedule cannot be more important than the Environment objective. This approach prevents tunnel vision, which reveals itself through the use of terms such as *cost-driven* or *schedule-driven* projects. These terms imply intent to deliver a project according to an approved budget or by a sanctioned completion date at all costs. Unfortunately, those costs would include lives, ruined organizations' reputations, environmental issues, or poor quality. Equally important project objectives impose healthy constraints on each other. This is supposed to isolate and avoid many sources and causes of risks and prevent, at least partially, negative impacts on multiple objectives.

Moreover, the same level of impacts for different objectives implies that those impacts are commensurate to each other. For instance, this means that a very high impact on Cost is equally unwelcome as a very high impact on Safety. (Corporate lawyers don't like this equality in the case of fatalities as it attaches a cost tag to them.) Following this logic, every project should be Scope-Cost-Schedule-Safety-Reputation-Environment driven.

The scoring method is not free of shortcomings and is characterized by a certain distance to project reality. Most of them boil down to the fact that selection of ranges for impact and probability categories is quite subjective. This distance could be maintained relatively short if project RAM is properly developed and updated when required. The shortcomings are balanced by the clear advantages of the scoring method, including handling multiple objectives. This balance could be clearly positive if the scoring method is considered a foundation for a more adequate Monte Carlo assessment method of cost and schedule uncertainties.

Decision Tree Analysis with Controlled Options

The deterministic scoring method is a powerful decision-making tool where several options should be considered. A set of options should be developed prior to analysis. We refer to those as *controlled options*, assuming that their set is known before risk-based option selection. Several bidders might respond to a request for proposal (RFP) or several engineering design options may be proposed. Very often costs associated with those options are very close to each other. What additional criteria or constraints should be used to make a right decision?

We discuss typical decision tree analysis later in this chapter. We refer to this as "decision tree analysis with chance events."[3] As discussed later, the decision tree analysis with chance events allows one to make decisions when external options are not controlled. Probabilities of their occurrences exist along with associated costs. Controlled option selection eliminates this lack of control. Instead, selection of any option is possible and depends on the risk analysis associated with each of them.

The principal difference between the two methods is that the controlled option method allows one to consider multiple objectives simultaneously,[4] not just Cost. All chance events are exported to the option's risk registers and treated as regular uncertain events and deviations from multiple objectives. Those uncertainties defining an overall option's uncertainty exposure become the option's differentiators.

Selection of controlled options starts with identification of risks associated with each option. Impacts on multiple objectives are considered, and not only on Cost. Probabilities of occurrences and associated impacts on objectives by identified risks should be done as a next step. All critical (red) and material (yellow) risks for each option should be reduced to the small (green) level through application of proposed addressing actions. Those actions may be used to reduce impacts of risks to Reputation, Safety, Schedule, Cost, Environment, and so on to an acceptably low level, whereas costs of those actions should be added to the option's cost baselines. Residual risk exposures of acceptable (green) risks are neglected. So, there is no need to make assessments of residual risks. This simplifies things a lot.

If some of the risks cannot be reduced to an acceptable (green) level, corresponding options should be disqualified. In some cases options with material (yellow) risks might be retained and selected. Decision makers might want to select those by accepting higher residual risks. That will be an informed decision of theirs.

Chapter 9 is devoted to selection of engineering design options. Procurement option selections is overviewed in detail in Chapter 10. Upon development of this method, I led several engineering design and procurement studies. The simplicity and top efficiency of the method for quick decision making was a surprise for participants. All decisions were quick, well structured, documented, and defendable. Although this is outside the scope of this book, any major decision made by an organization even beyond project management could be supported by this method, from entering new markets, to relocation of a production facility, to any decision associated with change management.

REVIEW OF DETERMINISTIC QUANTITATIVE METHODS

The next step in our discussion of risk methods should be an attempt to make deterministic qualitative methods more quantitative. Following Figure 3.1, we will consider three deterministic quantitative methods:

1. Questionnaire-based cost reserve assessment
2. Cost escalation and exchange rate uncertainty assessment
3. Project schedule project/program evaluation and review technique (PERT) analysis

The project risk register is a starting point for various project activities to assess and manage project uncertainties. One of them is assessment of a total project's risk reserve fund. When estimators develop project capital budgets, the most challenging activity for them is to develop those elements of the budget that are not part of the cost baseline and not directly aligned with CapEx elements. Uncertain events that make an impact on the Cost objective are major contributions to those extra elements. The best method to develop a project reserve is to use probabilistic analysis. However, the well-developed project risk register required for probabilistic analysis usually doesn't exist in the early phases of project development. A risk register "forefather" could be used in the form of a risk checklist. This method is still used by estimators in early phases of project development.

The difference between prices used in the base estimate associated with period of cost estimate development and prices really paid reflects changing market conditions for products and services. A lot of water may pass under the bridge before first purchasing is done. Cost escalation modeling anticipates base estimate evolution in time from the moment of base estimate development until those moments when particular project expenditures are done.

When a project schedule is developed, the project completion date requires some assurance and investigation of its confidence. Once again, the best method to investigate the project completion date confidence level is to use probabilistic analysis. However, deterministic PERT analysis is still widely used by schedulers. It may be understood as a method of project schedule validation, not schedule risk analysis. Using questionnaire-based estimating and schedule PERT analysis is similar to using less adequate methods of classical Newtonian physics in situations where more adequate methods of quantum physics should be used. Besides breaking with tradition, learning new techniques could be an obstacle to switching to new methods.

Questionnaire-Based Cost Reserve Assessment

Large organizations involved in capital projects for decades have been accumulating lessons-learned information about projects they did. Information about each particular project may be used to develop a rule-of-thumb project reserve evaluation tool. Several large organizations in the oil and gas industry I am familiar with did develop tools like this. Those tools are based on questionnaires that contain standard sets of questions. Each question can be answered using scores. Each question is assigned a weight that reflects the importance of the assessed factor and its contribution to the overall score. The latter represents overall project uncertainty and is used for evaluation of the reserve fund and its accuracy. Usually calculation of reserves and their accuracies is done for several different types of projects. The same questions in the risk questionnaire with the same scores would mean different reserves and accuracies for a shale gas production, an LNG initiative, or an off-shore oil project.

This is a purely empirical method based on the average performance of previous projects. Rules of recalculation from question scores to reserve numbers and accuracy levels are highly subjective although based on average performance data. Moreover, usually it is not possible to check or challenge those rules as they are considered highly confidential and proprietary. Those methods seem to be a pure reflection of the organizational bias introduced by the organization's top cost estimators. The greatest value of the questionnaire-based methods is consistency in rules, albeit biased rules, to define project reserves and accuracies across the corporate project portfolio. No doubt it is important to compare various projects in a portfolio in an apples-to-apples way, cost-reserve-wise, when selecting the most attractive ones. If the same type and degree of bias (a systematic error) is applied to all considered projects in portfolio, the method would be good enough for the ranking of projects. The same systematic error stemming from the bias should be applicable across the portfolio. However, no particular reserve number considered out of this portfolio context should be treated as too solid and credible. I tried to use two comparable questionnaire-based tools to evaluate the risk reserve for a project. The difference in risk reserve results turned out to be remarkably substantial.

The questionnaire-based risk reserve assessment method resembles the efforts of the arts scientists in the feature "Andrei Rublev versus 'Theophanes the Greek'" to declare the "truth" about an icon's authorship (the size of a project reserve) based on some indirect or very general factors. The difference in these two situations is that there are better methods for reserve development.

ANDREI RUBLEV VERSUS "THEOPHANES THE GREEK": WHO ACTUALLY PAINTED THAT 14TH-CENTURY RUSSIAN ICON?

This story was told by my former co-worker and mentor, Professor Valentine Naish, in the late 1980s. One of his close relatives was an arts scientist who studied the various schools and styles of Russian icon painting. If an unknown icon of the 14th or 15th century was discovered, top arts scientists presented their reasoning based on previous experience, indirect observations, precursors, and gut feelings on the most likely authorship of the ancient piece of art. They wrote scientific papers and had conferences and debates on the subject. As fully objective proof of any viewpoint would not be possible in most cases, the most reasonable viewpoint, usually belonging to the most authoritative and senior scientists, would eventually prevail. So the arts community would declare that this particular icon was painted, say, by Andrei Rublev and could not belong to Theophanes the Greek. After all, who could possibly know the objective truth? This is an example of when better justified or more consistent bias prevailed. However, if an additional piece of information or evidence related to the icon's origin did surface, they could change their minds and declare that Andrew Rublev had nothing to do with the icon. A new reality could be created that had complex relations with objective truth. The only justification of this method was that there were no better methodologies.

No one would argue with the result of the exercise as soon as a reserve number looked reasonable, to say, 10–20%. In any case, I assure you that those methods are calibrated to exclude any weird reserve numbers. On the other hand, in the early phases of project development this method might be considered legitimate enough as information about detailed risk exposure is not available, anyway. So this method is slightly better than allocating 15% reserve to any project or base estimate by default without any uncertainty considering or managing. Besides consistency of rules for project ranking and applicability to early phases of projects, this method has another justification. The set of questions used for scoring resembles risk breakdown structure (RBS). It looks like a risk register with all required categories but without risks. So, assessed are hypothetical contributions of risk categories (sources of risks) without identifying specific risks.

This method is limited to types of projects that were previously done by the organization. If a company moves to a new business, this method cannot be directly adopted without adding additional bias. For instance, if a company undertakes its first carbon-capture-and-storage project, corresponding questions and rules to develop a risk reserve using answer scores should be substantially conditioned. As a CO_2 sequestration project typically includes three components (capture, pipeline, and storage) it would be reasonable to consider three base estimates and risk reserves separately. However, unique integration and commercial aspects of CO_2 marketing will be missed, anyway. To overcome this issue more assumptions should be made, which inevitably introduces more errors and bias.

Another issue with the questionnaire-based method is that it does not take into account particular project execution strategies reflected in project execution plans. Particular engineering, contracting, construction, and other plans and their implementations make the difference in terms of real project risk exposure and required reserves. This level of detail could be taken into account only when using probabilistic methods based on well-developed risk registers. The questionnaire-based method produces project reserve numbers that, on one hand, may not be argued much as they all look somewhat reasonable. On the other hand, they cannot be taken too seriously. It sounds like that medical adage on the average temperature of patients in a hospital. It's about 99° Fahrenheit, so what? We need to know the average temperature of patients in *one* ward of the hospital at least, all the better if this is a private ward for one person.

Full justification of this method is questionable as there is a better substitute for it—the probabilistic Monte Carlo methodology discussed later in this chapter.

Cost Escalation and Exchange Rate Uncertainty Assessment

Project base estimates are done in currencies of base periods. These could be updated several times in the course of project development and execution starting with a Class 5 estimate.[5] Each new base estimate is done for a new base period. If a base estimate is done for a base period of Q4-2012, what will be the real project expenditures to buy materials and construction equipment and hire required labor according to the project cash flow plan, to say, in 2014–2017?

The next question would be about the meaning of the Cost category "Material," which is too general a category. This may include cement, gravel, structural steel, pipes of various diameters, valves, pressure vessels, wire, and cable.

Similarly, several categories of labor would be required, from general labor and engineers to welders, construction managers, and so on.

Generally, future prices for any material, equipment, or labor depend on market imbalances or imbalances of supply and demand. Markets for some products and services are global. This is the case for turbines for gas compressor stations or high-diameter line pipes. At the same time supply of and demand for rented construction equipment or some construction materials such as gravel or sand are local. In the case of the labor market it is usually regional in a particular country. Some projects and operations such as oil sands projects in Northern Alberta attract people from all over Canada and beyond, although migration of workers from other countries is not freely allowed.

If some materials, equipment, or services are bought abroad, additional cost uncertainties associated with the currency exchange rate volatilities of money markets might be relevant. Many factors, such as dynamics of trade balances among countries, countries' interest rates, and levels of inflation and debt, influence these.

Certainly project teams and decision makers should not spend most of their time on economic studies. There are methods to model cost escalation and currency exchange uncertainties using correct macroeconomic indexes from reliable sources. Qualified economists are developing and updating those indexes using quite sophisticated economic models. The issue is how to properly select and use the right indexes. This method is based on the representation of cost accounts of project cash flow forecast as composite indexes based on the time series of the macroeconomic indexes. This is the method to take into account future market imbalances.

We consider cost escalation and currency exchange rate modeling in more detail in Chapter 11. It will be seen that using inflation rates (consumer price index [CPI]) as a basis of cost escalation modeling is not adequate at all.

Project Schedule PERT Analysis

Introduced in the 1950s in the United States to manage major naval projects, PERT was a revolutionary method for several decades. It is not anymore; however, it still deserves a lot of credit as a predecessor of modern probabilistic schedule risk analyses. There are several reasons for this. I would not dismiss it entirely as I consider this not as a schedule risk method but rather a method to validate project schedules. As such it is still used by schedulers, especially those who started their career a while ago.

First, almost all major concepts of the PERT analysis such as most likely time (MT), optimistic time (OT), and pessimistic time (PT) for completion of an activity are used in modern probabilistic schedule risk analysis methods. However, using the same formula for calculations of expected time, TE = (OT + 4MT + PT)/6, always seemed too predetermined. As discussed in Chapter 12 this formula is just an attempt to approximate mean/expected values of durations of normal activities.

Critical path analysis (CPA), which was used in conjunction with PERT analysis, is also used in modern methods. However, if in the deterministic PERT method only one critical path is possible, using a probabilistic approach opens the possibility of switching several near-critical paths among each other when running multiple iterations of Monte Carlo analysis. The criticality index shows percentage of iterations when a particular near-critical path becomes critical.

It is not accidental that the original name of the most popular probabilistic schedule risk analysis software package was PertMaster. Developers of PertMaster did a really good job in the conversion of deterministic PERT analysis into a probabilistic schedule risk analysis technique. This conversion was made in two steps.

The first step of conversion was to replace the previous formula for TE with a simple three-point triangular distribution introduced for durations of each normal activity as (PT, MT, OT). Any reasons (general uncertainties or uncertain events, both upside and downside) were supposed to give rise to positive or negative deviations from the most likely time MT. So, in place of the deterministic TE formula a distribution was used that absorbed full information about the activity uncertainty. Figure 3.3 represents a case where two general

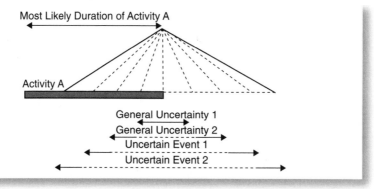

FIGURE 3.3 Representation of Activity Duration as a Triangular Distribution

uncertainties and two uncertain events make a contribution to the duration distribution. Such a distribution should be assigned to each normal activity of the schedule. After that a schedule is ready to take part in a simplified version of probabilistic schedule risk analysis. (We discuss correlations among distribution in Chapter 13, which is an additional requirement ignored here.)

Certainly, if a schedule has hundreds of normal activities, its preparation for risk analysis should take some time. Normal practice is to reduce a project master schedule to a more compact model, called a *schedule proxy* or just proxy. Proxies should fully represent the main logic of a project master schedule at a higher level. I like to call those proxy schedules "level one-and-a-half." Even in the case of a mega-project such a proxy should not contain more than 100 activities or so.

Figure 3.3 points to inconsistency as both general uncertainties and uncertain events are represented similarly as direct contributions to the overall duration distribution. But these two objects are quite different in terms of probability of occurrence. As discussed earlier, general uncertainties are absolutely certain in terms of probability of occurrence (100%). They are attached to baselines reflecting an associated impact range. Impact is represented by a distribution of all possible impacts belonging to a range between most optimistic (minimum) to most pessimistic (maximum) durations. The most likely (ML) impact is equal to a deterministic baseline activity duration. Any other impact from the range represents a deviation from the ML baseline value and is less likely.

Uncertain events may occur with some probability that is less than 100%. Possible impacts associated with an uncertain event is also represented by an impact distribution the same as general uncertainties.

One may argue that we are dealing with a distribution of Figure 3.3 that should represent probability of occurrence. Wrong! The distribution associated with impact represents the probability of realization of a particular impact, not the probability of occurrence. Durations that are close to the most likely one are more probable in terms of impact than durations close to optimistic and pessimistic limits. Probabilities of occurrence for both general uncertainties and uncertain events shown in Figure 3.3 are the same and equal to 100%. There is an explanation that contributions of general uncertainties should be placed closer to the most likely duration and contributions of uncertain events with lower probability of impact closer to extremes. This is still a bogus argument putting forward a sort of mixed impact-occurrence distribution (Figure 3.3), which is not solid mathematically but still widely used!

In practice, some uncertain events of the small, green level could be converted to general uncertainties as "uncertainty noise" to keep the overall number of uncertain events relatively low. For instance, there could be the possibility that a decision maker would be on vacation for one or two weeks, leading to the delay of a work package purchase order approval. This uncertainty could be implicitly taken into account as a general uncertainty. However, if we are talking about the possible delay of a final investment decision due to postponement of a board of directors' meeting for two or three months, that should be considered as a true uncertain event with some probability of occurrence.

This method is the basis of the QuickRisk functionality of PertMaster. This was a huge step from the deterministic PERT method to a probabilistic schedule risk analysis. It is still widely used by practitioners as a preliminary evaluation of project duration. There are some doubts about the adequacy of this method due to the blend of general uncertainties and uncertain events. This makes this method slightly speculative unless only general uncertainties are used as inputs. In this case it is an adequate method of project schedule validation in a "risk-free world." In other words, if a schedule completion date has a low level of confidence even in the absence of uncertain events, such a schedule should be further developed or optimized.

I know of attempts by some companies to come up with questionnaire-based methods for assessments of overall project durations using some RBS categories. All failed because, to the contrary to the cost questionnaire-based methods discussed above, the schedule risk methods strongly depend on schedule logic. In other words, different sequences of project activities could be proposed for a project that cannot be specifically told apart by questionnaires. To keep things simple, a modification of the PERT analysis could be used for this purpose as an analog of the cost questionnaire-based method. Three questions for each schedule activity should be answered: What are the OT (or minimum), MT (or ML), and PT (or maximum) durations? However, those input data could be better used as inputs to a probabilistic QuickRisk model instead.

"Modifying Mechanical Typewriters for the 21st Century" introduces an allusion on more exotic, "advanced" but desperate attempts to modify PERT methodology to compete with much more powerful probabilistic methods.

Hence, the second step in conversion of deterministic PERT to fully probabilistic schedule risk analysis was done when the functionality to map schedule risks from the risk register to particular impacted schedule normal activities was developed. Namely, an uncertain event of a schedule impact does not impact an entire project schedule as a probabilistic scoring method actually implies. It directly impacts one or several specific and relevant normal activities. For instance, a risk of permit delays should be mapped to permitting activities of the schedule as it has nothing to do directly with engineering or procurement

MODIFYING MECHANICAL TYPEWRITERS FOR THE 21ST CENTURY

As a reviewer of risk management papers submitted to the *International Journal of Project Management*, I reviewed a paper that considered modification of the deterministic PERT method, adding some stochastic distributions to each normal activity. I did not know the author(s) so I cannot cite this paper here even if it were published. It was similar in its intent to modifying and improving mechanical typewriters to compete with modern computers. Certainly, there would be a small number of interested clients who are accustomed to using typewriters (and PERT methodology) during the last 50 years. Even the simple QuickRisk-type of schedule analysis provides more realism to modeling than "stochastic modification" of a deterministic PERT method. Addition of functionality that allows mapping risks of schedule impacts to normal activities leaves no room for such competition.

activities. Overall impact of that risk on the project completion date will depend on several factors including schedule logic and belonging of impacted activities to the project critical path. This is discussed in the final section of this chapter and beyond.

REVIEW OF PROBABILISTIC QUALITATIVE METHODS

Probabilistic qualitative methods are an attempt to use a probabilistic technique without running probabilistic (Monte Carlo) risk analysis. For this reason they don't require any probabilistic software package. The key probabilistic concept utilized by those methods is *mean value*. In business its synonym, *expected value*, is used more often.

There are several mathematical parameters, including mean value, that describe probabilistic distributions. I will not introduce their mathematical definitions as I have no intention of talking about the so-called method of moments or the integral techniques of their calculation. Instead, I would point out that mean value is the best one-point representative of any distribution. It takes into account the shape of the curve and its spread. The mean/expected value of a probabilistic distribution is literally the center of its mass. Instead of using the method of moments, one may undertake an experiment using a pair of scissors to accurately cut a distribution curve and try to balance it on a pen. The balancing point will correspond to the curve's mean value. So, any distribution may be collapsed to a one-point value. For instance, if a cost distribution representing the possible impact of a cost risk had a spread from $10 million to $25 million, and due to its shape and skewing, had a mean value of $16.5 million, we would use $16.5 million as its representative.

Certainly, curves of different shapes and spreads may have the same mean value. This represents a limitation of the qualitative probabilistic methods as the degree of uncertainty reflected by a probabilistic distribution is represented by both the shape and especially the spread of the curve, and not just its mean value. A huge advantage of using qualitative probabilistic methods is the possibility of summing mean values for different curves. The resulting value will be exactly the mean value of the resulting curve as if we ran a probabilistic Monte Carlo analysis. This is not the case for any other values of distributions belonging to, say, its wings. We just cannot sum values on wings hoping to fully define a resulting distribution. For this reason we cannot evaluate the spread of the resulting distribution, which required a full-scale Monte Carlo analysis. The advantages and disadvantages pointed out earlier define how the qualitative probabilistic methods are used.

Expected (Mean) Value Cost Impact Assessment

This method may be thought of as an expansion of scoring deterministic methods for risks impacting Cost objectives. A project RAM may be used to define mean values of cost impacts assigned to each of 25 cells of RAM in place of corresponding scores. Usually the convention used is that a mean value of cost risk impact belongs exactly to the midpoint of the corresponding RAM's categories. If we go back to the RAM of Figure 3.2, all cost risks of the Very Low category should be assigned mean impact value $0.25 million, which is the average of $0 and $0.5 million. For the Low category it is $2.75 million (average of $0.5 million and $5 million). In the Medium impact it should be $12.5 million (average of $5 million and $20 million). Similarly, for High impact we may use $35 million (average of $20 million and $50 million). What should we use for Very High impact, though? The average of $50 million and infinity, which is also infinity? Or would $100 million be enough? (If yes, why? If no, why?) Any proposed number will look too voluntary and not quite justifiable. So, another convention is required, which means more bias. Okay, we may declare $75 million or any other number above $50M as mean value for every Very High cost risk impact. But any declared number will not look well justified anyway. The bottom line is that the Very Low, Low, Medium, and High categories resemble too closely a Procrustean bed, whereas the Very High category is too loose.

Now we need to recall that uncertain events have a probability of occurrence as another dimension. Similarly we should use midpoints of probability ranges as their representatives. The resulting cost risk mean (or expected) value is a product of impact mean value and midpoint probability. Such mean values could be calculated for each of the 25 RAM cells—only one value per cell, and no other values! Such certainty looks amazing and unbelievable in terms of precision and accuracy. Plus the method of deriving the mid-cell values is so dubious.

The first obvious issue was about selection of a mean value for Very High cost impacts. Selection of mean values for the other four impact categories implies that ranges of those impacts are always defined by the ranges of corresponding impact categories. That is how we calculated the impact's midpoints. What if a risk that fell into the Medium impact category during deterministic assessment has in reality a cost impact range, say, from $3 million to $8 million? Following the previous logic, $5.5 million should be assigned in place of a one-size-fits-all $12.5 million for the Medium category. Obviously, always using a cell's midpoint by default represents a sort of bias that cannot be meaningfully justified.

Second, if tomorrow we decide to change the RAM's ranges for any reason, all midpoints get changed as will all expected values for each RAM's cell. The uncertainty exposure would not change at all but the results of the quantitative assessment would.

This methodology absorbs very effectively all known shortcomings of the scoring method and amplifies them through introducing mid-cell numbers in place of RAM scores. It seems attractively simple. Some people even consider this smart and heuristic! The problem with this exaggerated simplicity is that this approach loses contact with reality. This reminds me of the icon-authorship identification exercise discussed earlier, not to mention the Cargo Cult. And yes, there is a much better method to evaluate cost risk impacts and develop project reserves, which is the probabilistic Monte Carlo method.

Decision Tree Cost Analysis

Decision making and selection of options related to project development and execution is usually done in situations of uncertainty. This means we cannot fully control their outcomes but may make assessment of probabilities of realizations and possible corresponding cost implications.

Let's contemplate a situation where decision making should be done (decision point) and two options seem viable, A and B. This could be a decision about purchasing equipment for a gas processing plant. The plant should be operational by the date defined by the commercial contract. Monthly revenue loss and penalties in case of delay are evaluated as $10 million a month. Cost of option A (purchasing, delivery, and installation) is $100 million, whereas cost of option B is $110 million. As both are long lead items to be delivered from overseas there could be delays in timely startup of the plans of particular probabilities stemming from possible procurement and logistics delays. Table 3.1 summarizes this information.

Options A and B are called chance events (or chance nodes) as they cannot be controlled by decision makers. Figure 3.4 represents the decision tree described earlier. This example is developed to demonstrate that the option of lower installed costs (option A) is not preferable if we take into account cash flow considerations. Despite the fact that option B has a higher installed cost its total cost ($121.5 million) is lower than the total cost of option A ($128.5 million).

This method seems quite effective in uniting the project's Cost (CapEx and OpEx) and Schedule objectives. Its key feature is the presence of chance events

TABLE 3.1 Information for Chance Event Decision Making

Parameter	Option A	Option B
Installed cost	$100M	$110M
Monthly cash flow and penalty losses in case of delay	$10M	$10M
Probability of one-month delay	5%	90%
Probability of two-month delay	10%	5%
Probability of three-month delay	80%	5%
Probability of four-month delay	5%	0%
Probability of five-month delay	0%	0%

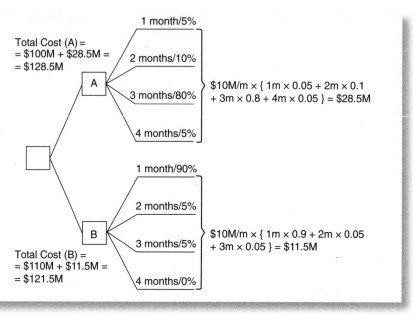

FIGURE 3.4 Sample Decision Tree with Two Chance Events

that cannot be controlled. If you asked me whether I use this method in my practice, the answer would be no. I prefer to use probabilistic models instead. In place of the possible monthly delays described in Table 3.1 and by branches shown in Figure 3.4 I would build distributions that matched the described delay's assessments. To do this I would identify and assess risks of schedule impacts that relate to two procurement options and map them to the procurement normal activities. The outcomes of these two schedule risk models could be used in the cost model to compare total costs. In other words, the more modern method of solving decision trees with chance events is based on a Monte Carlo simulation.

 REVIEW OF PROBABILISTIC QUANTITATIVE METHODS

Probabilistic quantitative methods are used for assessment of general uncertainties and uncertain events of a project's capital budgets and schedules. Application of probabilistic methods for optimization of a system's design through debottlenecking its elements is another application, which is outside the scope of this book.

If we assemble together 10 estimators or schedulers and ask them to come up with an estimate or completion date for a project, very likely we will get 10 different estimates and dates. What if there are 100 estimators and schedulers, or 1,000, or even 5,000? Not quite realistic, but, hypothetically, the distribution of estimates and dates resulting from this exercise will reflect the different methods, utilized information, experience, and features of the estimators'/schedulers' thinking processes. This example is a manifestation of various types of psychological and organizational bias as a realization of a general uncertainty.

What if (hypothetically) this project were executed by 10 different organizations so that no learning curve was involved? Again, very likely there will be 10 different final project costs and completion dates. What if 100, 1,000, or 10,000 organizations did replicas independently? Right: there will be a distribution of both final costs and completion dates. The different execution strategies and uncertainties that occurred during execution of projects will be factored into these final numbers.

Good benchmarking databases may contain information about a few projects that are relevant to the one an organization undertakes. But even in this case proper conditioning of data is required to compare projects on an apples-to-apples basis. Certainly, it is unrealistic to have information about hundreds of similar and relevant projects and their final costs and durations.

What if a project has a high level of novelty? Drilling in the Arctic or carbon-capture-and-storage initiatives may be put in this category. Available benchmarking information for more standard projects should be substantially conditioned to provide value, if possible.

Probabilistic Cost and Schedule Risk Analyses

We overview both cost and schedule probabilistic methodologies in this section. These will be introduced independently from each other. Strictly speaking, this is not quite an adequate viewpoint as schedule-driven costs and schedule-risk-driven cost uncertainties should be taken into account. This important link is overviewed in the next section, whereas here a disproven assumption is made that there are no schedule-driven costs and corresponding cost uncertainties.

A probabilistic method allows one to imitate statistical information on hundreds of relevant *hypothetical projects*. Simply speaking, each such project is an iteration of a Monte Carlo simulation. Each such iteration uses a unique random sampling of possible cost/schedule values defined by corresponding uncertainties.

Relevancy means that the baselines of all these hypothetical projects (Scopes, Costs, and Schedules) are exactly the same. Moreover, general uncertainty factors and sets of possible (known) uncertain events are defined the same way for all of those (hypothetical) projects. Obviously, if uncertain events have probabilities of their occurrences, they should not all happen in each project. In the case of general uncertainty factors, they are characterized by spreads or ranges of possible values around baseline costs and durations for each cost account and normal activity. Supposedly, values that are around baseline numbers are more likely, with values on both edges of ranges being the most unlikely. Those factors will not play out the same way for each project/iteration. For some projects/iterations corresponding values will be close to baselines, for some they will be closer to the upper end of the spreads, and for others they will be closer to lower ends.

There could be dozens of cost accounts in base estimates and hundreds of normal activities in project schedules. Each of them has a spread (min; max) around its baseline value to represent general uncertainty (see Figure 3.5). The baseline value is considered ML. Similarly, there could be dozens of uncertain events in the project risk register that may have an impact on Cost and/or Schedule. Each is characterized by a corresponding spread of impact (min; max) and most likely value. Any particular uncertain event may or may not

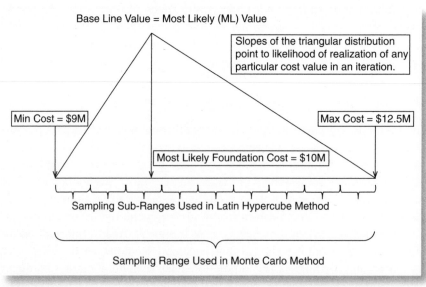

FIGURE 3.5 Example of Triangular Distribution for a Foundation Cost

occur in a particular "project." When it occurs, its impact could vary within the range.

The probabilistic Monte Carlo method is based on random sampling of values defined by (min; ML; max) distributions of all those cost accounts or normal activities and associated uncertain events. A combination or snapshot of sampled values for all cost accounts/normal activities is called an *iteration*. Any iteration corresponds to a full set of cost/schedule data used as inputs to a model for one of the hypothetical projects. The output of any iteration will yield final cost or duration for that particular hypothetical project. All inputs and outputs are one-point values for any particular iteration. There are no spreads around them. In other words, any iteration is fully deterministic. However, multiple sampling iterations give rise to a distribution of possible project costs or completion dates (see Figure 3.6).

Each value in the distribution has its likelihood depending on how often it occurs during sampling. Modern probabilistic software packages such as @Risk, PertMaster, or Crystal Ball installed on modern computers allow one to run thousands of iterations in just a few seconds or minutes depending on the complexity of a model. When computers were less advanced, running time was quite high even for relatively simple models. So, to accelerate modeling, a lower number of iterations was usually used, such as 500 or 1,000. Acceleration of running led to reduction of quality of results, though. Due to randomness of the sampling process that takes into account likelihoods of particular sampled values though, the less likely input data being close to minimal and maximum values of ranges became suppressed. They just did not get enough iterations to fully reveal themselves. As they are less likely to occur in inputs, they are less likely to contribute to the model outcome. As a result, the wings of project cost and schedule distributions became suppressed and not representative for low numbers of iterations. If the number of iterations increased, to say 5,000 or more, this issue was resolved automatically, but this required more running time.

To resolve this issue a modified Monte Carlo method was invented in the 1970s. The *Latin hypercube* method is based on breaking each input interval into several sample subintervals (Figure 3.5) to ensure that the whole range is sampled and represented evenly. This allows one to ensure that values on the wings of the input are represented more adequately in output distributions. If the number of iterations is high enough, results will be pretty much the same for both methods. As the issue of high running time for a high number of iterations is now resolved, it doesn't matter which method is used. I prefer to use the Monte Carlo method, which is more natural. However, if models are

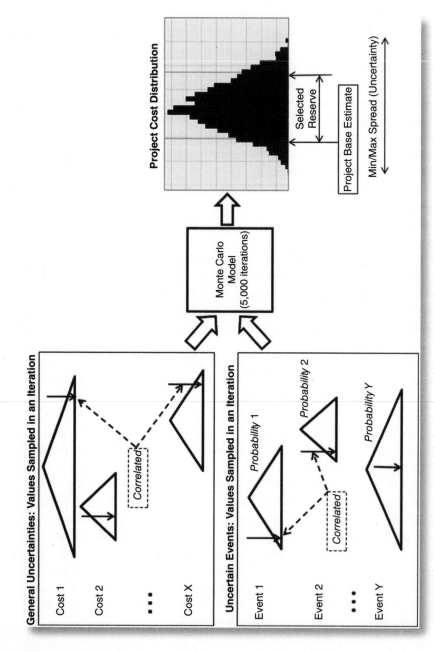

FIGURE 3.6 Overview of Probabilistic Cost Risk Analysis Inputs and Outputs

sophisticated and large enough, especially schedule models, it still could take a substantial amount of time to run them. This is especially the case when a local copy of a Monte Carlo software package is not available. So, the data transfer speed with a remote server could lead to even higher running times. To get preliminary results quickly it may stand to reason to use Latin hypercube sampling with 500–1,000 iterations.

Sampling of values should not be fully random for a simple reason. Some combinations of input values are not quite realistic. For example, due to uncertainty of space requirements for installation of equipment during the conceptual design phase, higher building footage should mean higher building costs. It is not very likely that higher building costs will result in lower foundation costs. So, sampling scenarios where higher building costs go along with lower foundation costs should be suppressed as rather unrealistic. A correlation between those two input distributions should be introduced. In any iteration, if a building cost is higher than its baseline value, foundation cost should be higher than its baseline value, too, and vice versa.

As some scenarios in sampling are suppressed by adding more realism to the model, the resulting cost or schedule distribution will have a broader spread. This usually corresponds to higher required project reserves as discussed in Chapter 12. In other words, correlations that add realism to the probabilistic models should be identified and added to the models. I reviewed several probabilistic models that did not take correlations into account, being well developed otherwise. Reserves coming from those models were unbelievably low and could not be seriously considered for decision making. Adding major correlations was a must to make models adequate for informed (not misinformed) decision making.

Figure 3.7 compares outcomes of a project probabilistic cost risk model for two cases. The narrow curve corresponds to a situation where no correlations were introduced at all. The wider curve represents the case where correlations were introduced. It is obvious that spreads of curves are remarkably different. As discussed in Chapter 12, this should lead to very different project cost reserves at the same level of confidence.

The probabilistic method allows one to identify uncertainty factors that are most sensitive for final costs/duration distributions. Sensitivity analysis highlights the rating of those uncertainty factors ("tornado chart"). The higher the rating, the higher the impact a particular factor has on project cost/duration. This means that even a smaller reduction of a factor's uncertainty may lead to a higher reduction of overall project uncertainty. This allows one to make

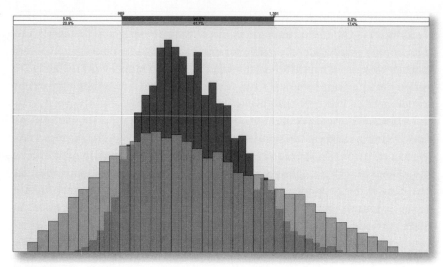

FIGURE 3.7 Comparison of Uncorrelated and Correlated Probabilistic Models

a decision about spending additional resources to improve outcome through development of corresponding addressing actions or optimization of baselines. If sensitivity of a factor is low, its addressing will not be effective. This topic is discussed in Chapter 14 in detail.

Integrated Cost and Schedule Risk Analysis

Most of the reasoning discussed in the previous section is applicable to schedule risk analyses. A higher uncertainty of project completion date is, of course, less preferable despite possible shorter deterministic project duration, and so forth. Two principal differences between cost and schedule risk analyses are as follows.

First, schedule risk analysis is schedule logic specific. Identified schedule uncertain events should be mapped to the impacted schedule normal activities. If those normal activities don't belong to a critical path or near-critical path, existing float may absorb the whole or part of the impact. There is no such schedule-type logic dependency in the case of cost risk analysis. Even though cost risks can be mapped to corresponding cost accounts of the base estimate, this doesn't impact the mathematical outcome of modeling.

Second, schedule risk analysis can be done independently of cost risk analysis. The reason for this is that normally the project schedule is done first to define sequencing and staging of activities. The cost estimate follows and depends on the features of the schedule. Obviously, schedule risks should feed some cost risks. Schedule-driven cost uncertainties are very often missed in probabilistic cost analysis, making it not fully adequate. We review integrated cost and schedule analysis in Parts III and IV. It will be seen that schedule-driven cost uncertainties belong to the cost general uncertainty category, and not uncertain events. A key point here is that completion date distribution presumes some delays for certain. Those delays will be translated to cost uncertainties through *burn rates*. For instance, if a construction team is deployed at a construction site, there is a cost of the team deployment, no matter whether they work or stay idle. Schedule-driven cost uncertainties are a realization of the situation where the team is idle and incurring capital costs due to delays.

This type of uncertainty is too often overlooked by project teams when developing project cost reserves. Because of this, it is critical that project teams and decision makers adopt adequate methods to pay heed to schedule-driven costs. The most adequate method to do so is integrated cost and schedule risk analysis. This topic is discussed in detail in Part III.

CONCLUSION

I am quite skeptical about modifications of scoring methods to make them semi-scoring, semi-quantitative, semi-probabilistic, and, hence, semi-efficient and semi-reliable. Some of them brought good value in the past when Monte Carlo methods were not available to risk practitioners. Some of them are inventions of estimators or schedulers turned risk managers, directors, or VPs and reflect corresponding personal and organizational biases.

We will not discuss deterministic quantitative and probabilistic qualitative assessment methods any further in this book. They absorb too much of the shortcomings of scoring and Monte Carlo methods without bringing enough extra value. Robust combination of scoring and Monte Carlo techniques is what is really required and will be discussed from here on. One exception is cost escalation modeling, which is a deterministic quantitative method in its own right (see Chapter 11). There is no viable substitute for this.

Part I has been a sort of "helicopter view" of project risk management. Now it's time to skydive down to the various terrains of risk management. Happy landings!

NOTES

1. A. Dubi, *Monte Carlo Applications in System Engineering* (Hoboken, NJ: John Wiley & Sons, 2000).
2. As will be discovered in Part IV of the book, this is a realization of RAM for a carbon capture and storage (CCS) project Curiosity discussed as a case study. Initially a generic RAM was developed for this chapter. It was eventually replaced by the CCS RAM when the decision was made to include the CCS project Curiosity case study in this book to exclude duplication.
3. J. Schuyler, *Risk and Decision Analysis in Projects* (Newtown Square, PA: Project Management Institute, 2001).
4. Y. Raydugin, "Consistent Application of Risk Management for Selection of Engineering Design Options in Mega-Projects," *International Journal of Risk and Contingency Management*, 1(4), 2012, 44–55.
5. AACE International Recommended Practice No. 17R-97: *Cost Estimate Classification System* (Morganton, WV: AACE International, 2003).

PART TWO

Deterministic Methods

A DETAILED REVIEW OF the major steps and tools of deterministic risk management is provided in this part. Based on Figure 2.1, risk management requires a high level of holistic integration of various project and corporate disciplines. It also should be very specific and well compartmentalized in all its realizations.

4

Uncertainty Identification

Questions Addressed in Chapter 4

- How should the three dimensions of risk management be used to structure uncertainty identification?
- How should uncertainty identification workshops be organized to be effective instead of boring?
- What is the difference between causes and sources of uncertainties?
- How may we identify the broiler black swans?
- Why should all risk management people get a bowtie?
- What defines room for unknown unknowns?
- What is a technology readiness level?
- What is the role of bias? ■

NTUITION IS A DOUBLE-EDGED SWORD. On one hand, it plays a key role in uncertainty identification, being an amalgam of our previous experience, education, and knowledge. On the other hand, it could be too selective, deceptive, or even blind. In other words, it could be extremely biased. Recognition of the necessity of using it, along with its utter unreliability, leads us to the need to better structure uncertainty identification activities.

This chapter compares worst and best practices of uncertainty identification. The three dimensions of risk management introduced previously serve as guidelines to keep uncertainty identification focused and specific. Simple but extremely effective uncertainty identification methodologies and tools such as the Delphi technique, risk breakdown structure (RBS), bowtie diagrams, three-part naming, and so on are presented. Various causes and sources that may lead to impacts on project objectives are discussed. Reasons why some uncertainties stay unidentified or unknown are also introduced. Influence of various types of bias on uncertainty identification is overviewed.

WHEN RISK MANAGEMENT BECOMES BORING

Many of us have attended grandiose risk identification workshops lasting sometimes two or more days. The major intent of these pompous shows was to demonstrate the importance of risk management or at least to show off that there was risk management of some sort. Two or three dozen people or more attended those workshops representing various project and near-project disciplines. Each participant would work actively for about one-tenth of the workshop duration as the rest of the time he or she was not interested in the topics discussed. For instance, people involved in permitting pretended that they were excited about features of technical risk exposure; project engineers found discussions related to nongovernmental organization activities "amazing," and so forth.

All risks were put into a "big bucket of risk soup" of corresponding "taste and smell." Risk facilitators (sometimes company employees, often external consultants) used sophisticated database tools to ensure that all the ingredients of the soup were visible on the screen, which made the process even more boring, slow, and depressing. Most of the participants' attention was focused on the misspellings or funny grammatical expressions used by facilitators who were desperate to capture discussed information. Multiple items could be identified during those workshops and put into huge project risk registers. As no one knew how to use them, they would be discussed again during the next workshop in a few months. Formally, all project disciplines were engaged; in reality, none were. What could be a more effective way to discredit project risk management?

A more structured organizational approach is required for real engagement of project teams in risk identification. Various ideas and tools that put forward required consistency, system, and structure to uncertainty identification are discussed in this chapter.

THREE DIMENSIONS OF RISK MANAGEMENT AND UNCERTAINTY IDENTIFICATION

One might guess that there is a fundamental connection between the RBS concept and the three dimensions of the risk management line-of-sight. This would be a correct guess as all relevant elements of these three dimensions must be reflected in the RBS. Uncertainties cannot be identified consistently and effectively if the three dimensions of risk management introduced in Chapter 2 (Figure 2.1) are ignored. We will not follow exactly the traditional thinking path when introducing RBS as a cousin of *work breakdown structure (WBS)*. Neither will we completely ignore the traditional approach. We will just take a fresh look at the role of RBS using the newly introduced three dimensions of organizational framework.

First, vertical integration at the work-package and project levels is a focus of this book and will be discussed later in detail. Integration at the business-unit and corporate levels should be subject to enterprise risk management (ERM) and is outside the scope of this book. It is reasonable to guess that all the vertical levels feed each other. Significant uncertainties identified at lower levels should be escalated to higher levels and uncertainties identified at higher levels should be watched at lower levels.

Second, a unique aspect of project risk management is that it cannot be just a standalone discipline. No doubt it should cast its 3D nets of Figure 2.1 broadly over all project disciplines and beyond to the external environment. This 360-degree scanning of internal and external project environments dictates integration of all involved disciplines. Often an identified general uncertainty or uncertain event would require implementation of addressing actions that belong to several project or corporate disciplines. The assigned uncertainty owner would be responsible for coordination of the efforts of multiple project specialists belonging to various project and corporate disciplines.

Third, relationships among project owners, members of consortia; investors; and engineering, procurement and construction (EPC) contractors and subcontractors depend on several factors. Types of contractual arrangements (lump sum, cost plus, unit price, and their modifications) influence risk identification by parties. Risk exposures of parties depend on contract types due to risk transferring (or risk brokering), which defines risk management responsibilities among the parties. For instance, project owners transfer the majority of risks to contractors that charge risk premiums in lump-sum contracts. Owners assume most of the risks in cost-plus contracts, though. Finally, project risk management systems adopted by partners could differ remarkably. Some parties do not have project risk management systems in place at all. Ideally, the project risk management systems of parties involved in a project should be synchronized by using a common project risk management plan, which promotes a common approach toward risk identification.

As a result, more structured and focused risk identification activities are promoted. They are not isolated from each other, being semiautonomous. Let's remember that we are talking about the dimensions of the line-of-sight. For instance, dozens of risks (or hazards) of Safety impacts could be identified for a particular construction package. Should they all be identified as project risks? Certainly not; otherwise the project risk register gets clogged quickly. They should be identified as package risks related to a particular construction package. This is one of the cells of Figure 2.1: Construction at the work package level.

Most critical identified package risks should be rolled up and promoted to the project risk register for visibility and reporting purposes. This can be done only after proper risk assessment. This should prevent the mass invasion of noncritical risks into the project risk register. Those promoted critical risks become project construction risks of Safety impact (the Construction-at-the-project-level cell in Figure 2.1).

Where several projects of a project portfolio have similar construction risks of Safety impact, those should be also rolled up into the business-unit level and placed in the corresponding risk register (the Construction-at-the-business-unit-level cell in Figure 2.1). For instance, one of most common construction risks of Safety impact identified for all three levels relates to traffic incidents. As such they should be visible and managed at all three levels. This example explains that risk identification includes rolling up risks and promoting them to higher levels of the *vertical line-of-sight.*

Similar examples could be provided regarding risks in the other disciplines, such as engineering, procurement, and so on, which accentuate the *horizontal* dimension of line-of-sight.

It is no secret that project owners and EPC contractors keep (or should keep) their internal project risk registers "close to their vests" without sharing with each other. Risks identified for those registers might have similar causes but lead to different identified uncertain events. For instance, a generally challenging economic situation may lead to identification by a project owner of the possibility of the EPC contractor's default. The contractor in turn may identify an event related to the project's delay, late payments or cancellation by the owner, and so on. Those internal risks are supposed to be identified before a contract is even awarded. It points to the need to keep in mind the in-depth dimension of the line-of-sight when identifying uncertainties.

In advanced risk databases (risk registers), RBS elements serve as attributes for data slicing and dicing. So the structure of a risk repository should reflect the three dimensions of risk management in a risk database through the RBS categories. In project portfolio management the same approach can be used in serving the business unit or corporate levels of Figure 2.1.

RISK IDENTIFICATION WORKSHOPS

The bottom line regarding the three dimensions is that specific risks should be identified in specific disciplines and at specific levels, separately. This does not require the grandiose risk identification workshops described earlier. Instead, the much more efficient activities based on the Delphi polling technique are required. Usually these correspond to one or a few cells in Figure 2.1. These focused Delphi workshops should not last more than two hours and could be undertaken frequently as part of the risk management routine. In my experience, in the early phases of project development, three or more workshops like this were held every week. Never more than a dozen participants took part. All those who attended were qualified participants working in the area of interest and adjacent areas. Full engagement of participants is a key requirement to ensure the required quorum for uncertainty identification (see "Typical Delphi Uncertainty Identification Workshop Agenda").

TYPICAL DELPHI UNCERTAINTY IDENTIFICATION WORKSHOP AGENDA

1. Safety moment and introduction of participants (5 min.)
2. Purpose of the workshop (5 min.)
3. Scope of the workshop (15 min.)
4. Review of the uncertainty identification methodology (10 min.)
5. Development of individual lists of uncertainties (3–7 items per participant) (15 min.)
6. Review of participant lists one-by-one (60 min.)
7. Next steps, wrapup (10 min.)

It is critical to properly define the purpose and scope of the workshop, otherwise participants will dissipate their attention and energies discussing irrelevant uncertainties. For instance, in a work-package risk identification workshop, the scope and features of products or services should be described, a general description of package schedule and budget should be provided, a list of qualified vendors should be reviewed, unique safety hazards or possible impacts on environment should be pointed out, and so on. Where there is a challenge involved in making a decision related to engineering design, the nature of the decision should be outlined and described in detail. Any relevant lessons-learned documentation should be reviewed. Lessons learned, or *postmortem* risk management, may serve as valuable providers of causes and sources of uncertainties related to a particular project.

When participants are on the same page about the purpose and scope of the exercise, they should brush up on risk identification methods and tools, including the implications of psychological bias.

As soon as participants know why they have assembled and how they should identify uncertainties, they have about a quarter of an hour to list uncertainties they believe are most relevant and critical to the discussed scope. ("Post-Its" are a very handy and efficient "risk identification tool" for this; these should be collected after the workshop.) Delphi polling sounds like a very biased exercise. It reflects participants' previous experiences, perceptions of risks, hidden agendas, and so on. But the beauty of the Delphi technique is that most biases are averaged out during the capturing, discussion, and processing of information. Discussion of points brought up by participants is a core activity. These are not necessarily fully developed uncertain events or general uncertainties. In fact, they are rarely identified like this. Very often they are just concerns, relevant facts, givens, and so on, that may be viewed as causes of uncertain events. The most critical skill of a facilitator is to capture those points quickly and jot them down, even before the participant has finished describing them. Some clarification questions could be asked by the facilitator and participants but normally without extensive discussion. There is no need to challenge the participants as this is merely a brainstorming activity.

Should a corporate or even simple Excel-based risk template be used during the Delphi technique exercise? Using a computer during any risk identification workshop is *detrimental* to effective risk identification. One of my co-workers regularly suffered from jokes about his spelling mistakes when he tried to capture information visibly on the screen. His knowledge of English was jokingly challenged many times by participants, who seemed more interested in his poor spelling skills than in uncertainty identification. Using computers for risk writing during a workshop should be avoided as this is an activity better done by a qualified facilitator *after* the workshop. If a dozen people take part in the workshop, at least a dozen extra person-hours of highly qualified people will be required to capture and write down risks during the workshop without adding much value. An experienced facilitator may do the writing after the workshop in two or three hours with much higher quality.

One might challenge the duration of the workshop proposed by the earlier agenda. If a dozen participants take part and each has 5 points to discuss, there should be about 60 points to discuss in 60 minutes! That's five minutes per participant and one minute per point! In reality, only the first one or two participants have to share all their points. The number of points per participant will drop as other participants find they have similar or the same items. Often, the final participant does not even have unique points to discuss at all. And, of course, there is no need to invite a dozen participants. I have run hundreds of workshops like this. On average there were 8–10 participants. Workshops that ran over two hours were very rare. The level of participant engagement was always close to 100% by default. Moreover, participants often argued over who should share identified risks first. Isn't that exciting in terms of engagement of participants?

The most critical activity for the facilitator begins after the workshop—writing down the identified risks properly. Three-part naming of risks (described later) should be used. Causes of risks, risk events, and impacts should be enumerated utilizing captured information. In my experience, in regard to the number of uncertain events or general uncertainties as outcomes of a typical Delphi technique workshop, as a rule, around 20–40 unique points typically raised by participants led to no more than 5–7 uncertainties.

On one hand, having the causes of uncertain events and general uncertainties properly grouped reduces the number of identified items dramatically. On the other hand, the level of detail during uncertainty identification is very important. One may break down an identified uncertain event into several more specific ones or could roll up several of them into one at a higher level. As there are no industry standards or established guidelines on the required level of detail, I present one here. An identified uncertain event or general uncertainty should be addressed. Are all its major causes and impacts listed? Addressing, as discussed later, is a process of breaking logical links between major causes and impacts. (We discuss the PETRA technique for the detailed addressing of risks in Chapter 5.) If all those links are broken, an uncertain event or general uncertainty could be considered avoided. In some cases, we might not know what event could occur. But if we know its causes as well as its impacts, we might come up with some reasonable addressing actions (barriers). The majority of standard risk checklists suggest causes of potential uncertain events and general uncertainties and imply impacts without even describing them. The intent of effective addressing through breaking all those logical links defines the preferable level of detail in identification.

A risk workshop is a major venue where various types of bias emerge and make an impact on the quality of risk management. The Delphi technique workshop is developed to minimize the impact of participants on each other. Key discussion points are jotted down first without any discussion or mutual influence. Although each opinion could be biased (and usually is), analysis of collected information after the workshop allows the averaging out of most of the bias impacts, which is a key role of the project risk manager or workshop facilitator.

 ## SOURCES OF UNCERTAINTIES AND RISK BREAKDOWN STRUCTURE

Work breakdown structure (WBS) is used by projects to properly represent project scopes in project schedules and estimates. This is one of the key planning tools that ensure that no project scope elements are missed. Various activities that make up project development and execution are covered by WBS. Following this logic it would be acceptable to use WBS as a basis for scanning the project for sources of risks as any project activity may reveal uncertainty. This approach is adequate but not the best or most practical. Project schedules may contain thousands of activities at levels 3 or 4. Investigation of uncertainties associated with them would be onerous and costly and without visible benefits.

Better trees-versus-forest balance is achieved in risk management if a higher level of detail is kept. For instance, all major project elements are grouped into major deliverables in the project schedule at level 2. The issue with using WBS directly in risk management is that some sources of uncertainties and associated activities are not explicitly represented by a project WBS. For instance, activities of external stakeholders that might be critical for project success cannot be part of the project schedule explicitly. Similarly, the general economic situation that impacts contracting and procurement activities cannot be represented directly. Moreover, some specific activities, such as change management, are not part of initial schedules. So, if we go back to the key uncertainties introduced in Table 1.2, we may see a requirement to describe some sources of uncertainties that may not be part of the WBS.

These two considerations—required level of detail and expected spectrum of uncertainties—lead us to the need to use a slightly different structure for identification of uncertainties. Even though it is traditionally called *risk* breakdown structure, we will understand this as *uncertainty* breakdown structure, although the latter term won't be used in this book.

Companies use various types of RBS. These depend on what they do and how they manage risks (organizational framework). Not unusual is a two-level RBS with a few RBS categories on the top. For example, it could be categories of the PESTLE (Political, Economic, Social, Technological, Legal, Environmental) analysis[1] used in business strategy development, or its shorter PEST version. To better reflect commercial and organizational aspects of project development and execution one may want to use the POCET (Political, Organizational, Commercial, Economic and Technical) categories invented for the purposes of this book. Up to two dozen (sometimes more) categories could be used at the second level of RBS grouped under the top categories. The level of RBS granularity should be explained in the project risk management plan. A generic RBS for a capital mega-project could be as follows:

1. Engineering
2. Procurement
3. Construction
4. Commissioning and Startup
5. Operations
6. Regulatory
7. Stakeholders
8. Commercial
9. Partner(s)
10. Interface Management
11. Change Management
12. Organizational

The first five categories resemble major WBS categories and project phases. If required, they may be further broken down to better reflect organizational context. For instance, for a CO_2 sequestration project, Engineering subcategories could include capture, pipeline, injection wells, and so on. As discussed in Chapter 10, the Procurement category may be specified through introduction of package-specific, vendor-specific, and external subcategories.

Strictly speaking, Operations are not part of a project. However, project development and execution activities are common sources and causes of uncertainties in Operations. For this reason Operations should be always part of the RBS. For instance, in a CO_2 sequestration project, containment, storage capacity, and infectivity as well as monitoring, measuring, and verification (MMV) are common subcategories under Operations.

The role of the Regulatory and Stakeholders categories cannot be over-estimated. It is well known by practitioners that nontechnical uncertainties are a primary reason for project failures. The permitting process and involvement of various stakeholders (local communities, first nations, nongovernmental organizations [NGOs], various activists, etc.) is a primary reason for project delays. (One may guess that "broiler black swans" introduced in Chapter 2 belong mostly to the Stakeholders category of RBS.)

Commercial aspects of project planning, including selection of the right partners, could be critical to the success of a project, especially if elements of commercial novelty are part of the picture. For example, one high-profile CO_2 sequestration project failed recently, canceled due to underestimating key com-mercial aspects. On one hand, the CO_2 market for enhanced oil and gas recov-ery is very immature. On the other hand, the project team was overly focused on the technical aspects of the project, with the commercial elements being virtually overlooked.

Unfortunately, Interface Management is a traditional source of risks. Although the main "soft" and "hard" interfaces usually seem to be planned among disciplines, owners, subcontractors, and vendors, the depth and sub-stance of such planning are rarely sufficient.

Change Management is another typical surprise in the form of uncertain events. As described by Cooper and Lee,[2] secondary change impacts (impacts of a changing part on the rest of the project) are regularly overlooked. This leads (what a surprise!) to extra person-hours and costs and schedule delays, which are not taken into account as part of the newly changed project base-lines. Cooper and Lee propose an excellent method to better take secondary impacts into account, which seems to still be ignored by the industry. This is an area of project services and not of risk management. However, this is a source of potential risks, depending on how change management is handled. And this is yet another illustration of the three-dimensional integration of risk management (Figure 2.1).

The Organizational category usually covers features of decision making and maturity of processes and procedures supporting project delivery. This is where the organization itself and its project governance are the sources of risks.

One mistake should be avoided when establishing the project's RBS. Namely, to avoid confusion, project objectives should not be included in the

RBS. It is not unusual for risk categories to include Schedule, Cost, Safety, and so on, along with Engineering, Procurement, Construction, and so on.

First, the terms *schedule risk, cost risk, safety risk* as names of categories are confusing risk jargon and should be avoided. These categories should be understood as uncertainties with impacts on project Schedule, Cost, Safety, and the other objectives. I am okay with using jargon if it reflects a true understanding of the subject. Unfortunately, jargon is often used in risk management as a substitute for understanding.

Second, even if those categories are understood correctly, the issue is that one such uncertainty could lead to deviations from several project objectives. So, it would be less confusing to say that there is "Schedule, Cost, and Safety risk" or "Schedule and Safety risk," meaning that it could lead to impacts on more than one project objective.

Third, impacts on/deviations from Schedule, Cost, Safety, and the other objectives may occur in Engineering, Procurement, Construction, and so on, or could come from Permitting, Stakeholder Management, and so on. This is a key reason why project objectives and RBS should be kept separately. The bowtie diagram introduced in the next section further clarifies this and introduces the required structure.

 ## BOWTIE DIAGRAMS FOR UNCERTAINTY IDENTIFICATION

We discussed the Delphi risk identification method earlier in this chapter. The purpose of this method is to collect pieces of information related to risk exposure. It was mentioned that dozens of points could be collected during the Delphi workshop leading to identification of only a few uncertainties. The bowtie diagram discussed in this section provides a consistent approach to collecting scattered uncertainty information ("uncertainty particles"), processing it, and coming up with a compact number of uncertainties. In other words, any uncertainty has a structure that should be captured for its proper identification. This is similar to the identification of the structure of a molecule, which is made up of several atoms. Each atom has a set of electrons surrounding its nucleus. Each nucleus is made up of a certain number of neutrons and protons. Each neutron and proton is a composition of quarks of various properties, and so on. Things are getting a bit complicated, you say? This analogy points to the dilemma regarding the correct level of risk identification again.

For instance, in a fault tree analysis, any required level of detail could be reached in risk identification depending on the task on hand. The reason for this is simple. All obvious risk events that could be represented by a simple logical link of a cause (basic event) and the risk event (top event) are usually believed to be trivial, well known, and taken care of. The situation where two or more causes (basic events) give rise to a risk top event is less common. The probability of the top event may be represented as sums and products of the probabilities of the preceding basic events. If two basic events are required simultaneously to give rise to a top event (AND gate), the probability of the top event will be a product of P_1 and P_2, where P_1 and P_2 are probabilities of the basic event's occurrences (see Figure 4.1).

If each of the two basic events might lead to the top event independently (OR gate), the probability of the top event is a sum of the basic event's probabilities. In Figure 4.1, basic event 3 may lead to the top event independently with probability P_3. However, the total probability of the top event is $P_1 \times P_2 + P_3$, because two independent branches may lead to the top event. In real fault tree analysis several branches containing multiple *AND* and *OR* gates could be considered. Getting back to physics, this may be perceived as a long chain of quarks–protons/neutrons–electrons–atoms–molecules, with the molecules being understood as the top events. The situation might be exacerbated by the fact that some otherwise independent basic events could be dependent or correlated. This will lead to additions (correlation coefficients) in assessments of

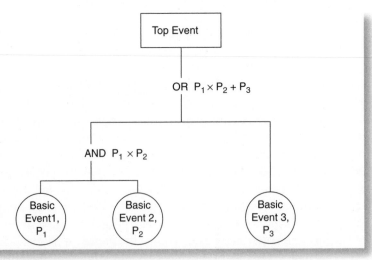

FIGURE 4.1 AND and OR Logic

probabilities. We will not follow this path, for a simple reason. Project risk management borrowed the fault tree analysis approach[3] but in a very simplified form—that of a bowtie diagram.

In terms of our physics analogy, a bowtie diagram consists only of atoms (causes in place of basic events) and molecules (risk events in place of top events). However, if in fault tree analysis a top event represents the end of the analysis as a system performance failure (impact on *Scope/Quality/Performance* objective), in a bowtie diagram multiple impacts on project objectives are weighed up instead.

As discussed in Chapter 3, besides Scope/Quality/Performance there are several other project objectives to be examined as impacted by a risk event, including Cost, Schedule, Safety, Reputation, Environment, and so on. Hence, possible causes of an uncertain event constitute the left part of the bowtie, whereas impacts on project objectives complete the right part of it. Figure 4.2 represents a sample bowtie diagram for project uncertainty identification.[4]

According to Figure 4.2, several causes are thought to lead to the same or similar uncertain event. This reiterates the topic of the level of detail in risk identification. At the work-package level an event may be very specific and have just one or two causes. Another risk event that resembles the first one but has different causes should be identified separately. For example, quality issues related

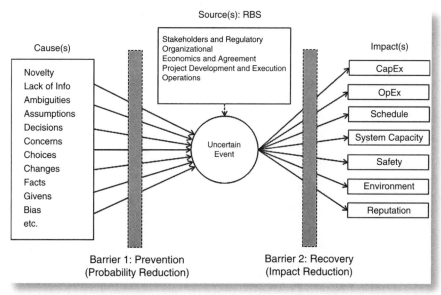

FIGURE 4.2 Bowtie Diagram

to two construction contractors delivering work packages of similar scope may have different causes but would lead to a similar uncertain event. At the project level those two uncertainties may be treated as one. Their causes are united, leading to more general or higher-level uncertainty. Corresponding groups of similar risks belonging to different projects may be rolled up as one, even more general risk at the business-unit level. This should lead to different probabilities of occurrence for an uncertain event at the work-package, project, and business-unit levels.

In traditional form a bowtie diagram contains only cause(s), risk event, and impact(s). I believe the addition of RBS doesn't complicate the picture but rather adds the other important angle: sources of risks. Although in the proposed form it resembles a bowtie less, it permits scanning a project's internal and external environments to identify sources (*where* deviations might occur) and causes (*why* deviations might happen) of possible deviations from objectives. Hence, the diagram should have four parts linked by a simple logic:

1. Cause(s)
2. Source(s)
3. Risk event
4. Impact(s)

Project team members should scan various causes of potential deviations relevant to various RBS categories. Among the possible causes there could be:

- Project novelty, including new geography and/or new technology
- Lack of information or ambiguities related to some RBS categories
- Lack of previous experience related to some RBS categories
- Assumptions and choices made when developing project baselines
- Concerns expressed by project team members or stakeholders (gut feelings)
- Lack of information encountered when developing project baselines or project execution plans
- Decisions made by project team
- Known facts or givens relevant to the project development or execution
- Changes (scope, regulatory, market conditions, etc.) relevant to a project

Novelty and lack of information or experience may characterize new commercial aspects of the project. It may be based on the absence of previous experience in working with particular major contractors, an immature market (as is true of the CO_2 market for enhanced oil recovery), and so on.

The bowtie diagram is applicable to both uncertain events and general uncertainties. The causes might lead to uncertain events that give rise to deviations from project objectives. The modal verb *might* in the previous sentence points out that those events are characterized by probabilities of occurrence. In the case of general uncertainties there are no events that might happen due to causes. Often they have already happened (issues) or have been givens all along. For this reason, modal verbs such as *might*, *could*, and *would*, which point to lower than 100% probabilities, should be replaced by verbs in the present tense.

If an uncertain event does occur, it makes an impact on project objectives and redefines impacted baselines. For instance, a schedule delay having occurred redefines the project schedule, or the project team has to accelerate some activities to obey the approved completion date, which usually costs money and redefines the project cost baseline. In other words, an uncertain event becomes an *issue* or a *given* (Table 1.2 and Figure 1.3) that should be reflected in amended baselines.

The bowtie diagram introduces two lines of defense to prevent impact on project objectives by an uncertain event. Those relate to two parameters of uncertainty: probability and impact. First, efforts should be planned to reduce the probability of an uncertain event's happening (preventive addressing actions). Second, along with this some steps should be planned for when an uncertain event does happen and becomes an issue (recovery addressing actions). For instance, blowout preventers (BOP) on a drilling rig are supposed to reduce the probability of methane or sour gas release, both of which are severe safety hazards potentially leading to casualties. The former could result in a fire at the rig; the latter could lead to poisoning of the rig's personnel by H_2S. We all know that in some cases BOPs don't work out as they are supposed to. To exclude the possibility of injuries and casualties, evacuation plans should be in place, personnel should be properly trained, H_2S sensors and personal protective equipment should be available, and so on. These measures are considered recovery addressing actions. They represent the second line of defense and could be thought of as part of crisis management.

If probability of occurrence is reduced to zero, the logical link between cause(s) and the uncertain event is broken, meaning the risk is avoided. That risk loses relevance to the project. This may be the case when the scope of a project is changed and the risk is pushed out of the picture.

If a relevant risk does happen but does not lead to any impact on project objectives, it may be considered fully transferred. In many cases this is achievable through transferring the risk to third parties. Transferring includes purchasing insurance or risk brokering, which are widely used in procurement.

The risk still may occur and make an impact on objectives but not on objectives of the organization that succeeded in full risk transferring. Risk transferring is not usually free, though. Insurance companies charge premiums to manage somebody's risks. Vendors usually charge additional risk premiums to accept and manage risks from project owners, and so on. A general rule in risk transferring is that a risk should be managed by the party that can do this in the most efficient way. In real life, full transferring of risks is not always achievable. Insurance policies normally have deductibles. Even in the case of liquidated damages paid by vendors, owners may still encounter severe project schedule delays, and so on.

In the case of general uncertainties and issues, preventive mitigation is not entirely possible as the probability of occurrence of a given is fixed and equal to 100%. At the same time reduction of the possible impact on objectives is still an option (barrier 2 of Figure 4.2), although the only option. This resembles crisis management in the case of the occurrence of downside uncertain events.

Uncertainty identification as discussed in this chapter is static and relates to a particular point in time. The dynamics of project uncertainty exposure were initially discussed in Chapter 1 where project uncertainty changers were introduced. The RBS that is part of the bowtie diagram defines whether particular changers belong to the external or internal project environment. Uncertainty addressing actions (internal changers) belong to two barriers of the bowtie diagram, whereas the rest of the changers reside in the Causes part of it. The role and importance of uncertainty addressing actions as major internal changers and risk controls are discussed in detail in Chapter 5.

It is common practice that in place of risk identification, standard checklists are used. By their nature the checklists may be understood as lists of possible causes of risks grouped according to their possible sources. The problem with using standard checklists is that some causes that are unique to a particular project could be overlooked. This is one of the reasons that some risks could stay unidentified (i.e., unknown). The value of using checklists is that some risks might be addressed even without their clear identification. This approach is based on breaking or blocking logical links between the causes and some unspecified uncertain events. However, this approach does not explicitly deal with specific impacts on project objectives. So, recovery actions cannot be consistently developed.

THREE-PART UNCERTAINTY NAMING

As soon as we know the causes of an uncertain event and understand where they might come from (sources), anticipate what event could happen, and realize the potential impacts on project objectives, we should use this information for clear uncertainty description. (In the case of general uncertainties there are no events, so direct impact of identified causes on objectives should be expected.) In other words, we should define an uncertainty in terms of cause(s), source(s), risk event (if applicable), and impact(s). Certainly, it is easier to operate with uncertainties that have a brief name (label or tag) that recaps the more detailed three-part definitions. But labels such as *schedule risk* or *safety risk* are not acceptable, being too general and confusing. A few more specifics would be required for a tag/label. "Example of Three-Part Naming of an Uncertain Event" represents a three-part uncertain event definition accompanied by a tag.

Here we need to tell apart notions of *consequences* and *impacts*. Often those two terms are used interchangeably. In the case of uncertainty identification, impacts just point to the possibility of deviations from particular objectives when an uncertainty does happen. Consequences are treated as expected values of impacts during uncertainty assessments. In the case of assessments of quantifiable impacts on Quality, Cost, and Schedule objectives, possible impacts multiplied by probability of occurrence produce the expected value. If impacts are not quantifiable, as in the case of soft objectives, there should be a more general definition in place of a mathematical *expected value* term such as *consequence*. Before assessments of uncertainties are undertaken the term *consequence* should be understood in a nonmathematical sense, even for quantifiable impacts.

We may describe consequences during uncertainty identification as short stories outlining qualitatively what could be observable. This is more informative than just having a list of impacted objectives. As the boxed example demonstrates, three causes (a)–(c) could give rise to an uncertain event, which, if it does occur, leads to three consequences (A)–(C). These three consequences result in two impacts on the project XXX objectives: Schedule (consequence A) and Reputation (consequences B and C). To be fully consistent, the impacted objectives are shown in parentheses. However, well-described consequences clearly imply impacted objectives without mentioning them.

EXAMPLE OF THREE-PART NAMING OF AN UNCERTAIN EVENT

*P*roject Sanctioning: Due to (a) general opposition by some NGOs to oil sands projects; (b) concerns in local communities about the project's environmental impact; and (c) environmental issues associated with a similar project in the past, **project XXX might be challenged during public hearings,** leading to (A) permitting and final investment decision delay (Schedule); (B) company's reputational damage in general (Reputation); and (C) complication of relations with local communities in particular (Reputation).

The benefits of three-part naming are:

- Uncertainty identification is specific and clear.
- This approach ensures relevance of identified uncertainty to the project.
- An identified risk is understood the same way by people of different backgrounds and experience.
- The same risk is understood by the same person the same way at a later time.
- This approach points out two barriers to addressing risks.
- The three-part naming of risks is becoming a standard that is understandable and adopted across the industry.

Although sources of risks are important for risk identification, they do not make it to the three-part naming. Otherwise, it would be four-part naming. Although the relevant element of RBS (where an uncertainty may happen or belongs to) could be easily mentioned when defining the uncertain event. In any case, the RBS element should be reflected as a standalone attribute in a corresponding risk register.

One might make the observation that three-part naming is relevant only to uncertain events. However, the same diagram should be used for general uncertainties. In the case of general uncertainties, events are absent. Instead there should be either an issue or a given. We tend to treat *issues* as former uncertain events that have occurred. *Givens* are facts in the project internal or external environment that should be taken into account when defining project baselines. Both issues and givens may be characterized by uncertainty of their

EXAMPLE OF THREE-PART NAMING OF GENERAL UNCERTAINTY (ISSUE/ OCCURRED UNCERTAIN EVENT)

Project Sanctioning (Issue): Due to (a) direct opposition by YYY NGO to the project during hearings and partnering with local communities; and (b) direct opposition in local communities to preliminary assessment of the project's environmental impact during hearings based on environmental issues associated with a similar project in the past, **project XXX is challenged during public hearings,** so that (A) permitting and final investment decision are delayed (Schedule); (B) damage to the company's reputation is done (Reputation); and (C) relations with local communities are complicated (Reputation).

impacts on project objectives (Figure 1.3). "Example of Three-Part Naming of General Uncertainty (Issue/Occurred Uncertain Event)" describes a general uncertainty associated with a recently realized uncertain event (now it is an issue at hand), the impact of which is yet uncertain. There is uncertainty of reputational damage and schedule delay associated with this issue.

Including causes in the definition of an issue is not mandatory: whatever the causes are, the previously uncertain event has just happened. So, it should be possible to switch to two-part naming: the issue ("project XXX is challenged during public hearings") and its impacts (A) – (C) as described above.

The previous example represents a specific case where a downside uncertain event has occurred. This leads to downside general uncertainty. Even though the initial uncertain event had nothing to do with baselines, the issue redefines corresponding baselines, although impact on those could be uncertain. In most of the other general uncertainty cases of Table 1.2 "true" general uncertainties assume the possibility of both upside and downside deviations. For instance, quotes received from vendors could be both lower and higher than the work-package cost in the base estimate. Similarly, one should exclude neither cost escalation nor de-escalation in the future, which defines the required escalation reserve range around the base estimate. Another example is the general uncertainty associated with labor productivity. There are usually no uncertain events associated with labor productivity. Labor productivity might be better or worse (which is usually the case)than assumed in project baselines, though.

In some cases the same uncertainty may be identified and represented twice: the first time as a general uncertainty, and the second time as an uncertain event. Let's exclude from consideration banal double-dipping, which should always be avoided. Then this may be a case where a general uncertainty defines reasonable limits of uncertainty associated with baselines. And an uncertain event points out the possibility of exceeding those. For instance, general uncertainty may define –15%/+5% variations of labor productivity for contracting work packages. A corresponding reserve could be put aside to cover the downside impact. However, in some cases labor productivity could be worse than defined by the general uncertainty. For example, extremely bad (cold, rainy, snowy, windy, hot) weather might be an additional event-driven reason for lower-than-assessed labor productivity. Or a less experienced contractor could be awarded a work-package contract because the more-preferred contractor was dropped from the bid as being too busy.

As previously discussed, one of the challenges in identifying and describing risks is selection of the correct level of detail. Work-package or safety uncertainties and hazards tend to be very detailed and specific. Project risks may be more general as they could be developed as rollups of several package risks. For instance, multiple hazards managed by the health and safety (H&S) department could be combined into a few major safety-related risks and placed in a project risk register for visibility and reporting purposes only. Risks at the business-unit level are usually generic and often look like givens or issues. A key criterion to pin down the right level of detail would be risk management intent. Specifically, whatever was identified as an uncertainty would be assessed, addressed, and reported. If an uncertainty was identified in a very detailed manner, more detailed actions would be appropriate to manage it. So it is not unusual that the original identified uncertainties are split up or bundled depending on how they should be managed and at what level (Figure 2.1). More detailed discussion on this is provided in Chapter 5.

 ## ROLE OF BIAS IN UNCERTAINTY IDENTIFICATION

Bias is a systematic error in risk identification, assessment, and addressing. This error could stem from several sources. It would be reasonable to distinguish organizational from psychological aspects of bias, although this is a conditional classification. Let's start with the usually milder form of bias in terms of impact on the risk management process, namely *psychological* bias.

Psychological bias could be both subconscious and conscious.[5] *Subconscious* bias could be perceptual and cognitive. *Perceptual* bias resonates with the emotional aspects of risk management and is based on personal previous experiences of individuals with a particular uncertainty, depends on its proximity and relevance to a project, and appeals to subjective understanding of its manageability. Overconfidence or lack of confidence is a common perceptual bias factor. One of the manifestations of perceptual bias is *anchoring*. First or previous impressions about an uncertainty may hold up even if additional information is available later. Even highly qualified specialists could be exposed to anchoring.

Cognitive bias may stem from a lack of practical knowledge of particular uncertainties or methods of their identification and assessment. That is why it is important that particular uncertainties are identified by people who are up to the task. Moreover, the influence of unqualified people should be reduced to a minimum. For these reasons, big workshops where representatives of many disciplines discuss specific uncertainties might distort the process. Some unqualified but outspoken participants could change group dynamics and overtake the process of uncertainty identification. A similar effect might happen if representatives of relevant disciplines are not attending a workshop. Some relevant uncertainties might just stay unidentified when there is no required quorum. In my experience, enthusiastic amateurs are innocent but major representatives of the cognitive bias.

Conscious bias is often called *motivational* or *hidden-agenda* bias. Jargon such as *double-dipping, exaggeration,* and *window dressing* is often used by practitioners to describe symptoms of conscious bias. This type of bias is less innocent than the subconscious types. Some "wrong" red-herring types of uncertainties could be identified in place of relevant ones on purpose. As a result, the wrong or misleading uncertainties could be managed due to overlooking right ones. For instance, if a group of stakeholders is not interested in the project's progress, some environmental risks might be enormously inflated while the more relevant commercial or technical risks are overlooked. In the case of oil sands, referred to by some stakeholders as "dirty oil," some environmental risks and stakeholder concerns might not be relevant to certain oil sands projects. However, identification of *those* concerns allows some major consumers to leverage lower prices for the "dirty oil," which is not really about environmental concerns.

Certainly, some projects might be engaged in window dressing, trying to assure stakeholders that real environmental problems are not relevant. Even though regulators are exposed to all the political tides and trends and "hidden agendas," their role in balanced rulings cannot be overestimated. Happy small groups of (biased) stakeholders or one satisfied major trading partner versus the overall competitiveness and prosperity of a country—this is a dilemma regulators are faced with when managing hidden agendas in project uncertainty identification. (But this is a topic for a different book on a different subject.)

Hidden agendas may be promoted by both individuals and organizations. This brings us to the topic of organizational bias.

What is the overall risk policy and risk appetite of an organization? What are the risk methods and tools an organization uses for risk identification? Is budget allocated to risk management sufficient for the activities and challenges the organization has in hand (organizational context)? What is the risk management culture of an organization? Is it ultraconservative, prudent, reasonable, aggressive, or negligence based? Is an organization very selective when picking projects to execute, or truly omnivorous? The importance of an individual such as the company CEO or the VP responsible for risk management cannot be underestimated. Herein lies the link between the psychological and organizational types of bias. Is it strange for an organization to pay attention only to risks of financial impact when its risk VP comes from the financial or cost estimating world? What might happen if the risk VP were to come from a scheduling or safety background? That's right—risks of schedule or safety impacts would suddenly become the most important. This type of corporate myopia (or risk tunnel or selective vision) leads to a situation when only risks of impacts on one or two objectives are at the radar screen of the organization. The rest of objectives and impacts on them indicated by a bowtie diagram (Figure 4.2) are just ignored.

Organizational bias of risk management should be considered a major cause of the Organizational risks in the RBS in Figure 4.2. The relatively good news is that if current organizational bias is recognized, the systematic error induced by it could be compensated for fairly well. Some additions to the existing risk management system should be applied and eventually taken into account in an updated version of the risk management system.

I could come up with examples of particular organizations where risk tunnel vision led to severe reputational damage, where billions of dollars were shaved from market capitalization as a result, and where some risks of reputational impact were just ignored in favor of doubtful initiatives and projects (i.e., in favor of greed). By the way, I am not talking here about some financial institutions in 2008; I refer to infamous activities and events related to capital projects.

All types of bias are highly interrelated; they feed and groom each other. Existing inferior risk management systems might be declared state-of-the-art, which could be used as an excuse to ignore more adequate and progressive methods. Being promoted from the top down, the inferior system becomes mandatory for all projects and activities in an organization, which in turn shapes perceptual and cognitive biases at lower levels of the organization, which reinforces the organizational bias from the bottom up. This picture is usually shattered in major project or organizational failures. But you are right: a new risk VP might appear instead, introducing a different type of bias.

The good news is that best industry practices do exist; but they are not quite well-known yet, which was one of the main reasons for writing this book. I would recommend using qualified third-party auditors and consultants to ensure the adequacy and health of an organization's risk management system. The key word in the previous sentence is *qualified*, to exclude indoctrination of various types of biases from outside in addition to existing ones. These cold-eye reviews might be very revealing, unless consultants succumb to organizational bias, too. At the end of the day, consultants need to be nice guys to ensure their future business with an organization. In any case, this book could be used as an additional source of benchmarking and insights based on best industry practices.

The key remedy against bias is awareness. Project team members should be aware of the main types of bias. They should be constructively suspicious about manifestations of bias as part of group dynamics. Better knowledge of each other and each other's backgrounds, motivations, and inclinations should help manage bias successfully or reduce it to an acceptable level. This is one of the key responsibilities of a project risk manager.

More on bias is provided in the next section, where we discuss unknown unknowns. Bias is not confined to risk identification. Even more surprising manifestations of bias are possible during the other steps of the risk management process (Figure 2.2), especially when assessing risks and developing addressing actions.

 ## ROOM FOR UNKNOWN UNKNOWNS

Table 1.2 introduced unknown uncertain events as opposed to known uncertain events. Actually, some general uncertainties may stay unknown, too. For instance, some factors of cost estimating and escalation as well as durations of normal activities could stay unidentified or unknown. This should be kept in mind, although we will focus mostly on unknown uncertain events in this section.

By its nature, dealing with unknown unknowns sounds mysterious. Unknown unknowns are what a project team did not even identify as uncertainty objects. As such they cannot be effectively managed. Generally speaking, possible room for unknown unknowns is an overall measure of the efficiency and quality of a risk management system. It is as simple as this: the bigger the room, the lower the quality and efficiency.[6] The room for unknown unknowns has four dimensions.

The first is project novelty. Intuitively one may guess that the unknown unknowns will be higher for a unique project. It may employ a new technology or be planned in a new geography, or both. When both new technology and new geography are involved, overall project risk exposure including unknown unknowns should be worst.

Obviously, a new technology may easily lead to some technical unknown unknowns if its level of maturation is not high enough. However, this might be a source of nontechnical unknown risks, too (e.g., environmental, permitting, commercial, and political risks). Similarly, the new geography seems to lead to nontechnical unknown unknowns related to political, organizational, commercial, or economic risks. For example, if two projects of a similar scope are planned in Western Canada and in Western Africa, the latter may have more nontechnical unknown unknowns than the former, including country risks, and so on. However, new geography may easily bring up technical unknown unknowns, too (e.g., subsurface risks).

Even though some industry lessons learned may be available, what is important is how they are adopted and utilized by an organization involved in a particular project. Any repetitiveness or standardization of projects reduces unknown unknowns to a certain level as some of them should have already occurred and been taken into account as known unknowns when planning similar new projects. Eventually, a particular type of project employing a proven technology and repeated several times in a given geography may be considered standard.

The second dimension relates to the phase of project development. When a project is in the earlier phases of development, say in Identify or Select (Table 1.1), it is reasonable to expect that unknown unknowns should have greater room for existence even in the case of proven technology or known geography. In the course of project development this room is supposed to shrink as some of them may have already occurred.

The third dimension relates to types of industry or even projects inside an industry (e.g., coal versus unconventional gas production or onshore versus offshore oil production, high-tech versus pharmaceuticals, space exploration versus railway transportation, etc.). It may provide additional insights when considering a project's unknown unknowns. This should shed light on the general maturity of the industry and accumulated project experience.

The fourth dimension points to several types of bias discussed in the previous section. First and foremost it is about organizational bias that points to shortcomings of risk methods adopted by an organization, shortage of budget or time allocated to identification and quantification of risks, and so on.

One example of the role of methods in producing unknown unknowns relates to using standard risk checklists. It is quite popular these days to use them; they are in essence causes of risks, in place of risk identification. This method might be justified in a series of very standard projects. In other words, checklists are quite reliable when projects are standard and have no uniqueness at all. This means the project environment is fully controlled and well known as in repeating operations. For instance, this could occur when an organization is involved in doing standard tie-ins using standard equipment and methods. However, it would be easy to overlook some causes and corresponding risks in case the next project is unique.

One of the most notorious examples of organizational bias is in the handling of change management. When a change to a project (change order) is initiated by a project owner or EPC contractor, it is not unusual for corresponding amendments to baselines to be made in an inconsistent (i.e., wrong) way. The fact that those changes are being made under a severe time crunch is an additional exacerbating factor. The major focus of a project team from both sides is on the changing part of the project reflecting the proposed change. Unfortunately, that primary change induces multiple secondary changes associated with the impact of the changing part on the rest of the project. Too often those secondary effects are overlooked, hiding as unknown unknowns. The good news is that most of them could be converted to known knowns if due consideration and modeling of the secondary changes are done. The bad news is that those extra costs are a major topic of disputes between project owners and EPC contractors, often leading to legal actions and damages, and damaged relations and reputation, not to mention schedule delays, lower quality, and so on. In some cases project owners tend to play down secondary impacts on purpose to reduce change order costs through transferring corresponding risks to contractors.

For the reasons specified, we singled out change management as a standalone source of risks in the RBS. Needless to say, those risks staying unidentified could eventually lead to impacts on several project objectives. A similar situation could occur when handling both hard and soft interfaces between project disciplines of owners and contractors. Interface management is another standalone source of uncertainties including unidentified unknown unknowns.

Besides the organizational bias, one cannot fully exclude some conscious bias factors such as hidden agendas, where some risks might be overlooked on purpose to make a project more attractive. This may be based on an explainable desire to get project funding or support from key stakeholders, which could make some risks unknown. Sometimes less relevant risks could be identified due to hidden agendas. Those politically motivated red-herring types of risks could be damaging to the sanctioning and execution of projects.

Two project teams developing similar projects in similar geographies but with different exposure to conscious and subconscious biases could have very different lists of identified or known uncertainties. Hence, these two projects should have very different exposure to unknown unknowns too. At the end of the day, a fundamental governance question every organization should keep in mind is: Which is preferable, to unexpectedly run into project failure or to adequately and timely address as many failure factors as possible?

The bias factors directly influence the quality of project risk registers. At the same time, phases of project development contribute to the quality of project risk registers. So, for purposes of this discussion we distinguish between bias and the phase of project development.

Room for unknown uncertainties will always exist unless a project is completely non-unique. It is possible to contemplate a natural or minimum room for unidentified uncertainties even if a project team does the very best job in uncertainty identification. This natural or irreducible room is based on the nature of project novelty, current phase of development, and type of industry. It also assumes that all types of psychological and organizational bias are fully addressed. Bias is supposed to make this irreducible minimum room bigger. This extra room above the irreducible level could serve as a measure of the health and quality of the project risk management system.

There is an infamous steam-assisted gravity drainage (SAGD) project that is considered a failure because it has not reached the planned level of oil production in several years. On one hand, it has world-class ground facilities. On the other hand, the subsurface conditions were a surprise. There were two contributions to this surprise as the project team was not fully unbiased. Out of several short-listed locations for drilling one was selected that provided good cost reduction due to shorter distances to processing facilities. This type of bias led to the worst short-listed although still somewhat acceptable spot geology-wise being selected. Plus the spot's geology turned out to be a bit worse than initially expected. Both legitimate unidentified unknowns and bias played ball together.

Some risks (either known or unknown) may have a catastrophic impact on project objectives usually having very low probability of occurrence. When they occur, they either significantly damage or destroy project baselines. They are usually classified as corporate risks. *Game changers* should be understood as potential events that require substantial rework of project baselines to continue project development and execution, if they occur. *Show-stoppers*, if they occur, lead to cancellation of a project.

Financial consequences of corporate risks are supposed to be borne not by a project but by an organization at large. Certainly, they may be delegated to be managed at the project level through purchasing insurance, for instance. As discussed in Chapter 2 and again in Chapter 5, some of both the known and unknown show-stoppers or game changers could be the result of the premeditated, focused activities of project stakeholders belonging to the external environment (broiler black swans), although some of them could be generic (wild black swans).

As briefly mentioned, R&D projects are aimed at elevation of the technology readiness level (TRL)[7] to get technologies ready for commercial applications. As a rule of thumb, a technology should reach a level of maturation corresponding to successful prototype demonstration to be adopted by a first commercial project (TRL score 8). However, at that level of maturation there still could be significant technology unknown-unknowns. Some of them may be revealed in the course of first commercial implementation (TRL score 9). Even in multiple commercial applications of a new technology (TRL score 10: proven technology) some unknown unknowns might still survive. These technology unknown unknowns can impact project objectives including Cost and Schedule.

The approach to developing unknown-unknown allowances for probabilistic cost and schedule models is discussed in Chapter 12. This is done only for commercial oil and gas (O&G) projects with TRL scores 8–10. Obviously, a standard project introduced there will correspond to a proven technology (TRL score 10). A high degree of novelty will correspond to first commercial application (TRL score 8).

It would be interesting to discuss and develop the cost and schedule unknown-unknown allowances for R&D projects (TRL score < 8) in various industries, including the O&G industry.

Even though a prudent rule is to exclude technologies of TRL < 8 from commercial projects, it is rather the owner's rule. Technology providers and EPC companies consider implementation of new technologies their key competitive advantage. This brings up the topic of the liabilities and responsibilities of each side when adopting new technologies. This is a major risk management activity adjacent to legal assurance of contracts among involved parties (technology licensors, project owners, EPC contractors, partners, etc.). As such it is one of five risk addressing strategies—risk transferring in the form of risk brokering—discussed in Chapter 5. It is trivial but correct to say that proper legal assessment of contracts involving implementation of new technologies is a must. It should reduce the room for surprises, including unknown unknowns in the form of low performance guarantees and legal damages, to a reasonable level.

CONCLUSION

Identification of uncertainties is the first step in the risk management process. Identification techniques and tools should be adequate enough to assure that most major relevant uncertainties get identified. Even if identified uncertainties are well assessed and managed, the weakest point of the project risk management system would be the ones that stayed unidentified. The good news is that now we are aware of all the major types of uncertainties and know what we should be looking for.

NOTES

1. R. Grant, *Contemporary Strategy Analysis: Concepts, Techniques, Applications* (London, UK: Blackwell, 1998).
2. K. Cooper and G. Lee, "Managing the Dynamics of Projects and Changes at Fluor" (Fluor Corporation, 2009; www.kcooperassociates.com/files/SD_Paper_for_Reprint_V3.pdf).
3. C. Ebeling, *An Introduction to Reliability and Maintainability Engineering* (Long Grove, IL: Waveland Press, 1997).
4. Seven project objectives shown by the bowtie diagram are the same as those included in the RAM in Figure 3.2. In place of 12 generic RBS categories introduced in the previous section, only five RBS categories are shown in Figure 4.2. The bowtie diagram of Figure 4.2 was developed for the case study of project Curiosity discussed in Part IV. A two-level RBS for that project is introduced there. These five categories represent the top level of the project's RBS. Initially a generic bowtie diagram was developed for this chapter. It was eventually replaced by the CCS bowtie diagram when the decision was made to include the CCS project Curiosity case study in this book to avoid duplication.
5. J. Hammond, R. Keenley, and H. Raiffa, "The Hidden Traps in Decision Making," *Harvard Business Review*, September/October 1998, 47–58.
6. Y. Raydugin, "Quantifying Unknown Unknowns in Oil and Gas Capital Project," *International Journal of Risk and Contingency Management*, 1(2), 2012, 29–42.
7. J. Malkins, "A White Paper: Technology Readiness Levels" (NASA, 1995; www.hq.nasa.gov/office/codeq/trl/trl.pdf).

CHAPTER FIVE

Risk Assessment and Addressing

Questions Addressed in Chapter 5

- What kind of measuring tool is required to assess uncertainties?
- What is the anatomy of a good RAM?
- Do we assess probability of a random event or possibility to discover a premeditated broiler black swan plot?
- Do we ask the right questions?
- Why did Italian geophysicists go to prison?
- What are five fundamental uncertainty addressing strategies?
- What is an *addressed uncertainty*?
- What are the roles of monsters, pets, diamonds-in-the-rough, and fine diamonds in risk management?
- What does a do-it-yourself risk register look like?
- What does *PETRA* mean and how should it be used for addressing?
- What is the role of bias? ▪

IDENTIFIED UNCERTAIN EVENTS SHOULD BE properly managed to decrease the overall uncertainty of project outcome and chances of failure. To understand how damaging downside uncertainties could be and how favorable upside uncertainties should become, project teams need a measuring tool. It should be adequate but simple to use. That measuring tool should be used even before any attempt to manage uncertainties is undertaken. However, the tool is as good as our understanding of the nature of measured objects. The right questions about uncertainties should be asked to carry out adequate measurements of their probabilities and impacts on project objectives.

To make managing uncertainties more proactive something should be done to address them. Five fundamental *addressing strategies* are discussed in this chapter. The key controls used for positive uncertainty exposure changing are *uncertainty addressing actions*. Expansion of the standard addressing approach based on the bowtie diagram (PETRA) is introduced to get to the next level of detail and efficiency. Comparisons of assessments before and after addressing are visualized to assess the efficiency of addressing as a major uncertainty control and changer.

DEVELOPING A RISK ASSESSMENT MATRIX

As we treat uncertainties as possible deviations from project objectives, we need corresponding grades to measure these deviations as well as their probabilities. What does "high impact on Reputation" mean? Which deviations from the Environment objective may be treated as very low? What probabilities could be considered medium? Either short stories or quantified ranges are required to introduce corresponding grades.

Selection of reasonable grades for deviations from all the selected objectives represents a significant challenge. Besides common sense, the following considerations should be taken into account:

- Understanding of project failure as related to each selected objective
- Risk appetite and tolerance the organization has in regard to its project portfolio
- Range of each deviation's grade to evenly cover the overall anticipated spread of deviations
- Comparability of deviation ranges describing the various objectives

A practical set of project failure definitions in terms of three hard objectives was developed by the IPA Institute:[1]

1. Budget overspending for more than 25%, and/or
2. Schedule slipping for more than 25%, and/or
3. Severe and continuing operational problems holding for at least one year

While failure thresholds for budget and schedule are clearly defined, a quantitative definition of "severe and continuing operational problems" could be challenging. A general risk appetite and tolerance that takes into account stakeholders' expectations may help to specify failure thresholds of a particular project.

Obviously, a risk that might lead to 25% or more deviation from the Cost or Schedule objective (or both) should be weighed as very high. But where should the line be drawn between the *very high* and *high* categories? The usual rule-of-thumb is that about two or three high or very high risks, if they occur, supposedly lead to project failure. This allows one to contemplate drawing the dividing line between high and very high deviations from the Cost and Schedule objectives at 8% to 12% of project budget and duration, correspondingly. If a project team decides that 5% or 15% deviations would be more appropriate to distinguish high and very high impacts, those should be acceptable, too. In any case, it should be an informed decision that takes into account expectations of stakeholders and the organizational context of risk management. Demarcations between high and very high impacts may be different in owner's and engineering, procurement, and construction (EPC) cases, reflecting on different organizational contexts. Degrees of deviations from well-quantifiable Cost and Schedule objectives could be assessed either as percentage points of baselines (project budget and duration) or in absolute numbers such as cost impacts in dollars and delays in days, weeks, or months.

Following this logic, the sample RAM of Figure 3.2 seems to be a good fit for capital projects (owner's environment) with CapEx of $0.5–$3 billion and duration of more than three years. A RAM of the same project for an EPC contractor might have a Gross Margin objective in place of CapEx. If, for example, contractual profit margin (objective) is 20% of $1 billion CapEx, the impact on profit of $10 million or more could be considered very high. Similarly, schedule ranges should reflect contractual obligations related to on-time completion of a project or possible liquidated damages. This is certainly the case for lump-sum contracts.

So, developed RAM should reflect on organizational context, as discussed in Chapter 2. Contractual obligations of parties, stakeholder expectations, and overall risk exposure should be taken into account when developing a good RAM.

Similarly, deviations from a Scope objective could be described in terms of either percentage points of an initially planned objective or absolute numbers. Let's say that a CO_2 sequestration project was supposed to capture and store one million tons of CO_2 per year in an aquifer. One major risk was identified by a project team that related to uncertainty of the reservoir's permeability. According to assessments, this could reduce planned annual storage capacity by 30,000–70,000 tons (3–7%). After completion of the project it turned out that only 950,000 tons per year could be stored due to the permeability issues. Missing 50,000 tons per year represented a 5% deviation from the planned objective. What if 100,000 tons (10%) or 250,000 tons (25%) were missing per year? What should be treated as a very high deviation from the objective? What could be considered very low? Whereas Scope ranges adopted by a project owner should cover the overall performance and capacity of a project, the ranges selected by an EPC contractor may cover only part of the scope it delivers. However, proper non-contradictive alignment of owner's and EPC RAMs should be considered and ensured (the in-depth dimension of risk management of Figure 2.1).

As soon as the demarcation lines between high and very high impacts are identified, three other demarcation lines (very low versus low, low versus medium, and medium versus high) should be set up. To keep things simple, the interval between corresponding project objective (no deviations) and the high/very high dividing line could be represented as three equal ranges that define these demarcation lines. If there is a reason to use unequal ranges, that should be discussed. (Usually it is based on project's risk appetite formally represented by so called risk utility curve. We will stay away from discussing theoretical utility curves in this book for simplicity purposes.)

In practice, it is not unusual that initially developed ranges of RAM are changed after an initial run of uncertainty identifications and assessments. It might turn out that the vast majority of identified and assessed risks before addressing belong to very low or low impact ranges. This is a sign that the demarcation lines between high and very high impacts should be reduced. Adjustments like this should allow one to introduce "high-definition" RAM by shrinking whole intervals down. As a result, the initial set of risks will belong to all five impact categories, from very low to very high.

Sometimes the vast majority of risks belong to high or very high ranges of the RAM. This indicates that the demarcation lines between high and very high impacts should be expanded. The amended RAM should evenly cover the same set of risks.

Negative impacts on soft objectives are not directly correlated with the scope, budget, or schedule of a project. Similarly devastating reputational, safety, or environmental risks might occur in projects regardless of their sizes. For instance, a single fatality could be understood as a project failure for any project. Usually this corresponds to a very high impact on the Safety objective. But this is not always the case. I came across the RAM of one project in Asia that defined one to five fatalities as a high safety risk. More than five fatalities was considered a very high risk. Regional differences for impact on Environment objectives could differ significantly, too. Environmental impact that is considered low somewhere else might be qualified as high or very high in North America.

Deviations from Reputation objectives usually reflect on the degree of damage to relationships with stakeholders, negative news coverage in mass media, and reduction in the potential to win future contracts. For oil and gas companies the latter also implies future difficulties in getting access to hydrocarbon reserves somewhere in the world. For EPC companies that would mean difficulties in winning future capital projects.

Another dimension of uncertainties is probabilities of their occurrence. For general uncertainties the probability is 100% by default while for uncertain events it could be anywhere from 0% to 100%. There are several approaches toward establishing probability ranges in project RAMs. One common approach is to associate probability with frequency of events as heard in the industry or similar projects. *Short stories* such as "happens to every second project" or "happens once in a hundred years" are sometimes used. A frequency-based probability assessment approach is good in the case of truly random events. Uncertain events relevant to projects are not necessarily truly random. For instance, if actions of the government or the competition are causes of risks, the frequency-based approach is not normally viable. Different methods, such as *game theory* or *scenario modeling*, would be more appropriate. Moreover, different companies manage their risks differently in different circumstances. It is also not clear which basis for frequency calculation to use. Should risks that occurred in civil engineering projects be counted for oil and gas projects?

Consistent application of the frequency-based method might produce probability scales that look compressed in the case of lower probabilities and too broad for higher ones. For instance, I observed a RAM probability scale for one mega-project based on a happens-once-in-X-years methodology that defined ranges as follows: Rare = < 0.1%; Low = 0.1–1%; Possible = 1–50%; Likely = 50–90%; Almost certain = > 90%. As a result, the vast majority of risks belonged to the Possible and Likely categories. This effectively reduced the initial number of five probability categories to two and produced a 2 × 5 RAM. An additional source of confusion was that some uncertain events that had probabilities of 5% and 45% belonged to the same probability range. That was an indicator that the *resolution* of the RAM was incorrect. More neutral is an approach where probability ranges are not directly linked to frequencies. This should help avoid compression of the probability scale as discussed earlier.

At the same time, using quite a low demarcation line between very low and low probability ranges at quite a low level could be somewhat reasonable. The reason for this would be a requirement to roll up Safety risks into a project risk register. The usual approach of the health and safety (H&S) discipline toward risk management promotes a much lower tolerance level in terms of both impacts and probabilities of H&S incidents. Safety specialists will not agree if a very low probability of risk occurrence were established to say < 10%. The sample RAM represented by Figure 3.2 is an attempt to combine a general project risk management approach with H&S, defining very low probability as < 1%.

As the same RAM should be used for assessment of both general uncertainties and uncertain events, very high probability is defined as > 90%. (In some cases projects define very high probability as > 99% or so.) So, selected probability ranges of Figure 3.2 are as follows:

- Very low: < 1%
- Low: 1–20%
- Medium: 20–50%
- High: 50–90%
- Very high: > 90%

Am I fully satisfied with the selected probability ranges? Not necessarily. But at the end of the day the ranges should be selected in a way that the project team members are comfortable with them. On one hand, they will inevitably reflect some types of organizational bias and risk appetite. On the other hand, as soon as they are established they will generate a good deal of consistency. Although such consistency will include persistently all possible systematic errors introduced by specific selection of particular RAM's probability ranges when assessing probabilities. However, those ranges could be amended after the first run of risk assessments similarly to impact ranges, although everyone understands that all those ranges are just a convention. It should not be taken too precisely. More precise evaluations of probabilities and impacts will be undertaken for risks of Cost and Schedule impacts when running probabilistic risk analyses.

Whatever the ranges selected for each category of impacts on project objectives and probabilities, each range gets a corresponding score. As we consider in this book only 5 × 5 RAMs there should be five scores, 1 to 5, for both impacts and probabilities. The *expected value* notion that is routinely used in statistics (a product of impact and probability) could be conditionally used for probability and impact scores, too. This could be understood as the *expected value score* or *consequence score*. Mathematically these terms sound terrible, but they are quite useful practically.

The resulting scores 1–25 represent 25 RAM cells. The standard approach is to group risks belonging to those cells into three or four risk-level or risk-severity categories based on ranges of scores. Common practice is that these three or four groups are associated with colors such as red, yellow, and green for a three-color code, and red, amber, yellow, and green for a four-color code. Obviously the four-color code brings more resolution to the project RAM. However, there is some doubt that a higher level of resolution is fully justifiable in a qualitative method like this, so we stay with a three-color code in this book. As an example, I have observed five categories of risks with five introduced colors. This is apparent overshooting in terms of precision of risk assessment. One aesthetic advantage of this five-color approach was that those RAMs and the corresponding risk registers looked so colorful and picturesque and seemed very "sophisticated, significant, and important."

Using an artistic analogy to define applicability of RAMs for assessment of project risks, a set of objectives could be understood as a simplistic project sketch drawn using project baselines. If only one or two baselines were used, a project would not be adequately depicted. If a dozen baselines were used to describe it, the sketch would become too busy. As discussed in Chapter 2, five to seven objectives are an optimal number. However, due to all those possible uncertainties associated with the objectives, this sketch will get blurred. Namely, uncertainties of all possible sorts and degrees will impact the baselines. In place of black-and-white baselines there will be blurred colored lines. Using the color semiotics analogy further, hues of green should mean benign deviations from the initial sketch, whereas hues of yellow and especially red should require special attention. A simple semiotics code of three colors is used in risk management to reflect the severity of project uncertainties and deviations from baselines.

Another reason I introduced this color analogy is that none of the illustrations in this book are in color (except the book jacket that depicts a four-color RAM for show purposes), although risk management extensively uses a color code for risk ranking. Three shades of gray are introduced in Figure 3.2 in place of the red, yellow, and green RAM cells. Accordingly, three categories of uncertainty scores—levels, severities, or colors—may be introduced (see Table 5.1) in case of the three-color RAM. The four ranking parameters (the columns of Table 5.1) defining the three categories (the rows of the Table 5.1) are virtually synonyms. Some people are more artistic and prefer more drama (Severity) and color (Color Code) when ranking risks. I prefer risk Scores and their Levels for ranking although all four parameters are used in this book interchangeably.

Short stories about various deviations from objectives included in the RAM in Figure 3.2 require further clarification. Similar to a description of project objectives, definitions of deviations' degrees should be included in a project risk management plan. This brings up a fundamental rule based on assessment of impacts on multiple objectives. Specifically, risks belonging to the same ranges of probability and impacts are fully comparable and commensurate with each other. For instance, if one risk has medium probability and high impact on Schedule and another one has medium probability and high impact on Reputation, these two risks are considered as being at the same level or severity. This allows apples-to-apples ranking of uncertainties of impacts on different objectives, which would not be possible without using a multi-objective RAM.

This implies another rule for assessment of overall level or severity. If an uncertainty is identified as having impacts on several objectives, the top impact is counted to represent this uncertainty as a whole. For instance, if an uncertainty is characterized as having low impact on Schedule, high impact on Reputation, and very high impact on Safety, the very high impact on Safety defines its overall severity after taking its probability of occurrence into consideration. This could be an uncertain event with Safety impact leading to a fatality. Reputational damage and stoppage of work for investigation are possible additional impacts.

TABLE 5.1 Three Categories of Uncertainties Depending on Scores

Score	Level	Severity	Color Code
1–5	Low	Small	Green
6–12	Medium	Material	Yellow
15–25	High	Critical	Red

Even though 5 × 5 RAMs seem to be the current standard widely used in capital projects, one might come across 3 × 3, 4 × 4, 4 × 5, 5 × 6, 6 × 6, 7 × 7, and other RAMs.

Based on my experience, 3 × 3 and 4 × 4 RAMs don't offer high enough resolution to distinguish risks. This situation is similar to the compression of ranges discussed earlier where risks of quite different impacts and probabilities could still belong to the same RAM cell. For risk addressing, and comparing assessments before and after addressing, risks might belong to the same cells and severity categories too often. (This may be the only justification to use four-color RAM containing four categories of risk scores/levels/severities/colors instead of three: better "resolution" like this should allow better distinguish uncertainties before and after addressing.) At the other end of the spectrum, 6 × 6 and 7 × 7 RAMs represent risk *micromanagement* and assessment over-shooting. So 5 × 5 RAMs with three (maybe four) risk-level categories seems to introduce the right balance.

Even though the value of using 5 × 5 RAM in assessment of risks is underscored in this section, we discuss a conditional sixth impact category in Chapter 7 to establish definitions of project show-stoppers and game changers. The reason is that very high RAM impact categories are unlimited (Figure 3.2). Answering the question "When does it become too much?" to keep impacted objectives still viable will provide guidelines to define project show-stoppers and game changers in a project RAM.

An additional complication when assessing the impact of risks on Schedule is that impact on Schedule is schedule-logic specific. If a risk impacts an activity that doesn't belong to the critical path, overall impact on project completion date could be lower than initially assessed or zero as the risk will be partially or fully absorbed by available float. If, however, a risk is mapped to an activity that belongs to a project critical path, this will impact the project completion date if it occurs. The general rule is that when assessing impact on Schedule, impact on a particular activity is evaluated as if it belonged to the critical path. This assessment will become input to probabilistic risk analysis when features of the impact are sized up while keeping in mind the schedule logic.

A scoring method could be used for assessments of upside deviations from project objectives, although the RAM discussed earlier apparently features *downside* deviation language. Ideally, another *upside* RAM should be developed that rewrites the downside deviation's ranges. This should be the mirror image of a downside RAM (Figure 3.2). An additional reason for its development is that it is more difficult to come across opportunities on the same scale as threats. For instance, it's easier or more likely to come across a risk that decreases performance by 5% than to run into an opportunity that increases it by 5%. The same reasoning is applicable to the other two hard objectives, Cost and Schedule. The situation is different with goal-zero-type soft objectives. If zero-safety-incident or zero-environmental-impact goals are project baselines, what could be opportunities to improve those? At the same time, the impact on Reputation could be positive. For instance, many of the current CO_2 sequestration projects are not expected to be terribly profitable. A breakeven level of profitability is often acceptable, with boost or improvement of Reputation being considered a top priority. So, four out of the six objectives we introduced are eligible for upside deviations.

I hesitated about whether a separate upside deviation's RAM should be included in this book. The decision not to include one could be understood as totally biased. This bias is based on the fact that there was no obvious need to develop a separate RAM for mega-projects I worked on. The same RAM could be used to assess upside uncertainties taking into account the need for more a prudent assessment approach, as discussed earlier. A possible error of assessments will be inside of the precision tolerance range of the scoring method, anyway. These scoring assessments will be reviewed and corrected when preparing for probabilistic cost and schedule risk analysis in any case. So, normally there is not much need to be excessively fancy unless there are some "sale and marketing" reasons.

Among the topics discussed in the majority of academic risk management books are *utility functions, risk aversion, risk appetite,* and so on. These are supposed to delineate organizations that are risk averse from those that are risk takers. This is a relevant topic that should be understood by project teams and decision makers. However, my practical experience of introducing mathematical definitions related to utility functions and using them in real projects was a complete disaster. Responses of project teams and decision makers (whether verbal or via body language) were "Are you kidding?" or "Forget about it!" My suggestion would be to include this angle through a well-developed RAM. If a project team is risk averse, all ranges of impacts should be shrunk down accordingly. Probability ranges could be compressed, too. For instance, a very high impact of more than $50 million (Figure 3.2) could be replaced by $30 million, which redefines the rest of the cost impact ranges. The safety example discussed in this section points out the different numbers of fatalities that could be considered very high in a project RAM. This is a very scary angle on risk appetite that reflects the variety of value-of-life utility curves in different parts of the world.

An extensive discussion on the validity of scoring methods based on using RAMs may be found in an excellent book by Doug Hubbard,[2] where the scoring method gets, using the words of Winston Churchill, "limited high respect."

Probabilistic assessment methods are proclaimed as the only viable alternative. Criticism of the scoring methods, associated drama, and elements of righteousness would be fully justifiable as a purely academic "ivory tower" exercise. I would join in this except that I have been involved in practical risk management of real capital mega-projects. Just as quantum mechanics is not required for mechanical engineering, probabilistic methods are not justifiable for all risk management challenges. Whatever assessment method is selected it should support the core risk management activity, which is uncertainty addressing. The scoring method is a wonderful match for this when handling multiple project objectives, whereas probabilistic methods are good only for quantifiable ones. New applications of the scoring method for engineering design and procurement option selection (introduced in Chapters 9 and 10) demonstrate the additional value and efficiency of the scoring method that cannot be effectively provided by a probabilistic one.

USING A RISK ASSESSMENT MATRIX FOR ASSESSMENT AS-IS

Assuming that a good RAM has been engineered based on recommendations of the previous section, the next step is assessment of identified risks before addressing (Figure 2.2). In practitioner's jargon it is often called *assessment before* or *assessment as-is*. This assessment is required to evaluate possible impacts without any additional attempt to manage a risk. However, all relevant controls and measures currently in place that seem to define this assessment as-is should be taken into account. According to Figure 2.2, risk response actions should be developed and approved that may be used for risk assessment after addressing (*assessment after* or *to-be*).

The assessment of impacts on objectives starts with a review of definitions of identified uncertainties developed using three-part naming. Supposedly, the third part (impacts) lists all relevant impacts. In other words, assessment depends on what has been identified and formulated.

There are four major sources of information that could be used for assessment of risks:

1. Historic data
2. Modeling
3. Expert opinion
4. Lessons learned

Consistent or relevant historic data are not always available. Modeling of risks is not often possible. Lessons learned are not always systematically collected and formalized although they are kept in the minds of specialists informally. So in the majority of cases the only source of assessment information relies on expert opinion. Being pretty subjective, these opinions are substitutes for possible objective historic data, lessons learned, and modeling. This again brings up the traditional topic of bias. The key challenge a facilitator faces is to collect biased opinions and average out elements of bias as much as practically possible. Uncertainty assessment is the business of quantification of stories and biases.

A facilitator who leads a risk assessment might want to use standard leading words and questions. These questions are based on discussions of possible scenarios of risks happening and their impacts. It is reasonable to start with evaluation of the probability of a risk happening. This parameter is attached to the risk and of course should be the same for all impacts. If it is discovered during discussion that some impacts seem to get different probabilities, this is a sign that the identified risk should be split into two or more detailed risks.

The first obvious guideline of probability assessments is based on the structure of the bowtie diagram (Figure 4.2) and probability rules reflected by Figure 4.1. Namely, each cause–event link of the bowtie may be viewed conditionally as a separate uncertain event. According to Figure 4.1, probabilities of all independent cause–event realizations should be summed.

For instance, let's distinguish four links, cause A–event X, cause B–event X, cause C–event X, and cause D–event X, as independent identified uncertain events. Let's also assume that the probabilities of these four risks are P_1, P_2, P_3, and P_4 correspondingly. Then overall probability of the risk X event should be $P_1 + P_2 + P_3 + P_4$. This is correct only if these four causes are independent, which is normally assumed when using a bowtie diagram. However, if only a combination of two causes, say A and B, can lead to the risk X event along with independent causes C and D, the overall probability of the risk X event should be $P_1 \times P_2 + P_3 + P_4$ according to Figure 4.1. Technically, causes A and B should be combined into one leading to an event of the rather lower probability $P_1 \times P_2$: a condition of the simultaneous happening (AND gate of Figure 4.1) leads to lower probability than probabilities of two independent events.

This leads us to the firm conclusion that probability of occurrence should depend on the level of an uncertain event definition and understanding. For instance, for assessments of quality related to construction contractors, one may guess that at the work-package level corresponding uncertainty should have quite a low probability. However, at the project level this might get medium likelihood if several contractors deliver construction packages. At the business unit/portfolio level this uncertainty could appear as almost certain! That is why some business-unit uncertainties or corporate risk look more like given issues or general uncertainties with probabilities close to or equal to 100% and not like uncertain events.

Another guideline that should be kept in mind when assessing probability of occurrence is that there are very few uncertain events in the project external or internal environment that are truly random. This brings up the question whether frequency-based historic data could be used for probability assessments of some events. By truly random probabilistic events I mean those that are comparable to the flipping of a coin.[3] For instance, there are probabilities that one gets heads two, three, four, or more times in a row, although those probabilities drop with an increased number of tries. So, the more tries, the higher the confidence level that heads and tails have equal 50–50 chances.

If a project team does not have a clue about probability of risk occurrence, the safest possible probability assessment would be 50%. If a right and objective assessment were 100% or 0%, maximum possible error would be no more than 50%. If instead an assessment is done to say 60% or 70%, possible maximum error might be 60% or 70% if a right assessment were 0%. I guess politicians should love 50% probabilistic assessments of some events in politics, economics, and society as being the most "politically correct." One should be careful when such 50% assessments are produced. Is this a reflection of the real nature of a possible event based on good analysis and justification as in the case of coin flipping, or a confession of complete lack of clarity and understanding or an attempt to hide information? "Broken but Safe Logic" contains a joke about unsubstantiated but scientific-like results.

BROKEN BUT SAFE LOGIC

The following is a common joke aimed at poorly justified results used by physicists. It sounds like a citation from a scientific paper, and includes a funny dichotomy and a "safe" assessment of expected results: "If we divide it into three unequal halves, the probability of desired outcome should be 50%."

Projects are managed differently by different organizations. Moreover, different projects are managed differently by the same organization. A competitor may react to a particular situation today differently than two years ago. One tries to assess a possibility that a project would be sanctioned by the government next year, keeping in mind that a similar project was sanctioned a few years ago. But the political situation today might be very different than it was, due to upcoming presidential elections. Moreover, a decision by the government to reject or put off a project might have been already made but not announced for political reasons at the moment when the probability assessment is undertaken.

So where is randomness, or the "game of chance," in all these examples? There is none. Assessment of probability is done based on the best available knowledge about a particular situation. Previous similar situations are not exactly relevant. In a way, the probability assessment is a measure of depth of knowledge and quality of information about a particular situation if it is not based on historic frequency data. We talked about unknown uncertainties in risk identification previously. Here we are talking about unknowns in probability assessment. We try to treat some actually known facts (but not to us) as uncertain events (to us) due to lack of information. (We refer again to our previously discussed broiler black swans.)

The bottom line of this discussion is that it would be necessary to answer a simple question first. Probability of *what* is assessed? In truly probabilistic events we are talking about the probability of a random event happening. Such an assessment should be based on historic frequency data. But in many cases of "untruly" probabilistic events we should be talking about probability of discovery of a particular outcome where outcome is predetermined and premeditated already.

This discussion points to rejection of frequency-based assessments of probabilities in most cases. It still could be used in true random situations when people have no control of or influence over their outcome. It looks like most of these situations belong to the technical area. However, I know of several technical examples where some events that previously were understood as perfectly random turned out to be more or fully predetermined. The level of predetermination is proportional to the depth of understanding and knowledge of those technical events.

First, in the case of a hydropower generation project I worked on, the probability of getting a water level higher than 20 m in each particular year was assessed as 5% based on 30 years of previous river observations. This information was important for design of cofferdams. Unexpectedly it was discovered that this assessment was no longer valid due to some recent hydro-engineering activities up the river. Risk of flooding got a much higher assessment, which had implications for cofferdam design. Previously perceived full randomness of flooding was rejected.

Second, previously hurricanes in the Gulf of Mexico were treated as random events. Their probabilities were assessed accordingly based on frequency data. Newly developed methods of forecasting based on extensive use of sophisticated computer modeling and satellite monitoring predict their occurrence and severity in a given period of time and place with amazing accuracy. Although accuracy is still below 100%, hurricanes are no longer seen as purely random uncertain events. The level of randomness is relatively low now due to the current level of understanding of the hurricane's mechanisms, which allows one to predict them with relatively high accuracy. Practically, this means the possibility of developing and implementing adequate and timely evacuation plans.

Third, similar trends are observed in the prediction of earthquakes. Advanced methods of monitoring, some knowledge about precursors, and sophisticated modeling techniques allow us to predict earthquake occurrences with some accuracy. This accuracy is not high enough yet due to the current level of understanding of an earthquake's triggers. In other words, the level of randomness of an earthquake occurrences seems still high due to a lower level of understanding of their mechanisms. The situation should eventually change for the better. However, some politicians overestimate the accuracy on purpose for finger-pointing purposes. I was surprised to discover that several Italian scientists had been jailed for their inability to predict the L'Aquila earthquake in 2009!

We just discussed three examples of technically predetermined or semi-predetermined events where the frequency-based approach for probability assessment is not adequate. In situations where people and their decisions, policies, biases, focused efforts, learning curves, competitiveness, and so on may influence an event's likelihood, the frequency-based assessments could be perfectly misleading.

Getting back to physics, it reminds me of the *Uncertainty* principle of Heisenberg and the related *Observer* principle. Measurement of a system cannot be done without affecting it. People's interference affects most of the events related to projects, making historic frequency data irrelevant. People's interference and influence make any uncertain event more unique and not directly comparable to similar previous events.

Using the frequency method for probability assessments of uncertain events that are not random in nature is a substitute for our knowledge about them.

Frequency data may be used as a starting point in probability assessments but only after corresponding conditioning. This conditioning should be an attempt to do an apples-to-apples comparison of previous risk occurrences with currently discussed ones, making the former relevant to current assessment. A better way to assess probabilities of untruly probabilistic events is by:

- Collecting more information
- Better learning and understanding their drivers and mechanisms
- Trying to influence their outcomes

In some cases, among the approaches to better understand those events there could be scenario planning and game theory modeling methods.[4] We won't discuss these in this book, although existence of the other methods of probability assessments and outcomes in case of untruly probabilistic events should be kept in mind.

Taking into account the earlier discussion, standard guiding questions should be used to assess both probabilities and impacts:

"Is the uncertain event truly random?"

"Do we assess probability of happening or probability of discovery of a particular predetermined outcome?"

"Are project stakeholders behind this event and do they define probability of its occurrence?"

"Do we have any knowledge of or historic data on this event?"

"What are elements of novelty in this project?"

"What potential steps, if any, should be undertaken to better understand this event and reduce its randomness?"

"Can we model this event?"

"What are the chances/odds/likelihood that this event happens or we discover its existence?"

"What is the worst/most expectable/least damaging scenario?"

"What makes you believe that?"

"What happens to that other project and is it relevant to ours?"

"What is your confidence level that impact will belong to this range and why?"

"What are the chances that real impact will be outside of the discussed range?"

"What types of bias might we come across when assessing this uncertainty and why?"

Questions such as "How often has this event happened previously?" or "Is this a one-in-five or one-in-ten-years event?" might not be appropriate, being based on the frequency method, which is frequently wrong.

The key intent in asking these questions is to provoke thinking but suppress bias, if possible. See the final section of this chapter for a discussion on bias.

As a result of assessment as-is, a project team justifies the most appropriate probability range for probabilities and ranges for corresponding impacts. While probability assessment is represented by one score (Figure 3.2), several different assessments are expected for impacts on corresponding objectives. For instance, in the case of risk discussed in Chapter 4 there are two impacts. One is on Reputation and the other on Schedule. Let's say that the project team assessed the impact on Reputation as high (score 4) and impact on Schedule as very high (score 5). If probability of this event were assessed as medium (score 3), the Reputation score would be 12 and Schedule score 15. According to the risk level rules of Table 5.1, the Reputation score gets a yellow color and the Schedule score gets red. Some project teams tend to consider these scores separately as manageability of corresponding impacts may be different. Some assign the highest score as representative of the whole risk. Figure 5.1 depicts this uncertain event and two impacts using a 5 × 5 format of RAM (Figure 3.2). The black star of Figure 5.1, which corresponds to the Schedule impact before

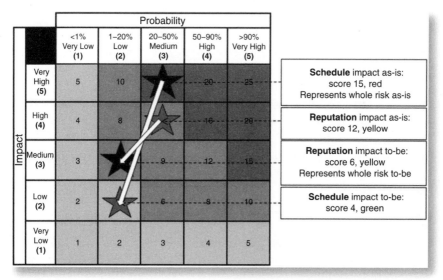

FIGURE 5.1 Depicting Downside Uncertainty Assessments

addressing (score 15), represents the entire uncertainty as-is. Another star represents the Reputation impact as-is (score 12). We discuss assessment after addressing in a later section.

To a certain degree assessment as-is is less important than assessment to-be. We may assign high or very high impacts and probabilities for the majority of uncertainties without much deep thinking. Most important is right assessment after addressing, which requires a clear-cut understanding of required addressing actions and their possible outcome. We introduce five main addressing strategies in the next section.

 ## FIVE ADDRESSING STRATEGIES

Recall that any uncertainty could be characterized by one (general uncertainty) or two (uncertain event) factors: uncertainty of likelihood and/or uncertainty of impact. If we succeed in influencing and managing those two factors, we may be sure that we are successful in managing any uncertainty.

As briefly discussed in Chapter 1, overall project uncertainty exposure is evolving in time due to the evolving in time of uncertainty objects that give rise to overall uncertainty exposure. Those evolve due to the presence of dynamic changers in the project internal and external environment, which were introduced in Chapter 1. The key types of uncertainty changers discussed in this section are uncertainty addressing actions. They are referred to in Chapter 2 in Step 5 and 7 of the risk management process (Figure 2.2).

It is important to keep in mind that any changer (an addressing action, a decision, a choice, or any relevant developments in the project external environment) could lead to a new or amended existing uncertainty. The possibility of such dynamics and transformations in the form of a domino effect is a major reason why the risk management process should be ongoing and evergreen (Figure 2.2).

The structure of the bowtie diagram (Figure 4.2) promotes such thinking, but only for uncertain events. Barrier 1 constitutes the first prevention line-of-defense. This barrier is supposed to reduce probability of an uncertain event happening by breaking or weakening logical links between causes and possible events.[5] Needless to say, barrier 1 does not work for general uncertainties that have irreducible 100% probability.

In some cases all those logical links could be successfully or naturally broken so that the event cannot happen. It becomes fully prevented or avoided, getting probability of occurrence equal to zero. This could happen mostly when initial causes become irrelevant to the project. Change of scope of a project is one such possibility. Sometimes the time window for an event happening could be past. This is often the case when project permitting is done. So, corresponding risks cannot occur anymore and their probabilities become zero.

Of course, a project team should not play a game of chance and just wait for the occurrence window to be past. Some focused preventive measures should be developed to at least reduce the probability of an uncertain event happening. Those measures are called *mitigation preventive actions*. Hopefully, due to reduced probability of occurrence, the risk did not happen. However, if it is not avoided or fully prevented, it still might occur. If the risk does happen, the second line-of-defense should be ready. Barrier 2 represents *crisis management measures* that should be in place if an uncertain event does occur. However, for general uncertainties it is not about crisis management as the general uncertainty has been there all along.

Addressing measures associated with barrier 2 are called *mitigation recovery actions*. However, for barrier 2 the mitigation relates to possibilities of reducing the impact of occurred uncertain events and given general uncertainties on project objectives. One such possibility is transferring the corresponding uncertainty to third parties. In some cases the project owner might keep some uncertainties for managing. In other cases these could be transferred to EPC contractors, joint venture (JV) or consortium partners partners, vendors, and so on. The process of uncertainty transferring is call *risk brokering*. The key principle is that the party that could manage the risk in the most efficient way should be assigned to manage it. What does this mean?

Let's assume that an owner could manage an uncertainty effectively but succeeds in transferring it to an EPC contractor. This may turn out to be quite expensive to manage for the contractor, so the contractor includes a substantial risk premium in the contract price. This will lead to an increase of the overall project cost. If the EPC contractor does not include a corresponding risk premium, it might encounter losses. This will give rise to an indirect impact on the project, through project delays, claims, change orders, sour relations with the contractor, damaged reputation, and so on. So transferring at all costs should not be an ultimate goal because there might be an unreasonably high cost for this. Smart optimization through risk brokering is required.

The most traditional way of transferring risks is purchasing insurance policies that cover specific types of risks. High premiums and deductibles could make this option unreasonable. As most insured risks belong to the corporate category, some companies choose self-insurance. If a company has a portfolio of projects supported by adequate financial resources, self-insurance of some categories of risks may be preferable.

If all economically viable addressing preventive and recovery actions are developed and an uncertain event still might occur and impact objectives, the last resort is to accept possibility of the residual risk occurrence and put away some risk reserve money. The risk reserve could be used to cover residual risks of various impacts, and not only of cost impact. Money is an addressing tool for residual risks of all impacts should they occur. For instance, reputational damage could be reduced through conducting a public relations or advertising campaign in the mass media, which requires corresponding expenses. Money spent or planned to be spent on any addressing action should be counted and included in the project budget (CapEx or OpEx, depending on when an action will be implemented). To sum up the discussion on uncertainty addressing, here are the five addressing strategies:

1. *Avoid* (barrier 1—preventive)
2. *Mitigate-Prevent* (barrier 1—preventive)
3. *Mitigate-Recover* (barrier 2—recovery)
4. *Transfer* (barrier 2—recovery)
5. *Accept* (barrier 2—recovery)

As pointed out, the Avoid and Mitigate-Prevent strategies of barrier 1 are not applicable to downside general uncertainties.

In practice, a combination of several appropriate addressing actions that are based on the five strategies should be developed by an uncertainty owner and approved by management, which corresponds to the Plan and Approve Response step of the risk management process (Figure 2.2). Obviously, actions based on avoiding risks are mostly viable in the early phases of project development. The second obvious choice and most popular strategy is Mitigate-Prevent, which might be supported by several actions for each particular risk. The Mitigate-Recover strategy is the most overlooked by project teams. One possible reason for this is overconfidence. There might be a belief that Mitigate-Prevent actions should be efficient enough to reduce probability to an acceptable level. But the question stays the same: What do you do if an uncertain event does happen, becoming an issue?

For instance, for the risk of H_2S release during drilling, the usual preventive measure would be using blowout preventers (BOPs). If BOPs do not work, proper training of the rig personnel, personal protective equipment, H_2S monitoring, and an evacuation plan establish a set of Mitigate-Recover actions.

Recently I was asked a question by one of my co-workers in one of the Persian Gulf states about addressing the risk of a new war in the region.

None of us were in the business of reducing the probability of such event. So, what could be done to address this? My response was that we needed to develop and implement business continuity and evacuation plans (Mitigate-Recover strategy). It seemed that no preventive actions were available to us unless it was decided that it was time to shut down operations in the region and run to fully avoid this risk.

Transfer strategy is widely used during negotiation of contracts among project owners, EPC contractors, vendors, JV partners, and so on. Corresponding risk assessments are required from the angles of the impacted parties. A tug-of-war usually follows to negotiate risk responsibilities versus risk premiums.

The Accept strategy is the last strategy that requires assessments of required project risk reserves to cover all assumed residual risks. It is important to remember that project cost risk reserves cover residual risks of various impacts, not only cost impacts. The cost of addressing should be included in a project's base estimate. The only exclusion here could be the addressing of Schedule impacts. Risk reserve might take the form of additional float in the schedule or different sequencing of activities on the schedule's critical path. But even in this case, schedule-driven costs should be kept in mind. Needless to say, schedule acceleration activities usually require additional spending (schedule-driven costs to crush the schedule), which should be taken into account in the base estimate, too.

Traditionally practitioners keep in mind only four addressing strategies: *Avoid, Mitigate, Transfer,* and *Accept.* Sometimes the mnemonic abbreviation *4T* is used to highlight *Terminate, Treat, Transfer,* and *Take.* It's nice to have mnemonic abbreviations like this. The problem is that the Mitigate strategy in this case is confusing and not clearly defined. According to the bowtie diagram, the Mitigate-Prevent strategy (barrier 1) and the Mitigate-Recover strategy (barrier 2) have totally different purposes, natures, and consequences. The former is part of proactive and efficient risk management; the latter is about reactive crisis management! The only link between them is the word *mitigate.* But this is again about linguistics and not the core essence of risk management.

All of those strategies are applicable to downside known uncertainties only. What should be our thinking for upside known uncertainties (Figure 1.2)? Our thinking should be the reverse or reciprocal. In place of attempts to reduce the severity of a downside uncertainty, one should try to increase the positive consequences of an upside one.

A downside uncertainty as-is might have a very high (red) level of severity (score 15–25), which is a major concern for a project team. Let's see that uncertainty as a *monster.* Assuming we have a good set of addressing actions based on the five strategies discussed earlier, one should expect the risk to become much less severe after addressing (green, score 1–5). In other words, the monster should get domesticated to become a nice pet. It still may bark and bite but nothing major is expected.

Reciprocally, an upside uncertainty before addressing is expected to have a smaller positive impact on the objectives ("diamond-in-the-rough") than after ("fine diamond"). As we decided not to develop a separate RAM for upside uncertainties, we may apply the RAM for downside deviations (Figure 3.2). Using the language of Table 5.1, an upside deviation before addressing could be small (score 1–5, green) and might become critical after addressing (score 15–25, red) or at least material (score 6–12, yellow).

Using zoological and diamond-cutting analogies, domestication of monsters through conversion of them to more predictable pets as well as polishing diamonds to make them fine highlights the essence of management of project uncertainties.

We have already discussed five addressing strategies for downside uncertainties; now, let's try to formulate them for upside ones. Here are five addressing strategies for upside uncertainties:

1. *Exploit* (barrier 1—magnify): to undertake actions to make it relevant to the project ("pull to the scope")
2. *Enhance-Magnify* (barrier 1—magnify): to try to increase probability
3. *Enhance-Amplify* (barrier 2—amplify): to try to increase positive impact
4. *Share* (barrier 2—amplify): to share it with partners for further amplification
5. *Take* (barrier 2—amplify): to accept it as-is ("do nothing more" strategy after the other strategies are applied) and reduce risk reserve accordingly

The Exploit and Enhance-Magnify strategies are not applicable to upside general uncertainties as those have 100% probability of occurrence.

The terms used for the definition of the five addressing strategies for upside uncertainties may sound inconsistent to some of my readers. I am a bit concerned about the terms *magnify* and *amplify*. I am not keen on particular labels; I would encourage readers to come up with better terms that reflect the nature of addressing actions more adequately.

It's the same for downside addressing strategies. The two Enhance strategies (in place of Mitigate) should be split and understood as totally different and belonging to two different places on the bowtie diagram. (Perhaps terms such as *trampoline* or *springboard* should be used for upside uncertainties in place of the word *barrier*.)

ASSESSMENT AFTER ADDRESSING

The next step in the risk management process (Figure 2.2) is assessment after addressing. The previous discussion on assessment as-is is fully relevant here. However, the assessment to-be should take into account both the initial as-is assessment and the approved set of addressing actions. As discussed in Chapter 2, any assessment to-be should be clearly linked with a particular point in time, which is usually associated with a particular decision gate or major project milestone.

The first complicating factor for such an assessment is that this should take into account the likelihood of successful implementation of approved actions. The second is that approved addressing actions may become causes of new uncertainties. The dotted line in Figure 2.2 reminds us about the need to keep an eye on new uncertainties generated by addressing actions in the course of their implementation. This includes the possibility of an action's implementation failures.

The importance of assessment to-be for project budgeting is dictated by the fact that decisions about project reserves are usually done based on assessment after addressing for a particular point in time. General efficiency of project risk management may be evaluated in monetary terms as follows:

[Project cost reserve as-is] – [Project cost reserve to-be] > [Cost of addressing]

Certainly, cost of addressing is an investment in reduction of overall project uncertainty exposure. If the difference in project reserves before and after addressing is higher but comparable with the cost of addressing the risk, management is not that efficient. Needless to say, if cost of addressing is higher than the difference, such risk management yields a negative value. This could be the case, for instance, when addressing actions introduce additional uncertainties or when risk management assumes mostly "ritual" functions (see "Cargo Cult Science" in Chapter 2).

The cost of addressing should include the cost of all addressing actions that address not only impacts on the Cost objective but also on Schedule, Scope/Quality/Performance, Reputation, Safety, and Environment. This approach is a basis for evaluation of engineering design and procurement options as discussed in Chapters 9 and 10.

Project teams should try to develop addressing actions that do not cost a lot of money. The most efficient and smartest addressing actions are those that are aimed at fulfillment of the same activities in different ways. For instance, engineers may carry out project design activities differently to address a particular uncertainty, which would not necessarily require extra costs. Certainly this is not always possible and extra spending is rather inevitable. Hence, the cost of addressing introduced earlier should be treated as additional budgets to be spent above previously approved annual budgets for project development and execution.

Assuming some addressing actions were developed and approved, an assessment after addressing could be done as if all or some of the proposed actions were already implemented. This defines timing that corresponds to the assessment to-be. Figure 5.1 depicts the situation where, after addressing, two impacts switch levels of severity. The Schedule impact, which was higher before addressing, became lower after addressing (score 4, green) than the impact on Reputation (score 6, yellow). So, the impact on Reputation having a higher score after addressing becomes representative of the entire risk.

This observation brings up *risk manageability*. In the previous example, Reputation impact has lower manageability, which is often the case in life. Schedule impact, on the contrary, seems to be better managed. Hence, the manageability of impacts of the same uncertainty can be very different.

Some risk management tools have manageability of an entire risk as a standalone parameter along with probability and impacts, which is quite confusing in light of this discussion. However, if just one objective is managed, which is an obvious manifestation of the previously discussed tunnel-vision organizational bias, this should be an acceptable concept. But what a "wonderful" but deceptive risk management system this should be: one would manage only impacts on a "favorite" objective (usually this is Cost) ignoring the rest of objectives.

Figure 5.2 is an illustration of an upside uncertainty assessment before (diamond-in-the-rough) and after (fine diamond) addressing.

To sum up the discussion, Figure 5.3 depicts the conceptual design of a project risk register representing assessment before and after addressing along with addressing actions. The uncertainty introduced in the boxed example in Chapter 4 is placed in the risk register for demonstration purposes. Six project objectives discussed so far are assessed before and after addressing using the RAM of Figure 3.2. Two sample addressing actions are proposed to distinguish assessments before and after addressing.

We discuss the very detailed specifications of the risk register template in Chapter 8.

Many major project management decisions, such as the final investment decision (FID), are done based on uncertainty assessments after addressing linked to those decisions. The three most typical assessments to-be are:

1. When a project passes a decision gate by the end of Select (assessment as-is), keeping in mind the expected uncertainty exposure to-be by the end of Define ("to-be-FID")

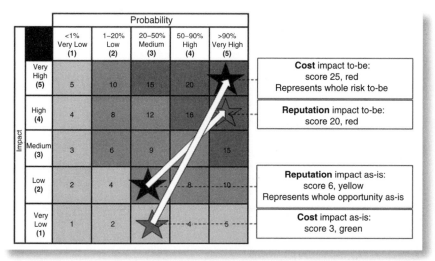

FIGURE 5.2 Depicting Upside Uncertainty Assessments

2. When a project reaches the end of Define to be considered for FID: an assessment as-is is conditionally considered an assessment to-be to define an approved project risk reserve for Execute.
3. Regular assessments in Execute which are used for forecasting of the risk reserve draw-down (Chapter 14).

In the course of the action's implementation they will move from assessment to-be to assessment as-is. Hence, assessment as-is is constantly changing being attached to "Now." The closer a project is to FID, the more similar assessments as-is and to-be at FID (to-be-FID) are supposed to become due to action's implementation in Define. By the decision gate preceding FID (the end of Define), both assessments should become equal and reflect residual uncertainty exposure for the rest of the project (Execute) if this is sanctioned. A set of addressing actions that have yet to be implemented in Execute should become an agreement of the project team with management: sanctioning of a project is subject to full implementation of the remaining approved actions. How often this promise is forgotten. This sort of "under-addressing" after sanctioning is one of the major sources of uncertainties of project outcomes and failures (Figure 1.1).

Assessments of uncertainties to-be that are used to develop project reserves are subject to assumed project execution efficiency. This must be factored into all to-be uncertainty assessments. Practically speaking, this means that project teams could assume excellent (at least good) project execution implicitly, which means hypothetically excellent project economics and

Table: Conceptual Template of an Uncertainty Register

DEFINITION						ATTRIBUTES			ASSESSMENT AS-IS								ADDRESSING								ASSESSMENT TO-BE							
ID	Upside or Downside?	General Uncertainty or Uncertain Event?	Title	Three Part Definition	Comments	Status	Owner	RBS Category	Level/Severity	Probability	Cost	Schedule	Product Quality	Safety	Environment	Reputation	Response Strategy	Action(s)	Cost of Action, K$	Start	Completion Date	Action Owner	Action Status	Comments	Level/Severity	Probability	Cost	Schedule	Product Quality	Safety	Environment	Reputation
1	D	UE	Project Sanctioning Delay	Due to a) general opposition by some NGOs to oil sands project; b) concerns by local communities about project's environmental impact; c) environmental issues associated with a similar project in the past, the **project XXX might be challenged during public hearings**, leading to A) permitting and final investment decision delay (Schedule); B) engineering, procurement and construction delays (Schedule); C) company's reputational damage in general (Reputation); D) complication of relations with local communities in particular (Reputation); E) extra owner's costs (CapEX).	In worst case of project cancellation or delay for more than one year this should be considered a show-stopper: to add to corporate RR and discuss with VP	Active	Mike Gorbiff	Stakeholders	15	3	2	5	0	0	0	4	Mitigate—Prevent	To establish community engagement and communication plan including schedule of open house meetings	500	25-Dec-12	25-Dec-13	John Lennin	Active	The plan is under review	6	2	1	2	0	0	0	3
																	Mitigate—Recover	To review sequencing of FEL/pre-FID works and develop additional float in the schedule to absorb schedule impact for a case the risk does occur	500	01-Jan-13	01-Jan-14	Ringo Starlin	Active	Review of main FEL/pre-FID activities schedule for next month								

FIGURE 5.3 Conceptual Template of an Uncertainty Register

performance. On one hand, the role of organizational governance is to assure proper execution. On the other hand, realistic and not utopian execution efficiency should be factored into uncertainty assessments to-be and clearly communicated. Unfortunately, bias based on pie-in-the-sky execution over-confidence gives rise to the good–bad execution gap depicted in Figure 1.1. A project that is prone to overconfidence bias usually needs more reserves than approved at FID. This is another major reason for project failures.

 ## PROJECT EXECUTION THROUGH RISK ADDRESSING (PETRA)

The addressing principles described in the previous section are applicable to any known upside or downside uncertainty. However, some uncertainties that are perceived as critical require special attention. Usually two or three top project uncertainties should be subject to more detailed addressing reviews. Let's call this *project execution through risk addressing (PETRA)*.

PETRA is no more than a very logical and simple upgrade of standard risk register templates to better accommodate the bowtie diagram philosophy.

As previously discussed, several causes may lead to an uncertain event. In turn, an event may lead to several impacts on project objectives. These many-to-one and one-to-many logical relationships need to be broken in a consistent way. There should be an assurance that all identified logical links will be broken or significantly weakened consistently. This could require development of several detailed addressing actions for each logical link. This sounds onerous, but is very consistent and effective. Figure 5.4 demonstrates the PETRA concept. This is a simplified and high-level example. Real PETRA could lead to dozens of preventive and recovery actions that have owners, start and completion dates, notes on progress, and so on. A risk practitioner could easily add required fields to the template of Figure 5.4 as soon as the concept is well understood. In essence, this is a fragment of a traditional project risk register but developed in a very detailed fashion. Its structure assures that every single cause and every single impact on objectives is properly and individually addressed. As I have not yet seen an adequate commercial application for the PETRA technique, for obvious reasons, project teams may use an MS-Excel template as introduced in Figure 5.4.

Should a regular uncertainty register template (Figure 5.3) be redeveloped the PETRA way? It is possible to do so, although not all uncertainties require this level of detail, only the most critical. Hence, the only constraint is about

CAUSES	PREVENTIVE ACTIONS	EVENT	RECOVERY ACTIONS	IMPACTS
a) general opposition by some NGOs to oil sands projects	To establish communication channel to engage most active NGOs in collaborative discussions	P r o j e c t	To accelerate permitting part of schedule and allocate part of project schedule reserve to most sensitive permitting activities	A) permitting and FID delay (Schedule pre-FID)
	To develop plan to address identified NGO's concerns		To get government engaged in discussion of ways to accelerate the process	
			To assure that application is prepared according to requirements and expectations	
b) concerns by local communities about project's environmental impact	To develop and implement communication plan to engage local communities in project discussions including regular open houses		To discuss early procurement of long-lead items before FID with management	B) engineering, procurement and construction delays (Schedule)
			Allocate part of project schedule reserve to most sensitive permitting activities	
	To communicate expected benefits for local communities related to the project (employment opportunities, support of small businesses, development of infrastructure, etc.)	S a n c t i o n i n g	To hold additional value engineering and constructability reviews to accelerate engineering, procurement and construction activities	
			To assure timely or earlier receiving of vendor data	
c) environmental issues associated with similar projects in the past	To inform interested stakeholders on recent progress of technology and methods to protect environment		To unite efforts with the other industry players in the region to communicate importance of oil sands projects	C) company's reputational damage in general (Reputation)
			To participate in the industry trade-shows to accentuate company's environment conservation approach	
		D e l a y	To develop employment and training plan for potential workers from local communities	D) complications of relations with local communities in particular (Reputation)
	To discuss details of incidents in previous projects and explain how similar issues will be handled by the project		To offer particular contributions in development of local infrastructure	
			To take into account schedule-driven costs related to delays in the project reserve	E) extra owner's costs (CapEx)
			To assure certain degree of flexibility in the pre-FID schedule to minimize impact on project budget in case of delays	

FIGURE 5.4 Conceptual Template for PETRA Methodology for Uncertain Events

the resources and time available to do such a detailed analysis. So, to avoid overshooting and overspending, normal practice is to have the regular risk register template shown in Figure 5.3 for all uncertainties and use the PETRA method for the very few critical uncertainties as an extra.

For general uncertainties the left part representing causes and preventive actions will be irrelevant. It is too late to prevent an event that has already happened or was there all along as a given. In place of an uncertain event there will be an issue/given/fact, and so on. So, only recovery actions should be considered as part of the barrier 2 (recovery actions) to rule out impacts on objectives. I came across an application of a similar methodology to develop addressing actions related to labor productivity uncertainties in a capital project. That was a really impressive and detailed document that contained 14 pages in an 11" × 17" format. I cannot share this information in this book due to confidentiality. However, this example demonstrates how detailed and sophisticated PETRA or a similar exercise could be.

There are several methodologies that resemble PETRA, which various companies have adopted and shared. Their origin is not exactly traceable. All of them look way more complex than really required. Most complicated versions are linked with WBS, project schedule, or budget in a similar way as nodes are used in hazard and operability (HAZOP) studies. Some utilize fishbone diagrams. All those fancy extras might yield 20% extra value but should generate 80% extra complexity, frustration, and time spent. It is amazing how a simple and effective idea can be overlooked or overloaded with extras to the point of impracticality! I feel that those futile bells and whistles may be left out for practicality and efficiency reasons. Once again, let's keep things simple or at least efficient. The lean PETRA methodology introduced in this section has nothing to do with those overcomplicated techniques. It is just a slight modification of a standard risk register template based on clear understanding of the bowtie diagram logic.

ROLE OF BIAS IN UNCERTAINTY ASSESSMENT

Uncertainty assessment is the business of quantifying stories and averaging out bias. As we all know, storytelling, even in the form of expert opinion, can be biased. We pointed out the manifestation of overconfidence bias when discussing decision making based on assessment of uncertainties after addressing. Let's discuss the main types of bias more systematically in this section.

The two most notorious manifestations of subconscious bias during risk assessment are *anchoring* and *overconfidence*. These seem to be linked to the frequency method, at least indirectly. Moreover, they seem to feed each other.

Anchoring is an interesting psychological effect based on previous or initial perception and overconfidence. I worked with one project manager who used to tell his team: "I am pregnant with this number!" This statement indicated that he was very aware of anchoring but could not easily overcome it due to his overconfidence. To convince him of any other assessment was extremely difficult but eventually possible. The questions listed in the previous section, and challenging his opinions, helped to do this.

Overconfidence is a characteristic of many technical people. Empowered by their previous training, knowledge, experience, and successes they follow a very specific and results-oriented thinking process. Any ambiguity would be judged as a lack of confidence. Any possibility of project execution lower than *good* would be dismissed right off the bat. This could lead to excessively narrow assessments of impacts and underestimating of probabilities. This looks like an almost quasi-deterministic and wildly optimistic semi-one-point value approach, which means overconfidence in terms of uncertainty assessment. I describe overconfidence bias partially from my personal experience and background. Overcoming overconfidence is a difficult exercise that requires special effort.[6] I tried to apply the calibration methods developed by Doug Hubbard on a couple of occasions. Although the calibration questions were not that project specific ("Please provide your estimate of the height of the Eiffel Tower in feet with confidence level 80%"), the results were real eye-openers for some participants. Some of the results made direct impacts on participants' egos and helped to manage overconfidence.

Conscious bias is very possible during risk assessments. It is usually observed in the form of hidden agendas and normally manifested as exaggeration (overly conservative assessments done on purpose) or window dressing (overly optimistic assessments done on purpose). The role of a facilitator is to recognize motives for conscious bias and to try to challenge and manage it, which could be an extremely political and not-too-lucrative activity.

My method of managing conscious bias is openness. When such bias is identified it should be discussed openly. I usually propose to take personal responsibility for its particular expression or a specific assessment and make the corresponding clear record in a risk register or minutes of a discussion. The efficiency and "success rate" of this method in avoiding hidden agendas is about 80%.

Using any RAM brings up a sort of organizational bias, too. There are five standard ranges for probabilities and impacts. Any assessed risk should be allocated to one specific cell of RAM. Let's say an uncertain event is assessed as having a probability of 5–15% and a cost impact of $7–$10 million. Using the RAM from Figure 3.2, one may easily assign this uncertainty to the medium category (yellow, score 6), because probability complies with a low range (1–20%, score 2) and cost impact with a medium range ($5–$20 million, score 3). What about a situation where probability is assessed at 10–30% and cost impact at $15–$25 million? Of course, a prudent approach would be to use higher probability and impacts ranges. But this might be overshooting, anyway. This Procrustean bed shortcoming may be fully resolved only when converting deterministic risk data to inputs to probabilistic risk analysis.

Another weak point of using RAM is that all assessments are RAM-range specific. If we redefine the ranges tomorrow morning, most of the assessment scores will be different. To address this changeability issue, we have discussed methods of RAM developing in this chapter. Those methods do assume the possibility of range changes if they are not developed properly in the first place. The bottom line of the discussion on organization bias is that project RAM is a convention that should not be taken as absolute truth written in stone. It is not an ideal but rather a useful tool that supports right thinking processes. At the end of the day, the most important part of risk management is implementation of addressing actions. The rest of it, including assessments, is supporting action implementation. If the assessments as-is and to-be are about right, they justify reasonable and viable addressing actions that should be consistently implemented to reduce overall project uncertainty outcome.

CONCLUSION

Along with their identification, assessment and addressing of uncertainties lays the foundation for a deterministic risk management method. In many organizations this is the only method used for risk management—no probabilistic methodology, no cost escalation modeling, no selection of options, and so on. Despite criticism of the deterministic method and its obvious shortcomings, I believe this is a very simple and adequate methodology that should be used as the basis of an overall risk management system. It provides clear guidelines on how uncertainties should be managed. When understood properly, it is not necessary to have sophisticated training or experience or software tools to start actively and successfully using the deterministic method.

No doubt though that some other more sophisticated and adequate tools should be kept in the risk management "tool box." I consider the deterministic method as a necessary input to those other methods including probabilistic ones. They will be discussed later in the book. The next chapter accentuates a need to make the deterministic method as practical as possible.

 NOTES

1. IPA Institute, "Successful Mega Projects" Seminar (Calgary, Canada, 2009), p. 18.
2. D. Hubbard, *The Failure of Risk Management: Why It's Broken and How to Fix It* (Hoboken, NJ: John Wiley & Sons, 2009).
3. J. Haigh, *Taking Chances: Winning with Probability* (Oxford, UK: Oxford University Press, 2003).
4. G. Owen, *Game Theory* (Bingley, UK: Emerald Group, 1995).
5. Readers who have had at least basic military training might recall the contents of the field manual for an infantry rifle platoon. The part on defense operations might provide additional insights on the topic.
6. D. Hubbard, *How to Measure Anything: Finding the Value of "Intangibles" in Business* (Hoboken, NJ: John Wiley & Sons, 2010).

CHAPTER SIX

Response Implementation and Monitoring

Questions Addressed in Chapter 6

- Where does the rubber meet the road in risk management?
- Why should addressing actions become part of project team work plans?
- Why is assessment after addressing (to-be) more important than assessment as-is?
- Do we keep our promise to successfully implement all approved addressing actions?
- When should uncertainties be closed or accepted?
- What is the role of bias? ■

EVEN THOUGH THIS CHAPTER is short, it is one of the most important chapters of this book. *Response implementation* is where the rubber meets the road in risk management. The rest is theory or auxiliary steps and methods. Only *development of project reserves using probabilistic methods* is equally important because that is about time and hard currency.

MERGING RISK MANAGEMENT WITH TEAM WORK PLANS

Three-dimensional integration of risk management (Figure 2.1) implies that any specialist at any level of the organization may become a risk or action owner upon approval by management (Table 2.1). The most sensitive challenge here is to ensure that risk or action ownership does not conflict with his or her direct responsibilities. Working on a risk or an action should become part of everyday activities and fully aligned with them. That is easier said than done. How often has a specialist who was assigned as a risk or action owner during one of those grandiose annual two-day workshops totally forgot about it afterwards and needed to be reminded during the next annual workshop? And sometimes uncertainty or action ownership is assigned *in absentia*, which makes forgetting about ownership even more convenient.

Unfortunately, it is not unusual for project risks to be identified and addressing actions to be proposed just for show. This show is called a *decision gate*. The top show of this kind is the *final investment decision (FID)* decision gate. I heard about a situation where a project team credibly reported to reviewers about identified risks, proposed risk response plans, and so on, with all those risks being identified a week prior to review sessions. Somebody had just discovered that risk review should be part of the FID review. The project was gloriously approved, with some decent and not-too-onerous recommendations to slightly improve the project risk management system, and miserably failed in the course of its execution. This tick-off-box type of organizational bias is not as rare as we might think and leads to quite predictable consequences.

Both the organizational framework and the tools of the risk management system should support merging risk management with working plans. The project risk management plan should contain general guidelines on frequency and triggers for reviews of risks of various severity and sources. But this is not enough. Ideally, the risk management plan should have an appendix with an annual schedule of reviews of particular risks of various severity and sources (risk breakdown structure [RBS] categories). This should include major expected milestones of project development or at least placeholders wherever exact dates are not yet defined. For instance, moving to a new phase, purchasing of major equipment, and signing of a major construction contract all could be triggers for risk reviews. The major source of such information is usually a software tool used by engineering and procurement for work-package development.

MONITOR AND APPRAISE

The loop of the risk management process in Figure 2.2 may repeat itself several times for each uncertainty until the uncertainty is finally accepted or closed. It reflects on amendments and transformations of a particular uncertainty due to the presence of various internal and external changers, including addressing actions.

When some addressing actions have been completed, the as-is assessment should be revisited to take completed actions into account in the updated as-is assessment. Some additional addressing actions could be proposed. Figure 2.2 points to the possibility of an extended loop that could head for Identify (dotted line) instead of Assess as-is. This reminds us about the fact that approved addressing actions are internal and often uncontrollable uncertainty changers (Figure 1.4): they could fully or partially fail or their implementation might lead to new uncertainties. This possibility should be checked during Monitor and Appraise. And, of course, new uncertainties are often identified during the Monitor and Appraise steps. The discussion about new uncertainties and failure of actions has practical ramifications when defining project reserves.

Decision making about risk reserves is normally done based on project uncertainty exposure to-be. Inputs to probabilistic cost models take in data on general uncertainties and uncertain events after addressing. This means credibility of developed cost reserve is subject to full implementation of all approved addressing actions and assurance that no new uncertainties are induced. In other words, credibility of developed project cost reserve has a condition: all internal uncertainty changers (addressing actions) should be fully controllable in the sense shown in Figure 1.4.

Moreover, this assessment is done before the FID, which is the end of the front-end loading (FEL) phases (Figure 1.1). By that time some of the addressing actions have been implemented or have failed and some of them have induced new uncertainties, which are all supposedly factored into the project reserve. This reserve is taken into account as part of the FID. However, the majority of approved addressing actions will be implemented after the FID in Execute. Some of them will fail and some generate new uncertainties, too. This situation provides room for subconscious and conscious bias when assessing the level of control over proposed addressing actions. The real required project cost reserve might be bigger than the one approved during the FID.

The bottom line is that adequacy of project costs and schedule reserves are a function of execution. If execution were not carried out as presumed explicitly or implicitly when developing the project reserve, the models to derive reserves would be at quite a big distance from future project reality. Such a project could become a failure due to overspending related to higher-than-anticipated uncertainty exposure in Execute, stemming from partial implementation of approved addressing actions. In other words, uncertainty exposure in Execute would not change to the extent contemplated during the FID.

The same could happen to the schedule risk analysis and the corresponding schedule reserve (floats). We discuss methods of handling project reserves in Chapter 12.

When all proposed addressing actions are implemented and no additional actions proposed, the as-is and to-be assessments of an uncertainty become identical, giving rise to residual uncertainty exposure. After this the uncertainty exits the risk management process, being either accepted or closed.

WHEN UNCERTAINTIES SHOULD BE CLOSED

The general rule for when an uncertainty may be closed is that it becomes irrelevant or insignificant. Technically a closed uncertainty is a nonexistent uncertainty. It is off the project risk management radar screen. It does not require addressing any more and does not contribute to risk reserves.

An uncertainty may be closed in only four cases:

1. When it is avoided and not relevant to the project any more (e.g., new reference case, change of design, etc.)
2. When it is fully mitigated or reduced to at least the green level after all the response actions are completed
3. When the time window that defines the uncertainty relevance is past (e.g., permits received, no permitting risks)
4. When it is fully transferred (e.g., good insurance policy purchased, no deductibles)

A closed uncertainty stays in the corresponding log as inactive and should not be erased. It becomes a part of the project risk management legacy system. This can be used by another project the organization undertakes in the future. It also could be reopened if risk exposure changes.

Possible confusion could stem from application of the *(as low as reasonably practicable) ALARP* approach toward addressing uncertainties. ALARP rarely means zero residual exposure. Very often risks that have reached the

ALARP level are being closed. But in many cases it means quite material possible downside deviations from the project objectives. For instance, the actual loss of two vehicles over 135 space shuttle missions produces a probability of 1 in 67.5. A Monte Carlo evaluation of the uncertainty distribution for the probability of loss of the space shuttle[1] produced a probability of 1 in 89 (mean value). This was quite a material risk, which was considered ALARP by NASA. Needless to say, it was certainly kept active and was never closed in NASA risk registers until the space shuttle program was closed in 2011.

Closed ALARP uncertainties mean uncertainties neglected from now on. The ALARP level depends on the risk appetite adopted by an organization or a project and does not necessarily mean zero exposure. If an uncertainty cannot be closed, it should be accepted.

There may be a tendency to close all risks that are qualified as *green* after addressing, according to the RAM of Figure 3.2. This may be done in most cases but not before all approved addressing actions are successfully implemented. Until then, the green status of that risk should be treated as conditional and that risk should stay active.

WHEN SHOULD RESIDUAL UNCERTAINTIES BE ACCEPTED?

The short answer is: when they cannot be closed after addressing. Once again, only active uncertainties give rise to project cost or schedule reserves. As discussed in the previous section, the ALARP concept might be a major confusion here. ALARP means *residual* exposure. The question is: Should this exposure be neglected? For instance, if it is not reasonable to further address some Cost and Schedule uncertain events or general uncertainties, their residual levels give rise to project cost and schedule reserves unless neglected. If those levels are low, they may be neglected in reserves. If an uncertainty is closed, it becomes inactive and does not give rise to reserves by default.

CONCLUSION

This chapter accentuates the obvious importance of proper uncertainty response implementation and monitoring. Whereas uncertainty implementation and monitoring is the single most important risk management activity, proper assessment of uncertainties is the single most important activity for development of project cost and schedule reserves.

 NOTE

1. T. Hamlin, M. Canga, R. Boyer, and E. Thigpen, "2009 Space Shuttle Probabilistic Risk Assessment Overview" (Houston, TX: NASA, 2009).

CHAPTER SEVEN

Risk Management Governance and Organizational Context

Questions Addressed in Chapter 7

- What risk management keys are required for decision gates?
- How unique should a project be allowed to be?
- What is the role of ownership in risk management?
- What is the terminology for various types of risks?
- What forms should risk reporting take?
- What sort of risk management system health self-check should be in place?
- Is a risk manager really a manager or a leader?
- What is the role of bias? ■

THE METHODS AND TOOLS described in this book should become part of project governance in order to assure their consistent application and real positive impact on project performance. Consistent development and execution of a project according to corporate processes enhances the predictability of the project outcome. Besides this, the role of project governance has two specific implications. First, project cost and schedule reserves approved as part of a sanctioned project budget and duration at the final investment decision (FID) are subject to presumed execution. Second, these reserves are meaningful only if project execution includes all approved addressing actions. These two additional conditions are crucial for credibility of project cost and schedule reserves derived from probabilistic models. Development of project reserves is discussed in detail in Chapter 12. In the meantime, we will overview risk management deliverables from the angle of organizational context and corresponding requirements in this chapter.

RISK MANAGEMENT DELIVERABLES FOR DECISION GATES

Table 1.1 describes the main phases of a project development. A decision gate follows each of these phases. The particular project development standards and requirements for various project disciplines depend on the size, scope, and complexity of a project. However, the key intent is to ensure an acceptable level of value after each phase. As a result a decision to proceed to the next phase should be made. The most important decision in terms of commitment to the project is the FID that should be made after Define.

The fundamental issue with the organizational context of project management relates to the definition of a project, which is a temporary endeavor to create a unique product, service, or result.[1] When a project attains its objectives it should terminate, whereas operations may adopt evolving sets of objectives and the work continues. The intrinsic "uniqueness and temporariness" of projects implicitly assumes a degree of uniqueness, instability, inconsistency, or "tailor-made-ness" of processes and procedures to deliver projects. This is a fundamental source for all kinds of surprises, unknown uncertainties, and deviations from project objectives, stemmimg from the organizational category of a project's risk breakdown structure (RBS). To a certain degree *uniqueness* is a synonym for *unpredictability* (and not only in the project environment). However, the intrinsic uniqueness of a project should be distinguished from inconsistent applications of project development and execution processes and procedures, if these are well developed at all.

In some cases project processes are well defined but not followed because of accentuating the uniqueness. In other cases the processes and procedures are not established at all. For instance, how many times have you heard about issues with change management, interface management, timely providing vendor data for engineering, and so on? Operations come across these on an everyday basis but have to react immediately. This allows one to sharpen and hone all aspects of operations permanently. Not surprisingly, the Six Sigma approach came from operations, not from projects. The statistical approach requires repetitiveness to promote the frequency-based evaluation of deviations from a norm, whatever the norm is.

Postmortem lessons-learned activities do not provide much value for a given project because they come too late. Benchmarking could be more relevant to a given project, although it usually requires some conditioning to be fully applicable to a particular project. If an organization has well-developed lessons learned and benchmarking processes, that would be the only analog comparable with ongoing operations. Some organizations develop and execute the same or very similar projects year after year based on the same technologies and construction methods and in the same regions. Such semi-operational projects or semi-project operations usually lose their uniqueness substantially, leaving little room for a very few uncertainties. However, even very standardized projects or operations will come across some uncertainties. Otherwise, there would not be a discipline called "operational risk management."

Hence, one of the key goals of project decision gates from the organizational governance viewpoint is to ensure that a project is not too unique to bring forth unexpected outcomes. The more it manifests that it is rather "an operation," the higher its chances of passing a decision gate. In a way, risk management along with benchmarking is a tool that allows one to fathom and cut the degree of project uniqueness, especially in terms of deviations from established practices, processes, and procedures in various disciplines. It is a Procrustean bed type of mechanism in quite a good value assurance sense. If the uniqueness of a project is too high and cannot be fully controlled, the substantial uncertainty exposure scares decision makers stiff.

It does not stand to reason to list all the value assurance requirements for all decision gates for all project disciplines. However, Table 7.1 points to the general project governance requirements related to risk management.

Although risk management should be integrated with all project disciplines, it closely supports estimating and planning in development of project budgets and schedules. The role of risk management is to justify required reserves based on uncertainty exposure. And in terms of organizational governance, exposure to uncertainty could be treated as exposure to uniqueness.

TABLE 7.1   Generic Risk Management Requirements for Decision Gates

Project Phase	General Requirement	Key Deliverables
Identify	Identification of major risks and their use for assessment purposes.	Preliminary risk management plan (RMP) approved for Identify; preliminary risk register.
Select	Identification, assessment as-is, development of response plans and assessment to-be for all main concepts/options; use of risk information for option selection.	RMP approved for Select at the beginning of Select; risk registers for each option; list of risks of Cost and Schedule impacts for probabilistic risk analysis for each option; project execution through risk addressing (PETRA) reviews for most critical risks; probabilistic Cost and Schedule risk analysis by the end of Select for a selected option; Cost escalation reserve.
Define	Full development of response plans and more precise assessment to-be for a selected option for Execute and Operate.	RMP approved for Define; expanded risk register; PETRA reviews for most critical risks; probabilistic Cost and Schedule risk analyses to develop project cost and schedule reserves; updated cost escalation reserve.
Execute	Management of risks to ensure project delivery as planned; transferring of risk information to Operations at end of Execute.	RMP approved for Execute; expanded risk register; PETRA reviews for most critical risks; regular probabilistic Cost and Schedule risk analyses and cost escalation reviews to draw down cost reserves.
Operate	Management of risks to ensure continued operations and planned value.	RMP approved for Operate; updated risk register containing only operational risks.

OWNERSHIP OF UNCERTAINTIES AND ADDRESSING ACTIONS

It is mandatory that each identified uncertainty and addressing action gets an owner. Combined, Table 2.1, Figure 2.1, and Table 5.1 promote a line-of-sight approach. Namely, the higher the severity of the uncertainty,

- The more-senior member of a project team should own it
- The higher in the hierarchy package–project–business unit it is reported
- The more frequently it should be reviewed

A risk owner is supposed to coordinate activities of action owners to ensure that all approved preventive and recovery actions are timely implemented. According to the 3D concept of risk management (Figure 2.1), a risk owner and action owners could belong to totally different disciplines and levels of the organization. Moreover, those individuals may work for different organizations. This implies a lot of dotted reporting lines in a virtually matrix-type "risk addressing organization." Following this logic, an uncertainty owner should be treated as the CEO of that uncertainty addressing organization with full accountability in uncertainty addressing.

Several similar risks could be managed by a category owner (Table 2.1). For instance, an engineering manager for the whole project could become a category owner for all risks stemming from the engineering category of the project's risk breakdown structure. The civil or mechanical lead could become a risk category owner for his or her discipline (corresponding engineering subcategory in RBS).

This picture could be complicated by the fact that estimators, schedulers, and procurement people are intimately involved in managing corresponding general uncertainties, too. Their responsibility and engagement should be clearly defined. So, interface management among disciplines risk-wise is a particular challenge that is the responsibility of the project risk manager.

For most critical risks that require addressing actions delivered from several disciplines, which may belong to different organizations, special task teams could be created. For instance, managing labor productivity uncertainty might require involvement of representatives of the owner's organization, consortium/joint venture (JV) partners, engineering, procurement and construction (EPC) contractor, and several construction subcontractors.

It is a must to establish a process that ensures timely implementation of addressing actions. Both the project risk manager and the risk owners should be interested in having one, which should be part of the RMP. This process could be supported by risk tools selected by the project. Most modern risk database software tools have variations of notification functionalities. Usually such functionality is linked to action completion dates. Two major types of such functionality are the sending of notification emails to action owners or the appearance of warning signs or marks in reports retrieved from the database. The first early alarm mark or notification email is triggered, say, two months prior to the planned action completion date. A pleasant email is sent to an action owner automatically or a green mark appears in front of the action in the report. Another (yellow) mark or a more formal email could be sent one month prior to the deadline. If a deadline is passed and an action is still not closed, a less-pleasant email or red mark could be generated. The email could also be sent to management. This functionality implies a clear requirement to maintain risk databases: all actions should have completion dates.

Some risk managers and especially corporate risk management could be obsessed with email alert functionality. This is a relatively new feature, not easily maintained by projects and not available in all commercial tools. It is a nice-to-have feature if properly used. Additional discussion on the required level of automation is provided in Chapter 2. Automation is a double-edged sword in terms of the adequacy of a risk management system.

 ## MANAGEMENT OF SUPERCRITICAL RISKS

Several terms related to the most critical uncertainties have been mentioned in this book. Black swans, broiler and wild black swans, show-stoppers, and game changers both known and unknown have been discussed. The purpose of this section is to provide an overview of the terminology for the most critical project uncertainties, the ones that I would call *supercritical*. This discussion is based on a 5 × 5 risk assessment matrix (RAM) (Figure 3.2) and on the possibility of its expansion for very high impacts.

Previously we discussed the three main categories of risks (Table 5.1) based on a ranking established by the use of RAM. Using three categories— *critical*, *material*, and *small*—is a major risk classification approach, although other ranking classifications could be used. Some of them are well justified, some not.

Identified or known show-stoppers and game changers should be listed by a project RMP to outline situations where project baselines would not be viable any more. An obvious contradiction from the RAM-based approach is that usually show-stoppers and game changers have very low probability of occurrence (score 1 of RAM) and very high impacts (score 5). This qualifies them as small (green) risks only (overall score 5). Even if we treated risks of score 5 as material (yellow), they would still be treated as relatively unimportant.

Recall that the very high impact range of RAM does not have a limit. In the sample RAM in Figure 3.2 any uncertainty with a possible impact on project objectives of more than $50 million, 6 months, one fatality, and so on should be considered very high. It was assumed that one or two events like this could be handled by a project without clear failure. What if overspending due to the occurrence of some uncertainties were to be $100 million, $0.5 billion, $1 billion, or more? What if the delay were nine months, one year, two years, or more? What if the number of fatalities were 5, 10, 100, and so forth?

One might imagine a sixth impact range in the RAM (Figure 3.2) that defines when a very high risk should be regarded as supercritical or a show-stopper or game changer.[2] So, let's treat show-stoppers and game changers as supercritical risks. These should be listed and communicated as a waiver or demarcation of responsibilities between a project team and corporate risk management along with the threshold definitions. These should become part of the corporate or business-unit portfolio risk management being promoted to the business unit or corporate risk registers. For instance, a project team may state, subject to agreement with corporate management, that if a delay related to project sanctioning by government is more than 12 months, this should become a game changer and be taken over by the corporation. If sanctioning is done after such a delay, previous baselines should be recycled and developed from scratch.

This angle has additional ramifications related to developing project risk reserves. Risk reserves underline the desired and reasonable level of confidence of baselines. Show-stoppers and game changers destroy these baselines, or mathematically speaking, they ensure that those baselines have close-to-zero confidence levels. For this reason, project show-stoppers and game changers, even if they are known, usually are not taken into account in project probabilistic risk models as they drastically redefine (knock down or knock out) project baselines. This outlines the limits of project probabilistic risk models through excluding certain known show-stoppers and game changers from probabilistic calculations.[3] Simply, it does not stand to reason to run a project model that includes factors destroying that project.

A good discussion on this is provided by Chapman and Ward in their great book on risk management.[4] Namely, if part of the corresponding reserve is esti-mated as the product of very low probability and very high impact, this reserve would not be enough to cover the catastrophic event, if it occurred, anyway. For instance, if an impact is assessed at $100 million and probability 1%, then the required risk reserve could be assessed at $1 million. On the other hand, if the catastrophic event is not happening at all during the project lifecycle, which is likely due to its very low probability, this reserve becomes free pocket money for the project. This is not an efficient way of doing business, and the better method is portfolio risk management at the corporate level through self-insurance or purchasing third-party insurance.

The issue with unknown-unknown corporate risks is that it is impossi-ble to come up with an explicit disclaimer as in the case of known-unknown show-stoppers and game changers. However, very general *force majeure* types of disclaimers would be worthwhile to develop. Project teams should learn this skill from contract lawyers. These generic demarcation-type unknown show stoppers and game changers should be taken into account when making final investment decisions. There is a method to evaluate project unknown unknowns if unknown show-stoppers and game changers are excluded. As discussed in Chapter 4, the room for unknown uncertainties could be understood as the measure of the quality of a project risk management system. The corresponding project-level unknown-unknown allowance is discussed in Chapter 12.

Some practitioners distinguish *strategic* and *tactical* risks. Tactical risks are general uncertainties related to the level of engineering and procurement development. In the course of project development these are permanently reduced. Corresponding engineering reviews (30%, 60%, 90% reviews) and major procurement milestones where prices for work packages are locked are major reasons to review and downgrade such general uncertainties. So, tactical risks are implicitly defined as package general uncertainties. According to this logic, strategic risks are possible uncertain events related to project development and execution (project level or higher). I have always had an issue with full justification of this logic as some general uncertainties that should be treated as tactical risks could be more devastating than most of the uncertain events or "strategic risks." For instance, labor productivity general uncertainty and, as such, a tactical risk by default may blow out any project if not managed properly.

If a project team elects to delineate strategic and tactical risks at all, clear rules defining what is considered strategic and tactical should be set up in the RMP. These rules should not contradict the line-of-sight approach and 3D risk management (Figure 2.1), the three risk level/severity categories (Table 5.1), and, most important, the six major types of uncertainties (Figure 1.2). I would call all the red uncertainties of Table 5.1 "strategic," although they are called "critical" in the table. I would not mind if they were called "critical/strategic."

 ## RISK REVIEWS AND REPORTING

Management has to keep its finger on the pulse of project risk management in order to make timely decisions. The nature of good risk management is that it provides ammunition for proactive decision making (preventive actions). But it should be ready for reactive recovery actions as part of crisis management, too.

This requires regularly answering various questions related to project uncertainty exposure and its dynamics. Is overall project risk exposure the same as last month or are there signs that it is evolving due to some uncertainty changers in the internal and external environment? Are there new uncertainties emerging, or are existing ones transforming their severities? Are some package or project uncertainties growing in their severity that should be reported (escalated) to a business unit or corporate management? Have some addressing actions failed, or been successfully implemented, to change the overall uncertainty exposure as-is? Should additional addressing actions be developed and implemented to ensure required assessments to-be in a particular moment in the future?

Timely answering of such questions requires the right frequency of uncertainty reviews and efficient methods of reporting and escalation, based on the previously discussed line-of-sight, the 3D risk management concept (Figure 2.1), and the classification of Table 5.1.

Normal practice is that a monthly risk report should be prepared by a risk manager. It should be based on the risk reviews and events that have occurred during the reporting period. Not all identified and managed active risks should be reviewed every month. Table 7.2 describes the standard frequency of reviews.

Table 7.2 is too generic to reflect all risk review possibilities but it sets up minimal formal requirements. In practice, risks may be discussed as part of engineering, constructability, package and so on reviews. Major project milestones including decision gates could be triggers and additional (not the only) reasons for risk reviews. Stages of package development, discussed in Chapter 10, contain a lot of risk review possibilities, too. Risk reviews of particular risk categories could be initiated by risk category owners and task team leaders. A project RMP should have a full description of rules on types and frequencies of risk reviews. Ideally, an annual schedule of those reviews should be part of the plan as a realization of those rules.

Information collected about risks should be included in a monthly risk report, which normally contains four main parts. First is an executive summary that describes current risk exposure and major developments related

TABLE 7.2 Standard Frequency of Reviews

Uncertainty Level	Uncertainty Severity	Color Code	Review Frequency
Low	Small	Green	Quarterly
Medium	Material	Yellow	Bimonthly
High	Critical	Red	Monthly

to project risk management. No more than two paragraphs should provide management at any level of an organization with an informative synopsis. Five to seven points on main risk management activities, highlights, lowlights, concerns, realized risks, failed or successfully implemented addressing actions, and so on may be added.

Second is a current snapshot of the current project uncertainty exposure. Statistics related to overall number of risks of various severity and RBS categories should be provided. Figure 7.1 is a sample of reporting charts developed for a mega-project that had four semi-independent components or subprojects.

Some software packages provide visualization statistics as part of their standard functionality. This can be easily done manually. Ideally, the risk database tool used by a project should be tailor-made to support the reporting required by management. All the charts in Figure 7.1 were generated manually using MS Excel. The beauty of MS Excel–based reporting is that slicing-and-dicing of information can be done exactly according to tailor-made project reporting requirements and not merely as the developers of a commercial risk database adopted by a project envisioned and imposed it.

Third, besides the static snapshot statistics of Figure 7.1, *dynamic statistics* on changes of uncertainty exposure during the reporting period should be provided. This usually reflects:

- New risks identified by RBS category and severity (assessments before and after addressing)
- Risks that changed severity (assessments before and after addressing)
- Risks closed during the reporting period by RBS category and severity (assessments before and after addressing)
- New and closed addressing actions

Fourth, it would be beneficial to include a list of all critical-red downside uncertainties (assessment before addressing) and upside uncertainties (assessment after addressing) accompanied by the names of their owners. All addressing actions for these, including action owners' names and completion dates, should be shown for accountability purposes.

Additional statistics based on plotting of uncertainties on a 5 × 5 RAM could be adopted. This approach is based on the visualization of uncertainties introduced by Figures 5.1 and 5.2. Uncertainties may be plotted in corresponding RAM cells depending on their probabilities and impacts before and after addressing. If an uncertainty has impacts on more than one objective, the top

XXX Project
Master Risk Register Statistics

Number of	Total RR	Comp 1	Comp 2	Comp 3	Comp 4
Upside and Downside Uncertainties (↑↓)	146	56	33	33	24
Upside Uncertainties Only (↑)	8	2	0	2	4
Addressing Actions	492	175	93	137	87
High Level Risks (red) Before Addressing (as-is)	78	28	22	17	11
High Level Risks (red) After Addressing (to-be)	28	8	7	6	7
Medium Level Risks (yellow) Before Addressing (as-is)	55	22	11	13	9
Medium Level Risks (yellow) After Addressing (to-be)	91	36	22	20	13
Low Level Risks (green) Before Addressing (as-is)	5	4	0	1	0
Low Level Risks (green) After Addressing (to-be)	19	10	4	5	0

RBS Category	↑↓	↑
Commercial	40	2
Commissioning and Start-up	6	0
Completeness	6	0
Construction	20	1
Environmental	6	0
External	5	0
HSS	22	0
Interfaces	6	1
Organizational	6	0
Operations	2	0
Regulatory	10	0
Technical	17	3
TOTAL	146	8

Number of Upside and Downside Uncertainties by RBS Categories

Number of Upside and Downside Uncertainties As-Is (All Impacts)

		Probability				
		Very Low	Low	Medium	High	Very High
Impact	Very High	1	6	26	6	2
	High	1	3	10	25	17
	Medium	0	1	5	8	3
	Low	0	0	9	3	0
	Very Low	0	0	0	0	0

Upside and Downside Uncertainties Before Addressing (as-is)

Upside and Downside Uncertainties After Addressing (to-be)

FIGURE 7.1 Sample of Monthly Risk Reporting

impact score is used to assign it to a particular RAM cell. If the number of reported uncertainties is high, such visualization could be done separately for each selected project objective. As an option, the total number of uncertainties belonging to each particular RAM cell could be shown. This statistic is shown in Figure 7.1.

Figure 7.1 as well as Figures 5.1 and 5.2 demonstrate options of possible statistical reporting and visualization of uncertainties. A particular project may develop its own set of standard charts and templates for monthly reporting to better reflect the organizational context of project risk management and the needs of decision makers.

The monthly risk report should be concise enough to provide decision makers with a quick uncertainty snapshot. However, it should be adequate enough to provide management with sufficient and comprehensive information for efficient and timely decision making.

BIAS AND ORGANIZATIONAL CONTEXT

Previously we discussed several expressions of *bias* in risk management, which is a systematic error in identification, assessment, and addressing risks. Obviously, if bias were in its most notorious form—organizational—the whole project risk management system could be compromised. However, the milder conscious and subconscious manifestations of bias that pertain to individuals involved in risk management should be properly managed, too. The dividing point between organizational and psychological types of bias is a gray area. For instance, if a project, business-unit, or corporate risk manager/director/VP is biased in any particular way, the corresponding psychological bias systematic error could be amplified when propagating across the organization to become an organizational bias. Some examples of this were discussed earlier.

One overconfident corporate risk manager enthusiastically developed and tried to implement a probabilistic schedule risk analysis guideline for a whole company. You might wonder, "What's wrong with that?" First, the guideline was remarkably inadequate. Second, it turned out that the risk manager had never before built or run probabilistic schedule risk models! These two points have a clear cause-and-effect link. But my point is that imposing guidelines like this on an entire organization is a perfect example of the conversion of personal cognitive bias into organizational bias. Lack of knowledge and experience combined with abundant overconfidence and arrogance in one individual became a cause of organizational bias.

It is not possible to exclude all kinds of bias for a simple reason. People who work in risk management are not robots. They have their unique experiences, backgrounds, education, preferences, psychological characteristics, and so on. Hence, we do not view bias of any type, including organizational bias, as an uncertain event. Being a given phenomenon, bias is a type of general uncertainty.

The general strategy to handle any type of bias is awareness. It is important to inform project team members and decision makers about the major types of bias. The main strategy to address manifestations of bias as a systematic error of the risk management system and a general uncertainty would be Mitigate-Recover through averaging out bias and calibrating it. This brings up three additional topics: (1) internal health self-checks, (2) external sanity checks, and (3) the role of the risk manager.

Internal Health Self-Checks

An organization may develop an internal health self-check list to ensure that there are no obvious or notorious incidences of bias in its risk management system. This should reflect all three components of the risk management system: organizational framework, risk management process, and tools. At a minimum it should indicate that all three components are in place, which is not always the case. The most important component—organizational framework—is often missed.

Table 7.3 represents a typical risk management self-check. It is based on a document developed for a CO_2 sequestration project I worked on as a consultant.

Despite the obvious importance and value of self-checks, including sanity self-checks, their role should not be exaggerated. They themselves could reflect organizational bias. One of the key expressions of this is the slogan, "That's our way of doing things!" Using this approach based on doubtful uniqueness, any lame risk management system could be announced as brilliant by default and the best in the universe. *External* health checks might be the only remedy against this type of psychological and organizational phenomenon.

External Sanity Checks

In order to reduce the possibility that an internally developed project risk management system will miserably fail, regular sanity checks should be undertaken. These may take the form of cold-eye and benchmarking reviews. Both could be done as related to either a risk management system at large or the particular results produced by it.

TABLE 7.3 Risk Management Health Self-Check

Aspect of Risk Management (RM)	Unacceptable	Acceptable	Excellent
Risk Register (RR) Quality	Only one or two objectives used.	Few objectives used.	Adequate set of multiple objectives used.
	Bowtie diagram and RBS not used.	Bowtie diagram and RBS used but not consistent.	Fully developed and consistent bowtie diagram and RBS used.
	Descriptions/definitions of uncertainties unclear.	Key uncertainty descriptions/definitions clear.	Uncertainty descriptions/definitions clear without further reference.
	Contains many non-uncertainty and common items (issues, concerns, etc.).	Contains less than 20% of non-uncertainty or common items (issues, concerns, etc.).	No non-uncertainty or common items (issues, concerns, etc.) in the RR.
	More than 300 open items.		Several (package, discipline, etc.) logs kept separately in the uncertainty repository to feed the master RR.
	Key risks not identified/understood.	A few upside uncertainties in the RR cover some aspects of the project.	Urgent/critical uncertainties and show-stoppers and "game changers" identified and highlighted.
	No upside uncertainties in the RR.		Upside uncertainties cover all aspects of the project.
Assessments	Less than 80% of uncertainties assessed.	Key uncertainties assessed and more than 50% of assumptions logged.	All uncertainties assessed and all assumptions logged.
	Assessment logic logged for less than 50% of risks.		Standard RAM in use.
	RAM inconsistent or incomplete.	RAM internally consistent.	Basis for assessments clear without further reference.
			All assumptions logged.
Addressing	Addressing plans not in place, approved, resourced, or realistic.	Addressing plans of key uncertainties approved and resourced.	All addressing plans approved and resourced.
		Residual uncertainties assessed and realistic.	All residual uncertainties assessed and realistic.
			PETRA methodology used to address the most critical uncertainties.
			Addressing costs and residual uncertainty levels integrated in project plans and probabilistic Cost and Schedule models.

Implementation	No reviews between uncertainty and action owners. Action closure not logged. Action deadlines not tracked.	Key actions tracked against their deadlines on regular basis. Action audit trails maintained. Reason for action closure logged.	Reviews between risk and action owners held regularly. Action deadlines tracked on regular basis. Action audit trails fully maintained. Reason for closure logged.
Review and Monitor	Uncertainties only drafted or reviewed prior to major decision gates or in (less than) quarterly meetings, resulting in only partial review of RR.	Uncertainties reviewed regularly. Management use RR information for decision making at decision gates.	Uncertainties reviewed continuously according to risk ranking, line-of-sight. and planned frequency. Risk manager leads review meetings and nominates uncertainties for review based on urgency/severity. Standard meeting structure employed. Schedule of reviews developed and followed. Team members have access to RR and are familiar with top project risks and those that impact their work.
Organizational Framework	Team members not aware of their roles and responsibilities in RM. No RMP developed.	All project uncertainties are explicitly approved, resourced, and tracked by project and risk managers. RMP available and used as basis for RM activities.	Uncertainty escalation rules established and in use. Management engaged in RM and explicitly approve, resource, and track addressing. RR information used for informed decision making and prioritization. Fully developed RMP available and consistently used as basis for all RM activities. Team member participation in RM is recognized and rewarded.

(Continued)

171

TABLE 7.3 (Continued)

Aspect of Risk Management (RM)	Unacceptable	Acceptable	Excellent
Risk Manager	Unfamiliar with rules of RM process, organizational framework, tools, etc.	Adequately understands theory of RM (process, organizational framework, tools, etc.).	Fully understands RM in projects (process, organizational framework, tools, etc.).
	Unfamiliar with principles of probabilistic risk analysis.	Supports project team, PM, and decision makers with training and information on uncertainty exposure and RM health.	Challenges and drives management to prioritize and resource RM.
			Tracks and highlights value of RM.
		Asks for help from consultants as appropriate.	Supports management team with training, quality information, and insights.
			Takes leadership role in RM company-wide and helps in setting company's RM policy.
		Adequately understands and applies principles of probabilistic risk analysis in most cases.	A recognized RM subject matter expert (SME) in the industry, including probabilistic risk analysis.
			Is sought out for opinions and advice by others.
Project Reserves and Execution Plan Integration	RR not used for development of project reserves.	Existing RR updated and used as basis of probabilistic risk analysis for development of project reserves.	RR is used as basis of probabilistic risk analysis for development of project reserves.
	RM not part of the project execution plan.	Adequate cost escalation model developed.	RM is integrated as part of project execution plan.
		RM included in project execution plan.	Cost escalation model fully developed.
			Project reserves are tracked and drawn down.

For evaluation of the risk management system at large, only external parties are unbiased to any degree. But even they might succumb to some form of nice-guy bias related to hope of getting repeat business from the organization.

Good external reviews are not cheap, which could be a major reason to refrain from them. However, their cost should be treated as the cost of addressing corresponding organizational risks and associated biases: risks related to the "insanity" of the risk management system in place.

For evaluation of particular results (quality of a project risk register, development of project reserves using probabilistic methods, etc.) specialists from other parts of an organization may be involved. These third parties bring a degree of their own bias to the reviews. But most likely, existing organizational bias will be identified and either calibrated or averaged out.

Efforts to manage bias using internal and external checks might be extremely political. This leads us to the role and job description of the project risk manager and his or her personal qualities and traits.

Leadership Role of Risk Managers

It would be an understatement to say that the leadership role of the project risk manager is important. What are the characteristics of leadership in a good risk manager? Here are five of them:

1. Independence
2. Confidence based on knowledge of risk management and psychology
3. Value proposition
4. Out-of-box (or no-box) thinking
5. Training and coaching skills

Let's review these in more detail.

Some project managers select risk managers that do not have independent opinions. Is it unusual for project risk managers to be part-timers who just started learning risk management few weeks ago? Those convenient nice-guys have low, zero, or negative value for projects, but they do not irritate management with independent viewpoints. Well, what could be more important than peace of mind for a project manager or business-unit manager? The obvious answer is that project success is of higher importance.

A key discrepancy here is the direct reporting of a risk manager to a project manager versus the need for "balance of power," "counterweights," "separation of powers," or whatever political terms you care to name. Dotted-line reporting to corporate risk management (if it is adequate) could be a solution. However, if a risk manager is independent and confident enough and represents real value not only for a project and an organization but for the industry at large, he or she should be ready to leave a project where risk management is not adequately supported. This type of positioning expressed even implicitly usually settles things down. But this is the last line of defense. More important is the ability to deliver added value.

The second major trait of a good risk manager is confidence based on deep understanding of risk management principles and psychological aspects, including biases. There should be a certain degree of technical leadership in development or adaptation of new risk methods. Technical leadership combined with understanding of psychology accentuates the requirement to have high regular and emotional IQs.[5]

Full integration of a risk manager into all project activities according to the 3D picture of risk management (Figure 2.1) is often not that easy. Personality and ego clashes are not unusual. A good risk manager should be able to recognize and manage manifestations of the main types of psychological complexes, including complexes of God, Hero, Napoleon, Ego, Superiority, Martyr, Inferiority, Guilt, and so on. Discovering and managing various manifestations of these complexes adds a lot of fun and furor to the lives of risk managers.

What is the most efficient way to overcome all these obstacles and get risk management integrated within the rest of the project? The short answer is the *value proposition*. This suggests the third major trait of a good risk manager. He or she should provide added value. The famous but loaded WIIFM question ("What's in it for me?") should be the key one a good risk manager answers for his or her co-workers every day.

The fourth important trait is out-of-box thinking. A risk manager should have a fairly high personal IQ. A good risk manager should be able to see interdependencies and logical links among possible causes, events, and impacts, even when most other people do not see them. As I mentioned earlier, I have a reservation about that *thinking out-of-the-box* buzzword. Working in science one assumes that there is to be no *in-box* thinking at all, because that is tantamount to "no thinking." (Otherwise, one would not be qualified for the job.) So, I would prefer "no in-box thinking" as part of a good risk manager's job description.

The fifth important trait of a good risk manager relates to training and coaching skills. This is a fairly obvious trait. A risk manager should be able to show the value of risk methods, ensuring their adequate implementation through building a *risk management culture* based on the four previous traits. Lack of independence, confidence, value proposition, or independent thinking should make this trait unnecessary or its lack even a positive thing: one should not expect that risk training and coaching would be based on or promote dependency, lack of confidence, no value, and narrow minded thinking,

A project risk manager should project credible leadership in order to establish an effective project risk management system integrated with all project disciplines. Real added value and a positive impact on project performance are the criteria of his or her success.

 ## CONCLUSION

The anecdote in "Incredible Leadership and Unbelievable Risk Addressing" could serve as the acid test of any leadership, including leadership in project and risk management.

INCREDIBLE LEADERSHIP AND UNBELIEVABLE RISK ADDRESSING

This anecdote was relayed to me by my old friend who used to work for the Russian Space Agency.

Soviet leader Leonid Brezhnev was personally challenged by the fact that NASA had successfully sent people to the moon. He called for his cosmonauts and ordered, "We need to beat the Americans! To do this, you men are ordered to fly to the sun!" After a moment of speechless silence, one of the cosmonauts dared to ask, "How would this be possible, Comrade Brezhnev? We will get burned up!" His answer revealed his *incredible* leadership and *unbelievable* risk addressing skills: "We took this into account—you guys will be flying at night!"

 ## NOTES

1. Project Management, *PMBOK Guide* (Newtown Square, PA Project Management Institute, 2004).
2. A project team may define both thresholds if it wishes, which will increase the number of impact ranges to seven(!) and produce a 5 × 7 RAM. So, just one extra threshold for game changers should suffice.

3. It would be easy to define Cost and Schedule show-stoppers and game changers mathematically if we did include them in Monte Carlo models. Using "reverse mathematics," any uncertain event that may lead to reduction of the baseline's confidence level to, say, 1% (P1) or lower would be declared a game changer or show-stopper. Corresponding Cost or Schedule impact thresholds could also be derived.
4. C. Chapman and S. Ward, *Project Risk Management: Processes, Techniques and Insights* (Chichester, UK: John Wiley & Sons, 2003).
5. D. Goleman, *Working with Emotional Intelligence* (New York: Bantam Books, 1998).

CHAPTER EIGHT

Risk Management Tools

Questions Addressed in Chapter 8

- Why should the structure of a project uncertainty repository be based on three dimensions of risk management?
- What commercial software packages are available for risk database management?
- How could automation make making errors more efficient?
- Why should the tail stop wagging the dog?
- Why is MS Excel still the best risk management software package?
- What is a detail specification for a do-it-yourself risk register?
- Why should we use commercial probabilistic Monte Carlo tools? ◼

THIS CHAPTER EXAMINES REQUIREMENTS and specifications to select or develop adequate risk management tools. Unfortunately, the available software packages force project teams to use risk management tools that support specific realizations of risk management systems as they are understood by their producers. Hence, the number of risk management systems supported by corresponding tools is equal to the number of producers. Each producer is heavily involved in sales and marketing activities to promote its own version of a risk management system as the only right one. Due to the general immaturity of risk management as a discipline, many project teams and organizations fall prey to these sales and marketing activities.

This chapter describes general requirements from early-introduced organizational context and risk management process. This is an attempt to preclude situations where sales and marketing define both. A generic uncertainty repository template is introduced that may be adopted by any project team.

THREE DIMENSIONS OF RISK MANAGEMENT AND STRUCTURE OF THE UNCERTAINTY REPOSITORY

An initial discussion on the structure of an uncertainty repository appears in Chapter 2. The repository should be organized as several logs, inventories, and registers to reflect the three dimensions of risk management (Figure 2.1) and in accordance with the other two components of the risk management system (the organizational framework and the process). This should reflect several key points, including:

- What does the project do in general (its scope, components, packages, etc.)?
- What are the project's stated objectives used in risk management?
- What are the main sources of uncertainties (risk breakdown structure)?
- What types of uncertainties does it manage ("objects" of Table 1.2)?
- How are the risks managed (the process and status of risks and action in various steps of the process)?
- What responsibilities do team members have in risk management (risk, action, risk category, and so on, ownership)?
- What is the level of integration of risk management with the other project disciplines, with package and business-unit risk management, and with risk systems of customers, partners, stakeholders, subcontractors, and so on (three dimensions of organizational context)?

This sounds very scientific. To keep it simple, Figure 8.1 represents a possible structure of the uncertainty repository and a hierarchy of uncertainty logs, inventories, and registers in full accordance with Figure 2.1. The *in-depth* dimension is not reflected explicitly in Figure 8.1 but could be added if required. Usually it is done by creating so-called *internal project risk registers* that collect uncertainties related to partners, investors, contractors, external stakeholders,

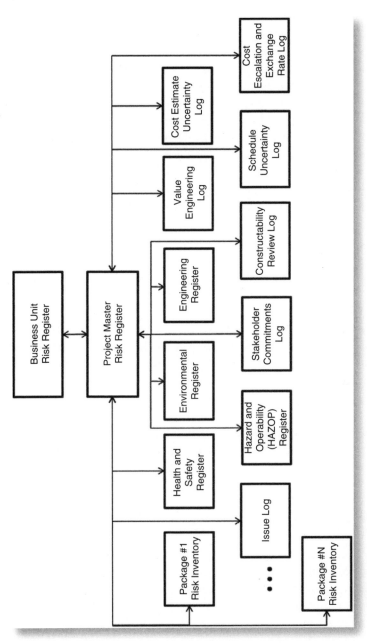

FIGURE 8.1 Sample Project Uncertainty Repository

and so on. Being highly confidential and sensitive documents, these are never shared with the other parties. Internal project risk registers feed business-unit risk registers. Elements of the advanced risk breakdown structure should be used as attributes of the risk database to slice-and-dice the repository information related to all three dimensions.

Depending on the contracting strategy, a capital mega-project may have several-dozen work packages. Some small and standard work packages don't require risk management and risk inventory development. The majority of them should be subject to risk management, though, which requires development of package risk inventories (see Chapter 10). One of the mega-projects I worked on recently contained about two dozen work-package inventories that were owned by small work-package development teams.

A health and safety (H&S) risk register should be part of the repository, too, but not part of the project master risk register. The H&S risk register may easily contain dozens and dozens of hazards. It seems to be reasonable to understand them as causes of project risks that may lead to impacts on project objectives. The key point here is that any of those risks may lead to an impact not only on the Safety objective but on Reputation, Schedule, and so on. For this reason we will not talk about safety, schedule, or reputation risks at all, which sounds like a lot of risk jargon. Instead, we will discuss risks of impacts on the Safety, Schedule, and Reputation objectives. As discussed in Chapter 5, conversion of H&S hazards into project risks is not straightforward.

I was the risk manager for a several-billion-dollar power generation mega-project a while ago. Corporate risk people came up with an initiative to automate a link between H&S and the project master risk register. They believed there would be great value in this. Despite my opposition to this low-value exercise it was implemented as a pilot. The result was a complete disaster as dozens of H&S hazards clogged up the previously neat master risk register. The link (mapping) between the two registers was not stable and generated unpredictable results every time we accessed the database. Everyone was happy when the pilot was scrapped.

We did include H&S-related risks in the master risk register and they were part of our monthly reporting. The key issue here is that this was done manually using analytical skills, and not automation. Multiple H&S hazards were rolled up intelligently to a few groups at a higher level and placed into the master risk register. The discussion regarding the first vending machines in Chapter 2 describes an almost-ideal automation solution for grouping and rolling up risks from lower levels and promoting them to higher levels of the repository. No need for blind automation just for the sake of automation!

Several logs should be maintained in the course of the base estimate and schedule development. For instance, general uncertainties of base estimate cost accounts and the schedule's normal durations are best understood by project estimators and schedulers and should be kept by them in corresponding logs.

It is very important to keep track of all commitments and promises made to project stakeholders in the course of project development and execution. I witnessed a situation where a midsized Canadian exploration and production company was purchased by the multinational oil and gas major I worked for at that time. Due to high turnover of employees following the acquisition, no records of previous commitments made by the company to local communities were kept. This became a major risk that impacted reputation and relationships with local communities and First Nations groups.

Value engineering and constructability reviews are a common source of project opportunities to reduce capital costs and accelerate schedules. The review records should be included in the repository. Engineering, HAZOP, environmental, project execution through risk addressing (PETRA), and stakeholder reviews should not be ignored by project risk management and should be included in the repository, too.

 ## RISK DATABASE SOFTWARE PACKAGES

All these files should be kept in web-based database applications. This would support multiuser access, which is especially important when project team members work in different locations. This also avoids problems with multiple versions of registers and logs when using MS Excel–based registers. Some of the logs in Figure 8.1 could be kept as MS Excel files. There is no need for overshooting and pushing all disciplines into using one tool or nothing. Moreover, for small or midsized projects that have all workers in one location, the Excel-based registers would be adequate.

Among the commercial web-based software packages, I would point out EasyRisk by DNV and Stature by Dyadem. These have database structures adequate for maintaining project master registers. Stature has several other applications including failure mode and effect analysis (FMEA) and HAZOP templates. The question with Stature is what kind of template should be developed to keep a risk register fully supporting the risk management process and organizational framework. My recommendation is that a risk register template in MS Excel should be developed and tried for several months before getting formalized in Stature. This should ensure that all organizational framework and risk process requirements are met and all organizational biases are averaged out.

EasyRisk has a very advanced risk reporting module that allows plotting risk data using several graphic output templates. It also has advanced risk breakdown structure (RBS) capability that allows one to slice-and-dice risk data for reporting purposes and consolidate them at the work-package, project, business-unit, or corporate level. Although far from ideal, this is the most adequate risk database software package available on the market (according to my biased opinion).

Besides EasyRisk and Stature, the PertMaster software package could be used for maintaining project master registers. The latter is mostly used for schedule risk analysis, though, due to its high price.[1] However, a common issue with all existing commercial tools is that they do not allow creation of uncertainty repositories as introduced in Figure 8.1, not to mention their complete lack of PETRA support (Figure 5.4). In addition, those tools do not have the functionality to support engineering design and procurement option selection, as discussed in Chapters 9 and 10. As a result (and according to my biased opinion), MS Excel is still the best risk management software package for keeping risk registers.

A general pitfall for project teams is too much focus on selection of risk database software tools, and not enough focus on risk process and organizational framework. Selection of the correct risk register tool is somewhat important. However, this should be established as priority #3 after the development and implementation of an adequate organizational framework (priority #1) and risk management process (priority #2). The ISO 31000 standard,[2] devoted to risk management, covers only the risk management process and the framework; risk tools are not even mentioned. They are merely supposed to effectively support the risk process and the framework.

Table 8.1 presents some general must-have and nice-to-have features and functionalities of a risk register database to support the risk process and the organizational framework described. Too many requirements or over-integration with some other risk tools (@Risk, PertMaster, Crystal Ball, etc.) may yield zero or negative value.

Keep in mind that a well-developed MS Excel–based risk register template would ensure much greater value to a project than would a commercial web-based application that does not support the risk process and the organizational framework. Moreover, the standard data management systems that many companies have in place could be used to keep the project uncertainty repository and, hence, provide access to multiple users. If required, only the latest version of documents could be visible.

TABLE 8.1 General Specifications of a Risk Register Software Package

Feature/Functionality	Purpose	Note
Web-based database	Access from multiple locations.	Assumes secured access.
Multiuser functionality	Simultaneous access for several users.	This assures that one version of a risk register exists.
Use of RBS	Introduction of major sources of risks.	RBS should be utilized for portfolio management to include several projects.
Assessment of impacts on several project objectives	Both hard (Scope, Cost, Schedule) and soft (Reputation, Safety, Environment) objectives should be in focus.	Including only traditional hard objectives is not enough and may lead to overlooking important parts of project risk exposure. Ability to manage upside uncertainties should be included.
Use of project risk assessment matrix (RAM)	Introduction of project RAM as a dropdown menu to assess impacts on multiple objectives and probabilities.	May include development of project-specific RAMs for each project in portfolio.
Various access levels	Access to defined areas of the repository (based on RBS) and various rights (read, read and write, custodian).	Important for confidentiality and tracking purposes, based on job descriptions of project team members and their roles and responsibilities in risk management.
Uncertainty and action ownership, action start and completion dates, types of addressing action, status of uncertainties and actions	To enforce responsibility of uncertainty and action owners to manage risks.	These fields are basis for action tracking.
Action tracking functionality	To enforce responsibility of action owners to address risks.	May include email alerts or alarm marks in risk reports.
Support of three-part naming	Specific definition and understanding of uncertainties.	This might not require specific functionality such as three separate windows for causes, events, and impacts, as the three-part naming may be written as a sentence in uncertainty description window.

(Continued)

TABLE 8.1 (*Continued*)

Feature/Functionality	Purpose	Note
Customization and flexibility	Amendment of input and output templates to accommodate specific requirements.	Tailor-made templates may be required for selection engineering design and procurement options (Chapters 9, 10) and PETRA.
Helpdesk support	To provide quick support with assignment of access rights to new users, briefing and training on functionality, etc.	If effective support is not provided, project teams tend to use MS Excel–based risk registers.
Exportation of data	Utilization of data from risk register in various applications including probabilistic Cost and Schedule risk analysis.	Integration of the risk register database with some other tools (@Risk, PertMaster, Crystal Ball, etc.) is not required. However, smooth output through MS Excel is a minimum requirement. Importation to the risk database is not usually considered important.
Reporting	Availability of visual and statistics reporting features based on RBS categories, project objectives, uncertainty/action owners, severity of uncertainties, etc.	This is important to support both risk process and framework including risk escalation and communications, responsibilities, etc. Reporting features should be flexible enough to accommodate data slice-and-dice requirements of project leadership and decision makers.

DETAILED DESIGN OF A RISK REGISTER TEMPLATE IN MS EXCEL

As discussed earlier, it would be beneficial to develop all components of the risk repository using MS Excel. The transition of adopted MS Excel templates to a suitable commercial application may be done later, if at all.

Figure 5.3 introduced a conceptual template for a project risk log, inventory, or register. Of course, this does not reflect the requirements for more specialized types of analyses such as process hazard analysis (PHA), HAZOP, and so on as those are outside the scope of this book. But the rest of the repository components described in Figure 8.1 may be based on the concept of Figure 5.3. If not, a tailor-made template could be used when required in MS Excel.

To be prudent the template of Figure 5.3 was introduced as conceptual. I believe though that this contains a minimal required set of fields that should not be increased or reduced. If even one of the fields is lost, the template may lose a significant piece of information. If any other fields are added, this should not yield much additional value. But, of course, this opinion is biased and may be ignored if there are reasons to think differently. I suggest using this template for most of the logs and registers of a project repository. I also believe that this template is much better and more consistent than all existing commercial software packages developed for risk databases. It would be interesting to discuss the development of this template as a part of a risk software package with representatives of corresponding IT companies. In any case, it takes into account all aspects of deterministic (scoring) risk management discussed in this book so far.

The purpose of this section is to provide a detailed description of the fields included in the template of Figure 5.3 when it is developed in MS Excel. Table 8.2 provides the required information for all fields of the template. Table 8.2 and Figure 5.3 could be used as do-it-yourself instructions for building simple and effective risk registers.

Table 8.2 looks quite detailed. However, any risk analyst who is at least a basic MS Excel user can develop the required risk register template according to the specifications of Table 8.2 in two hours or less.

COMMERCIAL TOOLS FOR PROBABILISTIC RISK ANALYSES

Earlier in this chapter I was skeptical about the need to use commercially available software packages for developing and maintaining uncertainty repository databases. Such fully adequate uncertainty repository tools do not yet exist. The situation is different for probabilistic applications. Virtually nothing can be done without a specialized probabilistic tool when developing project cost and schedule reserves unless some of the archaic methods described in Chapter 3 are used. Descriptions of the three probabilistic software packages I am intimately familiar with are provided in this section. Some users might like other probabilistic tools better, although they might not yet be as popular as the three that I mention here. In addition, a promising new tool is introduced at the end of this section.

TABLE 8.2 Specifications of the MS Excel–Based Risk Register Template

Group of Parameters	Field	Description	MS Excel Functionality	Standard Values
Definition	ID	Identification number according to rules adopted by a project.	Text or number.	1,2,3 etc. or combination of letters and digits.
	Upside or Downside?	Known deviations from project objectives according to Table 1.2, Figure 1.2. Both upside and downside deviations are possible for general uncertainties but issues/givens	Dropdown menu using "Data/Data Validation/ Setting/List" functionality.	US; DS; US and DS.
	General Uncertainty or Uncertain Event?	Known general uncertainty (impact uncertainty) vs. uncertain event (impact and probability uncertainty) according to Table 1.2, Figure 1.2.	Dropdown menu using "Data/Data Validation/ Setting/List" functionality.	GU; UE.
	Title	Short name/tag of uncertainty (2 or 3 words max.).	Text	N/A
	Three-Part Definition	Detailed three-part definition cause(s)–events–impact(s) for uncertain event and cause(s)–impact(s) for general uncertainties.	Text	N/A
	Comments	Any comment related to definition of an uncertainty, including description of show-stopper, game changer, or broiler black swan where applicable.	Text	N/A

Status	Status	Status of uncertainty according to risk management process (Figure 2.2).	Dropdown menu using "Data/Data Validation/Setting/List" functionality.	Proposed; Proposed Closed; Approved; In Progress; Accepted; Closed.
	Owner	Name of an individual accompanied by position and organization (not just position or name of organization).	Could be set up as dropdown menu using "Data/Data Validation/Setting/List" functionality.	List of names.
	RBS Category	RBS category from the list adopted by the project.	Dropdown menu using "Data/Data Validation/Setting/List" functionality.	Engineering, Procurement, Construction, Commissioning and Startup, Operations, Regulatory, Stakeholders, Commercial, Partner(s), Interface Management, Change Management, Organizational.
Assessment As-Is	Level/Severity	Score equal to product of probability and top impact score before addressing.	1. Formula Max (P × I1, P × I2, P × I3, P × I4, P × I5, P × I6), where P is probability score of an uncertainty; I1, I2,…, I6 are impact scores for six selected project objectives (RAM of Figure 3.2). 2. "Conditional Formatting/Highlight Cells Rules/Between" functionality according to Table 5.1.	0, 1, 2, 3, … 20, 25 Red, yellow, or green color of the cell depending on severity/level score.

(Continued)

TABLE 8.2 *(Continued)*

Group of Parameters	Field	Description	MS Excel Functionality	Standard Values
	Probability	Score representing assessment of probability of uncertainty before addressing using project RAM (Figure 3.2).	Dropdown menu using "Data/Data Validation/ Setting/List" functionality.	0,1,2,3,4,5 Score 5 for general uncertainty.
	Cost, Schedule, Product Quality, Safety, Environment, Reputation	Score representing assessment of impact before addressing using RAM (Figure 3.2).	Dropdown menu using "Data/Data Validation/ Setting/List" functionality.	0,1,2,3,4,5, where 0 corresponds to N/A.
Addressing	Response Strategy	Points out one of five main strategies for downside uncertainties and one of five strategies for upside uncertainties.	Dropdown menu using "Data/Data Validation/ Setting/List" functionality.	For downside uncertainties: Avoid, Mitigate-Prevent, Mitigate-Recover, Transfer, Accept. For upside uncertainties: Exploit, Enhance-Magnify, Enhance-Amplify, Share, Take.
	Action	Description of action.	Text	N/A
	Cost of Action, $K	Amount to be spent to implement the action.	Number	N/A
	Start	Indicates planned start of addressing activities.	Date	N/A
	Completion Date	Indicates a deadline when addressing action should be complete.	Date	N/A
	Action Owner	Name of an individual accompanied by position and organization (not just position or name of organization).	Could be set up as dropdown menu using "Data/Data Validation/ Setting/List" functionality.	Text or list of names.

Action Status	Status of addressing action according to risk management process (Figure 2.2).	Dropdown menu using "Data/Data Validation/Setting/List" functionality.	Proposed; Proposed Closed; Approved; In Progress; Completed; Closed.
Comments	Any comment related to addressing and its progress.	Text	N/A
Assessment To-Be	Level/Severity	Score equal to product of probability and top impact score after addressing.	1. Formula Max (P × I1, P × I2, P × I3, P × I4, P × I5, P × I6), where P is probability score of an uncertainty; I1, I2,..., I6 are impact scores for six selected project objectives (RAM of Figure 3.2). 2. "Conditional Formatting/Highlight Cells Rules/Between" functionality according to Table 5.1.	0, 1,2,3, ... 20, 25 Red, yellow, or green color of the cell depending on severity/level score.
	Probability	Score representing assessment of probability of uncertainty after addressing using project RAM (Figure 3.2).	Dropdown menu using "Data/Data Validation/Setting/List" functionality.	0,1,2,3,4,5 Score 5 for general uncertainty.
	Cost, Schedule, Product Quality, Safety, Environment, Reputation	Score representing assessment of impact after addressing using RAM (Figure 3.2).	Dropdown menu using "Data/Data Validation/Setting/List" functionality.	0,1,2,3,4,5, where 0 corresponds to N/A.

Crystal Ball is an MS Excel–based tool that has all the major Monte Carlo simulation functionalities. Its interface is very user friendly and intuitive. It is affordably priced. Crystal Ball is used for cost risk analysis. It was not developed for schedule risk analyses. Currently it is produced by Oracle.

Another spreadsheet-based tool is @Risk by Palisade. This is quite a sophisticated Monte Carlo tool. It has advanced Monte Carlo functionalities. Its interface is more sophisticated and less intuitive than that of Crystal Ball. Due to the high level of sophistication, MS Excel files loaded with @Risk data could get very big (15 to 25 MB). This causes problems with sending them by email. Otherwise, this is a very adequate cost risk analysis tool for advanced users. There is an @Risk for Projects module that allows carrying out schedule risk analyses using MS Project as a scheduling tool. I have not yet heard anything about applications of MS Project for capital mega-projects; @Risk for Projects doesn't seem to be terribly popular at the moment.

Both Crystal Ball and @Risk can be used in engineering for high-level integration of a system's components to identify and manage all possible performance bottlenecks. This topic is outside the scope of this book.

Another risk software package is Primavera Risk Analysis by Oracle, which had a different name (PertMaster) before its acquisition by Oracle. (Risk practitioners still call it PertMaster.) This seems to be the most sophisticated and adequate project risk analysis tool on the market that integrates deterministic (scoring) and probabilistic (Monte Carlo) methods. It has a risk register module that could be used for deterministic and probabilistic assessments of risks, but it does not support the variety of logs of the uncertainty repository introduced in Figure 5.3 supporting just a generic template. It enables building integrated cost and schedule risk models using its risk register module. Its functionality includes mapping of schedule risks to normal activities as well as resource-loaded schedule risk modeling. It has a seamless interface with the Primavera scheduling tool, which allows easy uploading of *.xer files from Primavera. This is the tool of choice for schedule risk analysis. However, it is not widely used for cost risk analysis or keeping risk registers. There are two reasons for this.

First, estimators use MS Excel and understand only the corresponding spreadsheet-based tools such as Crystal Ball and @Risk. The usual practice is that schedule risk data are retrieved from PertMaster and uploaded to Crystal Ball or @Risk to take into account schedule-driven costs (see Chapter 12). This is the current way to merge the estimating and scheduling worlds in project risk management practice. However, cost and schedule risk analyses are often done separately. It would be fair to mention that two traditional project services/controls disciplines—estimating/cost control and planning/scheduling—have an influence on the methods and tools used by project risk management. Representatives of those disciplines often become new risk managers. Due to tradition, or the lack of knowledge of advanced (probabilistic) methods on the part of some representatives of these disciplines, some outdated deterministic methods and tools discussed in Chapter 3 are still widely used in risk management instead of the more modern and adequate probabilistic methods.

Another obstacle to PertMaster becoming the only mass-market tool required for project cost and schedule risk analyses is its high price.

The recently developed Acumen Risk software package is an obvious attempt to minimize the shortcomings of PertMaster and compete with it. This new software package is positioned as a tool that does not require knowledge of statistics; hence, it has the potential to become a mass-market product. This positioning seems slightly deceptive as some mandatory functionalities of Pert-Master that do require some knowledge of statistics are missing. Lack of the functionality to take correlations into account is a fundamental issue with the current version of Acumen Risk. Additional discussion on this can be found in Chapters 12 and 13.

We discuss the required integration of deterministic (scoring) methods with probabilistic tools in Part III of this book. This integration does not presume integration of software packages, though. We instead discuss required inputs and their specs.

CONCLUSION

This chapter provides an overview of the software packages that could be used in risk management. This is a "cart" (tools) that is often put before "two horses" (organizational framework and process of risk management). Ideally, the cart should be put back in its place by using simple MS Excel–based risk register templates.

Probabilistic tools may be allowed to stay before the two horses for the purpose of probabilistic analyses and development of project reserves. But this is justifiable only when those two horses have already delivered the cart (a.k.a. the probabilistic tools) in to the correct location.

NOTES

1. The recent introduction to the market of Acumen Risk software is a good next step in support of risk register functionality with probabilistic capability, although it requires thorough testing. It looks like this tool has a different shortcoming related to lack of functionality to take correlations into account in probabilistic models.
2. ISO 31000 International Standard: *Risk Management: Principles and Guidelines* (Switzerland: International Organization for Standardization, 2009).

CHAPTER NINE

Risk-Based Selection of Engineering Design Options

Questions Addressed in Chapter 9

- Why is risk-based selection of options better than and preferable to risk management of a given option?
- How may a standard risk management methodology help engineers?
- What kind of template can be used for engineering design option selection?
- What is a controlled option selection decision tree and how might it help when there are numerous options? ■

THE TRADITIONAL SITUATION IN risk management is that project teams define baselines first and then investigate given project risk exposure. The usual logic is that project objectives and baselines are developed and all major project choices and decisions are made first by corresponding functions such as engineering, procurement, construction, and so on. Risk management steps in to manage given uncertainties that are predetermined by the preceding choices and decisions. It is certainly not proactive, but it is a common methodology. It is more reasonable to start using risk management methods at an earlier stage when options are being contemplated and selected. This is the most efficient way to control uncertainty changers.

Only project options with minimal risk exposure should be selected in the first place. This risk-based informed decision making is ideally applicable to options at both the work-package and project levels and beyond. Any decision made by a project, business unit, or corporation should ideally be informed risk-based. This should include the change management methodology at various levels of an organization, too.

As decision making at the business-unit and corporate levels is not within the scope of this book, this chapter and the following chapter are devoted to the proactive approach in selection of options at the work-package level.

CRITERIA FOR ENGINEERING DESIGN OPTION SELECTION

Engineers of a power generation mega-project I worked for had several technical challenges to selecting the most optimal engineering design options in several areas. One exacerbating issue was that there was interference from the project owner's representatives in the process. Those representatives did not have enough hands-on engineering experience to make informed engineering decisions, but they insisted on the cheapest options in every particular case. Debates related to several engineering studies continued for several months. Eventually, I decided to step in and help out. Five risk-based engineering studies were initiated and finalized in few weeks. All selection decisions were made, documented, and approved by the project owner. The corresponding work packages were on the street soon after. That was a remarkable achievement.

One $100 million decision was related to the selection of a major type of equipment. It will be used to introduce option selection methodology in this chapter. Another, smaller $10–$15 million decision related to reliability and maintainability of an electric transmission line in a particular geographic area depending on features of design and operations. This study should help us introduce decision tree analysis principles for controlled options, initially introduced in Chapter 3.

This method is based on the idea that each project objective imposes restrictions and constraints on the others. This allows one to consider all objectives as equal by default. For instance, using both CapEx and OpEx as equals allows one to consolidate the opinions of project and operations people while considering project lifecycle cost. Keeping in mind Reputation, Safety, and Environment objectives preclude options that are not acceptable from the reputational, safety, or environmental angles.

Criteria for engineering design option selection coincide with the project objectives selected for project risk management. These are all discussed in the first three chapters. For the studies mentioned earlier, they are:

- Cost: CapEx + present value (PV) of OpEx
- Schedule
- Quality
- Safety
- Environment
- Reputation

An additional point here is that according to the bowtie diagram (Figure 4.2), causes of uncertainties, uncertain events, and impacts might belong to different phases of project development. For instance, if engineering design option decisions are made in Select or Define (causes), associated uncertain events and general uncertainties make impacts on objectives in Execute or Operate.

Both option baselines and overall uncertainty exposures are option differentiators used for decision making. It is important to clearly define the scope of the study. Any part of a project that is not impacted by the option selection should be left out. In some cases the initially defined study scope should be expanded in the course of the study's progress because some parts of the project that were believed to be unchanging should be included due to identification of additional differentiators. Often these are newly identified uncertainties that should play a role as option differentiators.

The method discussed here is referred to as *controlled options selection* in Chapter 3. This implies that all options shortlisted for analysis should be well defined baseline-wise. Potentially any of them could be selected; this is not a roll of the dice. This should involve a diligent review of option baselines and overall risk exposures. Where options have additional sub-options (branching) with variations, especially in Operate, consideration of the corresponding decision trees should help. The decision tree samples are discussed in the final section of this chapter.

 ## SCORING RISK METHOD FOR ENGINEERING DESIGN OPTION SELECTION

There were three main options in selecting the major type of equipment mentioned earlier (no branching). In the transmission line study, there was branching that led to the development of a *controlled options decision tree*. This is discussed in the next section.

In the first step, project engineers, estimators, and schedulers developed baselines for three shortlisted options. Those options were selected taking into account preliminary feasibility studies as well as preferences expressed by a project owner.

In the second step, three Delphi technique risk identification workshops were held to identify uncertainties associated with each option. Needless to say, the majority of identified uncertainties were the same for all three options. However, some of them were unique and relevant only to one or two options. More than a dozen uncertainties were identified for the three options. Most of them were uncertain events.

In the third step, after validation of identified uncertainties another workshop was held to assess uncertainties before addressing. A risk assessment matrix (RAM) similar to the one introduced in Chapter 3 (Figure 3.2) was used. Only addressing measures in place and already included in the baselines were considered. No additional addressing was included in the assessment as-is. Some uncertainties that were relevant to two or three options had different assessments of probabilities and/or impacts. However, some had the same ones.

In the fourth step, after validation of the assessments as-is for all three options, addressing actions were developed for all identified uncertainties. Costs of addressing were assessed, too. When addressing was supposed to be applicable in Operate a model of OpEx was developed for project lifecycle (50 years). Corresponding annual OpEx expenses were rolled up to a base period (present value) using the agreed discount of about 7%. This allowed apples-to-apples comparison of OpEx and CapEx costs in dollars of the base period and evaluation of lifetime total costs for each option. Obviously, addressing actions were aimed at both cost and non-cost impacts (such as impacts on Safety, Schedule, and so on), although costs of addressing were obviously measured in dollars in both cases.

In the fifth step, after validation of proposed addressing actions to-be, assessments of all uncertainties were undertaken. This step as well as the previous one led to very intensive discussions and revealed several types of bias. For instance, representatives of the project owner tried to play down assessments of uncertainties and costs of their addressing for their favorite least expensive option. However, close monitoring of group dynamics and awareness of participants regarding bias helped to settle things down and produce relatively objective assessments. In addition, the structure of the discussion helped to compartmentalize topics and narrow them down to very specific technical tasks. That left little room for bias.

Assessment of uncertainties after addressing was eventually reduced to one uncertain event. The rest of the uncertainties were believed to be reduced to low (green) levels (Table 5.1) after application of all proposed addressing actions. Costs of those actions were added to the corresponding option's base estimates. While all uncertainties reduced to a low level were excluded from further consideration as differentiators, the costs of their addressing became differentiators instead. This approach assumes that low/small uncertainties have negligible and acceptable residual uncertainty exposures. This allows one to avoid making residual cost risk exposure assessments, which is in line with the overall precision of the methodology.

Figure 9.1 represents a simplified decision-making template that allows one to make an engineering option selection. This shows only one most critical uncertain event as a differentiator for three options. The only difference between this template and the register template of Figure 5.3 is that one uncertainty is assessed against each of the three shortlisted options. The template does not contain specific information about this particular risk and its addressing actions due to confidentiality. The specifics were replaced by "to be developed (TBD)."

According to Figure 9.1, Option 1 did not have economically viable addressing actions. Preliminary assessment pointed to the need for tens of millions of dollars to be spent in Operate to reduce the risk to a low level. Even though that option was actively promoted by the project owner as least expensive CapEx-wise, it was disqualified from further consideration.

Option 2 had a low risk level all along. If money were not a constraint, this would be the best choice. However, the problem with this option was that this was the most expensive one.

Option 3 had a material/medium level of risk exposure before addressing. However, two addressing actions were proposed that should reduce its uncertainty exposure to a low level. The cost of those actions was assessed at about $3.2 million. This included costs to be incurred in Engineering (CapEx) and Operations (OpEx). Comparison of Option 2 with Option 3 allowed us to select Option 3 as most preferable.

Figure 9.2 is a summary template used for decision making. Only cost of addressing of the most critical uncertain event ($3.2 million in case of Option 3) discussed earlier is included for demonstration and simplicity purposes. In reality, the other addressing costs did not lead to a different decision.

All assessments of uncertainties were done deterministically using the scoring method and RAM (Figure 3.2). All estimates of addressing action costs were done deterministically, too. Technically, all deterministic

FIGURE 9.1 Sample Template for Engineering Design Option Selection

	DEFINITION					ATTRIBUTES				ASSESSMENT AS-IS								ADDRESSING								ASSESSMENT TO-BE							
ID	Upside or Downside?	General Uncertainty or Uncertain Event?	Title	Three-Part Definition	Comments	Status	Owner	RBS Category	Option Description	Level/Severity	Probability	Cost	Schedule	Product Quality	Safety	Environment	Reputation	Response Strategy	Action(s)	Cost of Action, K$	Start	Completion Date	Action Owner	Action Status	Comments	Level/Severity	Probability	Cost	Schedule	Product Quality	Safety	Environment	Reputation
1	D	UE	TBD	TBD	TBD	Approved	TBD	Engineering	OPTION 1	16	4	4	3	3	3	0	3	Accept	No economically viable actions available	N/A	N/A	N/A	N/A	N/A	As no actions are developed the risk is accepted	16	4	4	3	3	3	0	3
									OPTION 2	2	1	0	2	0	0	0	0	Accept	Level of overall risk exposure is low as-is; no addressing required	0	N/A	N/A	N/A	N/A	As no actions are required the risk is accepted	2	1	0	2	0	0	0	0
									OPTION 3	9	3	3	2	2	3	0	3	Mitigate-Prevent	TBD	1,500	TBD	TBD	TBD	Approved	Actions relates to Engineering	4	2	2	2	2	2	0	2
																		Mitigate-Recover	TBD	2,700	TBD	TBD	TBD	Approved	Actions relates to Operations, lifecycle OpEx cost developed and rolled up as PV@7%								

	OPTION 1	OPTION 2	OPTION 3
Baseline lifecycle comparative cost	$90,000,000	$115,000,000	$100,000,000
Score risk assessment before addressing	16	2	9
Cost of risk addressing, $	N/A	0	3,200,000
Score risk assessment after addressing	16	2	4
Option is acceptable after addressing or not?	No: Disqualified	Yes	Yes
Option's lifecycle budget	$90,000,000	$115,000,000	$103,200,000
Decision	Disqualified	Rejected as too expensive	Most Preferable

FIGURE 9.2 Decision-Making Template

assessments of both risks and addressing actions could be done probabilistically if really required. Ranges around base estimates could be discussed. Uncertainties of impacts and probabilities could be discussed and introduced. Even the discounting factor used for developing PV of OpEx could be represented as a spread. This would be overshooting in most cases. However, in situations where the two most preferable options are close cost-wise, some additional probabilistic steps may be justified to accentuate the roles of some differentiators. However, finding more distinctive additional differentiators instead should be a better option.

Baseline cases for the study cited earlier were well defined and did not have branching in terms of sub-options. In some situations there could be sub-options based on the main ones. For instance, this would be the case for developing an oil or gas pipeline when there are options for some of its sections to use various rights of way. The example in the next section relates to developing and operating a transmission line in a certain geographical area.

DECISION TREE FOR ENGINEERING DESIGN OPTION SELECTION (CONTROLLED OPTIONS)

The example described in this section would be of particular interest to electrical engineers. Imagine that a transmission line crosses a strait between two Japanese islands. Two transition compounds should be designed and built to connect the underground cable with aerial transmission lines on both sides of the straight. A key decision factor for the transition compound location is distance to the shore. The reason for this is the saltwater spray effect, which impacts the reliability of electrical insulators.

Of course, a transition compound could be built several kilometers from the shoreline where the salt spray effect is negligible. Some studies indicate that locations that are three to five kilometers from shore would fully negate the saltwater spray effect. This would lead to very high costs for the underground cable, which makes such an approach too expensive. As an alternative, the electrical insulators in the vicinity of the transition compound and its bushings could be washed regularly, which would lead to an increase in operating costs. Another factor that must be taken into account is the acceptable level of reliability and availability of the transmission line, which is directly linked to Reputation of the transmission line owner. If a line were down, this would mean blackout for the whole island! The impact on sales revenue as part of OpEx and especially on owner's Reputation could be immense.

Three transition compound locations were initially studied: onshore, 900 meters away from the shore, and 1,800 meters away. These distances are defined like this due to the standard length of cable on one spool. Obviously, if two spools are used, a join between them is required and that is an additional CapEx expense. In the final study, only two options were considered: onshore and 900 meters from shore. However several sub-options were introduced for each of those relating to type and frequency of washing. Corresponding OpEx budgets were developed for the sub-options' lifecycles that took into account expected levels of availability (Quality) as well as sales revenues (OpEx). Those sub-options' OpEx budgets were rolled up to a base period as present values to be directly compared with the options' CapEx budgets. Sub-options' CapEx budgets included the purchasing of washing equipment where required.

In this study, the level of availability was directly linked to the Quality objective. It was also directly linked to the project Reputation objective. Any drop in availability was considered an impact on both OpEx (revenue) and Reputation. A risk assessment matrix (RAM) similar to the one in Figure 3.2 was used for risk assessments.

I will not further discuss the details of decision making but I would like to demonstrate a simplified decision tree used for option selection. Figure 9.3 introduces this.[1] Four nodes—1A, 1B, 2A, and 2B—represent four generic sub-options of two main options, although the number of options (nodes) in the real study was higher.

The method discussed in this chapter should be referred to as *controlled* option selection. Any option shortlisted for consideration could be selected after consistent comparison of the differentiators. Here, decision making is not a crapshoot. This is the first principal difference from the traditional decision tree cost analysis mentioned in Chapter 3, where "chance options" are reviewed

Parameter/ Factor	Option/ Node			
	1A	1B	2A	2B
CapEx	A	A	B	B
Lifetime PV of OpEx	C	D	E	F
Baseline Cost (CapEx + Lifetime PV of OpEx)	A+C	A+D	B+E	B+F
Top Risk Score Before Addressing	15	10	20	12
Cost of Addressing	G	H	I	J
Top Risk Score After Addressing	5	8	4	10
Is Option Acceptable After Addressing (Risk Score ≤5)?	yes	no	yes	no
Total Cost of Acceptable Option	A+C+G	n/a	B+E+I	n/a

Selection Criterion: MIN (A+C+G; B+E+I)

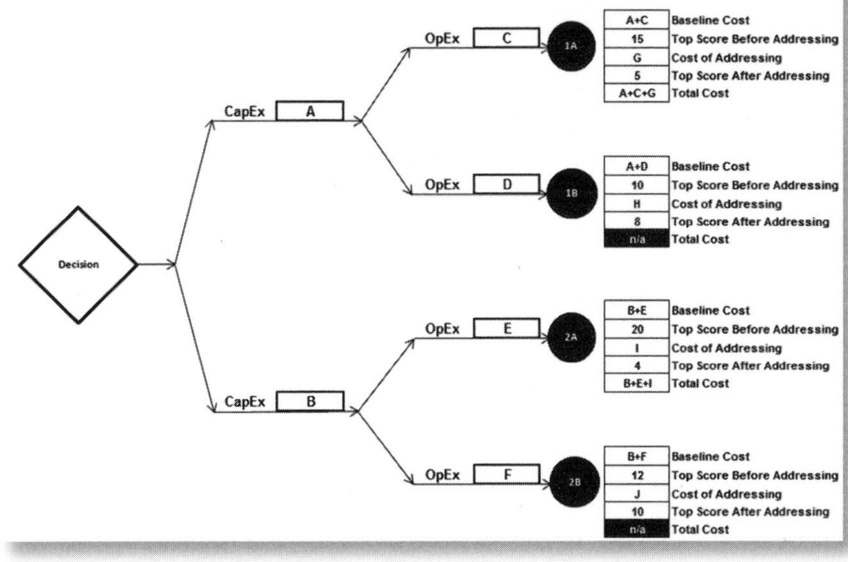

A+C	Baseline Cost
15	Top Score Before Addressing
G	Cost of Addressing
5	Top Score After Addressing
A+C+G	Total Cost

A+D	Baseline Cost
10	Top Score Before Addressing
H	Cost of Addressing
8	Top Score After Addressing
n/a	Total Cost

B+E	Baseline Cost
20	Top Score Before Addressing
I	Cost of Addressing
4	Top Score After Addressing
B+E+I	Total Cost

B+F	Baseline Cost
12	Top Score Before Addressing
J	Cost of Addressing
10	Top Score After Addressing
n/a	Total Cost

FIGURE 9.3 Controlled Options Decision Tree

Source: © IGI Global. Reprinted by permission of the publisher.

and each chance option has a probability of realization. The second principal difference is that only cost-related impacts are included in the traditional chance option tree analysis. The new method discussed here takes into account impacts on any project objectives, which makes it way more comprehensive and effective than traditional decision tree analysis.

One may guess that commercially available software packages are not suitable to support this method. The examples and MS Excel templates introduced in this chapter are the only viable solutions for the time being. It would be interesting to see what solutions might be developed by the corresponding IT companies to support this methodology.

CONCLUSION

The role of informed risk-based selection of engineering design options should not be underestimated. On one hand, no one is against informed risk-based selections. On the other hand, previously available methods had almost nothing to do with support of this declared approach. Methods proposed in this chapter are based on first principles of proactive risk management that allow one to shape baselines instead of merely identifying and managing deviations from given ones.

 ## NOTE

1. Y. Raydugin, "Consistent Application of Risk Management for Selection of Engineering Design Options in Mega-Projects," *International Journal of Risk and Contingency Management*, 1(4), 2012, 44–55.

CHAPTER TEN

Addressing Uncertainties through Procurement

Questions Addressed in Chapter 10

- How can we distinguish the contracts we should not touch from the ones we must win?
- Where do the uncertainties of procurement come from?
- What are three major groups of work-package risks?
- By what process do we manage risks in procurement?
- Why is risk-based selection of procurement options better than risk management of a given procurement option?
- How might a standard risk management methodology make procurement people's lives easier? ■

THIS CHAPTER IS DEVOTED to an overview of the applications of risk management in procurement. In some situations, a project or contract looks so attractive that a company jumps on it without diligent consideration. Then, its execution opens up a can of worms leading to huge impacts on the company's objectives.

For the most part, no one is interested in a contract that looks terribly risky. However, a company might be able to identify the key contract uncertainties and come up with smart and effective means of addressing them and this project or contract could become the most profitable one the company ever had.

Major steps of the procurement process are described in this chapter as related to risk management. There is a similarity in the risk methods used for selection of engineering design options[1] and selection of bidders. Their applications to procurement are outlined in this chapter. The *pre-award* part of the procurement process is the focus of this discussion. The application of the methodology presented in this chapter could be used by both project owners and engineering, procurement, and construction (EPC) contractors, and would require a bit of adjustment for every particular case. Ideally, cost escalation modeling (Chapter 11) should go along with this. The *post-award* part of the process is discussed at the end of the chapter.

SOURCES OF PROCUREMENT RISKS

The standard approach to project development and execution is that project scope is broken down into a number of engineering and construction packages. The role of procurement along with the other project disciplines is to ensure delivery of work packages according to project objectives. As discussed in previous chapters, a set of project objectives, besides Scope, includes Budget and Schedule as well as Safety, Environment, and Reputation. The main realization of this approach is based on the project's contracting strategy, which is part of the overall project execution strategy. The contracting strategy should be established as a *procurement baseline*, which is a combination of project objectives. Depending on its realism and consistency, its implementation might be characterized by some difficulties. In other words, some deviations from the assumed contracting strategy might occur. There are three groups of factors that may be treated as sources of deviations from the contracting strategy and project objectives. Using risk breakdown structure (RBS) terminology, the following sources of procurement risks may be defined:

- Package specific
- External
- Bidder specific

These three subcategories could be developed under the main Procurement category of the project risk breakdown structure.

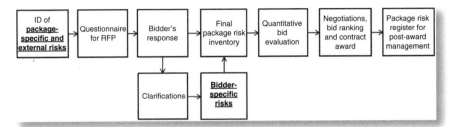

FIGURE 10.1 Simplified Bidding Process and Risk Management Prior to Contract Award

Figure 10.1 represents a simplified package bidding process from the risk management angle. Its steps will be explained in the following section.

Package-Specific Sources of Risks

The contracting strategy is supposed to provide the procurement baseline, which should address questions related to the work package such as:

- What should be the optimal size, scope, and schedule of the package?
- What interfaces should be managed due to selected size, scope, and schedule?
- What type of contract should be proposed and why?
- If applicable, how should technical novelty be handled?
- Are there severe or unusual safety hazards and how should they be managed?

Contracting strategy defines sizes of work packages that are believed to be optimal for a project versus types of contracts. This should comply with project schedule and budget, taking into account competition for vendor services. This may lead a project into cost escalation due to market forces, extra costs and delays due to lower contractor productivity, and so on. Proper sequencing of work should ensure timely delivery, especially if a work package belongs to critical path.

Assumed optimal sizes of work packages presume a number of soft and hard interfaces among the project disciplines and vendors.

For a technical novelty the contracting strategy should ensure that technology risks are properly addressed. Some construction work packages might involve unusual or severe safety hazards, which should be addressed by procurement, too.

For purposes of this discussion we treat a project-contracting strategy as a procurement baseline. There will be deviations from that baseline in the form of general uncertainties and uncertain events. All these uncertainties should be better identified beforehand (i.e., before a request for proposal [RFP] is on the street). Identified package-specific uncertainties should be collected in a *package risk inventory* (risk register). A two-hour Delphi technique workshop (discussed in Chapter 4) should be held to create the inventory. Identified risks should be reflected indirectly in the bidder's qualification questionnaire included in the RFP. Responses of bidders to the risk questionnaire will be used for bidder evaluations and ranking.

External Sources of Package Risks

External sources of package risks relate to the external environment of a project as well as to weather conditions or features of climate. These include:

- Various construction permits
- Related logistics issues where they are not part of the package scope, including delivery windows due to weather/climate constraints
- Weather at the construction site
- *Force majeure*
- Possibility of blockage of delivery routes and/or sites by protesters including representatives of a nongovernmental organization (NGO) and local communities that could delay the package execution

Some sources of the uncertainties just listed may be relevant to the delivery of a particular package. It would be prudent to know in advance how the bidder would handle various risks stemming from those external sources. External uncertainties should be added to the package risk inventory. Their identification should be part of the Delphi technique workshop held to identify package-specific risks. Corresponding questions should be also included in the RFP risk questionnaire.

Bidder-Specific Sources of Risks

When a bidder's RFP responses are received they should be evaluated against previously formulated package-specific and external questionnaires. The variety of responses to the risk questionnaires should become the basis for bidder rankings. Two additional sources of information may be also used to facilitate ranking.

First, assessments of the engineering, construction, safety, logistics, and other parts of the RFP responses could lead to identification of additional uncertainties. Second, clarification discussions with bidders may lead to either the addressing of previously identified risks or the identification of new ones. In both cases these could be considered bidder-specific risks that may be related to the following topics:

- Bidder's core competencies versus package size, scope, and schedule
- Availability of required skills and history of labor relations
- Workload forecast
- Concerns about quality assurance/quality control, technical capabilities, management efficiency, risk management, sub-vendors, financial stability, safety, and so on
- Lack of previous (or positive) experience with a bidder

Bidder-specific risks should be added to the package-specific and external uncertainty, forming the final package risk inventory. Although package-specific and external uncertainties could be the same for all bidders, the bidder-specific ones are unique by definition. In spite of this it is beneficial to develop a single final package risk inventory that will be used as common ground for the final quantitative evaluation of bidders. There is a simple key rule here: if a specific uncertainty is apparently relevant to at least one bidder, then the rest of the bidders should be evaluated against that uncertainty too.

QUANTITATIVE BID EVALUATION

As soon as the final package risk inventory is developed, quantitative bid evaluation is very similar to engineering design option selection. The main difference with engineering is that negotiations and clarifications are part of evaluations and may influence the contract award.

The structure of the risk register shown in Figure 9.1 could be used. The number of options should be equal to the number of shortlisted bidders prequalified for the bid using some standard procurement criteria. Addressing actions should be part of the risk register to develop and compare assessments before and after addressing.

Only uncertainties that could have impacts on the package owner's objectives are considered here. Bidders include risk premiums in their bid prices to manage the risks that are the result of risk brokering. Obviously, the amount of risk bidders assume depends on the type of contract. For lump-sum types of contracts, contractors assume most of the package risks. For reimbursable types of contracts, most of the risk exposure is kept by the package owner. A unit-price contract exposes the package owner to the number-of-units uncertainty but transfers the pricing risks to the contractor. Modifications to these basic types of contracts may make risk transferring very tricky. For instance, a reimbursable contract with a cap would return a lot of risks to the contractor.[2]

Any discrepancy between the letter and the spirit of a contract could be a major cause of risks. Be very careful with how a contract is labeled. For instance, a contract might be declared *reimbursable* or *unit-price* based but contain quite a few clauses that make it virtually a lump-sum contract. Development and review of contract drafts is within the domain of the legal department but should be done with the close involvement of risk management.

Take the *actual* package contract type into account when doing quantitative bid evaluation. As discussed in the final section of this chapter, the final risk exposure becomes clear only after the negotiations preceding the contract award. Part of the risks could be reassigned, along with acceptance of their addressing. This will define the actual demarcation of risk ownership among parties.

Only the uncertainties that are material or severe in the case of at least one bidder should be included in the evaluation. Usually there are fewer than a dozen. In reality, no more than two or three uncertainties are the real differentiators or game makers that define the outcome of the evaluation. The rest of them have the same or similar assessments for all bids.

Same as in case of engineering option selection (Chapter 9), if some risks for some bidders cannot be reduced to the low (green) level economically, these bids should be disqualified. For example, during the recent bid evaluation of a package to produce tanks for an SAGD project in Alberta, one of the frontrunners was disqualified due to its busy production program. Despite the location of the workshop in Alberta, the high quality of produced equipment, and the very reasonable pricing, a project delay of at least half a year was almost certain.

So, the contract award was played off between two other shortlisted bidders. One was located in Asia and the other in North America. The selection was based on a decision-making template similar to the one used for engineering option selection (Figure 9.2). However, in place of option base estimates, the bid prices found in the RFP responses were used. All risks associated with both bidders were reduced to a low (green) level. However, the costs of addressing were rather different. Costs of addressing for all uncertainties were added to the corresponding bid prices. Again, we are talking about risks that are kept by the package owner, not the bidders. This means that the bid price is not the full package lifecycle price for the package owner. Based on this pre-negotiation approach, one bidder was prequalified as the potential (preferable) contract winner.

However, following negotiations the picture changed. The other bidder agreed to accept some of the important risks and the costs of their addressing that initially were assumed by the package owner. As a result of negotiations, this other bidder was awarded the contract.

 ## PACKAGE RISK MANAGEMENT POST-AWARD

When a contract is awarded, the final package risk register should be cleaned to exclude bidders that did not win the contract. Only evaluations of risks that relate to the winner should be kept. For reimbursable contracts, risks that are transferred to the contract award winner should become subject to regular reviews. Ideally, the package risk management plan should be part of the final negotiations and the contract. This is to define the frequency of risk reviews, risk process, tools, and so on. It represents the *in-depth* and *time* dimensions of risk management as shown in Figure 2.1.

A standard contract is often used by organizations for all types of packages regardless of their size, scope, and so on. This is the way to get charged risk premiums for risks that are not relevant to a particular package. This is also the way to accept risks that are not identified beforehand. This inflexibility could lead to inadequacy of the procurement process. The clauses of the contract should result from consistent risk analysis and talks on optimal risk brokering.

The risk-based procurement process described in this chapter allows one to make informed decisions and *knowingly* identify, accept, or transfer relevant risks. This approach allows one to take on contracts that looked too risky initially. It is based on the idea that risk should be managed by the party that can do it in the most efficient way. Such optimization should lead to a more positive outcome—less expensive, higher-quality projects delivered on time safely and without damage to the environment or anybody's reputation.

 ## CONCLUSION

The method described in this chapter is a cousin of the method to select engineering design options presented in Chapter 9. It is becoming popular among the procurement people that I have been working with recently. This allows one to select successful bidders quantitatively and fully justify, document and defend such decisions. In some cases this should address risks related to ethics. The word *quantitatively* points to the possibility of coming up with the real (not as stated in the RFP response) contract price through the proper evaluation of uncertainty exposure that goes along with such a decision. Cost escalation modeling introduced in the next chapter is usually part of it.

 NOTES

1. Y. Raydugin, "Consistent Application of Risk Management for Selection of Engineering Design Options in Mega-Projects," *International Journal of Risk and Contingency Management*, 1(4), 2012, 44–55.
2. R. Wideman, *Project and Program Risk Management: A Guide to Managing Project Risks & Opportunities* (Newtown Square, PA: Project Management Institute, 1992).

CHAPTER ELEVEN

Cost Escalation Modeling

Questions Addressed in Chapter 11

- How average should an average really be?
- Why is consumer price index the worst possible macroeconomic index for evaluating project cost escalation?
- Why should first and second market transactions be delineated?
- How reliable can cost escalation modeling be?
- Should cost escalation modeling be probabilistic? ▪

O NE OF THE KEY PROJECT cost uncertainties that should be managed through the procurement process is cost escalation. This standalone project general uncertainty is directly related to the development of adequate project cost estimates and reserves.

 ## OVERVIEW OF THE COST ESCALATION APPROACH

Let's assume that all quotes received by a project owner in 2014 for a construction package are firm and valid for the next several weeks or months. Does this help to predict real expenditures? The answer is no. One reason for this is very basic. A dollar in 2014 will have rather different purchasing power in three or four years over the course of the project execution. So, quite often project teams use an average annual inflation rate to escalate future expenditures from the base estimate. In North America it is around 2% these days. In a few years, a smaller amount of goods or services would be purchased using the same amount of money as the value of money will be lower. The question is: What goods and services are we talking about?

General Inflation and Consumer Price Indexes (CPIs)

General inflation is directly measured (or well approximated) by the *consumer price index (CPI)*, which includes a standard set of goods and services the general population consumes on average. This set or *consumer basket* is usually different for various areas of a country. Moreover, the typical consumer baskets in Los Angeles and in Detroit would be different because the cost of living is different. Here we compare two major U.S. cities. What about the countryside in the U.S. Midwest? And are consumer baskets the same in North America as in the Middle East or Europe? It does not seem so. It would be reasonable to delineate CPIs for particular cities, for cities versus rural areas, and for different regions and countries.

In addition to the geographical dimension, economists exclude some products and services from consumer baskets on purpose to compare results. For example, some CPI variants may or may not include the price of gasoline. It sounds quite complicated. But wait a minute—what do all those consumer goods defining general inflation have to do with purchasing pressure vessels or line pipes and hiring welders to install them in a particular geographical location? Not a lot.

Market Imbalances and Macroeconomic Indexes

To continue the inflation analogy, we need to know the "inflation" for pressure vessels, line pipes, and hiring welders using "pressure vessel," "pipeline," and "hiring welders" baskets. Of course, there are no such inflations and baskets in economics. There is something similar, though. Macroeconomic indexes or rather their time series for the next several years are developed usually on an annual and quarterly basis. They are still based on the basket approach and organized in hierarchies and developed on a regional principle.

For instance, a general cost of labor index may be introduced for Canada. This is developed as an average for all Canadian provinces and territories and all major occupations. However, if a project is planned in Alberta, the Alberta cost of labor index would be more relevant. But if a project is planned in Northern Alberta somewhere around Fort McMurray to develop oil sands, even the labor index for Alberta would be rather misleading (too optimistic). Logically, the Northern Alberta or "Fort Mac" labor index should be used instead. However, escalation of labor costs in Northern Alberta would be more apparent in the case of qualified welders than for general labor, and so on. So, the Canadian labor index is a very big basket that contains various types of professions in various provinces of Canada. "Average of average of average of average, and so on" gives rise to an "undistinguished and calm" time series of the Canadian labor index, which has (almost) nothing to do with hiring welders in Northern Alberta. This index is better than the CPI index, but not much.

The next question should be about the method to define the right size of basket to adequately represent cost escalation for particular items. Natural limitation comes into play in the form of commercial availability of macroeconomic indexes.

Some consulting and research organizations provide indexes based on "midsized baskets." For instance, it could be a macroeconomic index to construct a refinery in the United States. It is still an "average of average of average," although it generally covers the relevant scope of a project. This index should be applied to a project's base estimate at large. Of course, it doesn't take into account the size of a refinery, a particular technology used, or the location of a project. It feels like a few more details are required, but how many more?

For instance, if we think about line pipes, there are pipes of various diameters. Intuitively, pipes of larger diameter (20″–48″), such as are used for large oil and gas pipeline projects, should be distinguished from smaller-diameter pipes. Usually they are produced by different mills, at least by their different divisions, and assume different technical and quality standards. At the same time, some averaging should be used as we don't want to use different macroeconomic indexes for 24″ and 36″ pipes. This means that our "pipe basket" for large-diameter pipes will be averaged for several diameters.

Supply–demand imbalances in smaller baskets are usually more acute as they are not subject to much averaging. For this reason, escalation of some products and services could be way more severe than the "calm"-averaged CPI index.

This discussion may be clarified by consideration of two types of macroeconomic indexes. All commercially available macroeconomic indexes are available in either "real" or "nominal" forms. Cost of money, which reflects general inflation and could be approximated by the consumer price index, is excluded from real indexes. In other words, general inflation is a bench-mark for real cost escalation. Simply speaking, nominal indexes are sums of real ones and general inflation. So if in place of a specialized microeconomic index a CPI index is used, its substantial and most informative portion is just missed, leading to incorrect conclusions about future cost escalation. The real escalation in the case of approximation by the CPI is always equal to zero by definition.

There are a finite number of macroeconomic indexes commercially avail-able to assess cost escalation. So if a project team would like to use a very spe-cific macroeconomic index for a particular product or service, there is a high likelihood that it is not available. There are four ways to resolve this.

First, a similar index might be found and used. Let's call it a *proxy* for the required index. Second, a higher-level (more-averaged) index may be a fit in some cases. Third, a similar index for a different geography might be selected. This situation is more easily resolved and more justifiable for products and services that are part of the global market. Turbine generators, compressors, or large-diameter pipes are examples of those. At the same time, markets for gravel, rented construction equipment, or construction labor are usually more local. Fourth, it is theoretically possible to engage an economic consultancy that would develop the required index using economic modeling and polling. However, this might become a substantial part of the project cost. This method is not often used. As an alternative, a project team may evaluate some indexes on its own. This approach is discussed in this chapter.

If purchasing of materials or services is done abroad using another cur-rency, additional contribution to cost escalation could stem from exchange rate volatility. The same approach is used to assess required exchange rate reserves as described above, although the discussion about secondary transactions is not relevant.

Selection of relevant macroeconomic indexes or their proxies for escala-tion modeling is always a creative process that should involve cost estimators. The best source of macroeconomic indexes for North America that I know of is Global Insight. All time series are represented as historic data for the previ-ous 10 years and as forecasts for the next 10 years on a quarterly and annual basis. Rolling updates of indexes are done every quarter. Global Insight provides almost 400 various indexes for the United States and almost 100 indexes for Canada. (The exchange rate forecasts for major world currencies are also pro-vided.) Unfortunately, the number of available indexes for other parts of the world is lower. It is still possible to get the required geographical indexes for an additional fee.

First and Second Market Transactions

A common issue with most of the available macroeconomic indexes is that they represent so-called *first transactions*. In other words, they are *producer price indexes (PPIs)* and reflect the prices paid to producers. As project owners usually use engineering, procurement, and construction (EPC) companies to deliver particular work packages, they pay to those companies, not to the producers, which is a *second transaction*. The differences between first and second transactions would be gross margin and risk premium. Both could be higher at the moment of purchasing than anticipated by the project base estimate. This is not only relevant to materials or equipment. The same situation normally occurs with labor hired by an EPC company for a project. Moreover, the situation could be exacerbated due to involvement of trade unions, employment commitments to local communities, aboriginal groups, and so on. Particular exposures of a project owner and EPC contractors depend on the nature of the signed contracts. Taking the second transaction into account is too often missed, which leads to rather optimistic or lower cost escalation assessments. At the same time, this is quite difficult to evaluate as the corresponding macroeconomic indexes that take into account the second transactions are rarely available. The example of cost escalation of line pipes in 2008 introduced in Chapter 1 is a good illustration of first and second transactions. Even though Global Insight predicted growth of pipe prices by 10 to 15% (PPI—first transactions), real growth in the first part of 2008 was 20 to 40% (owner's prices—second transactions). In any case, Global Insight pinned down the right trend.

There are several methodologies to evaluate additional contributions to the price volatility as differences of the first and second transactions. All of them are based on additions of multipliers that condition PPIs to take the second transactions into account. The development of multipliers and the methodology to justify them differ significantly. Any such methodology is based on a type of calibration. Due to lack of relevant historic data for calibration and their substitution by the judgments of specialists who are prone to various types of bias, the calibration of models is quite challenging and not always convincing.

It would not be an exaggeration to state that there is no fully consistent methodology to evaluate second transactions.[1] All of them have significant distances to reality. But it's better to take the second transaction into account even inaccurately than to just ignore it.

One of the methodologies is based on addition of a multiplier to all PPI indexes that is proportional to the speed of the index change. Mathematically, this multiplier is proportional to a derivative (dZ/dt) of a macroeconomic index Z by time.

As in the example of the growth of pipe prices in 2008, quicker growth of PPI (first transaction) should mean an even higher growth of the addition related to the second transaction. The same should be true for cost de-escalation: the quicker the PPI index declines, the deeper the cost reduction related to the second transaction.

The second method is based on evaluation of the multipliers depending on economic activity related to a particular PPI index. It is important to keep in mind that some PPI indexes are global in nature. For instance, production of line pipes or turbines for compressor stations is perfectly global. At the same time labor or rented equipment PPIs have clearly regional features. Various indexes of economic activities in particular countries or regions (growth of economy, capital spending, etc.) could be used to justify conditioning of PPIs.

Unfortunately, relevant indexes on capital project activities in particular regions are not usually available. Some consulting companies could carry out studies based on a collection of information about planned capital projects in a particular region, which would cost an arm and a leg. The reliability of such studies is not always clear. Polling of knowledgeable project specialists from engineering, procurement, construction, strategy and business development, and so on could be a viable and practical alternative to collecting the required regional macroeconomic information.[2] Governmental organizations that handle project permits are a common source of public information about planned projects. I have applied this method for several capital mega-projects, which produced somewhat credible results.

The two previous multiplier evaluation methods take into account the macroeconomic situation only. There is a third method to evaluate the second transaction multipliers that is based on a combination of microeconomic and macroeconomic factors. Besides the macroeconomic activities in a region related to capital projects, a particular competitive situation, contractual obligations and types of contracts define final contract prices that include the second transactions. If a type of contract is defined and fixed, it is important to understand how a particular project feels about the competitive situation. Three different possible competitive situations may be distinguished for particular work packages to evaluate local market factors:

1. Mass market
2. Oligopoly
3. Monopoly

If a project may receive the required services, materials, or equipment from multiple suppliers/vendors/contractors, such a competitive situation should not encourage large differences between PPIs and second transaction prices (mass market). The situation will differ if only three or four suppliers/vendors/contractors are available. Some of them could be quite busy. As a result, bidders may lean toward additional price increases. If there are only one or two prequalified suppliers/vendors/contractors available, the addition to the PPI price could be remarkable. So in many cases a local market factor depends on the number of prequalified bidders that are available and decide to reply to a particular RFP. There is a certain correlation between this and the regional economic situation, too. The local market factor is more important for a particular project than the regional economic situation in general. However, elements of double counting should be avoided when reviewing both factors.

In some cases a monopoly or oligopoly could be created quite artificially for a particular project regardless of the economic situation in the region. The following example led me to the conclusion that microeconomic local factors and regional macro-economic factors should be taken into account separately. I observed cases where projects were bound by labor agreements or arrangements with aboriginal groups, which led to remarkable spikes in contract prices due to inflated second transactions. A similar project across the street could get similar products or services on the open market at much lower prices. Artificial monopoly practices are normal in some regions of the world. They may take various forms, although the bottom line is always the same. Conditioning of PPI indexes for corresponding regions should take into account local features of second transactions realistically.

One of the challenges when handling the regional features of second transactions is defining the *region*. In many instances it is quite obvious. For example, when we are talking about a project in Northern Alberta, the Gulf of Mexico, or the Persian Gulf, the definitions of the regions are self-explanatory. However, when we discuss the continental United States or Europe, it is a different story. Some reasoning for the types and geographies of companies and labor force interested in and allowed to compete for the project works is needed. The degree of globalization related to the project should not be ignored, either.

As already mentioned, the biggest problem common to all three methods is the calibration of the second transaction multipliers. Historic data similar to those on growth of pipe prices in 2008, judgments of experienced procurement specialists and cost estimators, and the collecting of information about economic activity in the region a project is based in would help to properly develop and calibrate the second transaction multipliers for particular PPI indexes in some cases. However, according to my experience, the third method, based on evaluation of the competitive situation for a particular project, is most adequate and understandable by project teams. Project team members may actively contribute to evaluation of the second transactions for particular PPI indexes, which is important from the viewpoint of method's practicality and team member's engagement. Application of this method will be discussed in this chapter.

Credibility of Cost Escalation Modeling

I have a reservation about the value of macroeconomic indexes developed for the next 10 years. Usually, they represent a lot of dynamics for the first three to five years and then settle down ("flat and calm") afterward. This is an indicator that the economic models used for developing indexes represent future reality relatively well for the first few years and gradually lose their essence for the rest of the 10-year period. And of course they don't capture in advance a change in "economic paradigm" such as happened, for example, in 2008. If we look at the macroeconomic indexes developed in early 2000 for the next 10 years, of course there is no hint of the 2008 economic downturn. However, quarterly updates of all models and their outputs (indexes) allow one to capture signs and precursors of coming changes in advance, say for a year or a year and a half, as happened in case of the line pipes example.

Another point relates to the possibility of the selection of relevant PPI indexes. Proxies of desired PPI indexes are commonly used in cost escalation modeling; this leads to a certain degree of reduction in accuracy of modeling. However, such a reduction is not critical.

Obviously, cost escalation modeling including currency exchange rate volatility modeling does not look like a probabilistic exercise, although it could be developed probabilistically. It was pointed out earlier that the time series of commercially available macroeconomic indexes are sold as one-point numbers (i.e., one number per quarter or year). There is no uncertainty (ranges) around those indexes and exchange rate forecasts. It is possible to introduce those uncertainties (ranges) manually and run probabilistic models. A broader uncertainty should be used for later indexes in the series, with a zero range being assigned to the base period index. As there will be inevitable issues in justifying those growing ranges, probabilistic cost escalation modeling may be viewed as overshooting. Unfortunately, this means an absolute (+/–0%) level of accuracy in cost escalation modeling, which is not credible. Artificially introduced accuracy spreads do not help, either. The only reason to get involved in such an exercise is full assessment of primary accuracy ranges of a base estimate where all possible uncertainties, including cost escalation, should be counted. This challenge will be discussed in Chapter 14.

Instead, the one-point escalation numbers may be understood as *expected/mean values*, which are the best one-point representatives of distributions. The distributions (accuracy "ranges" around one-point values) of macroeconomic indexes are not available along with their one-point values, although I am sure economists who run economic models do derive the indexes and their accuracy ranges as outputs from their economic models. Developing expected values of cost escalation is sufficient for evaluating the contribution of escalation to the project cost reserve. However, the contribution of the cost escalation spread to the primary accuracy range associated with all cost uncertainties will not be taken into account (Chapter 14).

The weakest point in developing a reliable cost escalation reserve fund relates to taking second transactions into account. There is no straightforward and fully justifiable method to calibrate PPI indexes due to the impacts of second transactions. Too many talking points, assumptions, and non-substantiated calibrations are used to build these models. It is better to take second transactions into account somewhat inaccurately than to ignore them, which would be the wrong approach for sure. The best way to do this is to examine both the regional macroeconomic factors and the local competition factors that a project encounters.

Modeling cost escalation using macroeconomic indexes is not ideal. However, when used properly, it is the best available method to use for decision making.

EXAMPLE OF COST ESCALATION MODELING

Real cost escalation models could be quite large as dozens of macroeconomic indexes could be used to represent dozens of base estimate cost accounts. Let's review a simplified example related to the hypothetical concrete works of a capital project. This example may relate to an offshore concrete gravity-based structure, a dam at a hydropower-generation project, and so on. Let's also assume that according to the project cost estimate, the cost of concrete works is $100 million in prices of a base period. This was declared by estimating that the cost of labor is 40% of the base estimate. This could be broken down to 30% of construction labor plus 10% of engineering labor. The cost of construction equipment is 20% and the cost of materials is 40%. The two main types of materials are cement (25%) and structural steel (15%). A further breakdown of costs is possible, but for simplicity we will stay with just five cost components of the concrete works. These shares define the weight coefficients of a composite index for concrete works.

A *composite index* is a representation of a particular cost account of a base estimate through basic macroeconomic indexes. We use fictional macroeconomic indexes in this example. (It would not be prudent to use those in any real cost escalation modeling. Real indexes could be purchased from companies like Global Insight.)

As discussed earlier, finding macroeconomic indexes that are a perfect match to the modeling requirements is not usually possible. Proxies are normally used instead. Table 11.1 presents five hypothetical indexes that may serve as proxies for the five cost contributions to the overall cost of the concrete works. They are all normalized to the base period, which is 2014 in this example. Those indexes as well as the resulting composite index are time series for several years.

It is easy to construct the composite index for the concrete works I_{CONCR} where the weight coefficients and macroeconomic indexes are identified:

$$I_{CONCR} (t) = 30\% \ I_{CL}(t) + 10\% \ I_{EL} (t) + 20\% \ I_{CE} (t) + 25\% \ I_C (t) + 15\% \ I_{SS} (t)$$

As all five macroeconomic indexes represent PPIs or first transactions, they should be conditioned to include the second transactions. This should be done in two steps. First, the general economic situation related to overall capital spending in a region should be evaluated. Figure 11.1 plots the results of a regional capital expenditure (regional CapEx) assessment that could be done by any project team.

Second, the particular competitive situation should be discussed for every package cost component. Sometimes a project has no choice but to use a particular monopolist as a supplier or a contractor. Either very few or several vendors could be available. The level of competition will define the significance of the second transactions. In keen competition, the second transaction addition

TABLE 11.1 Macroeconomic Indexes Selected for Modeling

Index	Index Description	Weight	2014 (Base)	2015	2016	2017	2018	2019	2020
$I_{CL}(t)$	Construction labor	30%	1.00	1.03	1.09	1.13	1.17	1.21	1.26
$I_{EL}(t)$	Engineering labor	10%	1.00	1.03	1.06	1.11	1.14	1.14	1.18
$I_{CE}(t)$	Construction equipment	20%	1.00	1.03	1.06	1.11	1.14	1.14	1.18
$I_C(t)$	Cement	25%	1.00	1.03	1.07	1.11	1.13	1.19	1.20
$I_{SS}(t)$	Structural steel	15%	1.00	0.99	1.00	1.04	1.08	1.12	1.18

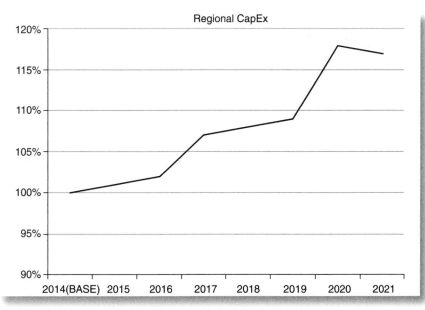

FIGURE 11.1 Assessment of Regional Capital Expenditure

might even be negative. Table 11.2 outlines three different competitive situations related to the five cost components of the concrete works. For this discussion, we treat these five cost components as relating to five different work packages.

Table 11.3 introduces the rules on how the local market factors used in Table 11.2 should be selected depending on the competitive situation.

As the composite index is a time series, it is important to know when corresponding concrete works and expenditures are planned. If the works are

TABLE 11.2 Local Market Factors

Macroeconomic Index	Local Market Factor	Rational
Labor	0.5	Unionized labor and agreement with aboriginal groups
Engineering Labor	0.5	Unionized labor
Construction Equipment	0.3	Three major providers in the region
Cement	0.1	Multiple suppliers
Structural Steel	0.1	Multiple suppliers

TABLE 11.3 Assessment of Competitive Situation

Competition	Local Market Factor
Monopoly (1 supplier)	0.4–0.5
Oligopoly (2–4 suppliers)	0.1–0.4
Mass market (multiple suppliers)	0–0.1

planned for several years, each annual portion will be escalated differently. Table 11.4 contains information about the cash flow for the concrete works and the results of the cost escalation calculations. The composite index in that example is already conditioned through taking into account both regional CapEx (Figure 11.1) and local market factors (Table 11.2).

In this example, the cost escalation of the concrete works is about 15% for the duration of the works, which is higher than if general inflation were used to evaluate escalation. The difference of that result and CPI defines real escalation that excludes inflation. Real escalation is often used in project economic models. In the example, all PPI indexes were assumed to be nominal, meaning that they included inflation. For this reason the escalation number derived is escalation in nominal terms.

Markets in equilibrium tend to give rise to escalation that is close to inflation. However, markets in equilibrium are rather the exception than the rule. There are always niches of the market relevant to a particular project that are out of equilibrium. The line pipe market in 2008 discussed earlier is one such

TABLE 11.4 Calculation of the Cost Escalation Reserve

Account	Estimate	2014 (Base)	2015	2016	2017	2018	2019	2020
Composite Index: Concrete Works	n/a	100.00%	102.69%	106.06%	112.14%	116.43%	120.23%	127.14%
Cash Outflow (Base), 000$	100,000	0	0	2,000	40,000	47,000	11,000	0
Cash Outflow (Escalated), 000$	114,926	0	0	2,121	44,856	54,724	13,225	0
Escalation, % of base estimate (BE)	14.93%							

example. This makes using CPI as a basis of cost escalation inadequate and irrelevant in most cases.

Most of the numbers used in the escalation modeling could be represented as distributions including macroeconomic indexes. Additional rationale would be required to justify all those ranges. This allows one to make cost escalation modeling a probabilistic exercise, which increases the complexity of models enormously. In my experience, I have built several models like this to include cost escalation (including exchange rate volatility in required cases) to the overall project cost reserve and evaluate its primary accuracy number. Even though those were quite successful efforts, I still recommend that escalation modeling be done deterministically as shown previously. This modeling should take second transactions into account to be adequate.

The terms *regional CapEx* or *local market factor* could be replaced by *macroeconomic* and *microeconomic factors of second transactions* if needed. As indicated previously, it is not about the terminology of particular uncertainty objects; it is about their essence.

 ## SELECTING THE RIGHT TIME TO PURCHASE

Using composite indexes is a basis for cost escalation modeling, which implies *downside* deviations from project base estimates in most cases. More fortunate, upside cost escalation situations may occur, too (cost de-escalation). This could be used for selection of the most favorable time to purchase some types of materials and services, assuming that the project schedule allows such flexibility.

The example of the huge cost escalation of line pipes in the first part of 2008 and prices dropping in the second part of the year is a practical one. It was recommended to delay the purchasing of line pipes for a mega-project in early 2008 and put it off until later that year. It was not exactly clear what would happen in late 2008, although some hints of an overall slowdown were there despite aggressive cost escalation in late 2007 and early 2008. In any case, implementation of this recommendation led to significant economy, which was even higher than the prediction was.

The approach for selecting the right purchasing time is the same as for modeling of cost escalation. (Taking into account exchange rate volatility could be part of this exercise when required.) The only difference is the running of several scenarios (early purchases versus late purchases) that are allowed by the overall project schedule and comparison of the results.

CONCLUSION

Project teams and decision makers understand the need to adjust the project base estimates that are made for any particular base period due to future price volatilities. The point is to select the right methods and macroeconomic indexes. Selection of the CPI index as a measure of inflation is inadequate but better than fully ignoring this topic. Assessment of the required cost escalation reserve as a part of the project cost reserve is not straightforward. However, this provides clarity regarding what should be the expected final project cost. Being able to proactively define the best time for purchasing is an additional bonus.

 NOTES

1. J. Hollmann and L. Dysert, "Escalation Estimation: Working with Economic Consultants," *AACE International Transactions* (Morgantown, WV: AACE International, 2007).
2. Consulting companies that sell corresponding economic indexes carry out these research activities on a broader scale.

PART THREE

Probabilistic Monte Carlo Methods

VEN STANDARD PROBABILISTIC METHODS for assessing project cost and schedule reserves are relatively sophisticated. Aside from their recognized power and value they entail several unwritten but fundamental rules to follow to stay adequate and avoid getting confusing results. The purpose of Part III is to summarize all the relevant rules for developing adequate probabilistic cost and schedule models. This includes discussion of the data specifications that should be used as inputs and outputs of probabilistic analyses.

CHAPTER TWELVE

Applications of Monte Carlo Methods in Project Risk Management

Questions Addressed in Chapter 12

- What is the value and power of the Monte Carlo methodology?
- How do 5,000 deterministic scenarios give rise to one probabilistic distribution?
- Why should deterministic and probabilistic methods be seamless?
- What are the origins and roles of general uncertainties and uncertain events in Monte Carlo models?
- What should be done to avoid double dipping?
- Why should correlations never be ignored?
- What is included in project reserves?
- What should project teams and decision makers know about probabilistic branching and merge bias?
- Is it really challenging to quantify unknowns?
- Why should integrated cost and schedule risk analyses come to maturity as soon as possible? ■

THIS CHAPTER EXAMINES UNCERTAINTY objects taken into account typically as inputs to probabilistic cost and schedule models. The major features of standard probabilistic cost and schedule risk analysis techniques are outlined. Some advanced modeling techniques are also introduced that might be regarded as either exotic or too complicated by some readers. Their application is a must in specific situations to adequately reflect reality in models. It is important to be aware of such techniques in the risk management toolbox.

FEATURES, VALUE, AND POWER OF MONTE CARLO METHODS

In the course of project development and execution an issue arises regularly regarding comparing its baselines with actual results and its actual results with the outcomes of other, similar projects. This relates to all project objectives but first and foremost to Cost and Schedule.

A company may have an internal database that collects information about its previous projects. Some of these are comparable with the project of interest. Some are not and either require proper conditioning of results to assure an apples-to-apples comparison or should not be used at all. Internal comparisons like this are not exactly bias free. One of the reasons is that all types of organizational bias that an organization has (quality of project management process and procedures, culture, risk appetite, etc.) would be factored in. This gives rise to systematic errors in the form of "standard" amendments of project costs and durations.

If an organization compares its project with similar projects of other organizations, those comparisons will have their own systematic errors. So additional conditioning will be required for an apples-to-apples comparison. Conditioning of data can be an additional source of bias.

Commercial consulting organizations may provide data about dozens of relevant projects in a particular industry. This allows one to identify a range of decent cost and duration outcomes using a higher number of projects in the sample. But apples-to-apples conditioning of data is inevitable there, too, due to the geographical and industry variety of projects' execution.

All types of benchmarking mentioned earlier are valuable to a certain degree. They provide additional insights on the project progress. However, all of them have a powerful competitor in the form of Monte Carlo statistical simulations for the following reasons.

First, this method resolves the issue of conditioning right off the bat. The reason for this is very simple. The Monte Carlo method, being an advanced sampling technique, is based on given project cost and schedule baselines, which excludes the need for any conditioning.

Second, all possible deviations from baselines would be evaluated at quite a detailed level. Each deviation would be identified, discussed, and assessed to ensure adequate sampling.

Third, practitioners who work with Monte Carlo models usually feel that any particular inaccurate assessment of uncertainties is not that important unless there is a systematic error across the whole process based on various types of bias. This ensures stability of results where bias is well controlled.

Fourth, random sampling of data, called *iterations*, can be done many times. The minimum standard in the industry is 1,000 iterations. But there are no visible restrictions to doing 5,000 or 10,000 iterations. Each of the iterations technically is fully deterministic and means a standalone relevant project based on the same scope as the investigated one. Moreover, the schedule structure and logic of each project are the same as those of the project of interest. It is the same with the structure of the base estimate. However, particular one-point numbers sampled in any particular iteration differ, belonging to assessed uncertainty ranges. So, in place of a few relevant projects to compare against during benchmarking, we may be talking about 1,000 or 5,000 or 10,000 fully relevant hypothetical projects that don't require any conditioning.

Fifth, what if our project is quite unique and no similar projects are available for benchmarking? What if we need benchmarking for a CO_2 sequestration project? What if the benchmark should be an Arctic drilling project? What if a new technology is used in a project of interest? In these cases, parts of a unique project could be benchmarked based on data conditioning but never the whole project. Therefore, the key value of the Monte Carlo method is the capability to mimic or imitate data statistically for thousands of fully relevant albeit hypothetical projects.

The essence of the Monte Carlo method is multiple sampling of uncertainties as inputs to the mathematical models to get information about possible overall project cost and schedule uncertainty. Each input requires due diligence and contributions from specialists of various disciplines. This defines the main power of the Monte Carlo method.

Specifically, the main power of the Monte Carlo method in project risk management is that it integrates opinions and inputs of multiple specialists belonging to various disciplines into decision making.

INTEGRATION OF DETERMINISTIC AND PROBABILISTIC ASSESSMENT METHODS

The levels of development and sophistication of deterministic and probabilistic methods adopted by organizations differ significantly. Sometimes either a deterministic or a probabilistic methodology (or both) has yet to be adopted. It is not uncommon that deterministic and probabilistic methods are developed and used independently by organizations. Sometimes an organization has a deterministic scoring methodology that is used along with deterministic quantitative methods for cost and schedule reserve development (see Chapter 3). In some extreme instances, fixed 15% or 20% cost and schedule reserves are applied across the board regardless of project scopes, budgets, schedules, complexities, and novelties.

A common situation is that project teams follow adequate deterministic risk management practices, develop good risk registers, and address risks. At the same time it uses qualitative probabilistic or very simplistic quantitative probabilistic methods such as QuickRisk (Chapter 3). But those methods do not utilize available project risk registers at all! One project manager who was not very advanced in risk management asked me "why an existing project risk register was not used in probabilistic schedule risk analysis for his mega-project." The answer was that his project services people were not well trained in probabilistic risk methods. They knew only the basics of QuickRisk and sold that to him as the most advanced probabilistic method ever known to humankind.

I am familiar with an organization that has been engaged in a number of mega-projects in North America and has a very strong probabilistic methodology. That sounds great except for the fact that it does not manage risks consistently using deterministic methods. This means that assessments of risk exposures before and after addressing are pretty much the same, at least during project development. Of course, experienced project managers manage risks in Execute regardless of corporate risk procedures. However, project baselines would be more aggressive and realistic if proper addressing of risks were done.

The previous examples are illustrations of various types of organizational bias that lead to lower efficiency of adopted risk management systems. We presented the 3D risk management integration approach in Chapter 2. Another integration effort should be undertaken to integrate both deterministic and probabilistic assessment methods. One without the other or without proper integration with the other leaves big voids in the credibility of the project risk management system. But their integration yields a robust synergy that drastically improves the quality and reliability of the overall project risk management system.

Figure 12.1 introduces a generic risk management workflow that integrates the deterministic and probabilistic steps. This describes the major steps in the risk management process (Figure 2.2) with a focus on the two assessment steps. In reality, this workflow may repeat itself several times and include several what-if scenarios. Moreover, it is not unusual that new uncertainties are identified or that existing ones are reassessed, accepted, or closed during the probabilistic steps of the workflow. Upon completion of the probabilistic activities both the deterministic and the probabilistic registers should be updated.

 ## UNCERTAINTY OBJECTS INFLUENCING OUTCOME OF PROBABILISTIC ANALYSES

The purpose of this section is to outline the major uncertainty objects that are commonly used as inputs to probabilistic models. Some objects (Table 1.2) are not subject to probabilistic cost and schedule risk analyses and will not be discussed in this section. However, a very important point is that in

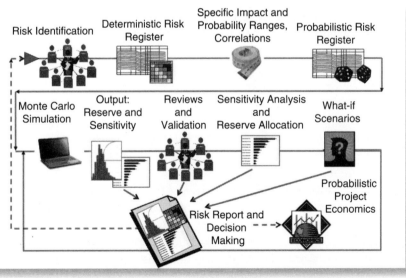

FIGURE 12.1 Integrated Deterministic and Probabilistic Workflow

spite of this they should always be kept in mind when working with uncertainty objects included in the analyses. The reason for this is the possible double counting of inputs. Practitioners call this *double dipping*. For instance, cost escalation uncertainty could be taken into account in a cost escalation model but also included in a project risk register as an uncertain event and/or ranges around costs of particular items in the base estimate as a general uncertainty. As a result, the same uncertainty object may be taken into account two or three times, hence the presence of double (or even triple) dipping.

Double dipping is a type of bias that could have both psychological (subconscious and conscious) and organizational roots. This is not the only type that should be managed in probabilistic analysis, though. Various systematic errors are imbedded in assessments of uncertainties due to various types of the previously discussed psychological and organizational bias. According to Table 1.2, these should be judged as general uncertainties that influence the accuracy of all inputs.

Some uncertainty objects of Table 1.2 should not be included in probabilistic models. As previously discussed, known show-stoppers and game changers should be listed explicitly as exclusions from inputs to probabilistic models. When they occur they destroy or drastically redefine Cost and Schedule baselines. So there is no uncertainty management of a project previously contemplated any more should a show-stopper or a game changer occur. In other words, the new reality should be dealt with that assumes that there is no previously defined project and no need in its uncertainty assessments. It will be either a cardinally re-defined project (in case of game changers) or no project at all (in case of show stoppers) . Such a situation constitutes the previously discussed corporate risks. Mathematically, it defines the limits of applicability of probabilistic cost and schedule models. We saw in Chapter 4 that various factors might lead to the situation where some project uncertainties stay unidentified. Project novelty, the phase of its development, and various types of bias may provide room for unidentified uncertainties. To a certain degree these define the level of adequacy, quality, and efficiency of the project risk management system. In a way, if the level of adequacy, quality, and efficiency of a risk management system were assessed, the impact of unknown uncertainties on results of probabilistic cost and schedule analyses would be assessed. Corresponding allowances may be introduced to the models as discussed next. This method of assessment of unknown uncertainties is already used by some multinational oil and gas companies as part of their corporate procedures for project probabilistic risk analyses.

To sum up, the following uncertainty objects from Table 1.2 will be taken into account when developing inputs to probabilistic cost and schedule models:

- General cost uncertainties (cost models)
- General duration uncertainties (schedule models)
- Burn rates (integrated cost and schedule models)
- Downside uncertain events
- Upside uncertain events
- Unacceptable performance uncertain events
- Organizational bias
- Subconscious bias
- Conscious bias
- Unknown uncertain events

Previously we discussed various types of bias when assessing uncertainties. This discussion is fully relevant to developing inputs to probabilistic risk models. Unacceptable performance uncertain events will be treated as part of a broader class of downside uncertain events. Burn rates will be examined when discussing the integrated model. In the next section we discuss the nature, origin, and examples of general uncertainties and uncertain events.

All inputs to probabilistic models are subject to types of contracts and particular contract terms, conditions, and clauses. For instance, let's consider a work package awarded to an engineering, procurement, and construction (EPC) contractor as a reimbursable, unit-price, or lump-sum contract. The same uncertainties would have different realizations and assessments for the project owner and for the EPC contractor due to the corresponding risk brokering and transferring. Additional negotiations and contract clauses could further change the overall uncertainty exposure of each side.

In other words, conversion of contract terms, conditions, and clauses into inputs to probabilistic models requires special attention and due diligence.

ORIGIN AND NATURE OF UNCERTAINTIES

As previously discussed, general uncertainties are characterized by ranges of impacts. The probability of their occurrence is totally certain, being equal to 100%. As such they are attached to project baselines. For uncertain events besides the uncertainty of impacts, the probability of their occurrence is uncertain and may be equal to any value that is less than 100%. To better understand the origin and nature of cost and schedule general uncertainties and uncertain events let's examine the following four examples.

Example of General Cost Uncertainty

Imagine that someone decided to renovate the basement in his or her house. Imagine that five contractors came up with their quotes. Those quotes took into account the general instructions of the homeowner. Let's say those quotes were $15,000, $19,500, $21,000, $23,000, and $35,000. An overly diligent homeowner might want to carry out an additional marketing study and ask about pricing from five additional contractors. Upon receiving their responses the owner gets the following numbers: $15,000, $16,000, $19,500, $20,000, $20,500, $21,000, $23,000, $27,000, $33,000, $35,000.

It seems that the majority of numbers concentrate around $20,000 to $21,000. Those look the most reasonable and natural for this type of work for the particular market. Lower numbers might mean great market opportunities but also inferior quality of materials and work. Higher numbers imply exceptional quality but might turn out to be just plain overpricing. Additional research to check the quality and reputation of contractors would be required to make a purchasing decision. This would narrow down initial options and allow one to come to a conclusion. But until this is done the numbers around $20,000 to $21,000 seem most reasonable and likely, the other conditions being equal. Those "other conditions" could become differentiators of options when an additional study is undertaken. Figure 12.2 represents the general uncertainty related to the cost of basement renovation after the initial collection of marketing information. Using the risk management process terminology of Figure 2.2, this corresponds to *uncertainty assessment as-is.*

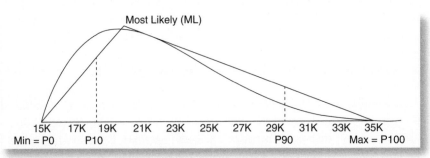

FIGURE 12.2 General Cost Uncertainty before Addressing

Triangular distribution was used along with beta distributions to represent the likelihood of particular costs. This should accentuate the fact that a set of statistical data may be approximated by several different distributions. The key point here is that some distributions may be fully defined by just three intuitively understandable parameters (minimum [min], most likely [ML], and maximum [max]) in the case of triangular distributions. Some other distributions require either three or more parameters that are not intuitively understandable as in case triangular distribution.

For example, the beta distribution shown in Figure 12.2 requires definition of parameters that are not that directly understandable by people without quite substantial mathematical background, which makes it impractical for everyday use in project risk management. The only justifiable use of sophisticated distributions like this in project risk management would be availability of relevant historic data about a particular uncertainty based on such sophisticated probability distributions.[1] Besides the triangular distribution, the other distribution commonly used in project risk management is the *trigen* distribution. This is also fully described by three parameters. As a matter of fact, the minimum and maximum values of a triangular distribution are too certain. They offer incredible precision when describing ranges associated with uncertainties. For this reason two probabilistic cutoff values on the wings of a triangular distribution are used as parameters along with ML value. After this the values outside of this cutoff range are not precisely defined. This reduces overshooting in terms of precision. These cutoff values are defined the following way.

The minimum number of $15,000 represents the 100% likelihood that all values of the range are higher than $15,000: there are no values below $15,000. A zero probability of the presence of values in the range that are lower than $15,000 is indicated in risk management as P0, which means here zero probability of presence of values below $15,000. In other words, there is a zero level of confidence that those values exist below $15,000. Similarly, a P100 level of confidence should be associated with value $35,000, meaning that there is an absolute (100%) level of confidence that all values of the distribution are below $35,000. The cutoff values usually used to define trigen distributions are P10 and P90 or P5 and P95. The reason why the P5 and P95 range is preferable is discussed in Chapter 14.

A P10 level of confidence associated with a value means that there is 10% probability that existing values are lower than this value, or 90% probability that they are higher than this. Similarly, a P90 level of confidence associated with a value means a 90% probability that existing values are lower than this value or a 10% probability they are higher than this. In Figure 12.2 the P10 value is about $18,300 and the P90 value is about $29,600. In any case, a particular level of confidence is associated with each particular value of the impact range.

When additional steps are undertaken to explore the possible renovation options it might be discovered that the two cheapest options are not acceptable due to low quality of imported materials and an unqualified labor force. It might be that these two contractors have bad records and reputations on similar projects. The two most expensive options included premium quality of materials and some extras and upgrades that were not initially required by the homeowner. The contractor that bid the price of $27,000 could not justify it by providing higher quality of materials or work. Quality seemed the same for options in the range $19,000 to $23,000.

Figure 12.3 represents the same general uncertainty but after additional study or addressing. Obviously, the spread of uncertainty has become narrower. More research could be required to make an informed purchasing decision, which should narrow the range to one option. One might guess that the remaining shortlisted options are characterized by different timelines and schedules of works, different borrowing options, and so on. As discussed in Chapter 10, these procurement options have different associated uncertainties. Hence, they could be used as additional differentiators to make a final decision. There will no longer be general price uncertainty when the job is completed. However, even if one option is selected, this does not mean that the uncertainty evaporates entirely. The selected contractor might come up with some change orders to adjust the pricing due to upgrades or substitutions of materials even after the contract is signed.

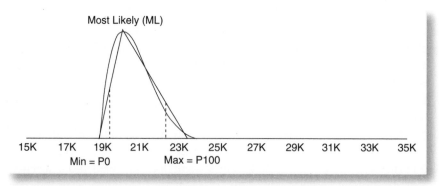

FIGURE 12.3 General Cost Uncertainty after Addressing

In real capital projects that have multiple cost accounts in the base estimates, their general uncertainties could be correlated. For instance, a larger building (its cost) is usually associated with a higher cost for the foundation. The paramount importance of correlations to ensure the realism of probabilistic modeling is discussed later in this chapter.

The key source of the general uncertainties of a capital project is the level of engineering and procurement development of a project.[2] Various factors from the uncertainty of labor productivity to the uncertainty and assumptions related to the scope of the project give rise to general cost uncertainties. All ranges are usually shrinking down while engineering is progressing, and solid quotes are received for work packages or package commitments are made, and so on. At the same time, methods and quality of data used for development of the base estimates define ranges, too. Various kinds of bias, from organizational to particular psychological types, are also always present.

The possibility of the double counting of general uncertainties along with some other uncertainties should be avoided. Design allowances, uncertain events, and cost escalation should be kept in mind.

Example of Cost Uncertain Event

The description of the selection of a contractor for a basement renovation looks like routine business-as-usual. No big surprises, just collection and analysis of marketing data, trying to reduce pricing uncertainty to an acceptable level. However, upon selection of a contractor and start of work, a big crack in the foundation could be discovered, leading to the need to repair it first before proceeding with the basement renovation. This might sound like a game changer if it redefines the initial project cost estimate, adding a substantial amount of money to the initial baseline.

Discovery of the foundation damage is certainly not a business-as-usual event. It is truly a "business-unusual" event. I am not sure about the exact statistics on the probability of such discoveries in particular areas but they could be assessed by knowledgeable specialists. Let's say the probability of this is 1–5% in a given area. This would depend on various factors such as age of the house, presence of groundwater, types of soil, type of foundation, differences in temperature in the summer and winter seasons, and so on.

The cost impact on the owner's budget will depend on the size of the foundation crack, access to the damaged area by excavation, and so forth. There is a certain range of possible damages and costs of repair. Even for a given damage there would be a spread of offers from contractors, the same as in the previous example. Now the homeowner should find another contractor that specializes in foundation repairing, undertaking the steps described in the previous section.

Potential events like these should be considered along with general uncertainties. First, they are characterized by their probabilities of occurrence or discovery (1–5% in our example) and the associated spread of impacts. The latter is general uncertainty (range of possible impacts) if the event or discovery does occur.

For a real capital project, multiple uncertain events might occur, both upside and downside ones. The impacts of some of them should be correlated. This means that if two risks occurred in the same iteration, their impacts would be synchronized in terms of magnitude. If the impact of one event belongs to the higher end of its range, the impact of the other should belong to the higher end of its range, too. For instance, an uncertain event of discovering poor sub-surface geotechnical conditions, say boulders, and an uncertain event of over-spending on the foundation should be correlated. Obviously, only distributions that have ranges can be correlated. One-point numbers cannot be correlated.

When assessing uncertain events, be sure that there is no double dipping with some other uncertainties, especially with general uncertainties as well as cost escalation.

Example of Schedule General Uncertainty

Imagine that an office worker commutes from her suburban home to down-town every working day of the week. Her method of commuting may include a bus, a streetcar, a subway, a bike, a car, and so on or any combinations of them depending on the town she lives in and her preferences. Commute times depend on these factors, too. Assume we are talking about Calgary; the average or most likely commute time is 30 minutes. However, depending on the day of the week, the season of the year, and the slight weather variations, the commute time actually belongs to a range of 25–40 minutes. We are not talking about a major snowstorm or traffic incident impacting the commute times. Small incidents like the bus or train the commuter was expecting to take being out of service may delay the commute time for a few minutes, but it's nothing major. This is an example of *general duration uncertainty*.

When a planner is developing a schedule for a project each normal activity is represented as a bar with absolutely certain duration. This duration is treated as most reasonable or most likely according to the project scope and data available for planning. Project specialists and the planner utilize their previous experience and some benchmarking data to come up with the most likely durations.

Of course, one-point duration numbers are utopian. Real numbers might be close to the proposed numbers but are almost never the same. The first reason for this is the intrinsic ambiguity of any input data used in planning, including the judgments of specialists. This is the case even if nothing unusual is contemplated, which is not linked with the schedule. Using risk jargon, this is a *risk-free* situation, meaning no uncertain events are possible, only general uncertainties. This is a business-as-usual case, based on a project schedule with some deviations from it. A business-unusual situation will be discussed in the next section.

Recall that a project schedule is a model of project execution. It has a certain distance to future reality, which is defined by several factors. In the same way as general cost uncertainties, the level of engineering development is a major cause of general duration uncertainties. Scheduling information from the subcontractors that are supposed to deliver the corresponding work package is also important. The qualifications and experience of schedulers and the information and methods they use for planning give rise to general duration uncertainties, too.

Example of Schedule Uncertain Event

Continuing the commuting example, let's imagine that a water-main break occurred in the early hours of the day so that the usual commuting route is blocked, causing a traffic jam. Now, instead of the usual commute time, it took two hours to get to the office that day. Traffic incidents may be other less exotic reasons for the delays. Let's say the incidents are observed on the way downtown once in one or two months. Based on 20 working days per month, the probability of occurrence may be assessed at 2.5–5% or so. Some of these incidents don't have any impact on commute times at all, some lead to modest delays, and some to major delays. The possible delay depends on its severity, the location of the incident, the level of blockage of the route, the availability of a detour, and so on. The most likely or average delay seems to be 20 minutes, although some incidents lead to major commute delays of two hours.

Identification of uncertain events with schedule impacts is a major task in investigating the level of confidence of a deterministic project completion date that is defined by a project schedule. As is true for uncertain events of cost impacts, uncertain events of schedule impacts may be correlated.

The cardinal difference between cost and schedule uncertain events is that a schedule uncertain event should be mapped to the normal activities it impacts. The possible delay of a particular impacted normal activity, if the event does occur, should be assessed by the project specialists. Such an assessment should include min, ML, and max impacts. Uncertain events may be also mapped to schedule milestones, although it is more logical to map events to corresponding impacted normal activities that are predecessors of the milestones.

ROLE OF CORRELATIONS IN COST AND SCHEDULE RISK ANALYSES

Let's review a general macroeconomics example of correlations and anti-correlations. If inflation rates start growing, it is expected that interest rates would grow, too. However, interest rates are established and used by central banks to regulate the growth of the economy. Inflation is a major but not the only factor in defining interest rates for a given period of time. To simplify, it would be fair to state that if inflation grows, interest rates should grow, too, in *most* cases. Both indicators are somewhat similar or comparable in behavior or are correlated to a certain degree.

Interest rates defined by a central bank or similar institution in a particular country define the mortgage interest rates the general public pays for borrowing money to buy real estate. The lower the mortgage rates, the higher the number of property sales. This is true in most markets, with some exceptions. Sales of properties in Beverly Hills or Manhattan are not that affected by the current level of mortgage rates, at least not in the same way as property sales in the rest of the United States. To simplify, mortgage rates and real estate sales are anti-correlated to a high degree.

Statistical methods allow one to discover correlations of two functions (indicators, parameters, time series, etc.) if required. They may be plotted against each other as two-dimensional charts or as time series. We will not review corresponding methods in this book but introduce correlation coefficients to measure correlations and anti-correlations. Figure 12.4 shows the concept of different correlation coefficients. Their spread is from 100% or +1 (full correlation) to −100% or −1 (full anti-correlation). The situation where correlation between two functions does not exist is described by the

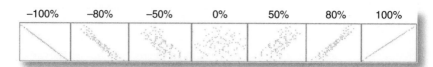

FIGURE 12.4 Correlation Coefficients

zero correlation coefficient. The behavior of the two functions looks perfectly random in this case.

The concept of correlated sampling of distributions in the cost and schedule risk analysis of projects was introduced in Figure 3.6. The effect of correlations on the results of probabilistic analysis is demonstrated in Figure 3.7. Figure 3.7 represents results of impact of general uncertainties (ranges around base estimate cost accounts) on the cost distribution of a capital project. One scenario is fully uncorrelated (all correlation coefficients equal to zero) and the other scenario represents the case where all cost accounts of the base estimate are fully correlated (all correlation coefficients equal to 100%).

Why should correlations be seriously taken into account at all? In the macroeconomic example, it is not quite realistic that higher mortgage rates are correlated with higher property sales. This requires suppressing such unrealistic scenarios in probabilistic models. In the case of evaluation of the costs of a building's foundation and the costs of the building itself, it should be expected that the higher the building's cost, the higher the foundation's cost in most instances. However, the higher foundation cost might be driven by geotechnical subsurface conditions only. Hence, these two cost distributions cannot be 100% correlated. A high enough (70–90%) but not 100% correlation coefficient could be applied.

Correlations bring realism to the models through suppressing unrealistic scenarios in probabilistic models. As such they reduce a model's distance to reality. The general rule-of-thumb is that probabilistic models with a higher level of correlations have wider distributions, which was demonstrated in Figure 3.7. The reason for this is that the width of a distribution coming from the correlated model is higher, being proportional to the correlation coefficients of the model.

If two distributions are convoluted to a resulting distribution by a Monte Carlo model, the width of the resulting distribution depends on three factors. The first and second factors are the widths of input distributions σ_1 and σ_2. The third factor is proportional to the correlation coefficient C between the two distributions. The following formula introduces the width of the resulting distribution:

$$\sigma = [\sigma_1^2 + \sigma_2^2 + C \times \sigma_1 \times \sigma_2]^{1/2}$$

This formula is correct if we understand σ, σ_1, and σ_2 as *standard deviations* of corresponding distributions. Standard deviations are measures of distribution width defined in a certain standard mathematical way.

Let's analyze this formula for the simplest situation where two equal distributions are convoluted ($\sigma_1 = \sigma_2 = \sigma_0$). In this particular case the previous formula takes following form:

$$\sigma = \sigma_0 \times [2 + C]^{1/2}$$

If these two input distributions are fully correlated ($C = 1$), then $\sigma \approx 1.73 \times \sigma_0$. If there is no correlation ($C = 0$), then $\sigma \approx 1.42 \times \sigma_0$. In the case of full anti-correlation ($C = -1$) the resulting distribution should have the width $\sigma = \sigma_0$.

This simple example demonstrates quite a broad range of possible widths of the outcome distribution depending on the degree of correlation. If the correlation is not properly analyzed and reflected through adequate coefficient C, the outcome distribution will have nothing to do with reality. A wrongly derived distribution would mean a wrongly derived project reserve. A wrongly derived project reserve would mean wrong decision making.

The higher the degree of correlations among the model's inputs, the wider the outcome distribution. Wider distributions mean bigger cost and schedule reserves. For anti-correlations the situation is reciprocal. Anti-correlations lead to narrower distributions and lower cost and schedule reserves. In real project probabilistic cost and schedule models that contain dozens of input distributions, both correlations and anti-correlations usually exist. So, the outcome of the model is the interplay of both. Incorrect handling of these, where unrealistic scenarios are not suppressed, will lead to unrealistic results and wrong decisions.

Hence the topic of correlations is not just mathematical theory; it has direct financial and planning implications.

The recently developed tool Acumen Risk seems to have entirely missed this point. It does not even have the functionality to set up correlations among input distributions! It looks like this feature has a sales-and-marketing origin as Acumen Risk is positioned as a tool for users who do not have knowledge of statistics and supposedly do not know what correlations are all about. The credibility of such a correlation-free marketing approach is doubtful when developing project cost and schedule reserves. I would pass on using such a tool until the adequate functionality to correlate inputs becomes a standard feature.

 ## PROJECT COST RESERVE

It is important to come up with a clear definition of a project cost reserve at this point. We need to be absolutely clear about all the contributions that give rise to the overall project cost reserve. It would be logical to do this based on the definitions of the uncertainty objects in Table 1.2 related to project costs.

The following components of an overall project reserve should be kept to cover residual uncertainties cost-wise, according to the objects in Table 1.2:

- *Design allowance:* Standard estimating term related to general uncertainties of scope; it is usually not subject to uncertainty management as estimators fear that it could be stripped when discussing the other contributions to the project cost reserve with decision makers.
- *Cost contingency:* Reflection of cost general uncertainties including schedule-driven costs. Design allowances should be kept in mind when developing cost contingency. In some cases costs of all addressing actions are included in the contingency.
- *Cost escalation reserve:* Takes into account a future change of project costs initially developed in money of a base period due to future market imbalances and volatility.
- *Exchange rate reserve:* In purchasing materials, equipment, and services in currencies different from the estimating currency, reflects future changes and volatility of currency exchange rates.
- *Cost risk reserve:* Takes into account all known uncertain events except show-stoppers and game changers. All components of design allowances, cost contingencies, cost escalation, and exchange rate reserves should be excluded from development of the project cost risk reserve.
- *Performance allowance and liquidated damages:* Usually part of project cost risk reserve but may be reported separately as required by corporate financial reporting; could be part of financial reporting of EPC companies. We consider this part of the project cost risk reserve.
- *Unknown-unknown reserve:* Used as a method to assess quality of project risk management system, project novelty, and the phase of project development as an additional cost allowance; usually relates to unknown downside uncertain events but could include unknown downside general uncertainties.

The project team should come up with a clear definition of the project reserve and its components in the project risk management plan. As will be discussed later, if integrated cost and schedule risk analysis is run, schedule-driven costs should become a contribution to project contingency. All components of project reserves except design allowance and cost escalation and exchange rate reserves should be developed using probabilistic methods. (As discussed in Chapter 11, it is technically possible to apply probabilistic methods to cost escalation and exchange rate reserve modeling, which seemed to be overshooting due to lack of required information.)

It is possible to build an integrated probabilistic model that produces an overall project cost reserve including all the components listed above including schedule-driven costs. I developed several probabilistic models like this that produced overall project reserves, including contingencies, cost escalation, exchange rate, cost risk, and unknown-unknown reserves. Even though such models bring a certain value they appeared appalling to anyone who looked at them. It is more reasonable to build corresponding models separately. One exception would be the development of an unknown-unknown reserve. As will be discussed, it is usually linked with project cost risk reserve development.

One important point related to general uncertainties is often missed when developing project cost reserves. As mentioned earlier, risk reserves are normally developed for to-be cases where all identified uncertain events were addressed through corresponding sets of response actions. The same approach should be taken toward general uncertainties, but usually this is not the case. The reason for this is the deficiency of the traditional risk management approach where ranges around cost accounts are not viewed as manageable uncertainties at all in probabilistic models. As a result, the as-is and to-be assessments differ only for uncertain events. In practice, timelines for as-is and to-be assessments should be clearly defined first. If assessment as-is relates to the end of Select and assessment to-be relates to the end of Define or final investment decision (FID), corresponding reductions of ranges for to-be-FID assessments should also be made. General uncertainties should get reduced in the course of project development. In other words, a project team should predict the uncertainty exposure that would exist in a particular point in the future (to-be).

This approach is widely used (or should be) for project reserve drawdown. The drawdown could be done for any part of the project reserve separately on a monthly or quarterly basis using models initially built to baseline the project cost reserves at FID. This topic is discussed in Chapter 14.

 PROJECT SCHEDULE RESERVE

A slightly different approach is used when developing schedule probabilistic models. Their primary goal is to investigate confidence levels of sanctioned completion dates. Their secondary goal is to estimate additional floats to ensure the required level of confidence. However, before these two goals are achieved it is necessary to ensure that the developed schedule is attainable despite the presence of general uncertainties. These tasks are usually pursued in three steps.

First, the proposed schedule is evaluated in terms of ranges around normal activities' durations (general uncertainties). Project planners and specialists evaluate those ranges based on uncertainty information used for development of durations of the normal activities. A simple probabilistic model utilizing the QuickRisk functionality of PertMaster is built and run to get distributions of possible project durations or completion dates. This is a model where no uncertain events are included. Such models are called *risk-free-world models*, or the "sniff test." Despite their apparent utopianism and long distance to reality, such models are used as quality checks of proposed schedules. If the level of confidence of a sanctioned project completion date is high enough, the schedule may be used for further probabilistic analysis. If the level of confidence is too low even in the risk-free world, the schedule should be recycled and redone, being unrealistic.

Second, when a proposed schedule passes the sniff test the project's uncertain events with schedule impacts should be added to the probabilistic model. The resulting distribution, which now includes both general uncertainties and uncertain events of schedule impacts, should be studied.

Third, by the end of the building and testing of the probabilistic schedule model, development of an unknown-unknown allowance to the model is required. This is discussed later in this chapter. After evaluating and adding the unknown unknowns to the model and running it, a distribution of project completion dates or durations will be obtained.

Needless to say, all relevant correlations should be included at each of these steps.

It is important to keep in mind that the functionality of PertMaster allows one to obtain distributions for completion dates for any project's milestone or normal activity. This may be used to investigate the level of confidence for milestones related to readiness for construction, turnaround, and logistics windows, or major decisions such as the final investment decision. A usual application of this functionality is to investigate the confidence levels of the mechanical completion dates or fulfillment of various commercial obligations and milestones.

To sum up, the following components of the schedule risk reserve should be kept in mind according to Table 1.2:

- *General schedule uncertainties:* Investigation of the attainability of the proposed project schedule in a risk-free world.

- *Project float:* Contribution of general uncertainties and uncertain events (except game changers and show-stoppers) to the definition of the desired confidence level of the project completion milestone.
- *Total project float:* Addition of an unknown-unknown allowance to the project float as a measure of the efficiency and quality of the project risk management system and project novelty. Total project float is used in decision making related to the project completion date.

The same reasoning in cost general uncertainties is relevant to assessments of general duration uncertainties as-is and to-be. In the course of project development, the general uncertainties usually get reduced due to better levels of engineering, procurement, and other types of development. As is true for cost general uncertainties, this point is often missed when making to-be assessments.

 ANATOMY OF INPUT DISTRIBUTIONS

We discuss key parameters of input distributions in this section. The discussion in this section is relevant to both cost and schedule distributions.

As discussed in Chapter 3, the mean value of a distribution is the best one-point representative of the whole curve. However, the true uniqueness of mean values is based on their features when input distributions are convoluted to produce probabilistic results. In business applications, the mathematical term *mean value* is replaced by *expected value*.

Assume that we have several distributions used as inputs to probabilistic models describing the general uncertainties of a project (Figure 3.6). If those distributions have mean/expected values $M_1, M_2, \ldots, M_n$, the curve obtained as a result of their convolution will have mean/expected value $M_1 + M_2 + \ldots + M_n$. For uncertain events with the same mean values of impacts the mean value of the convoluted curve will be $p_1 \times M_1 + p_2 \times M_2 + \ldots + p_m \times M_m$, where p_1, $p_2, \ldots, p_m$ are probabilities of uncertain events $1, 2, \ldots, m$.

This fundamental property of mean/expected values is a justification for all the probabilistic qualitative methods based on the evaluation of expected values (Chapter 3). If spreads of the outcome curves are ignored and the criteria used for development of project reserves are always based on mean/expected values, the probabilistic modeling will not be required. Potentially it is possible to use this for quick project reserve evaluations through evaluation of mean/expected values of inputs. This is exactly the approach of the project/

program evaluation and review technique (PERT)/critical path analysis (CPA) method, which is based on the approximation of the expected values of the general duration uncertainties. The problem with this is that three-point triangular distributions usually used as inputs to probabilistic models are based on (min, ML, max) not (min, mean, max) values, where ML is the most likely value corresponding to a peak of the input distribution. The ML value is also called the *mode* of a distribution. In general uncertainties (ranges around baseline one-point values) the most likely values represent the baselines, not mean values.

Figure 12.5 illustrates the difference between ML and mean values, which could be substantial for skewed distributions. Besides ML and mean values, Figure 12.5 introduces the *median value* that represents the middle of the (min; max) spread. A special term is used to mark median values: P50, where *P* means *probability*. In other words, there is 50% probability of finding a particular value below the median as well as 50% probability of finding it above the median value.

Some risk practitioners try to discuss the difference between ML, mean, and median values as related to inputs to probabilistic models. Such attempts turn off project team members pretty quickly even if some of them have engineering or mathematics backgrounds. So, mathematically, using mean values would be the right thing to do. However, it is not practically possible. It requires assessment of the input distribution using a fitting functionality of probabilistic software packages, which is quite beyond the discussed qualitative probabilistic methods. As ML values are much better understood and handled by project teams it is reasonable to stay with simple (min, ML, max) inputs.

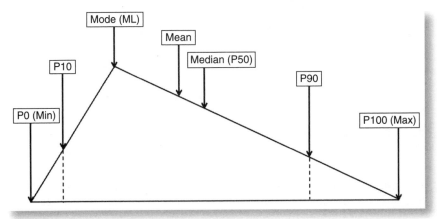

FIGURE 12.5 Triangular Input Distribution

For symmetrical distributions (bell curve, symmetrical triangular distribution, etc.) all three parameters (mean, median, and mode) are identical.[3] However, symmetrical distributions rarely exist as inputs to probabilistic models. Usually inputs are skewed to the right toward higher numbers (Figure 12.5). The general explanation for this is based on the presumption that it would be much more difficult to discover possible upside deviations from baselines (values lower than ML) than to run into downside deviations. In addition, zero values of impacts are natural limits for upside deviations, whereas downside deviations don't have such limits. Therefore, downside deviations could be much higher than upside ones. Usually this is true, but not always.

One of the situations where upside deviations should be higher than downside ones is where a project baseline (estimate or schedule) is way too conservative. Unusually high design allowances could be included and conservative quantities and prices might be factored into the base estimate for some reasons including bias. Durations for some activities could be quite conservative and seem to include some uncertain events implicitly. Ideally, the quality and integrity of the base estimate should be ensured through cold-eye reviews and benchmarking. However, the assessment of ranges may take this into account by application of distributions skewed to the left. So, in place of the usual ranges around the base estimate accounts or durations, say, −5%/+10% or −15%/+25%, ranges such as −10%/+5% or −25%/+15% could be used to compensate for conservatism or overshooting of the inflated baselines. Mathematically, this means moving the input distribution's mean/expected value to the left, toward the lower numbers.

If impacts around ML values are very likely by default, values close to min values (P0) or max values (P100) should be rather exotic. At the same time they are defined with amazing precision. This looks like another overshooting: a range of an uncertainty is defined with absolute precision as P0 and P100 one-point numbers. To avoid this sort of discomfort, practitioners use trigen distribution. So in place of P0 and P100 values determined with amazing precision used are P5 or P10 and P90 or P95 values. Figure 12.5 shows P10 and P90 values. In practice, P10 and P90 cutoff values are used much more often than P5 and P95. However, we discuss why values P5 and P95 are much more preferable when analyzing probabilistic model outputs in Chapter 14.

The P5/P10 value points to the situation where any value of the distribution could be found below that particular value with probability 5% or 10%, and with probability 95% or 90% above that value correspondingly.

Similarly, the P90/P95 values define the rule that any value could be found above that particular value with probability 10% and 5% correspondingly. Technically this means that trigen distributions stay uncertain on what should be P0 and P100 values. Such an understatement is a better fit for defining uncertainties.

Using the trigen input distributions is always preferable to using triangular ones if project team members are comfortable with estimating inputs as (P5, ML, P95) or (P10, ML, P90). One of the tricks risk managers use is to discuss inputs with project teams as (min, ML, max) as for triangular distributions but treat them as inputs to trigen distributions. Justification of this is based on recognition of subconscious bias. Namely, it is fairly normal that project specialists come up with too-narrow ranges of impacts of both general uncertainties and uncertain events. This allows one to address the systematic error related to overconfidence by applying systematic corrections like this. The project risk manager should make this call if such or a similar correction is appropriate based on assessment of the overconfidence bias. Namely, if P10 and P90 values were used in place of collected min and max data, the overconfidence bias would be addressed in a more radical way. In other words, if the overconfidence bias is not that severe, the P5 and P95 cutoff values of trigen distributions should be preferable.

Intuitively, one might dislike the shapes of both the triangular and the trigen distribution as they do not look smooth enough. It is true that it is quite unusual to observe phenomena in physics that have such unsmooth and rude dependencies and curves. Figure 12.2 introduces an alternative to the triangular and trigen distributions in the form of a beta-distribution. It looks more natural and smooth. However, using a beta-distribution requires definition of parameters that are not obvious or straightforward in interpretation by project teams, which is the normal price for higher aesthetics and lower efficiency.

A PERT distribution would be a good alternative to the triangular distribution if the project team is comfortable using it. However, replacement of all triangular distributions with PERT ones with the same parameters (min, ML, max) does not change the outcome curve significantly. It is counterproductive to spend too much time discussing exact shapes of input distributions. In the majority of situations it does not matter at all. Slight differences in shapes of output curves could be ignored as soon as about the same mean values of comparable input distributions are used. Much more important are correlations among distributions that make a real difference. I prefer to stay with trigen distributions unless some historic or modeling data are handy and dictate other choices.

 PROBABILISTIC BRANCHING

Earlier in the chapter it was mentioned that it would be important to investigate the readiness of a project for some construction, turnaround, or logistics windows. For instance, deliveries of installed equipment to a construction site somewhere in Alaska, Chukotka, or Labrador from overseas would not be possible during several winter months due to freezing of seaports. Such features of the project schedule should be realistically reflected in the schedule and the schedule risk analysis.

Figure 12.6 introduces an example that contains equipment delivery downtime in the schedule for five months from mid-November until mid-April next year. In case the delivery is not made by November 15, the next unloading of the equipment in the port could be done from mid-April on, which delays the equipment installation for five months. The date of November 15 serves as a trigger to initiate the delay in the probabilistic model.

Figure 12.7 shows the equipment installation completion date distributions. There are two peaks separated by several months of winter downtime.

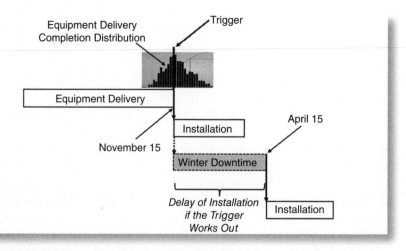

FIGURE 12.6   Example of Probabilistic Branching

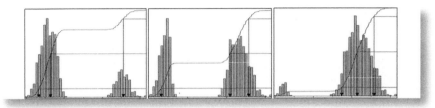

FIGURE 12.7 Probabilistic Branching

If the confidence level to meet the mid-November deadline is quite high, the likelihood that equipment installation will be done on time is high, too. The tall peak on the left side of the chart points this out. However, there is still the possibility that the deadline will be missed, which triggers a short peak on the right side of the chart. If the confidence level to be on time is around P50, either outcome is about equally possible. That is why the two peaks have comparable heights. If confidence level to meet the deadline is relatively low, the peak on the right side is much taller. In two extreme cases, which are not shown, there will be only one peak on either side of the chart. Obviously, if the confidence level to meet the deadline is about P100, there will be only one tall peak on the left. If the confidence level to be on time is extremely low (about P0), there will be one tall peak on the right side.

The origin and effect of probabilistic branching were introduced in this section to demonstrate that some very advanced modeling techniques might be required to adequately represent a project schedule and run its probabilistic analysis. The integration of the probabilistic branching to the schedule risk model requires advanced knowledge of macros in the PertMaster environment and can be adequately done only by a qualified risk analyst. Project team members and decision makers should be aware of this possibility and the corresponding modeling tool in the risk toolbox.

MERGE BIAS AS AN ADDITIONAL REASON WHY PROJECTS ARE OFTEN LATE

Merge bias has nothing to do with the various types of psychological and organization bias discussed so far. The merge bias relates to extra schedule delays when several paths are converged in a node.

Traditionally the baseline schedule of a project defines the project completion date according to the critical path method (CPM). A path that does not have

any float paves the critical path and stipulates the project deterministic completion date. General uncertainties and uncertain events associated with the project lead to delays in the project completion date identified by the CPM method
and shape more realistic distributions of possible project completion dates.

However, such delays could be further exacerbated where the baseline
schedule has parallel paths. Extra delays are generated in the path conversion
nodes. This type of delay is called *merge bias* in project management and *stochastic variance* in mathematics. As project schedules normally have parallel paths,
managing node convergence is vitally important to every project.

On one hand, it is possible to run standard probabilistic schedule risk analysis without paying special attention to converging of nodes. General uncertainties and uncertain events will work out in nodes automatically. The merge biases
belonging to the nodes will be factored into the final project completion date.

On the other hand, there is a way to proactively manage the merge biases
in order to reduce the associated stochastic variance delays. First, a proactive approach includes amendment of the baseline schedule to consider earlier
start dates for some activities belonging to the converging paths. Second, introduction of uncertainty addressing actions that reduce the impact of general
uncertainties and uncertain events associated with the paths would reduce
impact, too. Third, if quite a few paths are converging in a node, it would be
reasonable to split this node through reduction of the number of converging
paths. Fourth, additional float should be reserved right after the node according
to the results of the probabilistic analysis. The magnitude of the float should
be sufficient to provide the node's date with the required level of confidence.
A final simulation should be run to ensure that the effect of merge bias on the
schedule is reduced to a comfortable level.

The origin of the merge bias effect may be illustrated by a simple example. If
three people are to attend a meeting, the probability that they all show up on time
is reasonably high. If five people are expected, the probability that all of them
show up on time becomes lower. What if seven or ten people are expected? The
probability of all of them turning up on time would be even lower, and so forth.

Let's assume that there are no possible "correlations" among people such as
having attended a previous meeting, traveling from another location together,
and so on. We might evaluate the probability of each participant being on time as
90% (or 0.9). The probability assessments for all participants being on time may
be done as shown in Table 12.1. These simple calculations for independent simultaneous events are made according to the AND logic introduced in Figure 4.1.

The fundamental characteristic of elements of the discussed system,
such as the probability of being late for every particular participant, was not
changed, although the numbers of the elements/participants were. This gives

TABLE 12.1 Probabilistic Origin of Merge Bias

Number of Participants	Probability of All Being on Time
2	0.81
3	0.73
4	0.66
5	0.59
6	0.53
7	0.48
8	0.43
9	0.38
10	0.35

rise to a general rule on the merge bias effect. The more paths that converge in a node, the lower the confidence level that the conversion would be done on time.

Figure 12.8 provides an additional illustration on the origin of merge bias for two converging paths. Activities A and B in the schedule are representatives of two paths. They have their own uncertainties leading to a distribution of completion dates of those activities. The distribution of node *N* is a convolution of distributions of activities A and B.

INTEGRATED COST AND SCHEDULE RISK ANALYSIS

Needless to say, the downtime of construction crews deployed at a site due to schedule delays is not free. Every day costs a certain amount of money even if

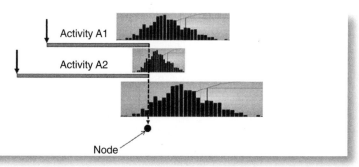

FIGURE 12.8 Merge Bias: Converging Two Paths in a Node

the crews stay idle (*burn rates* per day). Similarly, rented construction equipment not used due to delays or an idle engineering design team also costs money. However, some costs are not time dependent at all (fixed costs). The adequate representation of both fixed and variable costs in probabilistic models is a must to evaluate extra schedule-driven costs adequately. Unfortunately, schedule-driven costs related to project delays is one of the most important contributors to project cost reserves that is either regularly overlooked or taken into account inadequately.

It is standard practice that cost and schedule risk analyses are run independently. Two separate models are built using different software packages. Sometimes project risk registers that are used as inputs to cost risk models contain standalone items related to additional costs generated by schedule delays. Some probability and cost impact assessments are elaborated that don't look terribly credible or even adequate. But such an approach is still widely used, which is only slightly better than if schedule-driven extra costs are just ignored.

In the meantime there is a robust method to consistently take schedule-driven cost impacts into account in probabilistic cost models. Obviously, it is necessary to bridge the gap between the two types of probabilistic models. Integration of them allows one to adequately evaluate those schedule-driven costs.

First, it is not quite right to regard schedule-driven costs as a type of uncertain events. The causes of those have two origins: general duration uncertainties and schedule uncertain events. Those two factors give rise to duration or completion date distributions for the project as a whole as well as for any normal activity. Spreads of those distributions do predetermine possibilities of delays and upside deviations. In other words, the possibility of delays or accelerations has a 100% probability for a given distribution. Hence schedule-driven costs are quite certain; they are typical general uncertainties in cost models.

Second, to link cost and schedule probabilistic models it is necessary to clearly define cost per day, week, or month (burn rates) for all impacted normal activities. The problem here is that project schedules of level 3 or 4 may easily have hundreds or thousands of normal activities. Defining burn rates for all of them would be a problem even if the same work breakdown structure (WBS) was used in both the project schedule and the base estimate. (Unfortunately, they usually drift away from each other over the course of project development.) As we discuss in the next chapter, probabilistic schedule models are normally built based on high-level project schedules that are called *proxies* and correspond to level 1.5. Those level 1.5 proxies that should adequately reflect the main logic of project schedules still contain at least 40 to 70 normal activities. Development of burn rates for all those normal activities would still be onerous and impractical.

Third, as synchronization of cost and schedule probabilistic models though development of burn rates is a must, practically this could be done for a low number of activities. As a trade-off, synchronization of the models is done for major project deliverables. Those correspond to level-1 summary activities. Their number should not exceed a dozen. Those should have exactly the same definitions according to the base estimate and schedule WBS. Figure 12.9 demonstrates why it is important.

In place of the deterministic duration of construction activity (180 days) in the base estimate there will be input from the probabilistic schedule analysis in the form of a duration distribution for this construction activity. The deterministic duration of this activity is pointed out by an arrow in the distribution charts of Figure 12.9. The spread around the deterministic duration defines the range of possible delays/accelerations and corresponding schedule-driven costs/savings.

A key rule to exclude double counting in integrated cost and schedule risk analysis is that initial cost risk analysis should be carried out as if all schedule-driven costs are ignored. This corresponds to the project schedule completion by the deterministic completion date. All schedule delays should be taken into account only through inputs of schedule risk analysis results to the cost risk model.

One element of developing schedule-driven costs is proper allocation of fixed and variable costs. If this is not done adequately, the results of the

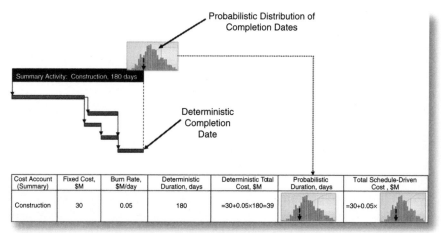

FIGURE 12.9 Origin of Schedule-Driven Costs

calculations of schedule-driven costs will be misleading. On one hand, if the variable part is inflated, the overall project cost will be excessively sensitive to delays and the model will produce huge schedule-driven additions. On the other hand, if the schedule portion of variable costs is underestimated, the sensitivity to delays will be played down. Such insensitivity will also lead to wrong results. A detailed and consistent consideration of burn rates as well as truly fixed costs for summary activities is required.

According to my experience, schedule-driven costs are one of the top uncertainty factors leading to project overspending. Strangely enough, this is one of the top factors that is systematically overlooked by project teams and decision makers. One of the fundamental reasons for this is lack of integration of several aspects of risk management, including integration of the cost and schedule modeling. Only integrated cost and schedule analysis can guarantee adequate representation of schedule-driven costs. In practice, even if those are not fully ignored they become semi-professional talking points that are not correctly represented in project reserves.

The good news is that the methodology to take schedule-driven costs into account does not have the same level of complexity as probabilistic branching. At the same time this requires knowledge of uploading of distribution data from PertMaster to @Risk or Crystal Ball and using function fitting. It has yet to become an industry standard although it should be kept in mind as the most adequate way of taking schedule-driven costs into account. This task is significantly simplified if both models are built in PertMaster. This is rarely a case as estimators prefer to stay with MS Excel–based applications such as @ Risk and Crystal Ball.

INCLUDING UNKNOWN-UNKNOWN ALLOWANCE IN PROBABILISTIC MODELS

An initial examination of unknown unknowns was made in Chapter 4. Four dimensions of unknown unknowns were introduced and discussed.[4] Novelty of the project (technological and geographical factors), phase of its development, industry a project belongs to, and various types of bias define room for unidentified uncertainties. However, it would not be a proactive practical approach to succumb to unknown uncertainties just because of their nature.

It is possible that two different project teams will manage these four dimensions with different levels of success. The main reason for this would be a difference in the quality of the two project risk management systems. The difference in quality will certainly define the amount of room for unknown uncertainties in these two projects. Unknown uncertainties cannot be fully eradicated even if a project enjoys an excellent risk management system. Residual room for unidentified uncertainties will always exist. The question is how big that room might be.

It is not unusual that some uncertainties occur during project development that were never part of the project risk registers. For instance, unidentified multi-hundred-million-dollar unknown uncertainties pop up every time a multi-billion-dollar offshore oil and gas project is undertaken. And every time they are different. This is especially true for "new frontier" Arctic drilling.

Due to the high level of uncertainty associated with unknown unknowns, development of corresponding allowances is not about a high level of precision but about the corresponding thinking process. It is certainly better to do the right thing not exactly right than to ignore the topic altogether. Moreover, high precision in evaluation of unknown-unknown allowances is neither possible nor credible due to the nature of the subject. More important is managing unknown unknowns (at least partially) through addressing various biases and properly addressing identified project uncertainties.

Some scarce historical data (all oil and gas [O&G] industry related) were used to very roughly calibrate the unknown-unknown allowances that are introduced in Tables 12.2 and 12.3.[5] These tables explicitly take into account only two dimensions of unknown uncertainties—novelty and phase of development. However, in each particular case this calibration should be challenged and revised by a project team and decision makers. There are at least two reasons for this.

First, type of industry and its maturity should be taken into account. For instance, a space exploration project should have far more unknowns than a railway transportation project. The numbers in Tables 12.2 and 12.3 are based

TABLE 12.2 Unknown-Unknown Allowances When One Novelty Factor Is Relevant

Novelty of a Project	Phase of Project Development			
	Identify	Select	Define	Execute
High degree of novelty	12%	9%	6%	3%
Medium degree of novelty	8%	6%	4%	2%
Standard project (technology readiness level [TRL] score 10/known geography)	4%	3%	2%	1%

Source: © IGI Global. Reprinted by permission of the publisher.

TABLE 12.3 Unknown-Unknown Allowances When Either One or Two Novelty Factors Are Relevant

Novelty of a Project	Phase of Project Development			
	Identify	Select	Define	Execute
High degree of novelty: two factors	18%	14%	9%	5%
High degree of novelty: one factor	12%	9%	6%	3%
Medium degree of novelty: two factors	12%	9%	6%	3%
Medium degree of novelty: one factor	8%	6%	4%	2%
Standard project (TRL score 10/known geography)	4%	3%	2%	1%

Source: © IGI Global. Reprinted by permission of the publisher.

on gut feelings related to the O&G industry. However, O&G has several sectors that are expected to have different allowances of room for unknown uncertainties (e.g., offshore vs. onshore projects, etc.).

Second, quantification of various types of bias as systematic errors in the identification and assessment of uncertainties should be tailor-made in each particular project as a measure of the health and quality of the project risk management system. Ideally, a third party should make recommendations about required unknown uncertainty allowance.

It is recommended to add a selected unknown-unknown cost allowance as a line into a general uncertainties ("ranges") model. A very broad range around this allowance is recommended, say +/−100% of the triangular distribution. The minimum number, −100%, will correspond to the situation where unknown-unknowns don't occur. (As an alternative, this allowance may be put into the project risk register with high probability. This adds another angle for consideration—probability—which seems to be an unnecessary complication or overshooting due to the nature of the discussed topic.)

There might be reasons speculated on to either correlate or anti-correlate this distribution with some or all ranges and/or risks. To keep things simple and exclude overshooting, keeping the unknown-unknowns allowance distribution non-correlated should suffice.

In schedule risk analysis the unknown-unknown allowance should be introduced as an additional normal activity at the very end of the project schedule. This allowance should correspond to the percentage of the project duration. Again, a very broad range around that additional activity duration (say, +/–100%) may be introduced. As an alternative, this allowance may be treated as an additional risk mapped to the project completion milestone.

It may be reasonable to assign some probability to that risk in the project risk register and schedule risk model. A very broad probability range (say, 0–100%) may be used. This approach reflects the difference between cost and schedule risk models as the latter is schedule-logic specific. The probability of much less than 100% (say, 50%) reflects the possibility that some unknown unknowns might occur out of the critical path, having minimal or no impact on the project completion date. Both alternatives may suffice due to the very high level of uncertainty associated with unknown unknowns. The risk register alternative seems to be a bit more justifiable for schedule models.

An additional challenge is to develop unknown-unknown allowances for R&D projects for various types of industries that may be used in probabilistic cost and schedule models. This topic is outside of the scope of this book, although we started with the example of a grandiose project failure related to the attempt to use unproven *in situ* technology in a capital mega-project.

Any company involved in capital projects will want the procedure that best reflects its risk culture and appetite as well as line of business. Guidelines introduced earlier provide enough ammunition for this. Such a procedure should be applied consistently across the project portfolio when developing the project cost and schedule reserves. Historic data on completed projects should be collected along the way. Along with managing various biases and the permanent improvement of the corporate and project risk management system this might be the best way to treat unknown unknowns as accurately as possible.

 CONCLUSION

This chapter introduces key objects that serve as inputs to probabilistic analyses and shape their outcomes. Several variants of probabilistic analysis are reviewed. Using some of them, such as probabilistic branching, could be overshooting. However, using cost and schedule risk analysis in isolation leads to inadequate representation of schedule-driven costs in project cost reserves.

This leads us to the conclusion that probabilistic integrated cost and schedule analysis should become the standard for capital projects for adequate assessment of project cost and schedule uncertainties and the development of project reserves.

NOTES

1. The correct mathematical term for curves discussed here is *probability density function*, not "probability distribution."
2. AACE International Recommended Practice No. 17R-97: *Cost Estimate Classification System* (Morganton, WV: AACE International, 2003).
3. The difference in these three parameters is a measure of distribution asymmetry or *skewness*.
4. Y. Raydugin, "Unknown Unknowns in Probabilistic Cost and Schedule Risk Models" (Palisade White Paper, 2011; www.palisade.com/articles/whitepapers.asp).
5. Y. Raydugin, "Quantifying Unknown Unknowns in Oil and Gas Capital Project," *International Journal of Risk and Contingency Management*, 1(2), 2012, 29–42.

CHAPTER THIRTEEN

Preparations for Probabilistic Analysis

Questions Addressed in Chapter 13

- What are the main goals of probabilistic analyses?
- What is the method statement in probabilistic analysis?
- What is the high-level workflow in probabilistic analysis?
- What factors influence the duration of probabilistic analysis?
- What is the typical specification of inputs to probabilistic models?
- Why must correlations never be forgotten?
- "Probabilistic analysis? What do you mean by that?" ■

T HIS CHAPTER IS DEVOTED to the steps in getting prepared for probabilistic risk analysis. The typical workflows of cost and schedule risk analysis will be outlined. Specifications of required input data will be introduced.

TYPICAL WORKFLOWS OF PROBABILISTIC COST AND SCHEDULE ANALYSES

Four major goals of probabilistic cost and schedule analyses are:

1. Investigation of confidence levels of planned or sanctioned project budgets and completion dates
2. Development of cost and schedule reserves to ensure the required or comfortable confidence level of total project costs and completion dates
3. Identification of the most sensitive general uncertainties and uncertain events for their further addressing, allocation of cost and schedule reserves against them, or optimization of baselines
4. Running and investigation of additional what-if scenarios to evaluate impacts of particular groups of uncertainties

The fourth point has not yet been discussed and requires some clarification. It concerns running probabilistic models with and without particular groups of uncertainties. For instance, it would be interesting to understand the role of uncertainties stemming from the governmental permitting process in a CO_2 sequestration project. Is this group of uncertainties a major driver of possible project delay or uncertainties associated with internal project development and execution? All uncertainties related to governmental delays may be excluded from the corresponding what-if scenario and such a *sequestrated* model could be run. The comparison of the results would be extremely informative. The number and scope of what-if scenarios depend on the level of curiosity of the decision makers. They should come up with a list of what-if scenarios for investigation.

Figures 13.1 and 13.2 outline typical workflows to develop and run schedule and cost risk analyses. These workflows come from Figure 12.2 and provide a higher level of detail and logic. They are almost identical at first glance. Their major difference relates to the modeling of schedule-driven costs.

Figures 13.1 and 13.2 accentuate the need for close integration of deterministic and probabilistic methods. General uncertainties and uncertain events initially identified and assessed are major inputs to probabilistic models. However, these require some conditioning when retrieved from the project uncertainty repository. Detailed specifications of inputs to probabilistic cost and schedule models will be provided in this chapter.

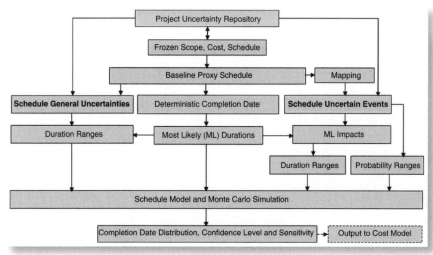

FIGURE 13.1 Probabilistic Schedule Analysis Workflow

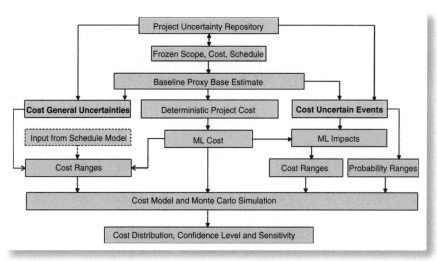

FIGURE 13.2 Probabilistic Cost Analysis Workflow

PLANNING MONTE CARLO ANALYSIS

Due to the need for integration of deterministic and probabilistic methods it is difficult to distinguish where planning of probabilistic analyses should really begin. The planned probabilistic analyses should be kept in mind when initial uncertainty identification is commenced to ensure a seamless integration of both methods. Some information that may be helpful when converting deterministic data to probabilistic inputs should be captured in the uncertainty repository in the form of comments and notes. Possible areas of double counting of uncertainties should be identified. Special attention should be paid to the approved addressing actions and assessments of uncertainties after addressing. At the same time, any probabilistic analysis should be managed as a small project that has a charter, schedule, start and finish milestones, interfaces with various disciplines, and a budget.

The method statement of a probabilistic analysis is developed in its charter. It defines the goal, scope, and methodology of the study. "Probabilistic Analysis Method Statement" examines a method statement for a hypothetical carbon-capture-and-storage project called Curiosity, which is discussed in Part IV of the text.

PROBABILISTIC ANALYSIS METHOD STATEMENT

Scope of the study: (A) Investigation of confidence levels of project budget and duration at the end of Select (case as-is) and at the end of Define/final investment decision (FID) (case to-be-FID); (B) development of cost and schedule reserves required to reach P80 confidence level of contractual project completion (sustained operations) for the to-be-FID case; (C) investigation of confidence levels of completion dates for planned FID milestone for the to-be-FID case; (D) evaluation of primary accuracy range of project cost estimate for the to-be-FID case.

Method of the study: Integrated cost and schedule risk analysis (CSRA).

Main scenarios: Before addressing and after addressing; additional after addressing scenarios, if required.

Baselines: Proxy base estimate (24 cost accounts) and proxy schedule (23 normal activities).

Selected uncertainties: Project downside and upside uncertainties of cost and schedule impacts selected from deterministic project register; schedule-driven costs impacts excluded from risk register, to be taken into account through integration of cost and schedule models.

Factors included in the cost analysis: General uncertainties and uncertain events and major correlations among those; schedule-driven costs will be taken into account as general uncertainties through inputs from schedule risk analysis; agreed unknown-unknown allowance to be included in cost model.

Factors excluded from the integrated cost and schedule risk analysis: Project show-stoppers and game changers according to approved list; cost escalation modeling to be modeled separately; a check to exclude double counting of input factors to be undertaken.

What-if scenarios: (A) Investigation of possible impact of governmental permitting delays on project completion and FID; (B) investigation of impact of upside uncertain event related to early procurement; (C) investigation of readiness for tie-in window.

Start date of the study: April 1, 2015
Completion of the study: April 24, 2015
Reporting: CSRA report validated by the project team and third-party reviewers.

The probabilistic analysis should have a well-defined and viable schedule. The following factors should be kept in mind when developing it:

- Is this exercise being done for the first time by the project team? If yes, special attention should be paid to training the team members, who should provide adequate and unbiased input information. This is the core message of this book. If most of the key members of the project team (project, engineering, procurement, construction, project services managers, and lead specialists, including estimators and schedulers) have never taken part in such activities, the schedule duration should be almost doubled in comparison with that of an experienced team.
- Are major interfaces and dates of key inputs clearly specified, including dates of freezing of project base estimate and schedule? It is quite common that changes to project base estimates and schedules are ongoing and never stop unless a project manager defines clear dates for their freezing. Normally, cost and scheduling development eats up 50–80% of the time allocated for probabilistic analysis. This is another reason to double the schedule duration, if possible. Stress is a major work hazard in risk analysis

when risk managers and analysts try to complete probabilistic analyses under a severe time crunch.

■ Is enough float allocated if additional probabilistic analyses were to be required? It is not unusual that probabilistic analysis based on initial to-be input data discovers that the confidence level of one or several milestones is unacceptably low. A full cycle of uncertainty reviews according to the risk management process (Figure 2.2) could be required. Additional addressing actions should be developed for the most sensitive uncertainties. This may include negotiations with subcontractors and stakeholders, better coordination among functional and support teams, additional engineering, constructability and value engineering reviews, and so on. This could be quite a lengthy process that requires a corresponding float in the schedule.

■ Are external stakeholders representing a major source for possible project delays? I took part in the development of a what-if scenario that resulted in cardinal amendment of a project schedule as related to permitting as well as restructuring of the project team. Often completion of one what-if scenario leads to new ideas about additional scenarios. Extra float should be reserved for tackling what-if scenarios.

Any practitioner who has taken part in real-life probabilistic analyses knows that most of these recommendations are nice but rather utopian. Any initially prudent schedule might quickly become unrealistic due to the causes listed above. There is a high level of furor and 14-to-16-hour work days for risk analysts and managers of capital projects during the period of the probabilistic analyses. Realistically longer workdays and ruined weekends are the only source of viable schedule floats.

A risk analyst who runs probabilistic analysis should be qualified to carry out adequate model building and interpret results meaningfully. He or she should have experience in running several models for similar projects under supervision of experienced specialists. There should be at least a sort of internal informal certification of analysts to permit them to run probabilistic analyses on their own. All results should be validated by peers or third parties. There is a clear reason for this. A well-developed model with several what-if scenarios would be a valuable source of information for decision making. Now let's imagine that both model and results are inadequate but taken seriously. The "Cargo-Cult"-types of analysis pointed out in Chapter 2 could be quite expensive in terms of project failures.

BASELINES AND DEVELOPMENT OF PROXIES

In an ideal world the probabilistic analysis workflows (Figure 13.1 and 13.2) start after the project scope, base estimate, and schedule are frozen. They will continue evolving during and after the probabilistic analysis. Hence, the analysis would represent a snapshot of the project baselines and uncertainties for a particular moment. Unfortunately, this rule is rarely obeyed in practice. For instance, a project team gets new information from vendors that changes equipment delivery timelines and risk exposure somewhat significantly. An attempt to amend the input data used in probabilistic models may be undertaken. Some changes are easy to accommodate. However, if a schedule logic is changed, the whole schedule model should be redone, leading to inevitable delays. In any case there should be a cutoff date that precludes any further changes of input data.

Base estimates might have hundreds of cost accounts and the project schedule might have even thousands of normal activities. Theoretically it is possible to run probabilistic analysis based on such detailed baselines. Technically there is no obstacle to doing this. The major constraint is time. Hundreds and hundreds of general uncertainties should be discussed and validated for each cost account and normal activity. Hundreds and hundreds of correlations among them should be also identified. After that, detailed uncertain events should be discussed as deviations from those hundreds and hundreds of cost accounts and normal activities, not to mention the correlations among them.

Besides time and level of effort, such granularization has intrinsic restrictions especially in the case of schedule risk analysis. If a project uncertainty repository contains 20 high-level uncertain events, those 20 should be mapped to hundreds and hundreds of detailed normal activities. There are two technical challenges with this.

First, the impacts of those high-level uncertain events should be scaled down to be commensurate with the durations of those normal activities. These events are a better match to the summary activities of the schedule, and not to very detailed normal activities. Second, as discussed previously, the probability assessment of an uncertain event depends on the level of its definition. The more general the event, the higher its probability. Initially assessed probabilities of high-level uncertain events will be all wrong when mapped to detailed normal activities. Due to these two points, the level of detail in the uncertainty repository and in the detailed schedule, including the level of detail of general uncertainties, will not be commensurate with each other. The results of such an analysis will be quite distorted, inconsistent, and misleading; they will be a waste of time and effort at best.

A similar situation may occur when running cost probabilistic models. A high level of detail in the case of general uncertainties developed for hundreds of cost accounts will conflict with the few uncertain events of higher impacts and probabilities. The resulting cost distribution curve might have two separate peaks, which is an indication of the presence of two groups of factors in the model that are not commensurate with each other. These groups should be in the same or a comparable "weight category." (This is usually the case when levels of detail are comparable.) Otherwise, they will not blend in the model and will produce distorted results.

The bottom line is that the level of detail in baselines should be comparable with the level of detail of uncertainty definitions kept in the project uncertainty repository.

There are two consistent possibilities to resolve this "incommensurability crisis."

First, an extremely detailed project uncertainty repository should be developed. Hundreds of detailed general uncertainties and uncertain events should be managed even before the probabilistic analysis is planned. They should be managed according to the risk management process in Figure 2.2, making the lives of the project team miserable. Each of those should be relevant to one or several detailed cost accounts and normal activities. This is absolutely the correct approach to match hundreds and hundreds of items in baselines with hundreds and hundreds of items in the project uncertainty repository, and is absolutely impractical. Months and months will be spent on such probabilistic analysis, which will have high complexity and likelihood of errors and omissions. The synchronization of cost and schedule models at such a level of detail in order to take into account schedule-driven costs would be a complete nightmare: hundreds of burn rates should be developed and justified to adequately integrate the two models.

Automation of this process would be bogus as good analytical skills cannot be replaced by a tool. Such an automated method will provide some results based on the infamous GIGO[1] principle that is so popular in the IT industry.

Second, the establishment of commensurability may be undertaken at a higher level. The detailed project base estimate and schedule may be rolled up to a much higher level that corresponds to a low level of detail. Similarly, the uncertainty repository should contain a lower level of general uncertainties and uncertain events. All relevant general uncertainties will be rolled up to ranges around one-point baseline numbers. A small number of relevant uncertain events with impacts and probabilities defined according to their level of definition will be a match with baseline items in terms of the level of detail. This simplifies probabilistic analysis enormously and makes it less onerous. Table 13.1 presents the general specification of inputs to such a probabilistic analysis.

TABLE 13.1 Specification of Inputs to Probabilistic Models

Input	Specification	Note
1. Proxy schedule	"Level 1.5" schedule: 30–150 normal activities (usually 40–70).	The same WBS at summary level for proxy schedule and proxy base estimate.
	Logic of master schedule retained.	Introduction of lags is required to keep logic and obey all milestones.
2. Proxy cost estimate	"Class 4.5" estimate: 15–50 cost accounts.	The same WBS at summary level for proxy base estimate and proxy schedule.
	Introduction of burn rates for summary accounts.	
3. General uncertainty register (deterministic)	Information required to justify ranges around cost accounts and normal activities of proxies.	Source: deterministic uncertainty repository.
		Full deterministic impact assessment for as-is and to-be cases.
		Set of approved addressing actions.
4. Uncertain event register (deterministic)	10–50 (usually 15–30) red and yellow uncertain events (assessment as-is for downside events and assessment to-be for upside events).	Source: deterministic uncertainty repository.
		Full deterministic impact and probability assessment for as-is and to-be cases.
		Set of approved addressing actions.
		Show-stoppers and game changers are listed and excluded as inputs.
5. Probabilistic general uncertainty register	Full definition of impact distributions.	Conversion of deterministic general uncertainty register to inputs according to PertMaster and @Risk/Crystal Ball specs.
	Main correlations (coefficient +0.8 to +1) and anti-correlations (coefficient −1 to −0.8) among distributions.	Usually triangular/trigen impact distributions used unless historic or modeling data indicate differently.

(Continued)

TABLE 13.1 (*Continued*)

Input	Specification	Note
6. Probabilistic uncertain event register	Full definition of impact distributions and probabilities.	Conversion of deterministic uncertain event register to inputs according to PertMaster and @Risk/Crystal Ball specs.
	Main correlations (coefficient +0.8 to +1) and anti-correlations (coefficient −1 to −0.8) among distributions.	Usually triangular/trigen impact distributions used unless historic or modeling data say differently.
	Mapping of schedule uncertainties to impacted normal activities.	Assessment of (min; max) probability range is required.
7. Description of probabilistic branching scenarios (if required)	Short description of construction/logistics/turn-around, etc. windows and associated triggers and delays.	Information according to PertMaster input requirements.
8. Description of what-if scenarios of interest	Short description of what-if scenarios of interest in cost or schedule models.	Groups of factors related to external or internal sources of uncertainties to investigate (e.g., permitting delays, engineering delays, etc.).
	List of key proxy milestones for investigation of their confidence levels.	Key milestones such as FID, mechanical completion, first oil, etc.

The schedule proxy introduced in Table 13.1 has a typical number of normal activities and a level of detail that is higher than level 1 but lower than level 2 typical project schedules. I call these "level 1.5" or "level one-and-a-half" proxies for probabilistic schedule analysis. A similar approach is used for development of cost proxies. They usually resemble estimates of class 4 or class 5 in terms of their level of detail. Let's call those "class 4.5" or "class four-and-a-half" proxies. This does not mean that all the ranges around cost accounts should comply with the typical accuracy ranges of class 4 or 5 estimates. Some parts of the cost proxies could have a higher level of detail to single out unique cost accounts that have anomalous wide or narrow ranges due to the current level of engineering and procurement development.

WHY USING PROXIES IS THE RIGHT METHOD

We saw in the previous section that commensurability between the number of cost accounts and normal activities in baselines and the number of uncertain events could be established at two levels: at a very low level with a very high level of detail, and at quite a high level with a low level of detail. A high level of detail makes building and running such models practically impossible. One of the additional contributions to the level of complexity would be the need to establish mandatory correlations among base estimate accounts and normal activity distributions. This comes from the high granularity of base estimates and schedules containing hundreds and hundreds of items and the need to compensate for such granularity mathematically. Here are the reasons for this.

Models that take in uncorrelated distributions produce much narrower distribution curves than models with a certain level of correlations (Figure 3.7). I do not intend to scare my readers away with topics such as the Central Limit Theorem, but it would be correct to state that uncorrelated inputs to probabilistic models will produce a narrow outcome curve that resembles a normal distribution (*bell curve*). As previously discussed, this should give rise to smaller-than-reasonable cost and schedule reserves.

Once upon a time I checked a project probabilistic schedule model that was run without any correlations among duration distributions and with a dozen uncertain events also uncorrelated. An amazingly low 0.8% schedule reserve at the P80 level of confidence was declared as an outcome of such analysis. And yes, the model had almost 1,000 normal activities with duration distributions around them. The distance to reality of this model was immense due to intrinsic granularity. The only benefit of this was the ease and speed of building and running this. The granularity of the model and the lack of correlations to compensate for it were among the key sources of its audacious inadequacy.

An additional reason why uncorrelated granularization should be avoided relates to the fact that a higher level of definition and detail in base estimates and schedules means narrower ranges around the most likely baseline values. For instance, ranges around the most likely values of level 4 schedules or class 3 estimates are usually narrower than the ranges of level 3 schedules and class 4 base estimates—they are better defined. If such inputs are not adequately correlated, sampling of narrow uncorrelated distributions will lead to a narrower outcome curve. That was exactly what happened in the previous example.

A word of caution relevant to the granularity of baselines: the transition from deterministic cost or schedule baselines to probabilistic models without proper correlations among components will lead to incorrect results. This just means that a deterministic baseline directly converted into inputs to a probabilistic model without proper compensation for the granularity will have nothing to do with the project probability-wise. Automation of modeling without proper correlations at the detailed level will consistently support producing wrong results. Automation will just make the production of wrong results easier and quicker.

Unfortunately the recently introduced software package Acumen Risk, which is positioned as a tool that does not require much knowledge of statistics, does not seem to address correlations properly. Even though it does have the functionality to condition the granularity of detailed schedules, it does not have the functionality to establish particular correlations among distributions in order to exclude unrealistic scenarios (!). It is not quite clear how Acumen Risk can produce realistic results. Sales- and marketing-driven user-friendliness and the targeting of laypeople as prospects seem to increase the distance of Acumen Risk models to reality to an unacceptable level. Hopefully, the next versions of Acumen Risk will get back to the correlating of distributions as a standard functionality to avoid this systematic error.

 ## MAPPING OF UNCERTAIN EVENTS

Uncertain events do not make impacts on a schedule as a whole. They make impacts on specific normal activities. If such an impacted activity belongs to the project critical path or near-critical path, there should be an impact on a project completion date. However, if an impacted activity precedes a substantial float in the schedule, there will be no overall impact at all. In other words, schedule impacts of schedule uncertain events are schedule-logic specific. This means in turn that any uncertain event of schedule impact should be mapped to one or several relevant normal activities to follow the schedule logic.

Such a probabilistic viewpoint conflicts with the deterministic method of schedule impact assessment discussed in Chapter 5. It was recommended there to regard schedule impact of any uncertain events as overall impact on the schedule completion date. This implies that such an impact belongs to a project's critical path, which is not always true. Technically, that corresponds to a recommendation to add contemplated overall impact to the project completion milestone, which belongs to the critical path for sure.

This contradiction dictates the need to substantially condition deterministic schedule impact data when converting them into inputs to probabilistic schedule models.

Any initially identified schedule uncertain event should be viewed from the angle of the normal activities it impacts. For instance, a delay in receiving vendor data may impact directly several engineering and procurement activities. Particular impacts (delays) for each of those activities could differ. So, a deterministically assessed impact should be reviewed and tailor-made (split) for each of these impacted activities. This makes the deterministic schedule impact assessment data unusable directly in the schedule probabilistic models. Some practitioners even believe that deterministic assessment methods are completely inadequate.[2] It's okay to engage in some drama when occupied with academic activities. I believe that the main practical value of deterministic methods is about addressing identified uncertainties using high-level rule-of-thumb assessments. They also provide some indicators of expected impact assessments, although those assessments cannot be used in probabilistic models directly without proper conditioning.

Existing probabilistic schedule risk analysis tools such as PertMaster correlate the impacts of an uncertain event on several normal activities with correlation coefficient 90% by default. This is a reasonable level of correlation. However, the correlation coefficients could be tailor-made if necessary.

Obviously, the same probability is used for all impacts of an uncertain event, which is the probability of its occurrence. A range of occurrence probability (min; max) should be discussed while assessing an uncertain event. When using a project RAM such a range is defined by one of five probability categories (Figure 3.2). When the conversion of deterministic data into probabilistic inputs is undertaken, the initially identified probability range should be challenged. A more precise or relevant range should be defined to get rid of certainty imposed by rigid RAM categories. For instance, if the initial probability assessment based on project RAM (Figure 3.2) were low (1–20%), a review of this RAM-based range could lead to a more specific assessment, for example, 5–15% or 10–30%. In the latter case, a new probability range covers two RAM categories (low and medium) and legitimately challenges the Procrustean-bed approach imposed by the deterministic RAM.

Technically, probability ranges are not required as inputs to probabilistic models. All existing probabilistic tools digest simple average values. For instance, the range 10–30% will be converted immediately by PertMaster into a single number, 20%. So, ranges are important and appropriate for assessment discussions, not for mathematical modeling.

The conversion of a deterministic uncertainty register (Figure 5.3) into probabilistic inputs to a schedule model is shown in Figure 13.3. Uncertain events of real project models could be mapped to several normal activities.

ID	Upside or Downside?	General Uncertainty or Uncertain Event?	DEFINITION		AS-IS		ADDRESSING		TO-BE		PROBABILISTIC TO-BE					
			Title	Three-Part Definition	Probability	Schedule	Response Strategy	Action(s)	Probability	Schedule	Probability	Mapping to	Min, days	ML, days	Max, days	Correlations
1	D	UE	Project Sanctioning	Due to a) general opposition by some NGOs to oil sands project; b) concerns by local communities about project's environmental impact; c) environmental issues associated with a similar project in the past, the **project XXX might be challenged during public hearings**, leading to A) permitting and final investment decision, engineering and procurement delays (Schedule); B) company's reputational damage in general (Reputation); C) complication of relations with local communities in particular (Reputation); D) extra owner's costs (CapEx).	medium (20%–50%)	very high (>6mos)	Mitigate-Prevent	To establish community engagement and communication plan including schedule of open house meetings	low (1%–20%)	low (0.5–1mos)	10%–30%	Engineering	5	10	25	
							Mitigate-Recover	To review sequencing of front-end loading (FEL)/pre-FID works and develop additional float in the schedule to absorb schedule impact for a case the risk does occur				Procurement	20	30	90	Construction. 80%

FIGURE 13.3 Concept of Conversion of Deterministic Data into Inputs to Probabilistic Schedule Model

As opposed to probabilistic schedule modeling, probabilistic cost modeling is not base-estimate-logic specific. Such logic in cost models does not exist. I mean there should be robust logic behind base estimates but not in the sense that the schedule logic is based on links among normal activities. It is still possible to associate some particular uncertain events with particular cost accounts of base estimates for tracking purposes. Moreover, this would be a good style when converting deterministically identified and assessed uncertain events of cost impacts into inputs to cost models. It could be easily done using mapping in the schedule model as cost impacts could be mapped to the same WBS accounts in the schedule model. However, such mapping makes no difference in terms of the mathematics of probabilistic cost modeling. In addition, there is no input functionality that allows one to take such cost mapping into account. This simplifies probabilistic cost modeling a lot. Figure 13.4 introduces a template used for developing probabilistic cost inputs.

A side by side comparison of Figures 13.3 and 13.4 reveals internal logic and links between impacts of the uncertain event on project cost and schedule. Obviously, the probability of occurrence of the uncertain event that has both cost and schedule impacts should be the same in both models. Mapping that is crucial in the schedule model is shown in the cost template for tracking purposes only. However, this event is mapped to the same activities: procurement and engineering. It would be logical to expect that there are the same correlations for this particular event with same other uncertain events in both models: to an unspecified construction uncertain event with correlation coefficient 80% in this example.

Once again, the probabilistic input data in both templates point to the fact that both probability and impact assessments ignore the Procrustean-bed ranges of the deterministic RAM. These should be used as starting points for development of probabilistic inputs and not as final inputs. A split of an initially rough impact is required to evaluate impacts on mapped normal activities individually. Strictly speaking, such individual impacts of one uncertain event on more than one normal activity should be treated as absolutely separate events, although correlated ones and of the same probability.

Both templates contain input data for probabilistic models for only the to-be case for simplification. If required, the as-is data could be easily added.

Obviously, mapping of general uncertainties is not required in either type of model as they are attached to the corresponding cost accounts or normal activities by default.

ID	Upside or Downside?	General Uncertainty or Uncertain Event?	Title	Three-Part Definition	AS-IS Probability	AS-IS Cost	Response Strategy	Action(s)	TO-BE Probability	TO-BE Cost	Probability	Mapping to	Min, $M	ML, $M	Max, $M	Correlations
					DEFINITION		**AS-IS**	**ADDRESSING**	**TO-BE**		**PROBABILISTIC TO-BE**					
1	D	UE	Project Sanctioning	Due to a) general opposition by some NGOs to oil sands project; b) concerns by local communities about project's environmental impact; c) environmental issues associated with a similar project in the past, the **project XXX might be challenged during public hearings**, leading to A) permitting and final investment decision, engineering and procurement delays (Schedule); B) company's reputational damage in general (Reputation); C) complication of relations with local communities in particular (Reputation); D) extra owner's costs (CapEx).	medium (20%–50%)	low (0.5M–5M)	Mitigate-Prevent	To establish community engagement and communication plan including schedule of open house meetings	low (1%–20%)	very low (<0.5M)	10%–30%	Engineering & Procurement	0.2	0.4	0.7	Construction. 80%
							Mitigate-Recover	To review sequencing of FEL/pre-FID works and develop additional float in the schedule to absorb schedule impact for a case the risk does occur								

FIGURE 13.4 Concept of Conversion of Deterministic Data into Inputs to Probabilistic Cost Model

BUILDING AND RUNNING MONTE CARLO MODELS

This book does not include the technical aspects of Monte Carlo modeling. This topic could easily become the subject for another book. I will reduce this topic to one bit of advice. As probabilistic output data are used for serious decision making that could predetermine a project's failure or success, employment of hundreds of workers, financial sustainability of a company, and so on, all probabilistic models should be built and run by fully qualified specialists.

When someone declares that he or she is capable of building and running probabilistic models, the first reaction should be skepticism. Different people imply different things when talking probabilistic modeling. This could be everything from qualitative "chance event" decision tree models to QuickRisk analysis or models based on general uncertainties only and without any correlations, and so on. Several examples of dubious modeling were provided in previous chapters. Simplistic models that do not require knowledge of mathematics and that have a huge distance to reality could be used to generate some talking points about project risk exposure and reserves. The same talking points could be generated without any probabilistic modeling. Project teams and especially decision makers should have strong immunity against such attempts at bamboozling. My method for preventing this is based on the simple request, "Show me your models." I am fully confident to show mine. Qualified and reputable third parties should be involved in the development of probabilistic models or at least in their reviewing and validation.

Validation of results is a major milestone in developing a probabilistic analysis report. The project team should review all the findings and conclusions of the third-party reviewers. Additional reruns or what-if scenarios are often required to clarify findings and provide clear recommendations.

CONCLUSION

This chapter does not get down to the technical level of model building. It would not be right to overload a book for project teams and decision makers with tons of mathematics. This chapter introduces all the main principles used to build probabilistic models that project teams and decision makers should be aware of. All input data specifications are introduced. This is done to ensure that project team members adequately understand the logic behind the input requirements. Input data are the main source of information for the modeling. Decision makers should be aware of the essence of the input data, which define the quality of the modeling outcome. A discussion on the interpretation of the probabilistic modeling results is provided in the next chapter.

 NOTES

1. Garbage in, garbage out.
2. D. Hubbard, *The Failure of Risk Management: Why It's Broken and How to Fix It* (Hoboken, NJ: John Wiley & Sons, 2009).

14

Using Outputs of Monte Carlo Analyses in Decision Making

Questions Addressed in Chapter 14

- What is the anatomy of output distributions?
- How may the overall project cost and schedule uncertainty be assessed?
- What is the primary accuracy range of a base estimate?
- Do we really need Association for Advancement of Cost Engineering (AACE) classes of base estimates in risk management?
- What are confidence levels of Cost and Schedule baselines and what are ways to make things better?
- How may criteria for project reserve be selected?
- Why do we need sensitivity analysis and what-if scenarios?
- Are we ready for construction, turnaround, and logistics windows?

N THIS FINAL CHAPTER of Part III we size up the value of Monte Carlo outputs for project decision making and methods of their interpretation. Some practical examples of interpretation of the results and their use for decision making are found in Chapter 16.

ANATOMY OF OUTPUT DISTRIBUTIONS

Figure 14.1 is a blown-up part of Figure 3.6, which represents typical output of probabilistic cost or schedule analysis. This figure shows the anatomy of the output distribution (the curve) at a higher level of detail. The curve could be used for assessment of overall cost or schedule uncertainty and the definition of project cost or schedule reserve. The selection criteria used for development of reserves should be part of the corporate risk management policy and the project risk management plan. The curve may represent any component of project reserve, combination of components, or the whole reserve, depending on what inputs were included in the probabilistic model.

A probabilistic schedule analysis can produce two versions of distributions for any project milestone or normal activity: distributions of durations and distributions of dates. The forms and shapes of both distributions are exactly the same. In most cases, they can be used interchangeably for the convenience of

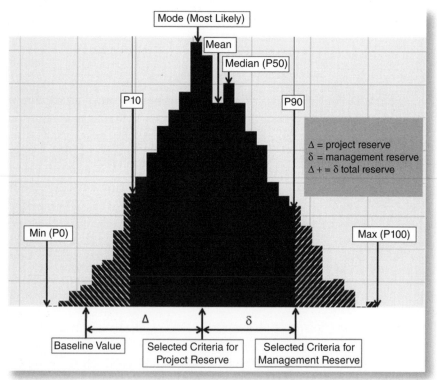

FIGURE 14.1   Typical Output of Probabilistic Analysis

decision makers. However, even though inputs to schedule analyses are done in the form of durations, decision makers prefer distributions of dates to more easily visualize the analysis outcomes and compare them to key project-related milestones.[1]

The output distributions are the raw material for decision making. A typical curve (Figure 14.1) shows the possible spread of project outcomes cost-wise or duration-wise. This means that if the distribution were developed adequately in terms of inputs, there would be zero probability to discover values higher than the maximum number or lower than the minimum number: values outside of the range are taboo. The maximum number provides us with 100% confidence or probability that the project cost or duration will be below that. To keep things short, we will not use long statements every time such as "The confidence level (or probability) is 100% that the possible project cost or duration will be below the maximum value of the curve." We will use the widely adopted risk term *P100* instead, where *P* stands for *probability*. (One might use *C100*, where *C* is for *confidence*. The C will not be used for the time being, though.) The reciprocal statement, "The confidence level (or probability) is 0% that the project cost or duration will be higher than the maximum value of the curve" is also true.

Similarly, in the case of a minimum number we should use *P0*. This is code for statements like "The confidence level (or probability) is 0% that the project cost or duration will be lower the minimum value of the curve."

The same logic may be adopted to describe any other probabilities/ confidence levels in the spread between P0 (min) and P100 (max). This implies that every value belonging to the spread P0–P100 should have its unique level of confidence. The level of confidence is the unique identifier of a value associated with each particular level of confidence, and vice versa. For instance, *P65* is code for "65% confidence level that the project cost or duration will be below this value," which is the equivalent of the reciprocal statement that there is "35% confidence level that the project cost or duration will be higher than this particular value."[2]

According to the shape of the curve in Figure 14.1, some values of the distribution are more likely than others. The peak of the curve represents the most likely (ML) value. It is called the *mode of the distribution*. Its confidence level depends on the particular shape of the curve. In Figure 14.1, the mode seems to have a level of confidence of about P40–P45.

Two other major mathematical characteristics of distributions are the *mean* and *median* values. The median value is associated with P50 by definition. This just represents the middle of the P0–P100 spread, with the shape of the curve being unimportant.

The mean value is a more complicated story. As discussed previously, this is the "center of the curve's mass." Hence, its position fully depends on the shape and spread of the curve. For instance, if the curve's right wing is spread significantly toward the higher numbers, the mean value should move to the right, too. If the curve has the left wing spread visibly toward the lower numbers, the mean value should become lower. As the mean value takes into account the shape and spread of the curve, it may be understood as the best one-point value representing the whole curve. Of course, it would be easy to come up with multiple curves that have the same mean value but totally different shapes or even a different number of peaks. So, the mean value does not serve as a unique identifier of a curve although it is still its best one-point-value representative.

Earlier we discussed the link between confidence levels and outcome values associated with the confidence levels. Another angle of this discussion concerns the likelihood of the realization of particular outcomes. Possible outcomes that belong to the curve's wings are less likely than curve's mode (most likely [ML] value). Outcomes that are close to P100 represent rather exotic cases where all downside uncertainties did occur. Apocalyptic scenarios like this cannot be fully excluded, though. If a project team is allowed to get a cost risk reserve that corresponds to the P100 level of confidence, all possible residual downside uncertainties should be nicely covered by such a reserve. Similarly, if a huge extra float is allowed in the project that compensates all possible schedule impacts of all downside uncertainties, the project team should be absolutely confident that the project will be completed on time or earlier. The problem with such "P100 confidence mentality" is that such a project becomes highly uncompetitive in terms of cost, schedule, and economics. Selecting very high levels of confidence such as P95–P100 to cover unlikely apocalyptic scenarios is unreasonable and too expensive.

Outcomes close to P0 values are not very likely, either. These are rose-colored-glasses scenarios based on the likelihood of all upside uncertainties being realized at once in one project with no downside uncertainties happening at all. This sounds even more utopian than the apocalyptic scenario discussed earlier, although both have the same (close-to-zero) probability of happening.

It would be weird for a project to bet on such a nice outcome. Such a bet would mean that a project team is comfortable with significant reduction of project budget or duration that is equal to the difference between the cost or duration baseline and the P0 value. No further comment is needed on such an unrealistic development.

In practice, project teams and decision makers ignore or should ignore outcomes that belong to the far-right and far-left wings so as to exclude exotic scenarios. To a certain degree those wings are harbors for all types of bias associated with the project uncertainty management. Cutoff values are usually established at P5 or P10 and P90 and P95 levels of confidence. Instead of the full spreads P0–P100, practitioners examine more the more practically significant spreads P5/P10–P90/P95.

OVERALL PROJECT UNCERTAINTY AND CONFIDENCE LEVELS OF BASELINES

The distributions produced from probabilistic models outline the overall or part of the overall project cost and schedule uncertainty, depending on the types of uncertainties included in the model (Table 1.2). Recall that cost escalation uncertainties are usually evaluated by separate models. Some types of uncertainties, such as game changers and show-stoppers, are normally not included in models on purpose. Sometimes schedule-driven costs are included, and sometimes not.

When a project reserve is discussed as the outcome of probabilistic analysis, a clear understanding of the inputting factors that gave rise to it is a must. This should be reflected in the probabilistic analysis method statement. Attempting to combine all types of uncertainties in one model is not practical. The standard set of uncertainties taken into account in probabilistic models includes general uncertainties in the form of ranges around baseline values and uncertain events of both the upside and downside type. A new trend is to include industry-specific unknown-unknown allowances as a measure of project novelty, phase of project development, quality of the risk management system, and so on. Whatever the contributors to a project reserve are, they also define the confidence level of the project cost or schedule baselines.

When a cost or duration distribution is developed as an outcome of a probabilistic model, the first step is evaluation of overall cost or schedule uncertainty associated with the project. We should go to square one (Figure 1.1) and associate the spread P0–P100 or the more practical spread P5/ P10–P90/P95 with the vertical spread of the project outcome in Figure 1.1. There is a tendency among decision makers (at least in the oil and gas industry) to prefer more expensive projects with a narrower spread of possible outcomes, rather than less expensive projects with a greater degree of uncertainty. For instance, project A has an estimated cost of $1 billion and a spread of possible costs from $900 million to $1.2 billion, whereas project B has an estimated cost of $960 million and a spread from $850 million to 1.3 billion. The former is much more preferable from the risk management viewpoint, despite the fact that it has a higher estimated cost (see Figure 14.2). The reason for this is the higher level of development of the first project and, as a result, the lower level of uncertainty. If the spread of final costs/durations is too big, additional measures may be required to reduce the uncertainty of the outcome to an acceptable level. Such a project might not pass the next decision gate if decision makers are not comfortable with the uncertainty of its outcome.

The next step would be the investigation of the baseline's level of confidence. Figure 14.1 shows a baseline value that has a very low level of confidence, below P10. It is not unusual to have a baseline confidence level in the range P1–P10 due to the overall uncertainty exposure, especially in the as-is scenario. Interestingly, the lack of correlations, which leads to narrow curves, may reduce the level of confidence. Including correlations produces wider curves with a higher spread of the wings in both directions. This usually corresponds to a higher level of confidence in the baseline. This observation points to the fact that the standalone confidence level parameter is not the ultimate measure of

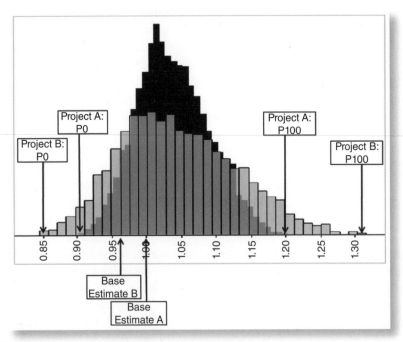

FIGURE 14.2 Comparison of Cost Uncertainties of Two Projects

project uncertainty cost- or schedule-wise. It should be considered along with the uncertainty spread.

There are three methods to increase the baseline's level of confidence. The first is to add a reserve above the baseline. The amount of required reserve will depend on the desired level of confidence and ultimately should be defined by a criterion stipulated by the corporate risk management procedures for project risk management. (Possible criteria to define project reserves are discussed in the next section of this chapter.) Throwing some extra money above the sanctioned budget or introducing extra schedule floats could contradict contractual obligations or previous decisions. Covering as-is uncertainties by reserves without any attempt to address them (Accept strategy) is the least efficient option.

The second method is to optimize the base estimate or schedule. Some value-improving exercises such as constructability and value engineering reviews, amendment of project execution strategy, and so on may be required. Technically, this corresponds to the situation where a distribution curve moves toward the lower values as a whole, with the baseline value staying put and gaining a higher confidence level. The distance of the curve's move is equal to a cost or duration reduction achieved as a result of the optimization as the curve follows the new optimized baseline. In reality, the proposed optimization measures could become causes of new uncertainties that would affect the resulting curve.

Third is to propose, approve, and implement additional uncertainty addressing actions (uncertainty changers) that would reduce overall uncertainty exposure. Some baseline optimization findings could be represented as upside uncertain events, especially if a project team does not have full control over their realization (Chapter 1). As the distribution curve would be favorably amended, the confidence level of a fixed baseline should be increased. At least the amount of required reserve should become lower.

Combinations of these three methods are commonly used. Trade-offs among them allow one to develop the most efficient approach. The sensitivity analysis of the as-is case helps one identify the most sensitive uncertain events and general uncertainties, which should be addressed first and foremost. Even slight improvements related to reduction of the most sensitive uncertainties would result in an disproportionately high improvement of the confidence level. What-if scenarios could be actively used to select and validate the most effective approach to improving baseline confidence levels. The three methods are demonstrated in Figure 14.3.

Going back to Figure 14.2 about comparison of two projects A and B, the manager of project B may initiate addressing actions to reduce the probabilities

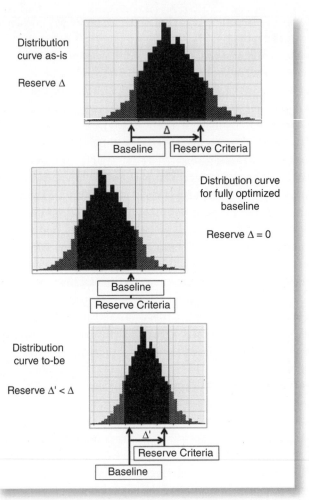

FIGURE 14.3 Three Methods to Increase Baseline Confidence Levels

and/or impacts of several top factors of project B. As a result, its estimated cost will be increased by the cost of addressing. However, the spread should become much narrower. For instance, the new estimated cost might be $980 million but the spread would shrink, getting a range from $930 million to $1.1 billion. Now, project B becomes preferable, having lower estimated cost and uncertainty. We can look at this example from a different angle and interpret this differently.

In practice, these two projects could be two different phases of development of the same project. Namely, the project B with the lower base estimate and the wider spread may be understood as the project in Select. The second project B, with the higher base estimate and the narrower spread, could be treated as the same project, but in Define, for instance. The difference in the two base estimates should include cost of addressing actions to manage project uncertainties.

Thus, the first method to increase baseline confidence level could be understood in most cases as the as-is scenario before any addressing, whereas the third method would mean the to-be case. In practice, two or more to-be scenarios could be run along with the baseline optimization to ensure the required confidence level of a baseline. A sequence of scenarios, as-is, to-be-1, to-be-2, and so on, could be run until the required level of confidence is achieved. Additional costs of addressing actions should be included in the cost baseline after optimization.

 ## PROJECT RESERVE CRITERIA

The criteria for the definition of project reserves that an organization adopts depend on several factors, including:

- Risk appetites and culture of the organization
- Size of the organization
- Number of projects in the portfolio under development
- Level of competition in the niches the organization works in
- Financial situation

Different criteria could be used for cost and schedule reserves or for different types of contracts. On one hand, the adopted criteria should be consistent across the project portfolio. On the other hand, the criteria should be flexible enough to take into account external factors such as competition and stakeholder expectations. For instance, for a competitive lump-sum contract bid, a proposal team could develop a comprehensive cost reserve at the confidence level P95 that includes all possible uncertainties, including possible liquidated damages, performance guarantees, and unknown unknowns. Everything would look fine except for the very high probability of losing the bid. Another organization might come up with a very competitive bid that includes a cost risk reserve developed at confidence level P20 or P30, which does not take into account liquidated damages, performance guarantees, and unknown unknowns. The latter organization would most likely win the contract ("buy

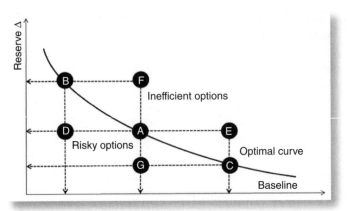

FIGURE 14.4 Optimal Risk Management Curve

it"), but it would start losing money over the course of project development and implementation.

Figure 14.4 represents a hypothetical optimal risk management curve that describes various scenarios related to this topic. It would be relevant to both cost and schedule reserves, although its application to cost reserves is intuitively better understood. An initial generic discussion of this is presented in an excellent book by Chapman and Ward.[3] Figure 14.4 is a further development of their generic idea.

The axes of Figure 14.4 represent levels of conservatism applied to the development of baselines and corresponding reserves. In other words, are baselines and associated reserves aggressive/low, reasonable/optimal, or conservative/inflated? An additional category, "acceptable," is used to mean "close to optimal" when the corresponding areas belong to the wings of the optimal curve. The preferable, or optimal, area belongs at the center of the chart (area A).

Table 14.1 analyzes seven characteristic areas on, above and below the optimal risk management curve and makes generic recommendations. In place of the proposed categories, other linguistic categories that describe the adequacy of the baselines and reserves can be used if needed. Unfortunately, it is not possible to express the optimal curve mathematically, but any project manager, estimator, scheduler, or risk manager could share his or her gut feeling about which area of Figure 14.4 a particular project belongs to.

Figure 14.4 and Table 14.1 provide a lot of food for thought. For instance, are options B and C, which both belong to the curve, equally attractive? Formally speaking, they are. However, it should be kept in mind that one dollar or day in a project reserve may correspond to more than one dollar or day

TABLE 14.1 Areas Related to the Risk Management Curve

#	Baseline	Reserve	Comments	Recommendations
A	Optimal	Optimal	Most efficient combination	Apply to your project
B	Acceptable	Acceptable	Second best to A	Move to area A
C	Acceptable	Acceptable	Second best to B	Move to area A
D	Low	Low	Risky option	Move to either area A or at least to area B
E	Inflated	Inflated	Inefficient option	Move to either area A or at least to area C
F	Inflated	Inflated	Inefficient option	Move to either area A or at least to area B
G	Low	Low	Risky option	Move to area A or at least to area C

in the baseline. The reason for this lies in the probabilistic nature of project reserves, at least of those parts of them that stem from uncertain events. In other words, if the baseline is inflated by an additional cost or duration Y due to taking an uncertainty into account, this corresponds to a P100 occurrence likelihood for such an uncertainty, regardless of whether it is a general uncertainty or uncertain event. This corresponds to the method of taking uncertain events into account along with general uncertainties discussed in Chapter 3 (Figure 3.3). This would mean that all uncertain events are counted in the baselines at confidence level P100, which is obviously overshooting. In the case of an uncertain event, its probability of occurrence Z is less than P100 (Z < P100). A rough assessment of the expected value required to cover such an uncertain event in the reserve would be the product (Y × Z), which is smaller than the initial Y. Such a compaction of project reserves leads to a lower overall project cost budget or duration in comparison with the case where uncertain events are taken into account in an inflated baseline at P100 confidence levels. This makes area B preferable to area C.

One of my co-workers pointed out that areas A, B, and C should belong to "most likely, mean or median optimal risk management parametric curves." Areas E and F should belong to the area around "P90/ P95 parametric curves." Similarly, areas D and G could be interpreted as close to "P5/P10 parametric curves." This is quite a valuable observation, especially to better understand relations between baselines and corresponding reserves. It also hints at the possibility of representing the optimal risk management curve mathematically.

If competition is not an issue, a bidding organization can afford to slightly inflate both Cost and Schedule baselines and reserves. This brings us back to the topic of second transactions to evaluate cost escalation (Chapter 11). However, in the case of severe competition, more risky options might be contemplated. This means that potential contract profit becomes associated with ("donated to") project reserve. Part of profit might be spent on occurred risks if the reserve turns out to be too low.

I would not call this a best practice for ethical reasons, but it is not unusual for bidding organizations to have two cost reserves. One is external, which goes to the RFP response and is based on a riskier option below the optimal risk management curve. The corresponding cost reserve is usually released to the project manager upon contract award; this plays the role of stretched target for the project team as imposed by decision makers. The other reserve is internal and often confidential. Usually, project team members do not even know exactly how far above the stretched target it actually goes. The confidential part of the reserve might be called "management reserve," "director's reserve," "VP's reserve," or "corporate reserve."

In some organizations the internal reserve is equal to a project contingency based on general uncertainty ranges plus the cost escalation reserve. Any uncertain event that is not directly linked with baselines ("business unusual") is treated through management reserve. I have doubts that such a demarcation is justifiable as some general uncertainties, such as labor productivity, could be the biggest project uncertainties and way more severe than all the uncertain events put together.

The introduction of management reserves that are kept unreleased to project teams leads to the idea of internal project insurance. All the management reserves of a project portfolio could be combined in an insurance pool unless the number of projects in the portfolio is not high enough to create such a pool. An organization should not keep such a big pool of money handy at all times as it would be quite expensive in terms of interest rates and lost investment opportunities. Only a small fraction of this is required, same as in the case of regular insurance companies

I know of an example of the implementation of such an approach by a major North American oil and gas company. Before the implementation of this approach, tens of millions of dollars were being released to projects annually as part of project reserves, which reduced the overall efficiency of the project portfolio management drastically. Upon the implementation of an approach based on much lower project reserves and proper tracking of funds released from the management reserve, it was discovered that only $10–$25 million per year should be kept and spent as management reserve.

Figure 14.1 illustrates the concept of distinguishing the project (Δ) from the management (δ) reserves, which together make up the total project reserve $\Delta + \delta$.

In practice companies often select project reserves Δ using the most likely (mode), mean, or median (P50) values plus the management reserve δ to reach very high confidence levels. This is a neutral option from the project governance viewpoint where competition is not a factor. Normally, mode, mean and median values are relatively close to each other. The median value or similar implies that there is a 50% chance that a project will end up with a lower cost or duration than sanctioned, and the same probability of overrun. Such a 50–50 chance represents the ideal option for a moderately stretched target.

In competitive situations any level of confidence from the range P5–P50 could be adopted for the project reserve. If competition is not an issue during bidding, the company can afford to select a project reserve from the range P50–P95. This would be the case if an organization is pretty busy with existing projects and can afford to win only highly profitable contracts. In both cases, there should be a management reserve above that complements the project reserve up to P90 or P95 confidence levels. Figure 14.1 illustrates the situation where the project reserve Δ is selected in the vicinity of the most likely value, which is complemented up to P90 by the management reserve δ.

Some companies do not split project and management reserves. Usually these are project owners who do not take part in project bids. In this case, project reserve Δ is usually selected at confidence levels P60–P90 (Figure 14.1), with the management reserve δ being equal to zero.

The project risk management plan should introduce a reserve selection criterion or methodology based on organizational framework of the project risk management as well as on corporate guidelines or recommendations and expectations of decision makers.

UNCERTAINTY OF COST OUTCOME AND CLASSES OF BASE ESTIMATES

According to standard estimating practice any base estimate should be affiliated with one of the five estimating classes promoted by AACE International.[4] Each class is associated with accuracy ranges around project base estimates. The purpose of this section is to fathom the applicability and value of such an approach imposed by estimating on project risk management.

The AACE classification is conditional as the edges of the AACE accuracy ranges are not very well defined, being sub-ranges or bands of values themselves. In practice low-low and high-high ranges are often ignored and low-high and high-low numbers are used to label associated classes and corresponding estimates.

Generally speaking, two approaches can be used to declare classes of particular estimates. The first is traditional and deterministic and well supported by the AACE methodology. When some relevant engineering, procurement, or construction activities are performed a class of a particular estimate is declared on the basis of completed activities, not achieved project development results. This is a traditional deterministic approach that justifies the presence of *ranges of accuracy ranges* (or bands) in place of clearly defined one-point numbers, as shown in Table 14.2. This makes definitions of AACE classes quite ambiguous and not specific. For instance, if 30% of engineering is done in two different projects, there will be differences associated with the real accuracy levels of those two base estimates. So, handy sub-ranges or *bands of accuracy ranges* (which sounds like a dichotomy to me) absorb any inconvenient differences. Moreover, ranges for different classes overlap. For instance, accuracy range −25%/+35% may belong to both class 5 and class 4. Isn't this too convenient? This is a traditional source of dispute between project owners and engineering, procurement, and construction (EPC) contractors when progress payments for EPC services are discussed. The discrepancy between the spent ("burned") hours that assume some level of project development and the actual level of project development can be astonishing. The ambiguity in selecting and declaring an AACE class of a base estimate resembles that of the methodology used to declare an icon's authorship by arts scientists (see Chapter 3).

TABLE 14.2 Primary Probabilistic Accuracy Ranges versus AACE Classes

AACE Class	Range for Primary Accuracy P5		Range for Primary Accuracy P95	
	P0	P10	P90	P100
	Low-Low	Low-High	High-Low	High-High
5	−50%	−20%	+30%	+100%
4	−30%	−15%	+20%	+50%
3	−20%	−10%	+10%	+30%
2	−15%	−5%	+5%	+20%
1	−10%	−3%	+3%	+15%
		Used for labeling of AACE classes	Used for labeling of AACE classes	

The second approach is new and probabilistic. The accuracy and class of a base estimate are not declared until accuracy ranges are calculated as outputs from probabilistic analysis, no matter what activities have been performed. Figure 14.5 illustrates the recalculation of the statistical data associated with a project cost distribution. (For simplicity, management reserve δ is not introduced here.) Besides representing project reserve funds graphically at all possible levels of confidence, it demonstrates the origin of the primary accuracy level of a project base estimate. Another example of this chart is discussed in Chapter 16 for the case study of Project Curiosity.

The shape of the curve shown in Figure 14.5 points to three distinctive areas. The dependency of the project reserves as a percentage of the base estimate on the confidence levels is almost linear for confidence levels between P5 and P95. Very different slopes of the curve are found on the wings of the curve for confidence levels P0–P5 and P95–P100. Such a change in the curve's behavior mathematically was quite common for curves developed previously for various projects I worked on.

First, wing areas P0–P5 and P95–P100 are harbors for improbable outcomes where all upside or all downside uncertainties are realized simultaneously. Second, these harbors also accept all overly optimistic and overly pessimistic uncertainty assessments fed by various types of bias. The manifestation

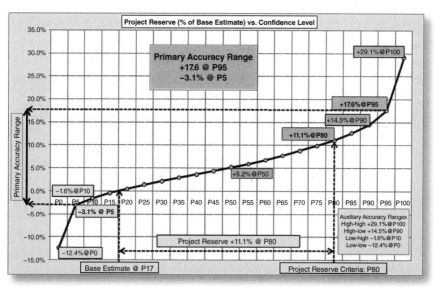

FIGURE 14.5 Project Reserves and Primary Accuracy Range

of those harbors through the changing behavior of the Figure 14.5 dependency is quite amazing mathematics-wise. I could come up with a more robust justification for this conclusion using standard methods of mathematical analysis, but I do not wish to get geeky and intimidate my readers with such an academic exercise, so I refrain from further mathematical justification of this point.

This sort of observation instigates the conclusion that a representative and practically significant spread of curves should be defined as P5–P95, with P0–P5 and P95–P100 wings being gently cut off. However, practitioners such as myself (a few years ago) have used P10–P90 spreads instead, which looks too narrow according to the shape of the curve in Figure 14.5.

Once again, the P5–P95 primary accuracy range of the base estimate must not be declared because of some undertaken activities; it is directly calculated without any phony declarations. It would be interesting (albeit not mandatory) to compare calculated primary accuracy ranges with AACE ranges, including ranges of ranges (bands). The following points should be kept in mind when doing such a comparison.

First, traditional AACE classes are used to define the accuracy ranges of base estimates only when the general uncertainties associated with the levels of EPC development are taken into account. Uncertain events usually are not included in the uncertainty assessments. Moreover, some general uncertainties, such as cost escalation and exchange rate uncertainties, are never included. So, based on the uncertainty object classifications of Table 1.2, traditionally, AACE classes are associated with general uncertainties that give rise to a project cost contingency. As we take into account uncertain events as well as schedule-driven costs and unknown unknowns (sometimes) in probabilistic cost analysis, traditional AACE accuracy classes and probabilistic primary accuracy ranges cannot be compared apples-to-apples, having different natures and inputs.

Second, due to the behavior of the curve in Figure 14.5, range P5–P95 is ideal for the definition of unambiguous probabilistic primary accuracy ranges. Again, there is no need for AACE-type accuracy range declarations as they would sound like "I have a gut feeling and belief that this is rather a class X estimate (the "Andrei Rublev" estimate) than a class Y estimate (the "Theophanes the Greek" estimate)." I have a feeling that the box in Chapter 3 on "Andrei Rublev versus Theophanes the Greek" is relevant to this discussion, too. There is no need for vague "art science" statements like above. Much better statement would be "It is what it is (P5 and P95), according to Monte Carlo calculations."

The probabilistic primary accuracy range definition is fully self-consistent and mathematically justified and elegant. In place of the vague AACE classes, which are slightly archaic, risk management should just calculate the percentage of deviations from the base estimate at P5 and P95 confidence levels using Monte Carlo modeling. That's it!

Third, there is no need to divide the estimating people from the risk management people. We are all comrades-in-arms fighting the overall uncertainty of project outcomes, although we work in two adjacent but separate and "sovereign" areas. Table 14.2 proposes a link between traditional AACE classes and the new, probabilistic definition of the primary accuracy range. According to the previous discussion, it looks natural to associate low-low edges of AACE classes with the P0 level of confidence in the probabilistic case. Similarly, the P100 confidence level could be interpreted as high-high edge. The P10 and P90 confidence levels should be interpreted as low-high and high-low edges, which corresponds to the traditional labeling of AACE classes. The link between primary accuracy range P5–P95 and the AACE classes could be established in a simple way. As Table 14.2 suggests, the calculated P5 value should belong to the (low-low; low-high) AACE interval. This should correspond to the probabilistic P0–P10 range. And the calculated P95 value should reside in the (high-low; high-high) AACE interval corresponding to the P90–P100 range.

As Figure 14.5 points out, AACE classes play a secondary role in risk management but could be used as the liaison between estimating and risk management worlds for labeling purposes. In reality, P5 and P95 values calculated probabilistically are not obliged to belong to the same AACE class. For instance, Figure 14.5 points to two AACE classes. The P5 value (−3.1%) belongs to class 1, whereas the P95 value (+17.6%) belongs to class 2. A simple explanation would be that more downside uncertainties are taken into account in the probabilistic analysis than in the traditional AACE assessments based on some general uncertainties and the level of project development. The whole distribution has moved toward higher required reserve numbers due to additional downside deviations. No explanation is required for the calculated (not declared) primary accuracy range. It is what it is. Using the AACE estimating labels of classes is nice but not mandatory for imposing on project risk management.

Fourth, Figure 14.5 introduces an example where the confidence level of a project base estimate is relatively high (P17). This outcome was obtained for a case after addressing (to-be-2) in Execute when well-developed addressing actions were proposed. For this reason the primary accuracy range is quite narrow. In as-is scenarios it is not unusual for the confidence level of the base estimate to be quite low. For instance, it could be below P5. In this case, the low edge of the primary accuracy range would be positive. This means that the base estimate is outside the primary accuracy range, which is a clear sign of trouble. Addressing actions and some upside deviations from the cost objective should be developed to get the base estimate back into the primary accuracy range. Some baseline optimization steps could be also undertaken. It is quite common for the confidence levels of baselines to belong to the range P5–P10. This is another manifestation of the preference for having P5 as a low cutoff value over the P10 values.

Fifth, as discussed, it is not justifiable to compare AACE classes with their probabilistic analogs directly as far more uncertainties are taken into account in probabilistic analysis. A direct apples-to-apples analogy is possible only where traditional general uncertainties are taken into account in a probabilistic model. This means that the definition of the primary accuracy range is input specific in the sense that it is type-of-uncertainties-included-in-probabilistic-analysis specific. The weakest point in this logic is that the cost escalation uncertainty is not probabilistically treated (Chapter 11).

 ## COST RESERVE DRAWDOWN

The project cost reserves developed initially for decision making at the final investment decision (FID) should not be kept intact until project completion. Project uncertainty exposure changes constantly. For instance, any permitting, engineering, procurement, or construction milestones achieved are reasons for the review and update of a project cost reserve. The representatives of corporate finance would be keenly interested in releasing part of the project cost reserve to profit over the course of project development and execution. Such reviews can be done on either an ad-hoc or regular basis.

If according to corporate procedures the drawdown reviews should be done on a regular basis, particular points in time of to-be assessments should be advanced to be specific in developing the project reserve forecasts. For instance, if the drawdown reviews are being done on a quarterly basis, the corresponding forecasts of the required cost reserves should be done for the to-be-Q1, to-be-Q2, and to-be-Q3 scenarios, and so forth. A review of the corresponding inputs should be undertaken for those scenarios that are supposed to take into account upcoming achieved milestones, expected reductions in uncertainty exposure due to implementation of addressing actions, uncertainties that cannot happen any longer, and so on. Even though the input templates are supposed to be regularly reviewed and updated, the initial mathematical models for the probabilistic cost and schedule risk analysis may stay the same. If an integrated cost and schedule model is used, the schedule analysis should be rerun correspondingly and the burn rates should be updated to come up with an adequate drawdown forecast.

Cost escalation models should be updated, too. These updates have two levels. First, cash flow forecasts should be renewed as required. Second, macroeconomic indexes that are used to program the project cost escalation should be also updated regularly because the providers of these indexes update them on a quarterly basis.

The drawdown calculations depend on what is included in the definition of the project cost reserve. The drawdown could be forecast either for individual contributions or for the whole reserve. It is important to use the same confidence level to define the required reserve for all periods. For instance, if the cost reserve at FID was approved at confidence level P60, the same confidence level should be used for all to-be forecasts for financial reporting. Along with this, high and low end values for the required reserves could be represented. The most reasonable would be the cost reserve values that correspond to P5 and P95 confidence levels that define the primary accuracy levels.

Project risk practitioners develop so-called "banana curves" to illustrate the forecast results for the corporate financial people to properly manage their expectations and appetites. Those banana curves also resemble funnels, becoming narrower for future forecasts. This increasing narrowness represents the increase of expected primary accuracy levels. Eventually, by project completion, absolute accuracy or zero uncertainty exposure will be reached, which will correspond to a project cost reserve equal to zero.

It is obvious that the reserve drawdown should be done by organizations that take on corresponding uncertainties according to contractual obligations. For the lump-sum type of contract, the EPC contractor owns the reserve and calculates the drawdown forecasts. For a reimbursable type of contract, the project owner is supposed to do this. However, for a unit-price contract both organizations would be exposed to specific uncertainties that give rise to their cost reserves.

As previously discussed, labeling contracts by their types can be quite misleading. Similarly features and dynamics of the project execution strategy are behind of many project uncertainties and so on. The specific details of an organization's uncertainty exposure and its dynamics should be adequately represented in the corresponding uncertainty logs and taken into account during reserve drawdown.

SENSITIVITY ANALYSIS

The application of the three methods to increase the confidence levels of Cost and Schedule baselines introduced in this chapter requires some tips and guidelines. Which particular uncertainty should be further managed first and foremost? Which particular element of a base estimate or normal activity of a schedule should be picked up for baseline optimization as a priority?

It seems clear that if a cost element or a normal activity has a significant general uncertainty attached to it through ranges, even a relatively modest reduction of such an uncertainty would improve the project outcome substantially. However, there seem to be some exceptions.

First, if a significant uncertainty is associated with very low cost or a short normal activity of just a few days, overall improvement will not be that exciting. Second, if a normal activity of significant uncertainty does not belong to the project's critical or near-critical path, the available float should absorb this. Near-critical paths may switch from one to another in iterations of probabilistic analysis. As a result, some normal activities and the uncertainties associated with them may belong to the critical path in some particular iterations. Depending on the frequency of belonging to the project critical path, the influence of particular normal activities and their associated uncertain events could vary.

What if a project uncertain event is mapped to quite a few normal activities? This could become quite influential in terms of the impact on overall project duration. But the devil is in the details! Again, do all those mapped normal activities belong to the project critical path? If most of them do, that uncertain event might keep its top-influencer status. Otherwise, it will get a lower ranking. As in social or political life, networking is important for being influential. But this will also depend on the frequency of occasions to influence and the magnitude of the influence as well as on quality of the network. As in politics, some uncertainties create "coalitions" through correlations and have greater influence due to the degree of alignment. The cost impacts of uncertain events are not schedule-logic specific. So, the probability of their occurrence and impacts should be a primary factor of influence along with correlations, and so on.

Intuitive speculations above have quite robust realizations in probabilistic analyses. There are several types of mathematical sensitivity analysis methods used to find the most sensitive baseline elements and project uncertainties. These are based on modifications of regression analysis and correlation ranking. Several parameters and indicators could be used to measure levels of sensitivity. Some of them are derivatives of each other and are not used in practice very often. The two most valuable and popular types of sensitivity analyses are:

1. Cost or duration sensitivity ranking
2. Criticality indexes ranking (only for schedule analysis)

Introduction of additional sensitivity indexes to project teams and decision makers does not offer extra value and can be a source of confusion.

Any type of sensitivity analysis is usually run by probabilistic software tools in parallel with the development of cost and/or duration distributions.

Duration sensitivity of an uncertain event or a general uncertainty of a normal activity is a measure of the correlation between its duration and the overall duration of the project. In cost sensitivity it is the measure of the correlation between the overall project cost and the impact of the cost uncertain event or cost general uncertainty, correspondingly.

Cost or duration sensitivity ranking may be done for general uncertainties only, for uncertain events only, or as a combination of general uncertainties and uncertain events. Criticality index ranking cannot be done for probabilistic cost analysis as such ranking is schedule-logic specific. Criticality index ranking can be developed for three situations: for schedule normal activities with their general uncertainties only, for schedule uncertain events only, or for a combination of both.

The results of sensitivity analyses are usually represented by "tornado charts" that show the sensitivity ranking of the corresponding uncertainties. It is possible to compare the sensitivities of general uncertainties and uncertain events by putting them both in the same tornado chart. The following figures demonstrate various options for tornado charts. These charts directly relate to the hypothetical case study of Project Curiosity discussed in Part IV.

Figure 14.6 depicts the sensitivity ranking of the general uncertainties associated with the normal activities belonging to the project proxy schedule. No uncertain events are included in this analysis.

Figure 14.7 shows the sensitivity ranking of only schedule uncertain events. None of the schedule general uncertainties are included. It is important to note that upside uncertain events have negative sensitivity. Their presence gives rise to shorter project durations. The uncertain events are shown in association with the normal activities they impact. For instance, uncertain event R1 (Regulatory Approval Delay), which is mapped to normal activity 022, (it refers to review and approval of project application by government in this example)

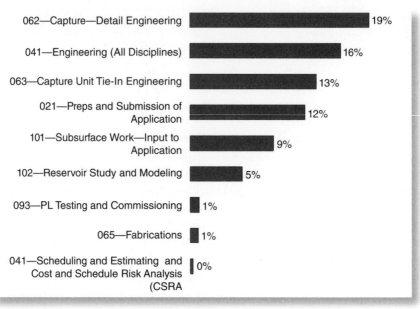

FIGURE 14.6 Sensitivity Chart of Schedule General Uncertainties

has top sensitivity ranking in Figure 14.7. Figure 14.7 also reflects the fact that some uncertain events are mapped to several normal activities.

Figure 14.8 is the combination of sensitivity rankings for schedule general uncertainties and uncertain events. Different colors are used to represent these two categories of uncertainties in the tornado chart. It is important to remember that uncertain events and general uncertainties do not have a level playing field. Uncertain events are counted only in iterations when they occur according to their probability of happening. General uncertainties are sampled in all iterations, having 100% probability by default.

Additional valuable information would be gained by figuring out which normal activities or uncertain events appear on the project critical path in most iterations. As in the case of sensitivity charts, criticality indexes may be developed for three major situations: (1) when only normal activities with their general uncertainties are included; (2) when only uncertain events are taken into account; and (3) when both give rise to the ranking. As opposed to normal activities with general uncertainties, uncertain events do not show up in all iterations. The frequencies of their appearance in sampling depend on their probability of occurrence. For instance, there could be an uncertain event that always appears on the critical path. However, due to

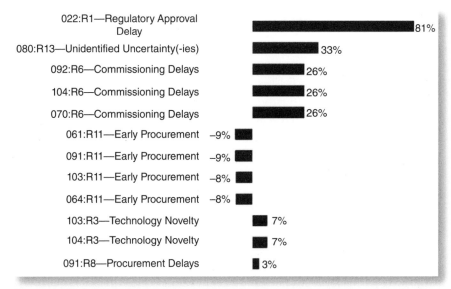

FIGURE 14.7   Sensitivity Chart of Schedule Uncertain Events

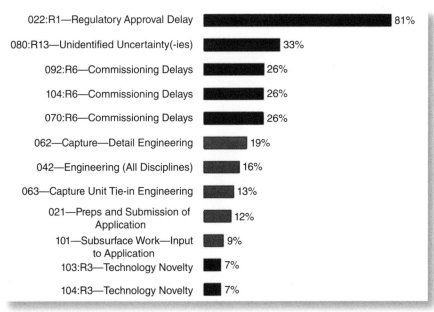

FIGURE 14.8   Sensitivity Chart of Schedule General Uncertainties and Uncertain Events (Negative Sensitivities Excluded)

its probability of occurrence being equal to 5%, it has a 5% criticality index. At the same time a normal activity should be represented in all iterations. If it belongs to the critical path in 30% of the iterations, its criticality index (30%) would be six times higher than the criticality index of the uncertain event (5%).

Top criticality points out those normal activities and uncertain events that should be addressed first when optimizing the project schedule and addressing uncertainties. Figure 14.9 introduces a criticality index that takes into account both normal activities with general uncertainties and uncertain events.

In cost sensitivity analysis it is also possible to distinguish general uncertainties from uncertain events in the tornado charts. However, there is no specific functionality for distinguishing these two main types of cost uncertainties. Namely, a sensitivity analysis can be done for any particular output from the cost model. This output may contain contributions from both general uncertainties and uncertain events depending on how the model was built. As a result, sensitivities of all contributions to the output will be analyzed. Hence, the result of the sensitivity analysis will depend on how a

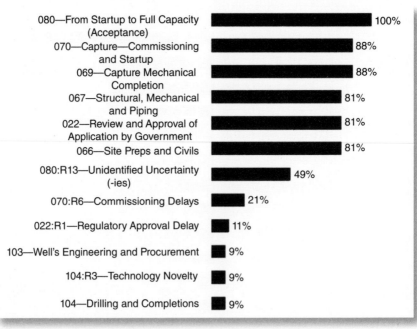

FIGURE 14.9 Criticality Index Chart for Normal Activities with General Uncertainties and Uncertain Events

particular output is programmed. For instance, one output may include only ranges around the baseline costs. Its sensitivity analysis will obviously contain only general uncertainties. The other output may include only uncertain events coming from the project risk register. Sensitivity analysis of such an outcome will obviously show the rating of uncertain events only. However, it is easy to program a third output as a summary of these two outputs. The resulting output will represent a united sensitivity analysis that comprises both types of uncertainties. This means that any output may be created in a probabilistic cost model to investigate particular combinations of uncertainties of interest. Figure 14.10 represents a sensitivity tornado chart for a Project Curiosity model output that is a combination of cost general uncertainties (GU) including schedule-driven costs (SDC), unidentified uncertainties (UU) and uncertain events (UE).

Information on sensitivity is used to further support steps based on the three methods demonstrated in Figure 14.3. Optimization of baselines, allocation of required project reserves, or development of additional addressing actions can be done in a most efficient way when keeping in mind the most sensitive uncertainties.

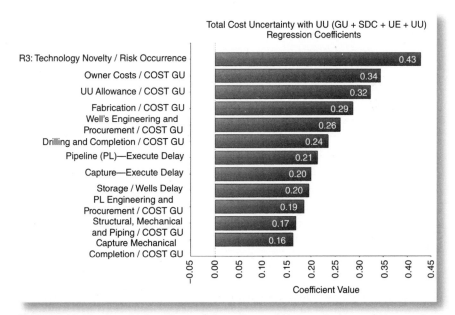

FIGURE 14.10 Sensitivity Chart of Cost General Uncertainties and Uncertain Events

USING WHAT-IF SCENARIOS FOR ADVANCED SENSITIVITY ANALYSIS

The cost and schedule uncertain events associated with a project belong to various risk breakdown structure (RBS) categories. Together they result in the overall cost and schedule uncertainties of the project. In many cases it is worthwhile to single out all uncertainties of a particular origin. How would a project be doing if all regulatory uncertainties vanished? What might be the expected project outcome if all procurement uncertainties were gone? Questions like this can be asked and reflected in the method statement. Often those questions are raised in the quest for further clarification when the primary probabilistic risk analysis activities defined by the method statement are completed.

As opposed to the standard sensitivity analysis discussed in the previous section, advanced or what-if sensitivity analysis is based on the behavior of the uncertainty population of particular RBS categories. Several uncertain events could be left out to compare the difference with a scenario where they are part of the model. Probabilistic software packages allow such modeling to be easily done.

Some practitioners see standard to-be cases as part of what-if scenarios. I am not against this classification, although the roles of the more unique what-if scenarios could be understood differently. For instance, the efficiency and capability of a project team to meet the approved project completion date and the role of the permitting process in timely project completion could be investigated. One such scenario could be the hypothetical situation where the permitting timelines are guaranteed through excluding any associated uncertainties. Such utopian "written-in-stone" permitting timelines would reveal the confidence level of project completion depending on the efficiency of the project team activities only. At the same time, as-is and to-be cases should be investigated as a standard set of probabilistic analysis scenarios.

Standard sensitivity analysis may provide guidance for the development of what-if scenarios. For instance, if regulatory or procurement uncertain events occupy the top positions in the tornado charts, these could be selected as the subject of what-if scenarios to better understand the overall role of uncertainties belonging to such RBS categories. Decision makers may express their interest in particular scenarios and should clearly formulate them.

The outcome of what-if scenario modeling usually provides valuable information for the next steps, such as negotiations, restructuring the project, optimization of the base estimate and schedule, and so on. The scopes of particular what-if scenarios depend on the curiosity of decision makers and the challenges surfaced or anticipated in the course of project development and execution. Three practical what-if scenarios will be discussed in Part IV for Project Curiosity.

 ## ARE WE READY FOR CONSTRUCTION, LOGISTICS, OR TURNAROUND WINDOWS?

Figures 12.6 and 12.7 depict the possibility of modeling and visualizing specific schedule windows where some activities are or are not possible. Modeling based on probabilistic branching requires advanced skills. Not every project team will have a specialist at that level. The good news is that a quite adequate analysis of readiness for a window or preparedness to complete works before a downtime period could be easily done utilizing standard PertMaster functionality. The confidence level of a milestone that precedes the downtime window or a milestone that precedes the construction, logistics, or turnaround window could be easily investigated. In addition, a milestone that succeeds an allowed window should be investigated, too. The latter should ensure that all works are done by the end of the window. If the confidence level for being on time for either of those milestones is below around P50 or P70, a red flag should be raised and either the schedule should be accelerated or additional actions addressing schedule uncertainties should be developed and implemented (or both) to reach a comfortable confidence level close to P100.

Usually schedulers introduce start and finish milestones of corresponding windows as constraints. Technically, this guarantees a confidence level of P100 for each of those milestones, no matter what. Nothing could be more confusing than this for investigations of realistic confidence levels! All constraints like this should be removed. (Actually, the only constraint that is acceptable for a schedule used in probabilistic analysis is the project start date. The presence of any other constraint will ruin the probabilistic schedule analysis as the constraints will not allow the uncertainties to play ball.)

One example of a narrow turnaround window would be a one- or two-month tie-in period to hook up a CO_2-capture unit to an existing power plant or refinery. Usually such a "special period" takes place once in 1.5 to 2 years if we are talking about preplanned windows. According to standard rules, a notice about the coming tie-in should be submitted to the facility owner 1 to 1.5 years before the turnaround window. The equipment and all parts for installation should be on site, say 6 to 12 months before the window. Any delay or missed deadlines could lead to a critical project delay of 1.5 to 2 years, respectively, which can become a project game changer if not a show-stopper. This example will be discussed in Chapter 16.

The investigation of readiness for the turnaround window is reciprocal to the investigation of completion of works prior to the downtime window (Figure 12.6).

The investigation of readiness for the turnaround window is discussed in Part IV for Project Curiosity.

VALIDATING RESULTS AND CLOSING PROBABILISTIC ANALYSIS

Part IV is devoted to a practical if simplified business case that illustrates most of the key concepts and methods introduced in this book. Before we get to this case study, it is important to accentuate the validation of the outcome and reporting of the probabilistic analysis results.

First, when we talk about schedule and cost probabilistic analysis we are talking time and money. If such results are not well substantiated, we are also talking quality, reputation, safety, and environment. Sometimes, the results of such an analysis mean canceled projects and higher unemployment. Besides the application of the line-of-sight concept (Figure 2.1) and the development of roles-and-responsibilities matrixes (Table 2.1) there should be internal responsibility of each project team member for providing unbiased and reliable information as inputs. The role of the risk manager is to explain the logic behind the required input information and ensure the collection of the required unbiased input data according to specifications.

Second, the project risk manager should be completely unbiased, honest, and realistic about his or her experience and capabilities to carry out an adequate risk analysis. The development of models that have near-infinite distances to reality just to justify one's existence is unacceptable. The involvement of specialists from other divisions of an organization or from third parties is the most reasonable thing to do in many cases. Cold-eye reviews of results should be mandatory in all cases no matter who carries out the probabilistic analysis. Checking the results is also a great opportunity for coaching risk managers and analysts.

Third, the project risk manager should be absolutely sure that decision makers are comfortable with the concepts used in the modeling and interpretation of the results. This point is absolutely crucial. All the activities described in this book have one ultimate purpose: decision making. In deterministic analysis it is about the approval and implementation of addressing actions. In probabilistic analysis it is about the optimization of baselines and allocation of adequate reserves to ensure a high level of confidence in project success.

An informative briefing or training that explains the details of the method statement and ways to interpret the outcomes should be provided for decision makers. This should be done either by the project risk manager or by more knowledgeable third parties, if required.

The validation of the probabilistic analysis is the culmination of all previous activities, from the initial uncertainty identification to defining cost and schedule reserves. Some of the findings will not be pleasant for some project team members and decision makers. The role of the risk manager in handling various types of bias is especially important during the validation period.

When the validation of results is done, three things are left to complete. First, all project uncertainty repositories should be updated using the most recent information obtained during the probabilistic analyses. Some what-if scenarios could be especially valuable in updating assessments of probabilities and impacts. Additional addressing actions developed as part of consecutive to-be scenarios should be approved and included in the uncertainty repository, too. Working plans to implement new addressing actions should be specified. Some uncertainties and/or addressing actions could be closed, and so forth.

Second, a lessons-learned session should be held to reflect on risk management activities and identify the highlights and lowlights. Areas of improvement should be outlined to be taken into account during the next rounds of probabilistic analyses.

Third, a concise but comprehensive report should be prepared, supported by all relevant templates and input data as backup. This information should be available for future audits. This report should serve as an effective source of information required to sanction project reserves and evaluate the confidence levels of the final project baselines. The report should summarize the method statement and major activities (workshops and discussions) to collect and validate input data. Special attention should be paid to presenting information normally used in decision making. This should include information on key risks included in and excluded from the analysis (game changers and show-stoppers), main scenarios (as-is, to-be-1, to-be-2, etc.; all what-if scenarios), main statistical data of final output curves, sensitivity analysis outputs (tornado charts), selected project reserve, primary accuracy range, and so forth. Five or six pages accompanied by half a dozen of the most relevant charts and tables are what decision makers usually require to be sure that all input and output data are robust and trustworthy. Some reporting charts and tables are presented in Chapter 16.

 ## CONCLUSION

This chapter is devoted to the briefing of decision makers on ways to use the information obtained from probabilistic cost and schedule modeling. Along with results of cost escalation modeling (Chapter 11) and information about key project uncertainties, including corporate risks (show-stoppers and game changers), this could be used for decision making at any project decision gate or when a project reaches a major milestone. Practical applications for decision making will be discussed in Part IV of the text.

 ## NOTES

1. We use distribution curves in this book that are called *probability density distributions* in mathematics. Having a peak and wings, such a distribution resembles a bell curve. In input distributions, probability density distributions are usually triangular/trigen distributions, although smoother types of curves could be also used as inputs when required. The other types of distributions used in practice as outputs from probabilistic analysis are *cumulative probability distributions*. These are S-shaped and are produced along with density distributions automatically by probabilistic tools. It is impractical to use S-shaped distributions as inputs to probabilistic analyses. So, the density-type distributions are preferable for consistent use as both inputs and outputs of probabilistic analyses. However, if density curves are selected as the output format from the probabilistic schedule models in PertMaster, both curves will be shown, anyway, helping to define the confidence levels of particular dates. This feature will be depicted in the figures in Chapter 16.
2. It is obvious that the discussion about the anatomy of output curves strongly resembles the corresponding discussion about the anatomy of input distributions in Chapter 12. We keep both discussions to reiterate the major distribution characteristics and better accentuate the differences between input and output distributions. In any case, repetition is the mother of knowledge and skills.
3. C. Chapman and S. Ward, *Project Risk Management: Processes, Techniques and Insights* (Chichester, UK: John Wiley & Sons, 2003).
4. AACE International Recommended Practice No. 17R-97: *Cost Estimate Classification System* (Morganton, WV: AACE International, 2003).

PART FOUR

Risk Management Case Study: Project Curiosity

I T WAS A DILEMMA TO ME WHETHER a practical case study on major applications of project risk management should be included in this book. The major argument not to include was that project team members and decision makers will not do such exercises on their own, usually being led by project risk managers. A major argument to include was supported by my previous experience. There was a high interest on the part of many project team members and decision makers I worked with in understanding risk management via practical examples. After all, no one appreciates driving courses based solely on theory, important as theory is, without the opportunity of actually driving.

After I had decided to include a case study, the next challenge was to select a type of a project for this. As I had worked on a variety of capital mega-projects, making the choice was pretty difficult. The final decision was encouraged by my former co-worker, Dr. Bill Gunter, who kindly agreed to write the foreword to this book. Being a top world specialist in carbon capture and storage (CCS) and greenhouse gases (GHG) projects and initiatives, he expressed an interest in finding a topic that is close to his professional activities. How could I ignore the wish of my first reader?

As a risk specialist I took part in more than one CCS project. Some information about this can be found in the public domain.[1] At the same time the format of this book and existing confidentiality agreements do not allow me to be terribly specific. So any similarity to any real project is accidental albeit some public domain information was certainly used.

The simplified version of CO_2 sequestration Project Curiosity, discussed in this part of the text, lost most of the factual features of the real projects I worked on. Moreover, all the actual numbers in Cost and Schedule baselines were replaced by fictional numbers that have nothing to do with real CCS projects. So there is no need for benchmarking of the baselines used in this case study. However, the study keeps the main uncertainties and methods to manage them relevant to real CO_2 sequestration projects. It should be encouraging news for my readers who work on other types of projects, from onshore and offshore oil and gas exploration and production, to pipelines, to power generation, and so on, that all those methods and many uncertainties are relevant to their projects, too.

Chapter 15 introduces a CO_2 sequestration project case study. Chapter 16 is devoted to the practical application of several methods discussed in this book and their results. It also outlines the process of risk-based informed decision making. The decision presented by a decision review board concludes Chapter 16.

---

[1] Y. Raydugin, Y. "Developing a Risk Program for a Carbon Capture and Storage Project: A Case Study of Project Pioneer" (A report prepared for TransAlta Corporation. Global CCS Institute, 2013).

Putting Together the Project Curiosity Case Study

Questions Addressed in Chapter 15

- What are the objectives and baselines of the project discussed in the case study?
- What is the deterministic uncertainty management approach adopted by Project Curiosity?
- What is the probabilistic uncertainty assessment approach adopted by Project Curiosity?
- What are the main templates used for preparing input data to probabilistic modes?
- What are the what-if scenarios used to further investigate project uncertainty exposure? ■

T HIS CHAPTER INTRODUCES THE SCOPE and goals of a case study to demonstrate most of the methods and tools introduced in this book. It also introduces the risk management system adopted by a hypothetical project. The integration of deterministic and probabilistic methods is accentuated.

This hypothetical case study is a simplified carbon capture and storage (CCS) project called Curiosity. Its description, including baselines, is provided. A high-level base estimate and schedule are introduced in this chapter for demonstration purposes. Normally, the number of identified project uncertainties is measured in the dozens. Only a dozen of the most critical uncertainties were highlighted for this case study. Some of those are included in the probabilistic cost and schedule models. Features of these models bear the stamp of simplicity, which is inevitable when a low number of uncertainties is included. However, these models are informative enough to demonstrate all the major features of probabilistic analyses and decision making.

SCOPE OF THE CASE STUDY

Based on the country's obligations to obey the Kyoto protocol requirements, the country's local and central governments initiated a program to facilitate the development and implementation of CCS projects. The program, financed by government grants, was aimed at proving CCS technologies on a commercial scale. This was considered a major step in CCS technology maturation through moving it from the pilot development phase to commercial applications. Although this program did not support commercial aspects such as the maturation of the CO_2 market, it did not preclude participating companies from improving project economics through the selling of CO_2 for enhanced oil recovery.

Companies interested in obtaining financing were obliged to demonstrate that:

- A full-scale industrial facility (refinery, upgrader, power plant, etc.) that was a significant source of CO_2 would be selected.
- Appropriate subsurface reservoir(s) could be identified for either CO_2 storage or enhanced oil recovery (EOR).
- Adequate monitoring, measurement, and verification (MMV) methods could be applied to control the behavior of stored CO_2.
- A reliable and economically viable transportation method would be used to deliver captured CO_2 to the injection site(s).

At least 700,000 tons of CO_2 should be captured and injected each year during the project lifetime.

This case study relates to a diversified energy and utility company that won the grant with intent to develop CCS Project Curiosity, which had the following features:

- To use a company's power generation facility as a source of CO_2 that currently is released to atmosphere
- To install CO_2 capture equipment based on a new, advanced carbon capture technology in order to capture about 1 million tons of CO_2 per year
- To inject about 800,000 tons of CO_2 into an aquifer reservoir in a location about 80 km from the power plant
- To sell the balance of the captured CO_2 (200,000 tons) to one or several oil and gas companies engaged in enhanced oil recovery in the area to improve the project economics
- To define the project lifetime by the remaining lifetime of the power plant (about 35 years after project completion)

For simplicity, the type of contract that the project owner has with the engineering, procurement, and construction (EPC) contractors is a reimbursable contract which is taken into account during uncertainty assessments.

The case study covers the Select phase of the project development and ends with the decision gate review preceding Define.

The primary goal of this case study is to demonstrate the power of probabilistic cost and schedule modeling for decision making. This includes development of project reserves, sensitivity analysis, what-if scenario development, and assessment of the primary accuracy ranges of cost and duration distributions. Along with these, key points of deterministic risk analysis will be reiterated to accentuate the integration of deterministic and probabilistic methods (Figure 12.1). However, some methods discussed in this book, such as cost escalation modeling, are not included in the study for simplicity. As demonstrated in Chapter 16, the conclusions and recommendations advanced by the decision review board are based on the results produced by both deterministic and probabilistic methods.

 ## PROJECT CURIOSITY BASELINES

Engineering Scope

Major decisions on the engineering scope were made to comply with requirements stipulated by the funding agreement with the government. A CO_2 capture technology was selected that was proven by a pilot test at a small refinery. The pilot was based on a fraction of CO_2 volume that was planned for the full-scale CCS project (1 million tons per year). Although the pilot project was successful, the scalability of the equipment to full capacity seemed to be an issue.

The injection site selection was based on several technical parameters, such as capacity of reservoirs, their permeability and injecting efficiency, as well as containment. The possibility of application of effective MMV methods was also taken into account. Additional parameters used for the selection of suitable injection sites were risk based. These additional criteria were included to reflect project objectives such as Cost, Schedule, Reputation, Environment, and Safety. An uncertainty assessment of shortlisted sites was undertaken to narrow down the possible options. As a result, a quite suitable aquifer reservoir was identified with possible injection sites 80 to 100 km from the power plant. A corresponding reservoir study and modeling were initiated to narrow down injection site options and define the required number of injection wells and prepare for the project application to the government.

The design of the 80–100 km 18-inch pipeline from the power plant to the injection area was based on the expected specification of CO_2 captured at the power plant. A better than 95% CO_2 purity was guaranteed by a capture equipment producer. Such a level of CO_2 purity was suitable for enhanced oil recovery. In fact, several oil reservoirs suitable for miscible CO_2 flooding were identified in the vicinity of the pipeline's right of way. The possibility of improving the project economics through selling CO_2 to oil producers was included in the scope of the project. It was one of the factors when selecting injection sites. Selection of the pipeline diameter was based on the possibility of increasing sales of CO_2 in the future.

According to the funding agreement with the government, the overall amount of CO_2 stored in subsurface reservoirs should be 1 million tons per year during Project Curiosity's lifetime. Besides this, several acceptance criteria were advanced by the government as related to capacity, injectivity, and MMV aspects of operations.

Hence, the Scope objective of Project Curiosity was formulated by the project team as a *System Capacity baseline*:

- To ensure that overall System Capacity of three project components (capture unit, pipeline, and storage) is 1 million tons per year of CO_2 captured and stored
- To store about 80% of captured CO_2 in subsurface reservoir(s) according to government acceptance criteria
- To sell about 20% of captured CO_2 to oil and gas producers for their CO_2-EOR projects

Project Schedule

The project team developed a project work breakdown structure (WBS) that reflected the four major deliverables of Project Curiosity. The following summary activities became the basis for the project schedule development:

1. Regulatory
2. Capture
3. Pipeline (PL)
4. Storage/wells

Even though the government was a major stakeholder of the project its various branches should review the project application and approve it. The issue with this was that the level of maturity of existing regulations was low, which could cause project sanctioning and final investment decision delays.

Each of the three components of the project has activities related to engineering, procurement, and construction followed by the final integration. The sustained operations milestone was introduced as the end of the project. As detailed acceptance criteria on sustained operations were included in the contract with the government, special activities to ensure full acceptance were planned after startup and before the finish milestone.

A government grant was provided to cover all major development and execution activities to ensure a breakeven point of project profitability. However, a final investment decision should be done by the end of Define to sanction the project internally. The possibility of project cancellation would also be considered then if project economics were to look poorer than expected.

Strict timelines for sustained operations were stipulated by the funding contract with the government. According to the contract, sustained operations should be reached by December 1, 2018. Any possible delay in securing sustained operations on time could lead to severe penalties (liquidated damages). To increase the chances of meeting the stipulated deadline, a three-month float was added to the schedule prior to the contractual completion date, which defined the schedule completion date as August 30, 2018.

The importance of a timely final investment decision from the angle of effective corporate governance was recognized by the project team. The final investment decision (FID) milestone was scheduled for February 3, 2016.

The project schedule developed by the project team contained several hundred normal activities. According to broadly accepted practice, its concise version (a "proxy of level 1.5") was developed as a basis for schedule risk analysis (Figure 15.1). It contained five milestones, five summary activities, and 23 normal activities.

One of the factors that could lead to a catastrophic project delay was associated with the need to complete CO_2 capture unit tie-in during a very short turnaround window. A missed turnaround window would mean the project would be delayed for more than a year. Two milestones to delineate the beginning (068SM: Jan. 1, 2018) and the end (068FM: Feb. 15, 2018) of the turnaround window were introduced to the project schedule to monitor compliance with this important constraint.

The overall project Schedule objective of Project Curiosity was formulated as follows:

- To ensure that FID milestone is timely achieved according to the project schedule (Feb. 3, 2016)
- To ensure that all three components (capture, pipeline, and storage) are timely in sustained operations to meet government timeline requirements and acceptance criteria by Dec. 1, 2018.

Project Base Estimate

The nature of the funding agreement with the government assumed a zero level of profitability of the project. However, to reach breakeven and avoid losses it was required to develop, execute, and operate the project keeping in mind various cost reduction and cost control methods. It was not precluded by the agreement with government to improve project economics through selling part of the captured CO_2 to oil and gas producers in the area for enhanced oil recovery.

A detailed base estimate was developed by the project team that contained hundreds of cost accounts. A proxy base estimate that was rolled up from the detailed base estimate contained 24 cost accounts and 6 summary accounts. The number and types of cost accounts are the same as in the case of the proxy schedule. However, one additional cost and one summary account were added. These two represented owner's costs that were not included in the other cost accounts.

Table 15.1 represents cost estimating information for Project Curiosity at the summary level. It has the same WBS as the project proxy schedule. The base estimate is represented also as the sum of fixed and variable costs, where variable costs are the product of summary activity durations and corresponding burn rates. The summary activity durations are taken from the project schedule proxy. This representation of the base estimate is required for building

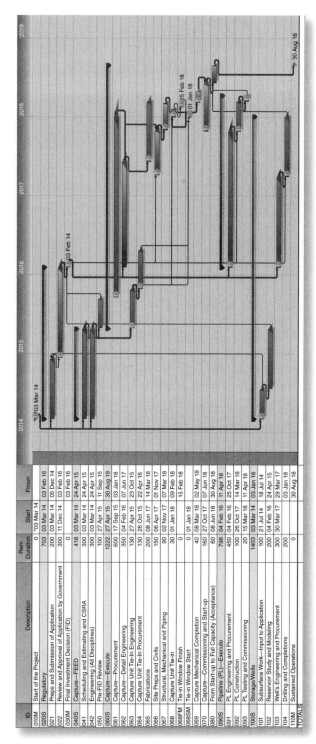

ID	Description	Rem Duration	Start	Finish
010M	Start of the Project	0	'03 Mar 14	
020S	Regulatory	703	03 Mar 14	03 Feb 16
021	Preps and Submission of Application	200	03 Mar 14	05 Dec 14
022	Review and Approval of Application by Government	300	11 Dec 14	03 Feb 16
030M	Final Investment Decision (FID)	0		03 Feb 16
040S	Capture—FEED	418	03 Mar 14	24 Apr 15
041	Scheduling and Estimating and CSRA	300	03 Mar 14	24 Apr 15
042	Engineering (All Disciplines)	300	03 Mar 14	24 Apr 15
050	Pre-FID Review	100	27 Apr 15	11 Sep 15
060S	Capture—Execute	1222	27 Apr 15	30 Aug 18
061	Capture—Procurement	600	17 Sep 15	03 Jan 18
062	Capture—Detail Engineering	350	04 Feb 16	07 Jun 17
063	Capture Unit Tie-In Engineering	130	27 Apr 15	23 Oct 15
064	Capture Unit Tie-In Procurement	130	26 Oct 15	22 Apr 16
065	Fabrications	200	08 Jun 17	14 Mar 18
066	Site Preps and Civils	150	06 Apr 17	01 Nov 17
067	Structural, Mechanical and Piping	90	02 Nov 17	07 Mar 18
068	Capture Unit Tie-in	30	01 Jan 18	09 Feb 18
068FM	Tie-in Window Finish	0		15 Feb 18
068SM	Tie-in Window Start	0	01 Jan 18	
069	Capture Mechanical Completion	40	08 Mar 18	02 May 18
070	Capture—Commissioning and Start-up	160	27 Oct 17	07 Jun 18
080	From Start-up to Full Capacity (Acceptance)	60	08 Jun 18	30 Aug 18
090S	Pipeline (PL)—Execute	798	04 Feb 16	11 Apr 18
091	PL Engineering and Procurement	450	04 Feb 16	25 Oct 17
092	PL Construction	100	26 Oct 17	14 Mar 18
093	PL Testing and Commissioning	20	15 Mar 18	11 Apr 18
100S	Storage/Wells	1403	03 Mar 14	03 Jan 18
101	Subsurface Work—Input to Application	100	21 Jul 14	18 Jul 14
102	Reservoir Study and Modeling	200	04 Feb 16	24 Apr 15
103	Well's Engineering and Procurement	300	30 Mar 17	29 Mar 17
104	Drilling and Completions	200		03 Jan 18
110M	Sustained Operations	0		30 Aug 18
TOTALS				

FIGURE 15.1   Proxy Schedule of Project Curiosity

TABLE 15.1 Project Base Estimate and Project Duration at Summary Level

ID	Description	000$	Fixed Cost, 000$	Duration, day	Burn Rate, 000$/day
020S	Regulatory	8,406	7,000	703	2
040S	Capture—FEED	41,254	40,000	418	3
060S	Capture—Execute	306,110	300,000	1,222	5
090S	Pipeline (PL)—Execute	137,990	134,000	798	5
100S	Storage/Wells	177,015	170,000	1,403	5
OC	Owner's Costs (items not included above)	63,780	60,000	1,890	2
	Total Base Estimate	734,555			

an integrated cost and schedule model. Another representation of summary cost accounts was done as a percentage of installed materials, construction equipment and labor. This breakdown is required for the development of the project's cost escalation model.[1]

The overall project capital cost (CapEx) objective of Project Curiosity was formulated as follows: to ensure that all three components (capture, pipeline, and storage) are delivered according to the approved capital budget to maintain at least zero profitability of the project or better.

Project Operational Budget Estimate

The standard evaluation of project economics includes the overall project lifetime costs and profitability. The proper trade-off between CapEx and OpEx budgets and their optimization is the way to ensure the best possible project economics and profitability. Several engineering design and procurement options selection activities were undertaken by the project team to ensure a proper trade-off. One feature of the CCS project is that decisions made in Select, Define, and Execute and factored into the CapEx could impact Operate during project lifetime. Such an impact might be realized not only through increased OpEx and poor System Capacity but through impacts on a company's Reputation as well as Environment and Safety objectives.

An operational budget baseline for Project Curiosity was developed by the project team to ensure that the project CapEx and the present value of OpEx supported at least a zero level of project profitability. This approach was also based on taking into account additional constraints related to Reputation, Environment, and Safety objectives.

Other Project Baselines

In addition to the Scope, Schedule, and Cost (CapEx and OpEx) objectives and baselines, three other objectives were presented for project development and execution. These were Reputation, Environment, and Safety, which were understood as goal-zero objectives. Namely the three soft objectives of the project pointed to the need to develop and execute the project without any:

- Reputational damage or negative impact on relations with major stakeholders
- Negative environmental damage during project development and execution
- Safety incidents at project sites

It is important to make it clear that special attention was paid to ensure the absence of negative reputational, environmental, and health and safety impacts in Operate. Due to the nature of Project Curiosity addressing uncertainties related to cap rock integrity, CO_2 plume propagation, containment, and MMV, the reliability of the capture, transportation and storage operations was a major part of the project activities.

An upside deviation from the goal-zero Reputation objective in Operate was implied by the project team. Proving CCS technology at the commercial scale should contribute to improving the company's reputation as a leader in innovation and technology and enhancing its "green" image. This in turn should improve the company's chances to get access to new oil and gas reserves and power generation contracts globally. In addition, the company would become a profitable licensor of a proven CCS technology to be sold to other organizations and governments interested in CCS projects.

PROJECT RISK MANAGEMENT SYSTEM ADOPTED BY PROJECT CURIOSITY

The project team developed a project risk management plan for Project Curiosity that covered the three main components of a project risk management system.

Organizational Framework

First, organizational framework was formalized. Seven project objectives and baselines were formulated as discussed in the previous section. Roles and responsibilities of team members were formalized (Table 2.1). A two-level risk breakdown structure (RBS) that reflected the nature of the project and its three distinctive components was developed (see Table 15.2). The RBS (level 1) and seven objectives were integrated in a project bowtie diagram for uncertainty identification and management (Figure 4.2). A corresponding risk assessment matrix (RAM) was developed and approved (Figure 3.2).

TABLE 15.2 Risk Breakdown Structure of Project Curiosity

Level 1	Level 2	Uncertainties Related to:
Stakeholders and Regulatory		Local communities, industry, government and NGOs
Organizational		Project development and execution practices adopted by the company, features of decision making as well as business culture aspects
Economics and Agreements		Project economic model, funding agreement, and contracts
	Funding/Grant	Contract with government on funding of the project
	Acceptance Criteria	Part of contract with government on major project deliverables
	Commodity Marketing	CO_2 marketing and contracts with oil and gas (O&G) producers to sell CO_2 for EOR
Project Development and Execution		
	Capture	EPC of capture component
	Pipeline	EPC of pipeline component
	Wells	EPC of well's drilling and completion
	Integration	Integration of three components
	Startup	Activities from mechanical completion to sustained operations
Operations		From sustained operations to decommissioning of the project
	Capture	Capture unit operations
	Containment	CO_2 sequestration in a reservoir (cap rock integrity)
	Injectivity	Speed and stability of injection of CO_2 to the reservoir

TABLE 15.2 *(Continued)*

Level 1	Level 2	Uncertainties Related to:
	Capacity	Volume of CO_2 accepted by the reservoir
	MMV	Measurement, monitoring, and verification of CO_2 sequestration and CO_2 plume propagation
	Asset Integrity	Integrity of the capture unit, pipeline, and wells

Five grades of deviations from the OpEx objective due to uncertainties should be understood as accumulated deviations from the annual operating budgets during project lifetime that are rolled up as present values related to the baseline period.

Five grades related to the System Capacity objective are understood as deviations from the budgeted capacity of 1 million tons per year during at least one year of project lifetime. The project team examined an alternative to assess accumulated deviations from the planned System Capacity during project lifetime. This alternative was rejected as not being specific enough for managing the project in Operate.

The frequency of uncertainty reviews kept in various logs of the project uncertainty repository was established. Uncertainties of higher severity and their addressing actions should be reviewed more often than less severe uncertainties.

The project risk management plan was developed to describe all elements of the project risk management system. It contained reporting requirements, including reporting templates.

Risk Management Process

A standard risk management process was adopted by the project team (Figure 2.2). Several Delphi technique workshops were held to identify uncertainties related to the project. The bowtie diagram (Figure 4.2) was used as a major identification tool that included approved project objectives and RBS. Several-dozen upside and downside uncertainties were identified and categorized using the two-level RBS (Table 15.2). A series of uncertainty assessment workshops were held that included development of various addressing strategies and actions (Chapter 5). The majority of identified and assessed uncertainties seemed to have a low level of severity after addressing. Table 15.3 is a list of the most significant uncertainties that will be further described in this case study. For the purpose of this case study, the list contains only a dozen uncertainties.

TABLE 15.3 The 12 Most Critical Uncertainties of Project Curiosity

ID	Upside or Downside?	General Uncertainty or Uncertain Event?	Title	Three-Part Definition	RBS Category
R1	D	UE	Regulatory Approval Delay	Due to (a) immature regulatory framework for approval of CO_2 sequestration project; (b) stakeholder intervention and objections; (c) requirement of Environmental Impact Assessment; (d) difficulties demonstrating containment, **project approval by the government could be delayed**, leading to (A) project schedule delay; (B) reputation damage; (C) schedule-driven costs.	Stakeholders and Regulatory
R2	D	UE	Missed Tie-in Window	As (a) the plant's shutdown window occurs earlier than planned; (b) engineering and procurement activities are not complete by the beginning of the shutdown window, **the tie-in window could be missed**, leading to (A) critical project delay; (B) recycling of project baselines; (C) financial losses; (D) reputation damage.	Organizational
R3	D	UE	Technology Novelty	As (a) this type of project brings up a significant level of novelty with regard to capture and storage; (b) some subsurface studies are planned after completion of engineering, **late change of engineering and drilling scope of works could be required**, leading to (A) rework and extra costs; (B) schedule delays; (C) lower quality of integrated system.	Project Development and Execution
R4	D	UE	Subcontractor Default	As unknown instability of some bidders was not identified during prequalification, **selected subcontractor(s) might become insolvent or bankrupt during project execution**, leading to (A) the need to find a substitute and schedule delays; (B) extra (premium) costs for quick mobilization; (C) lower quality of work; (D) reputation damage.	Project Development and Execution

R5	D	GU	Low Productivity	As (a) some construction contracts are reimbursable; (b) subcontractors are not able to attract and retain qualified workers; **subcontractors are not able to maintain expected level of productivity**, leading to (A) schedule delays; (B) extra schedule-driven costs.	Project Development and Execution
R6	D	UE	Commissioning Delays	Due to (a) novelty of capture unit compressor applications; (b) issues with quality of pipeline construction; (c) issue with quality of well's completion, **commissioning delay could occur,** leading to (A) rework and extra costs; (B) schedule delays; (C) reputation damage.	Project Development and Execution
R7	D	GU	Cost Escalation	Due to (a) development of project base estimate in money of Q1 2014; (b) volatility of market prices for materials, equipment, and labor, **purchasing prices will differ from budgeted ones,** leading to extra capital costs.	Project Development and Execution
R8	D	UE	Procurement Delays	As (a) several types of equipment and materials are delivered from overseas; (b) selected vendors have lack of production capacity; (c) equipment arrives damaged at the construction sites, **timely installation of equipment would not be possible,** leading to (A) overall schedule delay; (B) extra schedule-driven costs.	Project Development and Execution
R9	D	UE	Reservoir Geology	Due to misunderstanding of various aspects of sequestration (injectivity, capacity, heterogeneity, cap rock integrity, plume propagation, wells completion, etc.), **poorer-than-anticipated geological characteristics of the selected reservoir might be discovered,** leading to (A) environmental damage; (B) reputation damage; (C) health and safety impact; (D) lower system capacity.	Operations

(Continued)

TABLE 15.3 (Continued)

ID	Upside or Downside?	General Uncertainty or Uncertain Event?	Title	Three-Part Definition	RBS Category
R10	D	UE	Immature CO_2 Market	As (a) infrastructure to deliver captured CO_2 to injection wells for EOR purposes does not exist; (b) delivery of CO_2 to EOR injection sites by trucks is too expensive; (c) development of horizontal directional drilling technology becomes an alternative to CO_2-EOR; (d) O&G companies do not consider CO_2-EOR a primary option; (e) there is a gap between economic expectations of the project owner, oil producers, and the government, **marketing of CO_2 by the project could be unsuccessful**, leading to (A) poorer project economics; (B) lower attractiveness of the project for stakeholders; (C) reputation damage; (D) redefinition or cancellation of the project.	Economics and Agreements
R11	U	UE	Early Procurement (Opportunity)	As (a) funding of procurement of capture, pipeline, and storage long lead items is planned after FID; (b) several types of equipment and materials are delivered from overseas, **pre-FID procurement could be sanctioned by management,** leading to (A) acceleration of schedule; (B) better chances to meet government commitments; (C) improved reputation; (D) schedule-driven cost reduction.	Project Development and Execution
R12	D	UE	Safety Incidents	Due to (a) presence of standard safety hazards at construction and well drilling sites; (b) potential violations of safety procedures by contractor's personnel; (c) possibility of catastrophic incident at the power generating facility, **safety incidents might occur at the project construction sites,** leading to (A) injuries or fatalities; (B) stoppage of works for investigation; (C) reputation damage; (D) environmental impact.	Project Development and Execution

Risk Management Tools

The project team investigated various risk database software packages available on the market. None of them adequately supported the organizational framework and risk management process adopted by Project Curiosity. It would have been possible to build the required bowtie and RAM for some of the databases, but the costs of such tailor-made adjustments and consecutive support turned out to be unreasonably high. Eventually, the project team adopted a generic MS Excel–based template (Figure 5.3 and Table 8.2) as the basis for the project uncertainty repository (Figure 8.1). All seven agreed project objectives as well as the RAM categories were included in the template. The list of uncertainty and addressing action owners was built into the template as a dropdown menu.

The company's document control system was used to publish the repository templates on its intranet. This system had a good tracking functionality that allowed control of all the changes in the templates. The most recent versions of the templates were visible to users who had the corresponding access rights. All previous versions of templates were also available. It was decided to revisit the decision to select a generic MS Excel–based database tool upon project sanctioning.

One of the options studied when selecting a database management tool was using PertMaster or another comparable package as a single risk management tool. Technically, it would have been possible to develop a deterministic risk register and run cost and schedule risk analyses. Such a solution was rejected for several reasons, including the following.

First, several licenses would be required to allow access to multiple users. It turned out that the price per license was too high.

Second, the adopted structure of the project uncertainty repository (Figure 8.1) could not be built in PertMaster, which supported a single risk register. Some applications (PHA/HAZOP, safety, value engineering, etc.) could not be supported by PertMaster templates at all.

Third, although project planners and schedulers did not object to using PertMaster, cost estimators and the majority of the other project specialists were not comfortable with this. They preferred MS Excel–based probabilistic software packages.

As a result of the obstacles and shortcomings listed above, it was decided to use PertMaster for probabilistic schedule risk analysis only and @Risk for probabilistic cost analysis. The schedule analysis output data would be used in @Risk template to carry out integrated probabilistic cost and schedule analysis.

Additional MS Excel–based templates for collection of probabilistic cost and schedule input data would be developed. These were adaptations of the basic MS Excel template (Figure 5.3) for probabilistic analyses.

A standalone cost escalation model would be developed based on the project base estimate and the cash flow forecast. The latter would indicate when the corresponding purchasing commitment should be locked. The required composite indexes would be developed utilizing macroeconomic indexes from a reputable source.

OVERVIEW OF PROJECT UNCERTAINTY EXPOSURE OF PROJECT CURIOSITY

While the majority of the identified uncertainties could be managed at the work-package or project levels successfully, some of them (Table 15.3) represented a supercritical challenge to the project. Some of those uncertainties stemmed from the work-package level and some from the project level. At the same time some uncertainties should belong to the corporate level. Moreover, some identified uncertainties could become game changers or even show-stoppers if manifested in the form of the most unfavorable scenarios. The issue with the proper evaluation of corporate risks is that they require a different set of objectives because not all project-level objectives are relevant. Corporate RAM should not keep CapEx, Schedule, or Scope objectives. However, Reputation or Safety should be kept. In addition, Legal, Profit Margin or ROI, Employee Retention, and so on could be considered, which is outside the scope of this book.

Most of the uncertainties of Table 15.3 should be taken into account when developing the cost and schedule reserves of Project Curiosity through probabilistic modeling. However some of them (game changers and show-stoppers) should not be part of the corresponding probabilistic models. If at least one of the game changers or show-stoppers were to occur, all baselines should be recycled and redeveloped if the project still exists.

The rest of this section is devoted to an overview of each of the uncertainties listed in Table 15.3.

Regulatory Approval Delay (R1)

This downside uncertain event will be included in the schedule analysis along with or above general uncertainties associated with duration ambiguities of the permitting process. Four causes (a–d) were identified that may lead to such a delay. Each of them could give rise to a very high impact on the project schedule of more than six months (Figure 3.2). The project team came up with a reservation, though, declaring that if the delay were more than 12 months, this should be regarded as a game changer and a corporate risk. This disclaimer meant that in the worst manifestation of this uncertainty the schedule and cost baselines should be revised and redone as Project Curiosity would not be able to absorb or manage such a devastating impact.

Missed Tie-in Window (R2)

A month-and-a-half turnaround window was planned for the tie-in of the capture unit at the power generation plant. Such planned turnaround windows were used for maintenance of major equipment at the power generation plant every 18 to 24 months. If the tie-in works were not started on time or not completed on time for any reason, the impact on project schedule would be devastating. Enough float was reserved before the turnaround window in the project schedule to get prepared. At the same time, all preceding steps such as timely submitting a notice, carrying out tie-in engineering, and procurement should be obeyed to avoid such a risk. A bigger concern was the completion of all required works during that short period of time. The availability of required materials and qualified workers should be ensured. Special attention should be paid to the confidence levels of the tie-in window's start and finish milestones.

Technology Novelty (R3)

Two out of the three major components of Project Curiosity (capture and storage) were characterized by a high level of technology novelty. This could lead to late engineering changes and corresponding impacts on project Cost and Schedule. For this reason this uncertainty should be taken into account in probabilistic cost and schedule models as an uncertain event. Such uncertainty could exist even in projects with a lower level of technical novelty, just due to the selected sequence of works. In a CCS project some particular unknown discoveries could be made that would lead to a drastic schedule delay, cost increase, or decline in System Capacity. As declared by the project team, any such discovery that could lead to more than 12 months' schedule delay and/or $75 million of extra capital costs and/or reduction in System Capacity by 0.2 million tons per year should be sized up as a game changer if not a show-stopper. Lower-than-anticipated efficiency and reliability of the capture unit in commercial operations as well as poorer-than-initially-assessed characteristics of a selected reservoir could give rise to that outcome. The replacement of capture equipment or additional drilling might be undertaken, leading to additional delays and costs.

Subcontractor Default (R4)

This is a typical execution risk that could happen to any capital project. Delays to find a replacement that would require premium pricing due to urgency should be taken into account in cost and schedule models.

Low Productivity (R5)

This general uncertainty is typical in the execution of any capital project. Lower productivity should be taken into account as ranges around durations of all construction normal activities. The corresponding extra costs will be taken into account as schedule-driven costs.

Commissioning Delays (R6)

This type of uncertain event could occur in any capital project even if standard technologies and equipment were used. The technical novelty of the capture unit technology and CO_2 sequestration aspects of Project Curiosity could exacerbate this uncertainty. The corresponding cost and schedule delays should be included in the probabilistic models. This uncertainty is interdependent with the technology novelty uncertainty (R3). Mathematically, these two uncertainties should be correlated in the models.

Cost Escalation (R7)

This is a general uncertainty that pertains to any capital project.

Procurement Delays (R8)

The delivery of the equipment (capture unit compressor, line pipes, casings, etc.) delay is a common uncertainty for any capital project. The corresponding extra costs will be taken into account as schedule-driven costs.

Reservoir Geology (R9)

This uncertain event might occur in Operate. This could be a severe corporate risk. At the same time it cannot be treated as a project show-stopper or game changer due to its window of occurrence. For the same reason it should not be taken into account in probabilistic cost and schedule models.

The corresponding addressing actions should be developed and implemented during Select, Define, and Execute using the project execution through risk addressing (PETRA) methodology (Figure 5.4).

Immature CO_2 Market (R10)

This uncertainty could be a game changer if lower-than-expected interest in buying CO_2 for enhanced oil recovery were manifested by oil producing companies. The lack of infrastructure to deliver CO_2 to EOR injection sites as well as the growing popularity of horizontal directional drilling to improve oil production could be major factors. The fact that the government grant did not support the marketing aspects should not be underestimated. Being a game changer that could redefine project baselines, this uncertainty should not be included in the probabilistic models. There were signs that oil producers that might use CO_2-EOR methods had different economic expectations from Project Curiosity than the project owner and the government. Some of them even expressed a general interest in becoming Project Curiosity partners instead of being the project's customers.

Early Procurement (Opportunity) (R11)

As a rule the company did not allow entering any contractual agreements with vendors until the project final investment decision was done. However, there were a few exceptions previously when project teams built strong cases to demonstrate the benefits of pre-FID procurement funding. This opportunity should be common in any capital project, although the benefits of risking a substantial amount of money before project sanctioning should be explained to management. This opportunity should be strongly anti-correlated with procurement delays (R8) as these two uncertainties work against each other.

Safety Incidents (R12)

Safety incidents could occur in any capital project, especially in the Execute phase. An additional cause of safety incidents for this project could be the proximity of the capture unit construction site to the existing power generation facility (a *brownfield* project). A major safety incident at the main facility might impact Project Curiosity. Besides the obvious impact on Safety, it could lead to stoppage of the construction works for the investigation and corresponding impacts on Schedule.

Unidentified Uncertainty(ies) (R13)

The 12 uncertainties in Table 15.3 represent the most critical factors of the overall project uncertainty exposure. Besides those, a few dozen less critical uncertainties were identified and kept in several project logs. A cold-eye review of these logs was undertaken by a third party. It was stated that the risk management system of the project could be qualified as adequate and efficient. Some traces of organizational and psychological bias were detected but seemed to be well managed. At the same time, due to a certain degree of technical novelty and the early phase of project development some uncertainties of Project Curiosity could stay unidentified.

It was agreed that supercritical unidentified uncertainties that could be qualified as show-stoppers or game changers should be accepted by corporate management. The definition of show-stoppers and game changers was developed and agreed as:

▪ More than 12 months' schedule delay, and/or
▪ More than $75 million of extra capital costs, and/or
▪ Reduction in System Capacity by more than 0.2 million tons a year

To respond to any less severe unidentified uncertainties that might be run across, the project team and corporate management agreed that unknown uncertainty allowances based on 3% of the project base estimate and duration should be added to the probabilistic cost and schedule models according to common practice (Chapter 12).

 TEMPLATES FOR PROBABILISTIC COST AND SCHEDULE ANALYSES

The 13 uncertainties discussed in the previous section were put into a project master uncertainty register. According to the risk management process of Figure 2.2 they were assessed before addressing first. A comprehensive set of addressing actions based on the strategies discussed in Chapter 5 was developed for uncertainties R1–R12, which are outside the scope of this case study. Based on a newly developed set of addressing actions, assessment of uncertainties R1–R12 was done to reflect an expected snapshot of their implementation by the end of Define (FID), which corresponds to the to-be-FID assessment.

The project master uncertainty register (Log #1) became the source of seven additional logs:

1. Register of corporate risks, show-stoppers, and game changers (Log #2)
2. Register used as input to the probabilistic schedule model (Log #3)
3. Register used as input to the probabilistic cost model (Log #4)
4. Log of ranges around proxy schedule normal activities used as inputs to the general schedule uncertainties model (Log #5)
5. Log of ranges around proxy base estimate used as inputs to the general cost uncertainties model (Log #6)
6. Log #3 converted to Log #7 to comply with PertMaster input requirements
7. Log #4 converted to Log #8 to comply with @Risk input requirements

Log #2 was discussed with corporate management and established as a demarcation line between the project and corporate risk management responsibilities. On one hand, the project team should exercise due diligence when managing these show-stoppers and game changers. On the other hand, corporate management should provide leadership and support in managing these supercritical uncertainties. If these uncertainties do happen and damage project objectives, the company should be ready to accept them.

Unknown uncertainty R13 was added to the probabilistic models. The main correlations among the input distributions were identified and included in the corresponding logs. All schedule-driven cost impacts identified in the project master risk register were excluded from the probabilistic cost register on purpose. Those should be taken into account through the proper integration of schedule and cost models (Figure 12.1).

In addition to these main logs, several auxiliary logs were developed to upload the results (statistics) of the schedule analysis to the probabilistic cost model, to take the project cash flow into account in the cost escalation model, and so on.

BUILDING AND RUNNING PROJECT PROBABILISTIC COST AND SCHEDULE MODELS

This section is devoted to a high-level description of the integrated probabilistic cost and schedule model of Project Curiosity. I did not have to represent detailed modeling mathematics as this book is for project team members and decision makers. Excessive mathematical details are not required for deep understanding of the main steps to develop probabilistic models.

Probabilistic cost and schedule models were built in accordance with the method statement introduced in Chapter 13. Their integration was undertaken to properly take into account schedule-driven costs. The probabilistic schedule model was built first. It was developed in PertMaster based on the project proxy schedule (Figure 15.1). Initially, a general uncertainty model was developed based on Log #5. Then Log #3 was converted to Log #7 and transferred to PertMaster. A loaded version of the model was created that took schedule uncertain events into account along with general uncertainties. It was done through mapping of uncertain events to the corresponding proxy schedule normal activities (Log #7). Two versions of the loaded model were developed according to PertMaster functionality. The first was based on assessments of uncertain events as-is; the second took into account assessments to-be-FID (Log #7). All correlations identified in Logs #3, #5, and #7 were also programmed to exclude unrealistic sampling scenarios. Finally, the agreed unknown uncertainty allowance distribution was added to the model.

The results of the probabilistic schedule analysis for summary activities were uploaded to the probabilistic cost model to take schedule-driven costs into account.

The probabilistic cost model was built for general uncertainties based on Log #6. Ranges around the most likely cost numbers were developed by the project team to reflect the current level of project development. Ranges of some accounts reflect the fact that corresponding costs were initially overestimated.

Schedule-driven costs for the to-be-FID case were also included in the cost model based on the information of Log #6. Namely, each summary cost account was represented as the sum of fixed and variable costs (Table 15.1). Variable costs were introduced as the product of the corresponding burn rates and the most likely durations from the proxy schedule. Distributions around the most likely durations came from the schedule model as outputs. As burn rates cannot be defined with absolute accuracy, ranges around their most likely values were introduced (Log #6).

The initial deterministic cost risk register (Log #4) was converted to the format required to build a probabilistic cost model (Log #8). Also two cases were built in: one for cost assessments as-is and the other for the to-be-FID case.

Logs #6 and #8 were used as the basis for development of the overall probabilistic cost model in @Risk. All correlations identified in those logs were programmed in the cost model to ensure its realism. Finally, the agreed unknown uncertainty allowance was added to the model.[2]

 ## THREE WHAT-IF SCENARIOS

In addition to the standard probabilistic modeling described in the previous section, the project team and decision makers were interested in investigating the impact of uncertain events related to the permitting process, early procurement, and the tie-in window.

Permitting

The purpose of the first what-if scenario was to compare project completion and FID milestones in the presence and absence of uncertain event R1 (Regulatory approval delay). The government played a dual role in the project. On one hand, it provided a grant to support development and implementation of Project Curiosity. The government's full support was offered along with financing. On the other hand, the government had to follow standard permitting procedures. To a certain degree, the word *standard* in the previous sentence was a challenge as finalized standard permitting requirements for CCS projects had yet to be developed and approved. In combination with the possible interference of the general public and NGOs this could become a most uncontrollable uncertainty to the project and potentially might be a game changer or show-stopper.

This what-if scenario was thought out as a foundation for building a case study and discussing this with the government, appealing to its role as the project's major stakeholder and partner. The intent would be to engage the government in accelerating and streamlining the permitting process.

Technically this scenario was developed on the basis of the existing project schedule to-be-FID model. Uncertainty R1 was mapped to normal activity 022 (Review and approval of application by government) of the proxy schedule (Figure 15.1) in the main model. It was excluded from the to-be-FID model in this what-if scenario using PertMaster functionality. Confidence levels of the project completion date (milestone 110M [Sustained operations]) and the FID date (milestone M 030M [FID]) were investigated and compared with the main to-be-FID case.

Early Procurement

Although the purchasing of any products or services prior to the final investment decisions was not the usual practice adopted by the company, there was some interest in verifying the possible positive impact of early procurement (upside uncertainty R11) on improvement of project completion milestone 110M. Uncertainty R11 was mapped to several procurement activities of the proxy schedule (Log #7). Just as in the permitting what-if scenario, the upside uncertainty R11 was excluded from the what-if model. Again, the confidence level of the project completion date of Project Curiosity (milestone 110M [Sustained operations]) was investigated and compared with the main to-be-FID case.

Readiness for Turnaround Window

This scenario did not require amendment of the main to-be-FID probabilistic model. PertMaster functionality allows one to obtain completion date distributions for any normal activity, summary activity, or milestone. Its purpose was to ensure that uncertainty R2 (Missed tie-in window) was fully addressed. Otherwise, it could result in a supercritical uncertainty as previously discussed.

Distributions for milestones 68SM (Tie-in window start) and 68FM (Tie-in window finish) were retrieved from the main model to investigate the confidence levels of these two milestones.

 ## CONCLUSION

A simplified business case for the hypothetical Project Curiosity was introduced in this chapter. Its primary goal was to demonstrate applications of the probabilistic method to develop project reserves and evaluate the overall cost and schedule uncertainty of the project outcome. The secondary goal was to reiterate some of the deterministic methods introduced in this book. Adaptation of the bowtie diagram, RBS, RAM, and major templates for Project Curiosity was done. Some methods (cost escalation, selection of engineering design and procurement options, etc.) are merely mentioned to avoid excessive complexity.

To eliminate a resemblance to any real CCS project, the Cost and Schedule baselines of Project Curiosity are fictional. They cannot be associated with any real CCS project. This is done on purpose. In any case, I hope that those baselines would not pass any serious benchmarking.

The number of discussed uncertainties is very low—just a dozen. Some of them were not even included in probabilistic models, which made modeling a bit artificial. However, the results of the modeling were informative enough for the purpose of this study and are discussed in the next chapter.

NOTES

1. Cost escalation modeling is outside the scope of this case study.
2. A simplified approach was taken toward addressing general uncertainties in both cost and schedule models. An assumption was made that ranges stayed the same in both loaded models. As previously discussed, this is not quite a consistent approach as general uncertainties should get smaller in the course of project development. It was used here for the sake of simplicity.

CHAPTER SIXTEEN

Decision Making

Questions Addressed in Chapter 16

- What are the key findings of the risk report prepared by the Project Curiosity team?
- What recommendations were made by the decision gate review board? ■

WHEN PROBABILISTIC COST AND schedule modeling was done, the Project Curiosity probabilistic risk report was prepared by the project team and validated by a third party. It became part of the project risk report prepared as part of the package of documents for the decision gate preceding Define. All probabilistic modeling scenarios were done for two cases: uncertainty exposure as-is and uncertainty exposure anticipated for the end of Define (to-be-final investment decision [FID]).

Some of the recommendations of the decision gate review board were a surprise to many Project Curiosity stakeholders and the project team.

KEY POINTS OF THE PROBABILISTIC ANALYSIS REPORT

Schedule Analysis Outcome

The results of the schedule risk analysis for the two main cases, as-is and to-be-FID, are represented by Figures 16.1 and 16.2. The as-is case is based on current uncertainty exposure by the end of Select. The to-be-FID case is thought as anticipated uncertainty exposure by the end of Define, which corresponds to FID.

The project completion date according to the proxy schedule (August 30, 2018) has a low confidence level of P2 and P6 for both cases. The contractual completion date (December 1, 2018) has confidence level P16 for the as-is case and P43 for the to-be-FID case due to the three-month float built into the schedule. The two-peak shape of the as-is curve points to the presence of standalone considerable uncertainty, which lingers even after addressing (case to-be-FID). Sensitivity analysis for the to-be-FID case (Figures 14.7 and 14.8) reveals the most likely reason for this. This should be uncertain event R1 impacting activity 022 (R1:022), which occupied the very top of the tornado charts. In other words, it was an impact of regulatory approval delay. This relatively obvious hypothesis required confirmation. The results of the what-if analysis that excludes uncertainty R1 from the model are shown in Figure 16.3.

Figure 16.3 shows that the confidence level of the contractual completion date improves from P43 to P49 if uncertainty R1 gets excluded. The overall spread of uncertainty P5–P95 corresponds to the time interval from August 27, 2018 to April 11, 2019, even if uncertainty R1 disappears. In the presence of R1 this spread is much worse: from August 27, 2018 to October 9, 2019 (Figure 16.2), not to mention the quite appalling spread for the as-is case: from September 28, 2018 to June 2, 2020 (Figure 16.1). These spreads, which could destroy the schedule baseline of Project Curiosity, should alarm any decision maker.

An immediate impact of uncertainty R1 was even more obvious when analyzing the FID milestone. Figure 16.4 shows the FID date distribution for the to-be-FID case when uncertainty R1 was part of the model. The possibility of a terrible delay in the final investment decision is shown by the standalone additional peak. Its dates do not have probabilities comparable with the main peak although the overall spread of possible outcomes is alarming. The planned FID date (February 3, 2016) could be delayed for more than a year! This game-changer R1 was excluded from the what-if scenario, leading to a much narrower spread in the FID date outcome (Figure 16.5). The additional peak on the right wing of the distribution stemming from R1 is gone.

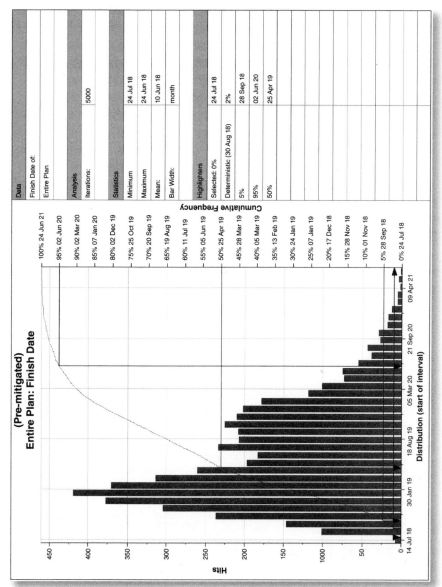

FIGURE 16.1 Project Curiosity Completion Dates As-Is

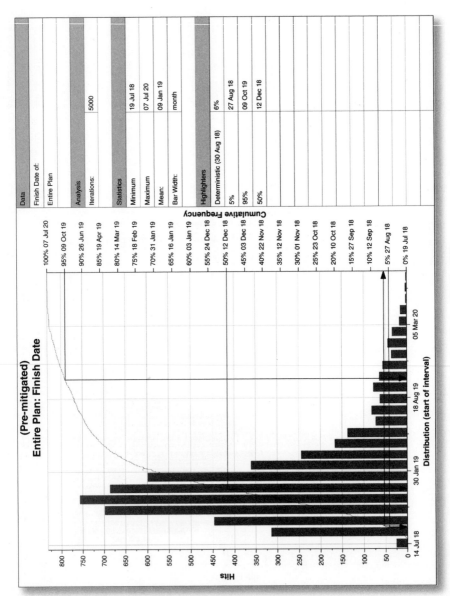

FIGURE 16.2 Project Curiosity Completion Dates To-Be-FID

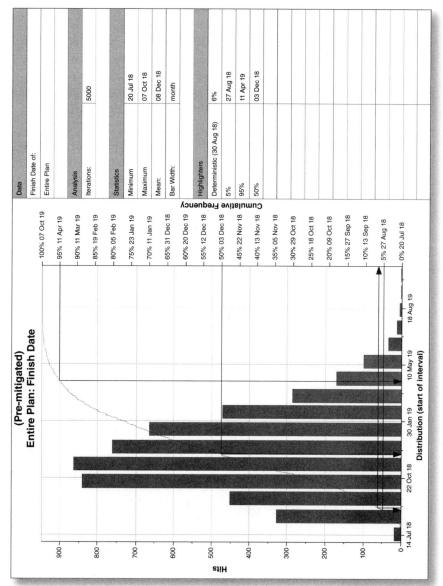

FIGURE 16.3 Results of What-if Scenario: No Regulatory Delay (R1)

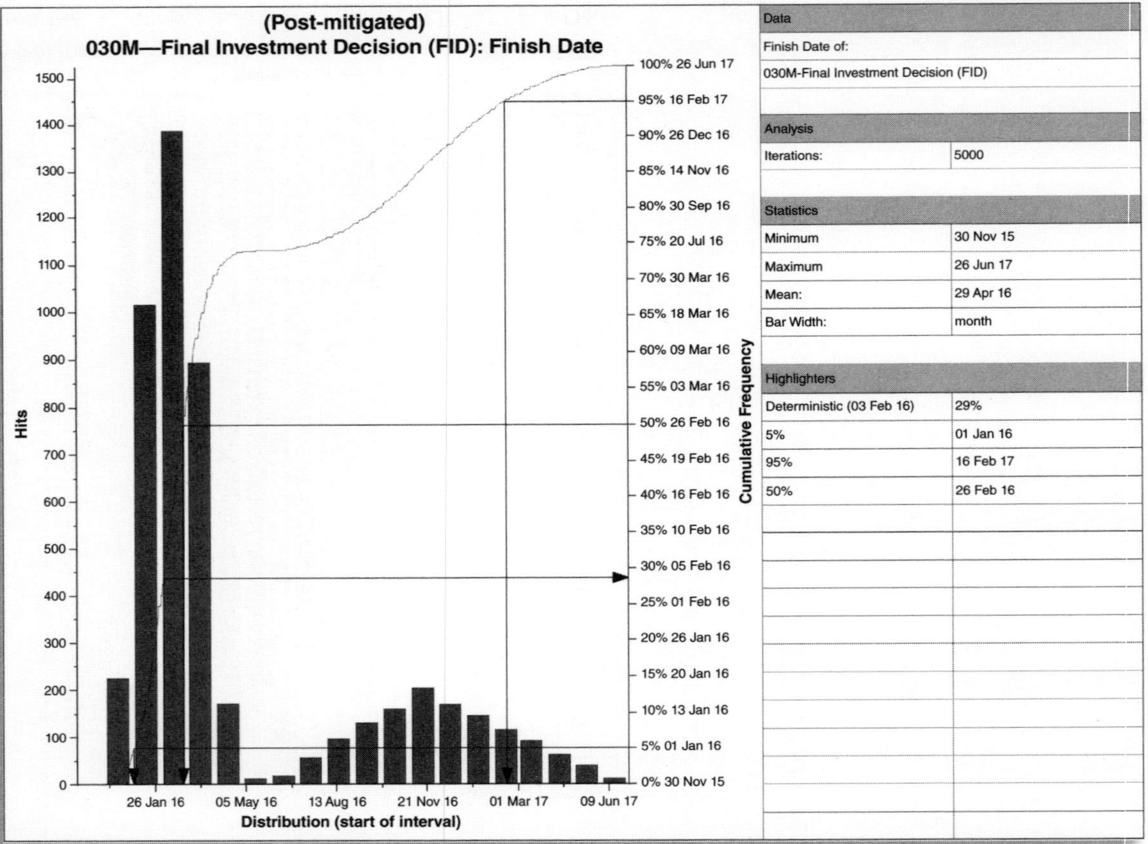

FIGURE 16.4 FID Dates in Presence of Regulatory Delay (R1)

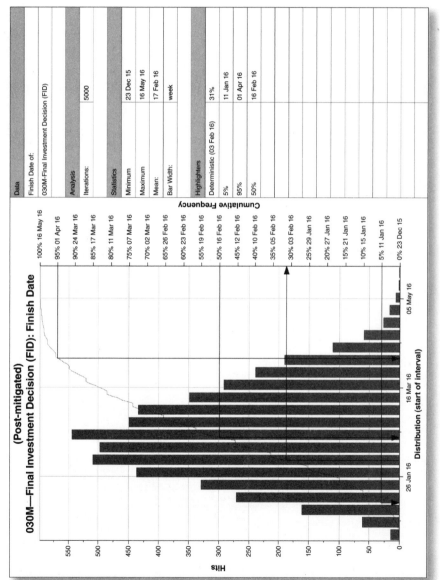

FIGURE 16.5 FID Dates in Absence of Regulatory Delay (R1)

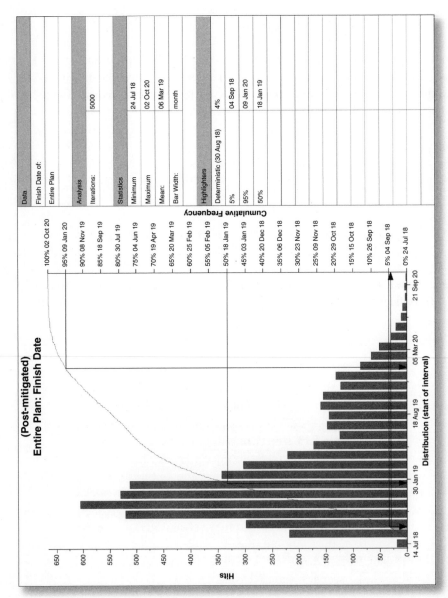

FIGURE 16.6 Project Completion Dates if Early Procurement (R11) Is Not Approved

The to-be-FID distribution of Figure 16.2 was developed when the possibility of early procurement R11 was factored in. The sensitivity chart of Figure 14.7 shows that its impacts on procurement normal activities, 103:R11, 064:R11, 061:R11, and 091:R11, are not impressively high. This led to the necessity to evaluate whether it was worth it to bend the company rules and allow early procurement prior to the FID. Figure 16.6 demonstrates results of the what-if scenario when early procurement R11 is not allowed.

Comparison of Figure16.6 and 16.2 points to the reduction of the contractual completion date confidence level from P43 to P33. This was not a critical reduction, especially in the presence of much more sensitive schedule uncertainties. This meant that the possibility of allowing early procurement was not that attractive. More sensitive possibilities should be explored first.

Presence of a narrow turnaround window in the project schedule to tie in the capture unit dictated the necessity to investigate confidence levels of milestones of the start and finish of the window. It turned out that the start milestone 068SM got a P100 level of confidence. Floats in the schedule preceding this milestone should absorb any identified uncertainty. This should not be a reason for complacency as all the steps to get prepared for the tie-in activities should be timely undertaken. It looked like only negligence could drop the confidence level of this milestone.

It was a different story about the finish milestone 068FM. It turned out that the tie-in completion date of February 15, 2018, had quite a high level of confidence close to P70. At the same time, the possibility of up to 10 days' delay to reach P100 confidence level should make the project team and management slightly nervous. Extra few days could result in realization of corporate game-changer R2 leading to destruction of the schedule baseline. A confidence level close to P100 was required. The obvious low-hanging fruit was to apply a seven-days-a-week schedule in place of the five-days-a-week one used in the proxy for the duration of the tie-in works. Some other measures and controls required to increase the confidence level to the comfort zone should be also implemented.

The allowance to cover unknown uncertainties was included in the schedule model as uncertainty R13. Being a measure of Project Curiosity novelty and its risk management system quality, this uncertainty occupies the second top position in the sensitivity charts (Figures 14.7 and 14.8). This uncertainty is much smaller than the top uncertainty, R1 (regulatory approval delay).

The information about key project milestones discussed earlier is summarized in Table 16.1. If milestones of the proxy schedule are all represented by distributions of dates, the contractual completion date (December 1, 2018) is a given fixed date. Its confidence level was evaluated every time a new distribution for a particular scenario was developed.

TABLE 16.1   Summary of Major Project Dates

Milestone	Deterministic Date (DD)	DD Confidence Level	Date @ P5	Date @ P80	Date @ P95
Completion (110M) As-Is	Aug. 30, 2018	P2	Sept. 28, 2018	02-Dec-2019	02-Jun-2020
Completion (110M) To-Be-FID	Aug. 30, 2018	P6	Aug. 27, 2018	Mar. 14, 2019	09-Oct-2019
Contractual Completion To-Be-FID	Dec. 1, 2018	P43	n/a	n/a	n/a
FID (030M) To-Be-FID	Feb. 3, 2016	P29	Jan. 1, 2016	Sept. 30, 2016	Feb. 16, 2017
Contractual Completion/ No R1	Dec. 1. 2018	P49	n/a	n/a	n/a
FID (030M)/ No R1	Feb. 3, 2016	P31	Jan. 11, 2016	Mar. 11, 2016	Apr. 1, 2016
Contractual Completion/ No R11	Dec. 1, 2018	P33	n/a	n/a	n/a
Tie-in Start (068SM)	Jan. 1, 2018	P100	Jan. 1, 2018	Jan. 1, 2018	Jan. 1, 2018
Tie-in Finish (068FM)	Feb. 15, 2018	P70	Feb. 7, 2018	Feb. 16, 2018	Feb. 21, 2018

Cost Analysis Outcome

There were four main factors that were taken into account in the probabilistic cost model and included in the project cost reserve:

1. Ranges around base estimate cost accounts
2. Schedule-driven costs (assessment to-be-FID)
3. Uncertain events of cost impacts (assessment to-be-FID)
4. Unknown uncertainties

Figures 16.7 and 16.8 represent cost distribution results based on these four factors.

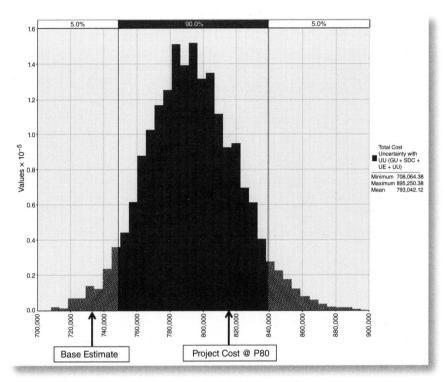

FIGURE 16.7 Project Curiosity Cost Distribution (Unknown Uncertainties Included)

Figure 14.10 comes up with sensitivity analysis results associated with the cost distribution of Figure 16.7. This tornado diagram contains interesting information about some factors giving rise to the cost distribution.

As expected, the technology novelty (the cost uncertain event R3) got top ranking. Third place was occupied by unknown uncertainties (R13). Interestingly, three schedule-driven costs made seventh, eighth, and ninth in the ranking. They came from schedule analysis.

Figure 16.8 shows the Project Curiosity cost distribution when unknown uncertainties are excluded from the model. It has a similar sensitivity chart, although without the unknown uncertainty category.

Figure 16.9 depicts the required project cost reserves depending on the desired levels of confidence for the two cases of Figures 16.7 and 16.8. Statistics associated with these two cases is collected in Table 16.2.

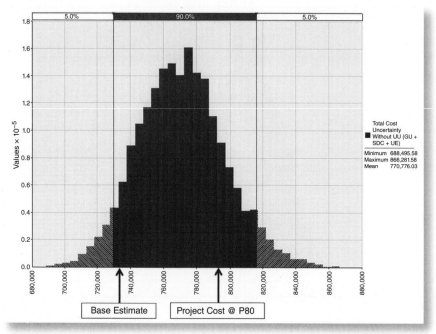

FIGURE 16.8 Project Curiosity Cost Distribution (Unknown Uncertainties Excluded)

TABLE 16.2 Statistical Data for Probabilistic Cost Analysis Outcome

	Project Costs (Unknown Uncertainties Included)			Project Costs (Unknown Uncertainties Excluded)		
Confidence Level	Project Cost, $000	Cost Reserve, $000	Cost Reserve, % of Base Estimate	Project Cost, $000	Cost Reserve, $000	Cost Reserve, % of Base Estimate
P5	747,746	13,191	1.8%	727,221	−7,334	−1.0%
P10	757,504	22,949	3.1%	737,650	3,095	0.4%
P15	764,335	29,780	4.1%	743,493	8,938	1.2%
P20	769,651	35,096	4.8%	748,580	14,025	1.9%
P25	773,766	39,211	5.3%	752,665	18,110	2.5%
P30	777,877	43,322	5.9%	756,477	21,922	3.0%
P35	781,543	46,988	6.4%	759,969	25,414	3.5%
P40	784,914	50,359	6.9%	763,458	28,903	3.9%
P45	788,595	54,040	7.4%	766,535	31,980	4.4%

TABLE 16.2 (*Continued*)

Confidence Level	Project Costs (Unknown Uncertainties Included)			Project Costs (Unknown Uncertainties Excluded)		
	Project Cost, $000	Cost Reserve, $000	Cost Reserve, % of Base Estimate	Project Cost, $000	Cost Reserve, $000	Cost Reserve, % of Base Estimate
P50	791,813	57,258	7.8%	769,985	35,430	4.8%
P55	795,359	60,804	8.3%	772,910	38,355	5.2%
P60	799,281	64,726	8.8%	776,508	41,953	5.7%
P65	803,117	68,562	9.3%	780,083	45,528	6.2%
P70	806,953	72,398	9.9%	783,998	49,443	6.7%
P75	811,421	76,866	10.5%	788,566	54,011	7.4%
P80	816,707	82,152	11.2%	793,492	58,937	8.0%
P85	822,455	87,900	12.0%	799,125	64,570	8.8%
P90	829,928	95,373	13.0%	806,125	71,570	9.7%
P95	841,786	107,231	14.6%	818,006	83,451	11.4%

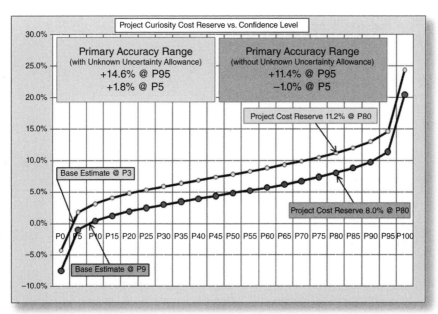

FIGURE 16.9 Required Project Curiosity Cost Reserves versus Levels of Confidence

According to Figure 16.9 and Table 16.2, confidence levels of the base estimate of Project Curiosity ($734,555,000) is P9 when unknown uncertainties are excluded and P3 when they are included. The role of the unknown uncertainty allowance is not simple addition of an extra 3% to the base estimate. If we compare the spreads P5–P95 for both cases in dollar values using the data of Table 16.2, this spread is $90,785,000 (12.4% of base estimate) where unknown uncertainties are excluded. It becomes $94,040,000 (12.8% of base estimate) when they are taken into account. The primary accuracy range for the case where unknown uncertainties are excluded is −1.0% /+11.4%. Including unknown uncertainties, which calibrates the whole distribution, gives rise to a positive lower range value. Namely, the range becomes +1.8% /+14.6%.

The required Project Curiosity cost reserve to reach a P80 confidence level would be 8.0% of the base estimate or $58,937,000 when unknown uncertainties are excluded and 11.2 % when they are included or $82,152,000. The contribution of unknown uncertainties to the project cost reserve at confidence level P80 is 23,215,000 or 3.2% of base estimate.

The contribution of cost escalation to the project cost reserve was done separately.

DECISION GATE REVIEW BOARD FINDINGS AND RECOMMENDATIONS

The decision gate review board evaluated the information on project uncertainty exposure provided by the Project Curiosity team and came up with the following observations, conclusions, and recommendations.

Highlights

- Project adopted a comprehensive risk management system that was consistently implemented.
- Set of identified uncertainties adequately reflected project uncertainty exposure according to the novelty of the project and phase of its development.
- Assessment of identified uncertainties was done correctly using adequate deterministic and probabilistic methods.
- The Project Curiosity team was not fully free from some types of psychological and organizational bias when identifying and assessing uncertainties, although all manifestations of bias were well managed.
- Primary accuracy range is narrow enough for this phase of project development. It reflects successful efforts of the project team to reduce the project's uncertainty outcome.

- Probabilistic schedule and cost analysis was carried out according to industry standards, providing robust results.
- Project cost reserve was developed adequately and should be approved at confidence level P80, which includes unknown uncertainty allowance.
- Cost escalation contingency was adequately developed deterministically and should be added to the final project budget, which should correspond to the confidence level at the expected (mean) value.

Lowlights

- Uncertainty related to regulatory approval was a top schedule uncertainty that could not be well controlled by the project team. This significantly reduces confidence levels of the FID milestone and contractual project completion date. In the worst-case scenario such uncertainty could become a project game changer or even a show-stopper.
- Confidence levels of the FID milestone and the contractual Project Curiosity completion date were not high enough.
- Although the confidence level to complete capture unit tie-in was quite high it was not at level P100. Any delay in completing the tie-in may become a game changer.
- Early procurement proposed by the project team does not seem to drastically improve the confidence level of the project completion date.
- Uncertainty related to level of maturity of the CO_2 market is a very top uncertainty that could become a project game changer or show-stopper. Current assessment of interest from the side of oil producers to buy CO_2 for enhanced oil recovery was unfavorable. Some oil and gas producers expressed general interest to become project partners. The lack of infrastructure to deliver CO_2 to enhanced oil recovery (EOR) injection sites, growing popularity of horizontal directional drilling for improved oil production, growing interest to develop heavy and shale oil deposits instead of depleted conventional reserves, the lack of economic incentives to use CO_2-EOR, and so on prevented development of the CO_2 market.[1]

Recommendations

Project Curiosity was permitted to proceed with Define keeping in mind the following recommendations:

- To negotiate with government the steps to streamline and accelerate project application review and approval.

- To discuss with government the possible incentives for oil producers to use CO_2 for EOR as expansion of the current round of the grant program.
- To explore possibilities to engage oil producers as partners of the project, including possibilities of public-private partnerships (PPP).
- To intensify talks with oil producers on long-term CO_2 purchasing contracts.
- To engage major external stakeholders that oppose or could oppose Project Curiosity in constructive consultations to demonstrate benefits of the project.
- To modify the existing project schedule in order to ensure the required confidence levels for all significant milestones.
- To develop an alternative variant of Project Curiosity (Curiosity-B) that could be based on injection of 1 million tons of CO_2 to aquifer due to failure to develop its commercial aspects. The decision on which variant would be sanctioned as the FID should depend on success of steps to make commercial aspects of the project viable.

 CONCLUSION

The purpose of Chapter 16 was to shed light on a risk-based way of thinking and informed decision making that could be positioned as typical for capital projects. Even this simplified version of the case study of Project Curiosity provides enough flavor for evaluation of the decisions to be made and the methods to substantiate and justify them. Both deterministic methods and probabilistic techniques contributed to the decisions made by the decision gate review board. A comprehensive list of project game changers and show-stoppers as well as the most critical (red) risks should be available along with the report on cost and schedule reserves.

I would not insist that a similar process should be adopted by any company managing its projects. It was successfully applied in the majority of capital projects I worked on. A certain degree of uniqueness in decision making took place occasionally, dictated by the requirements of project stakeholders according to the "in-depth" dimension of risk management (Figure 2.1). Neither the natures of the projects nor their sizes resulted in a uniqueness of decision making that differed significantly from the approach described in this book. The methodology presented in this book is quite stable and has merit for project teams and decision makers.

I am committed to supporting any intent or attempt to implement the methodology introduced in this book. For those readers who are not LinkedIn users, the following email address could be used for 24/7 helpdesk support: yuri.raydugin@risk-service.com.

 NOTE

1. Some of the causes mentioned led to a commercial uncertain event that did occur in the case of one CCS project I worked on.

About the Author

Dr. Yuri Raydugin is Principal Consultant of Risk Services & Solutions Inc., a Canadian consulting company. He has an engineering degree in nuclear physics from Urals Polytechnics Institute, Russia, a Ph.D. in physics and mathematics from Russia's Academy of Sciences, and an MBA in business strategy from Henley Management College in England. He is a member of the Association of Professional Engineers and Geoscientists of Alberta (APEGA).

Before establishing his consultancy business Yuri worked for TransCanada Pipelines and Royal Dutch Shell managing risks of several major and mega-capital projects. Currently he works with a number of major oil and gas and engineering companies as a project risk management consultant.

Yuri is the author of several articles on project risk management as well as on various aspects of physics. He is a member of the editorial board of the *International Journal of Risk and Contingency Management (IJRCM)* and a reviewer of risk management publications for the *International Journal of Project Management (IJPM)*.

Born and raised in Ekaterinburg, Russia, Yuri lives with his wife, Irina, and sons, Eugene and Roman, in Calgary, Alberta, Canada.

Index